THE SPRING

A visual journey into this season

KIMA
STUDIO
SAGU

THE COFFEE TABLE BOOKS

Copyright @ 2024. All rights reserved. KIMASAGU STUDIO

All rights reserved. No part of this book may be reproduced or transmitted in any form or by any means without written permission from the author.

ISBN: 9798883993168
Printed in the USA by KIMASAGU STUDIO
Check for more of our books on Amazon

Spring, also known as springtime, is one of the four temperate seasons, succeeding winter and preceding summer. There are various technical definitions of spring, but local usage of the term varies according to local climate, cultures and customs. When it is spring in the Northern Hemisphere, it is autumn in the Southern Hemisphere and vice versa. At the spring (or vernal) equinox, days and nights are approximately twelve hours long, with daytime length increasing and nighttime length decreasing as the season progresses until the Summer Solstice in June (Northern Hemisphere) and December (Southern Hemisphere).

Northern temperate zone
Astronomical season 21 March – 21 June
Meteorological season 1 March – 31 May
Solar (Celtic) season 1 February – 30 April

Southern temperate zone
Astronomical season 23 September – 22 December
Meteorological season 1 September – 30 November
Solar (Celtic) season 1 August – 31 October

"The Spring: A Visual Journey into this Season" is a photography book that invites you to experience the beauty and colorful atmosphere of this gorgeous season. Enjoy yourself and relax looking at the pages of this book full of images showing blooming flowers, green landscapes, and the luminous play of light passing through the blossom trees. You will enjoy and relax looking to the beauty of fields full of colorful flowers and the delicacy of the new growth coming from the land, this book shows and celebrate the uniqueness of the spring season. This is a gorgeous piece to keep on your table or shelf and to sit and relax passing every page of, "The Spring" and enjoying the magic and pure spirit of this renewal and growth of this new season.

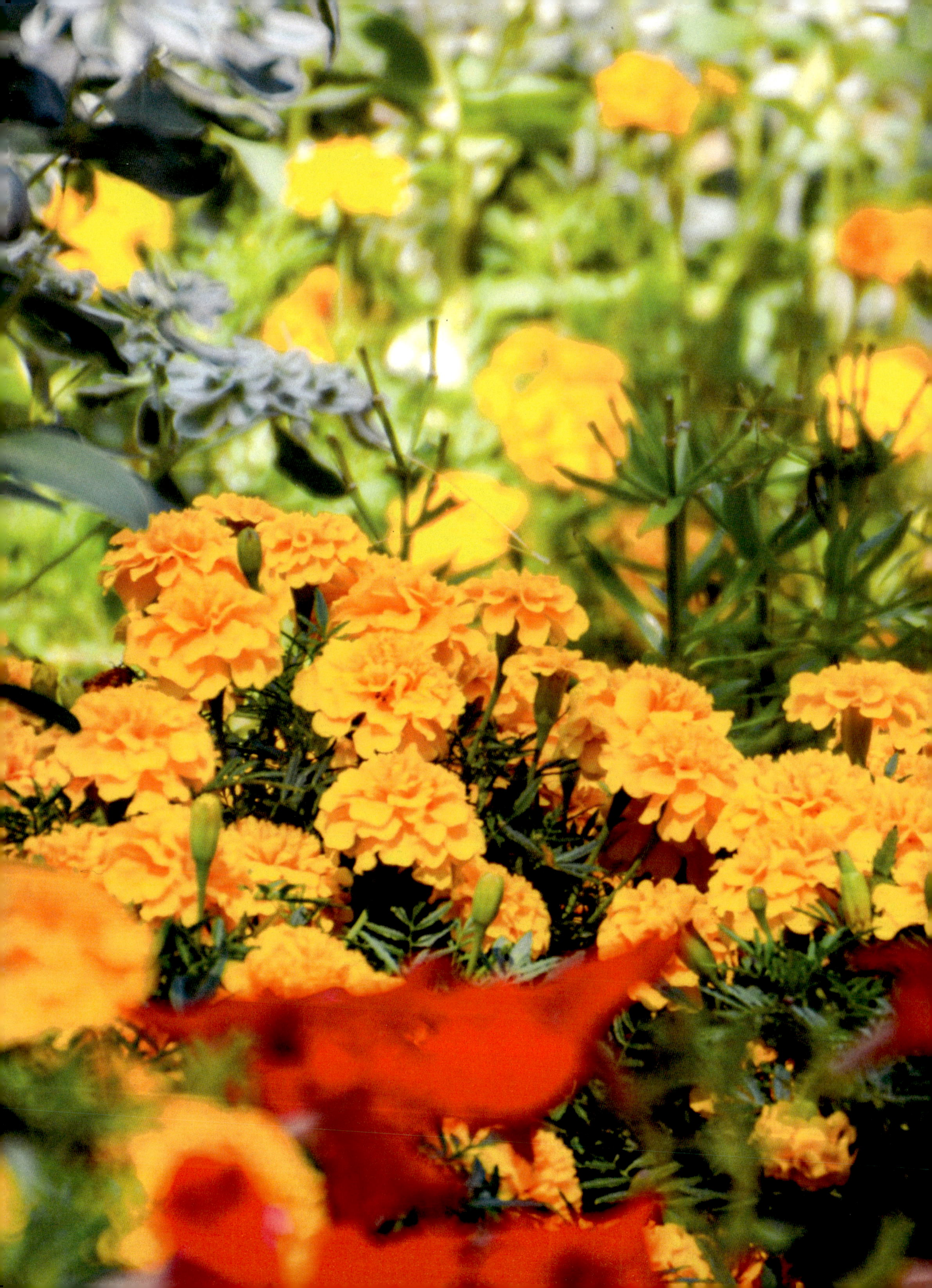

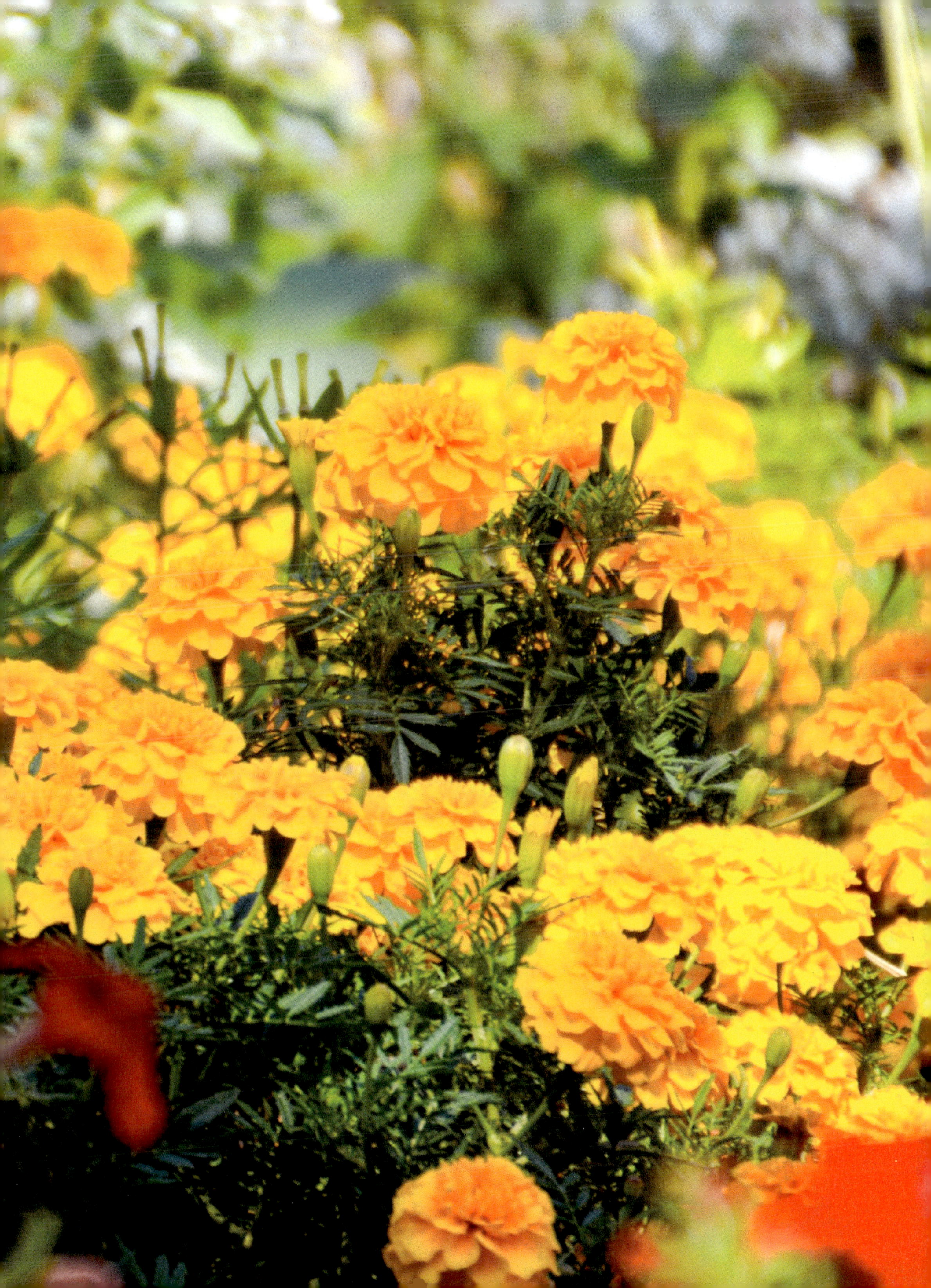

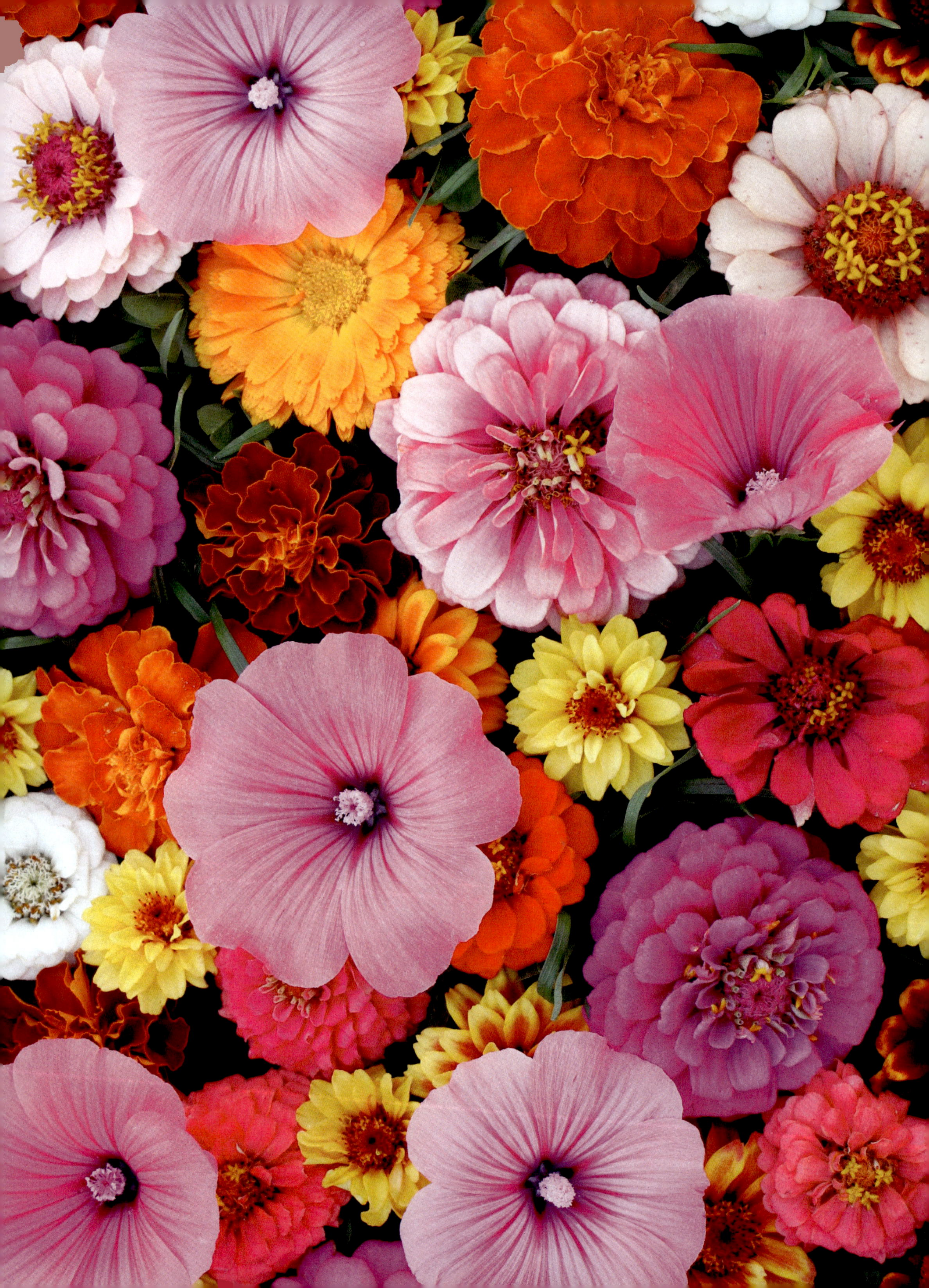

the spring

Spring is the season of new begins as the flowers start to bloom and the weather becomes warmer. The landscape transforms with bright colors, bringing a sense of renewal and change.

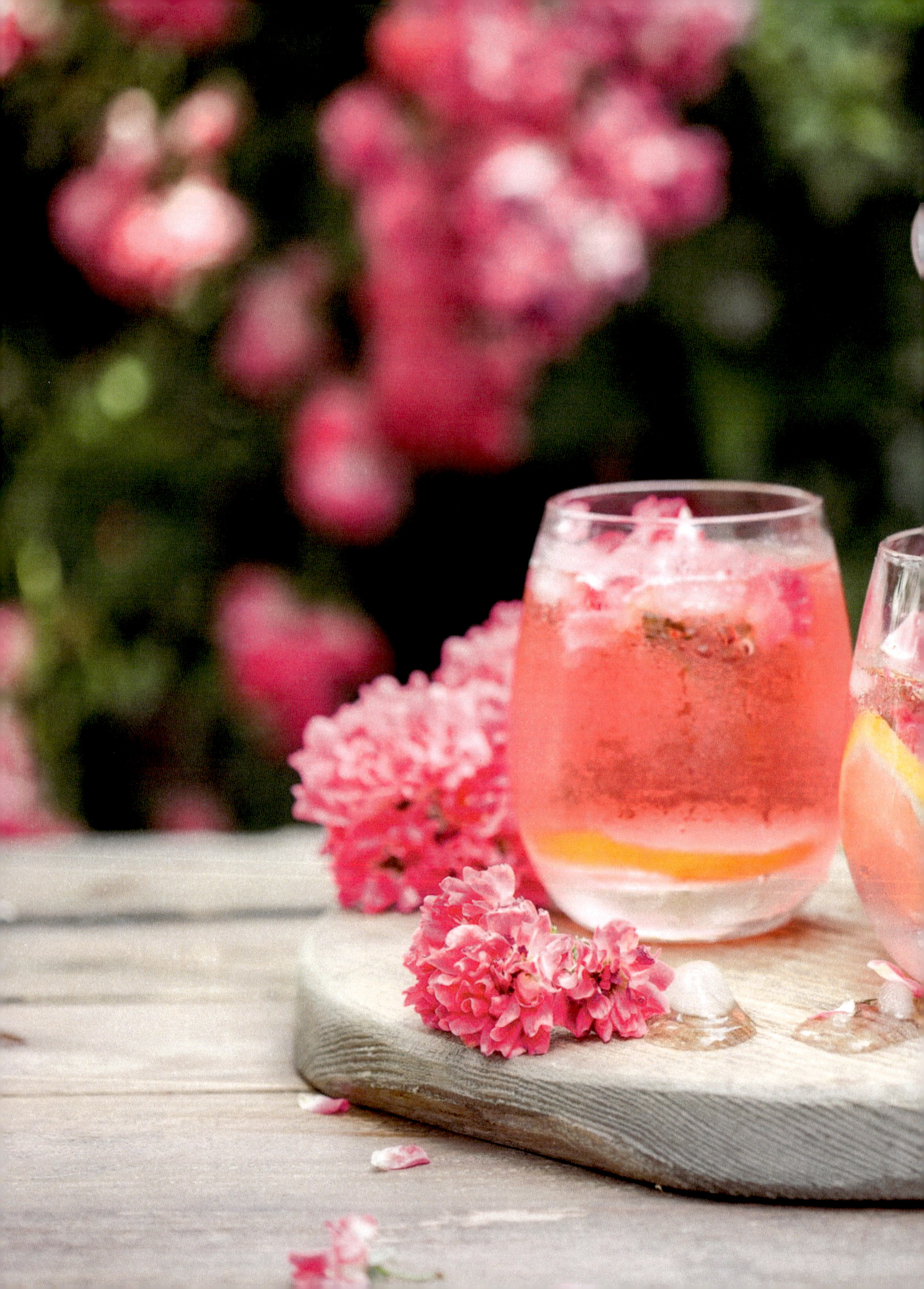

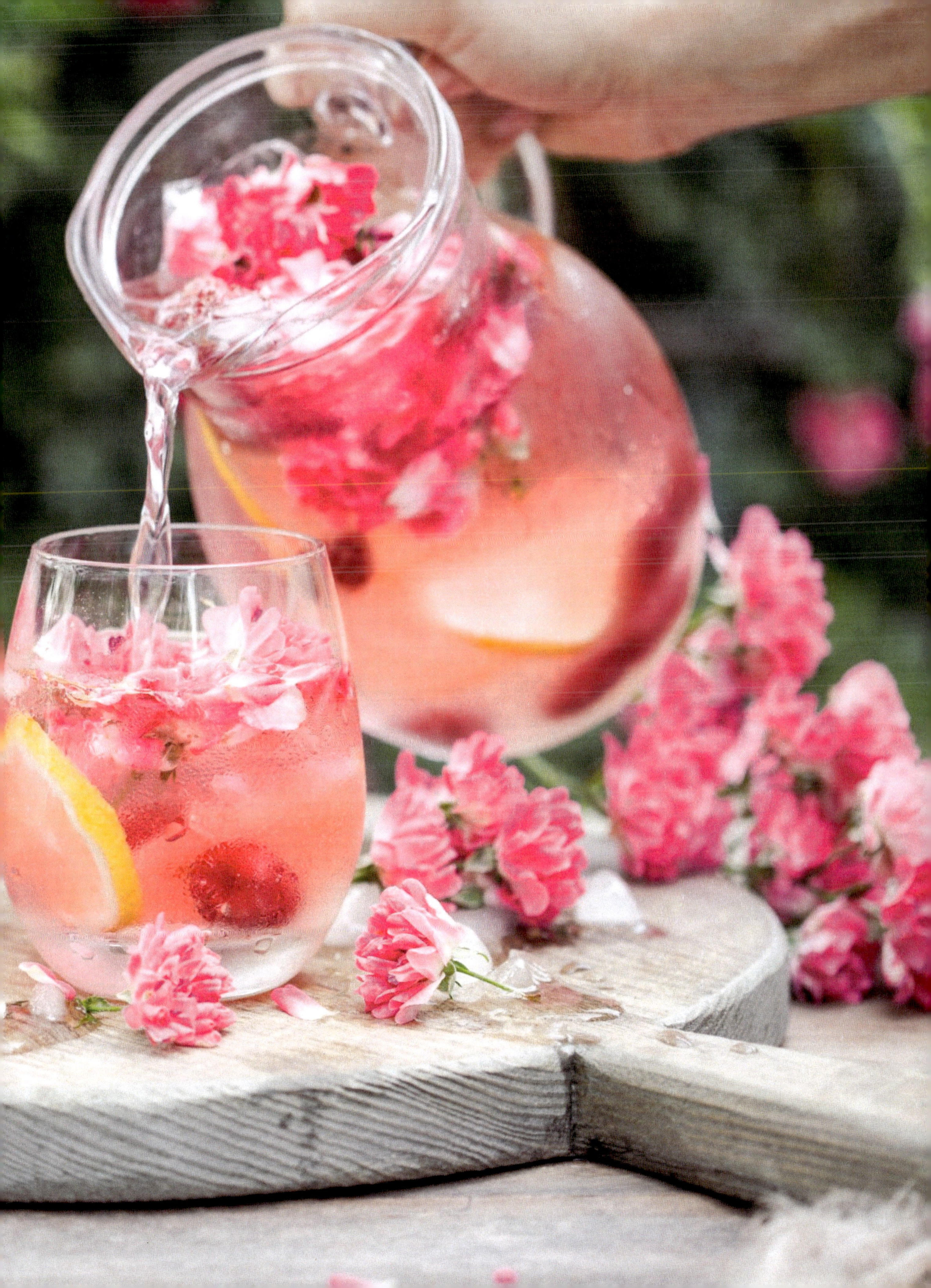

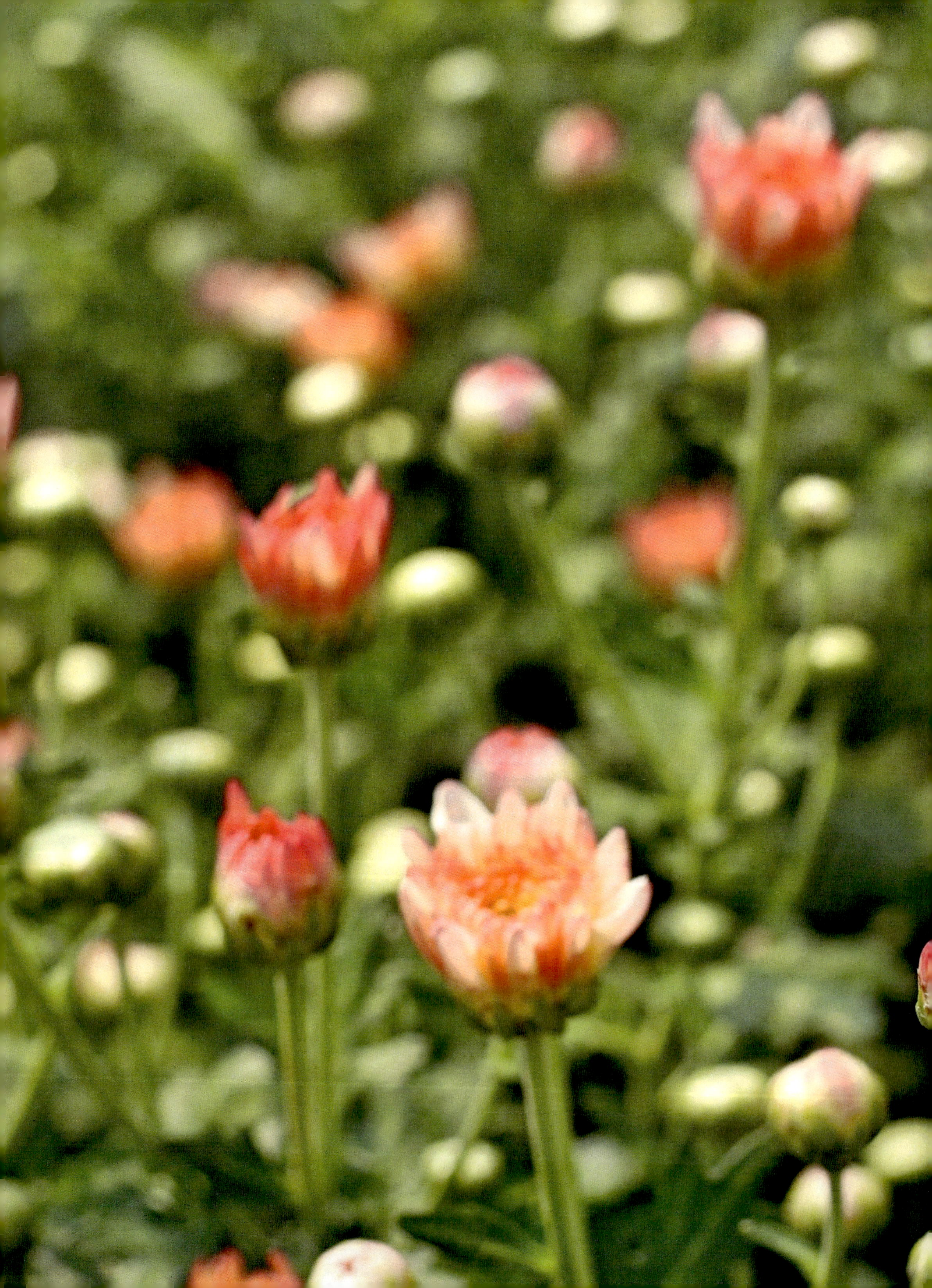

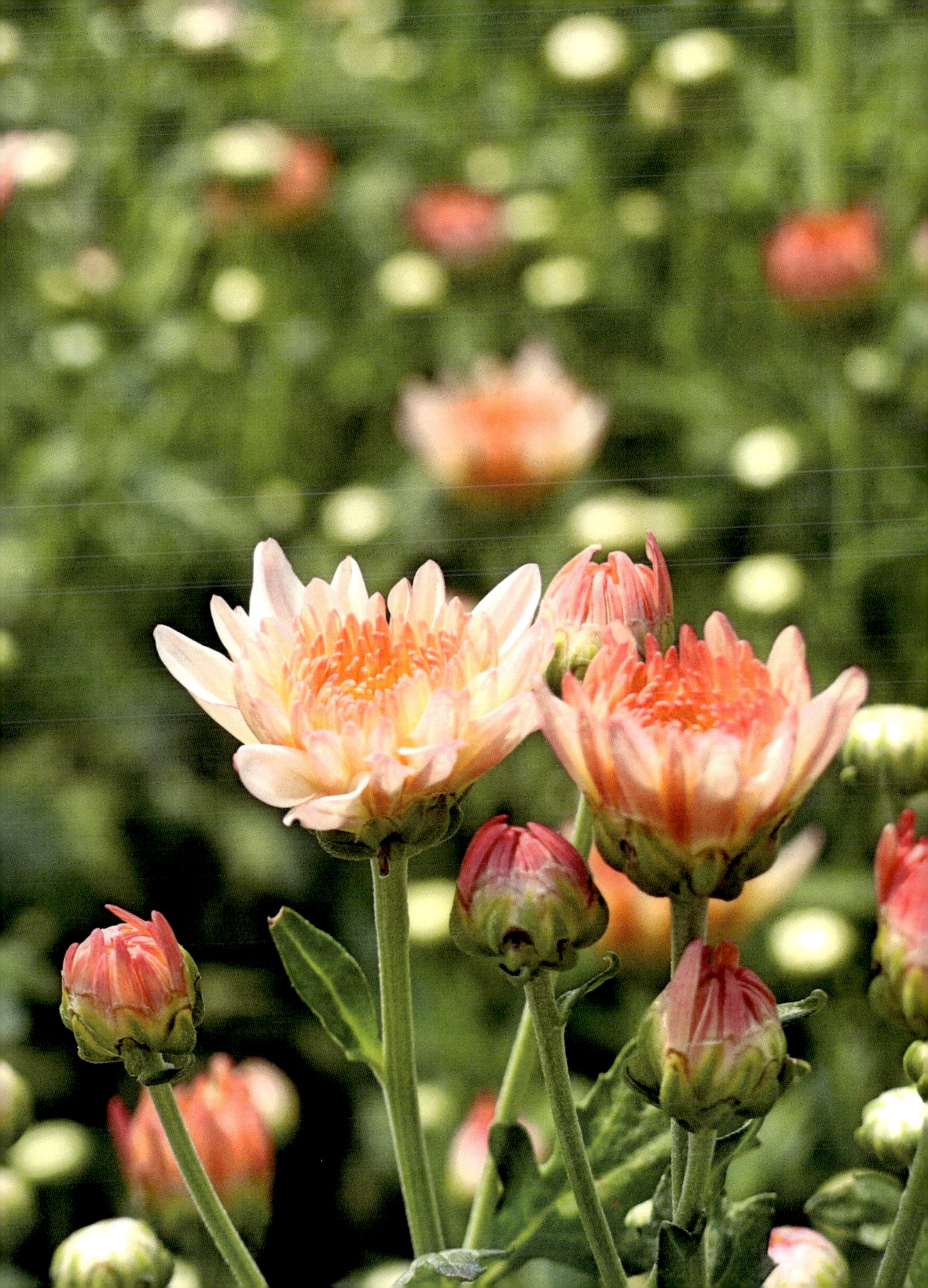

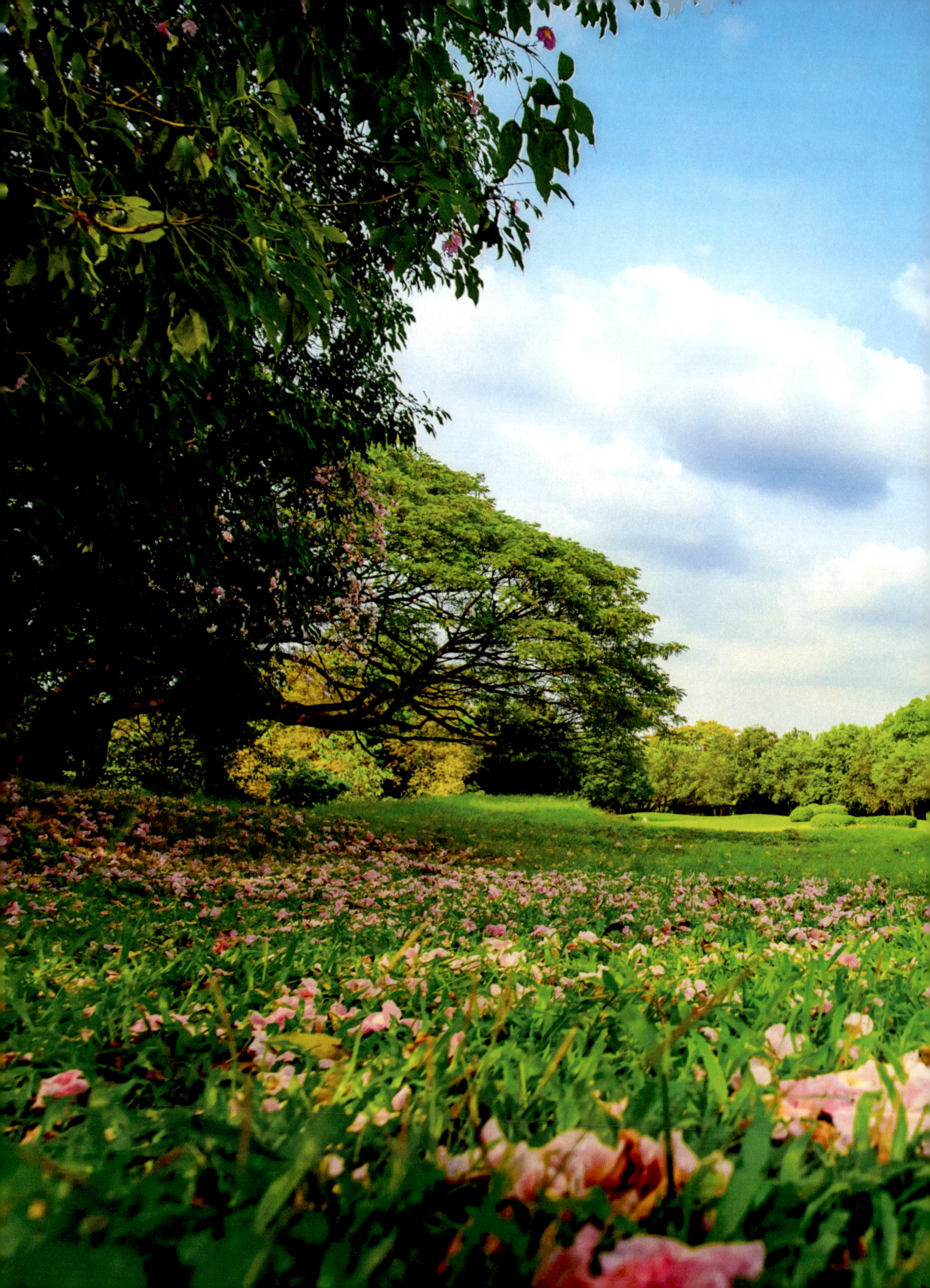

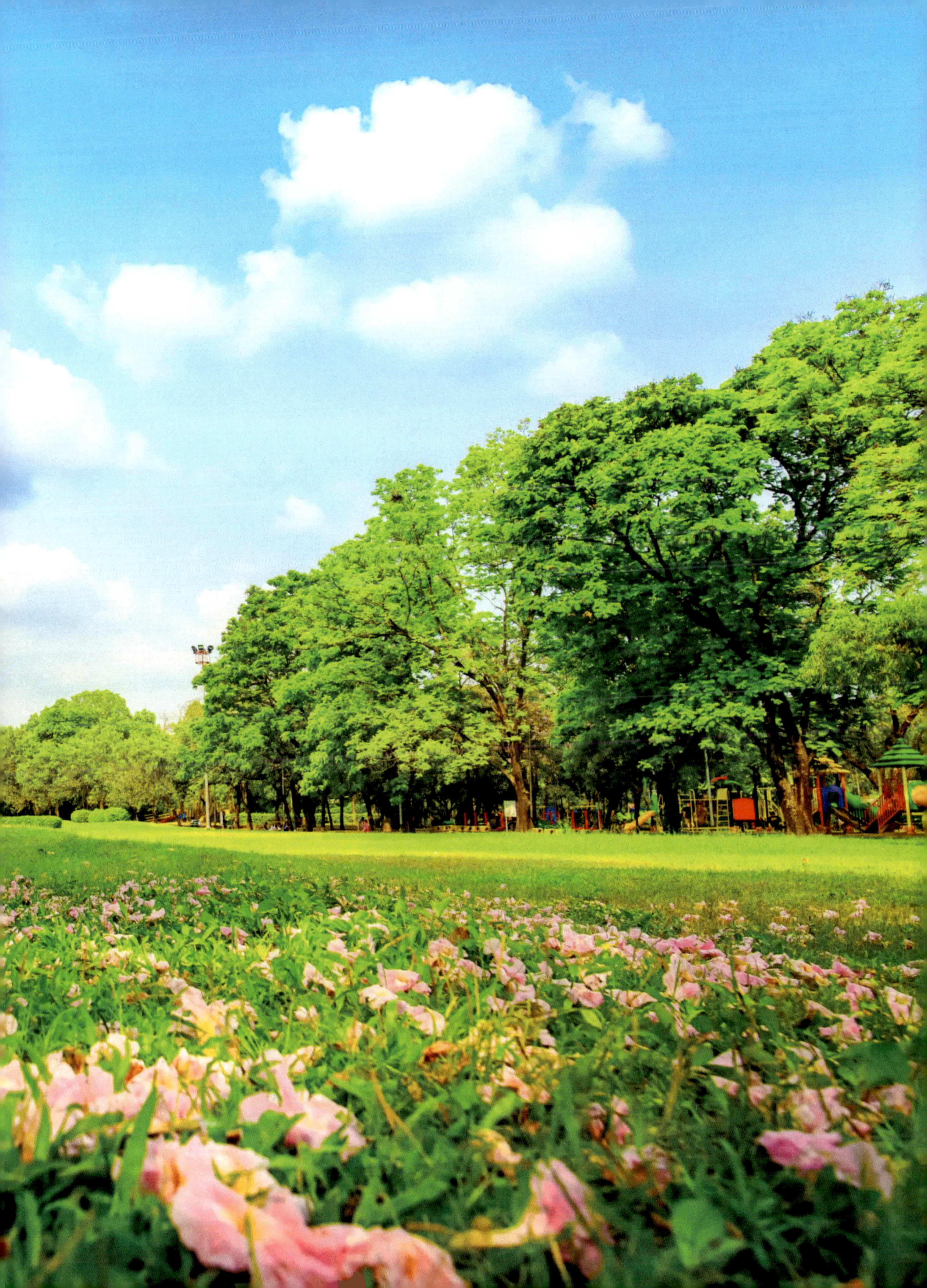

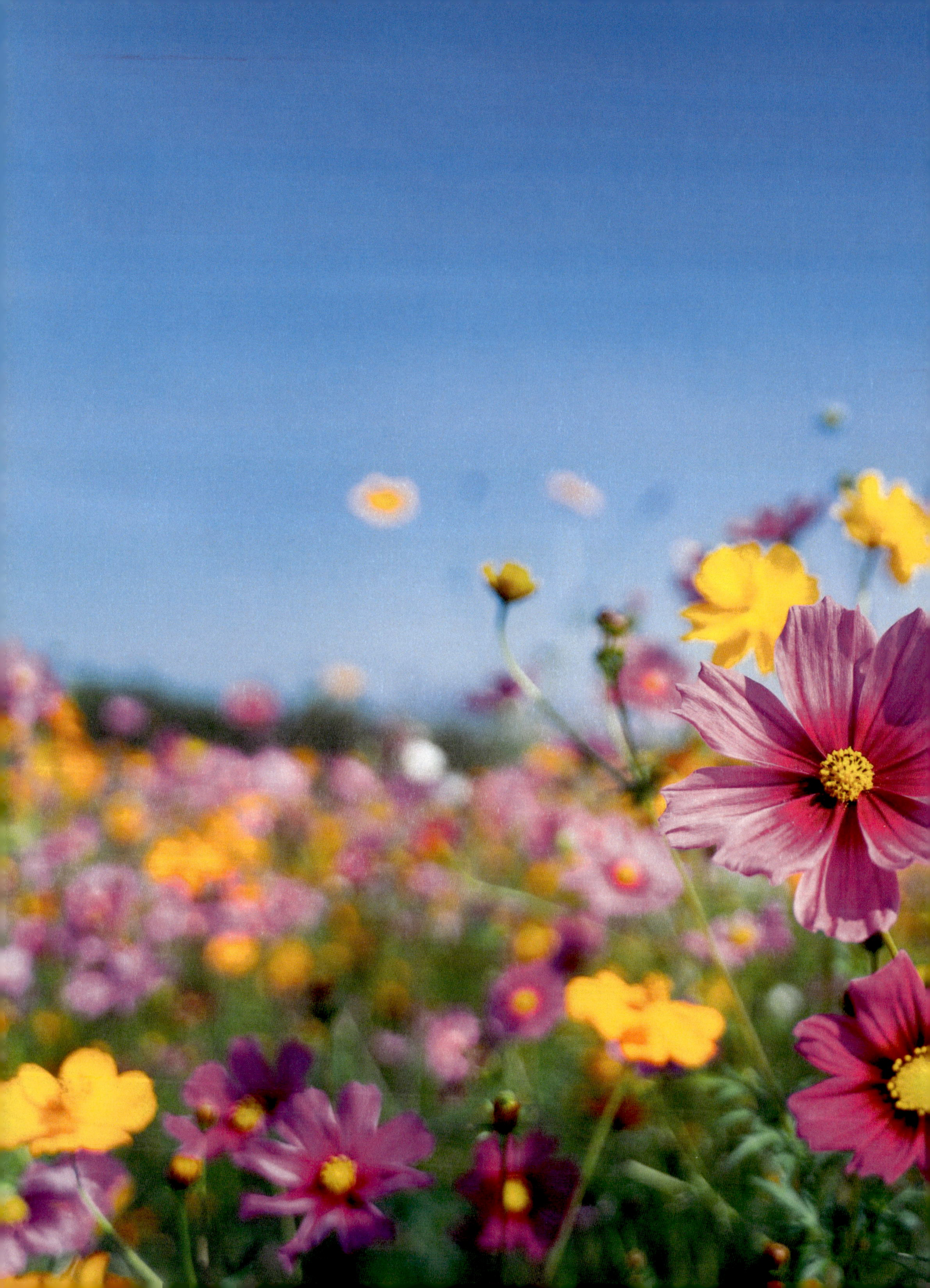

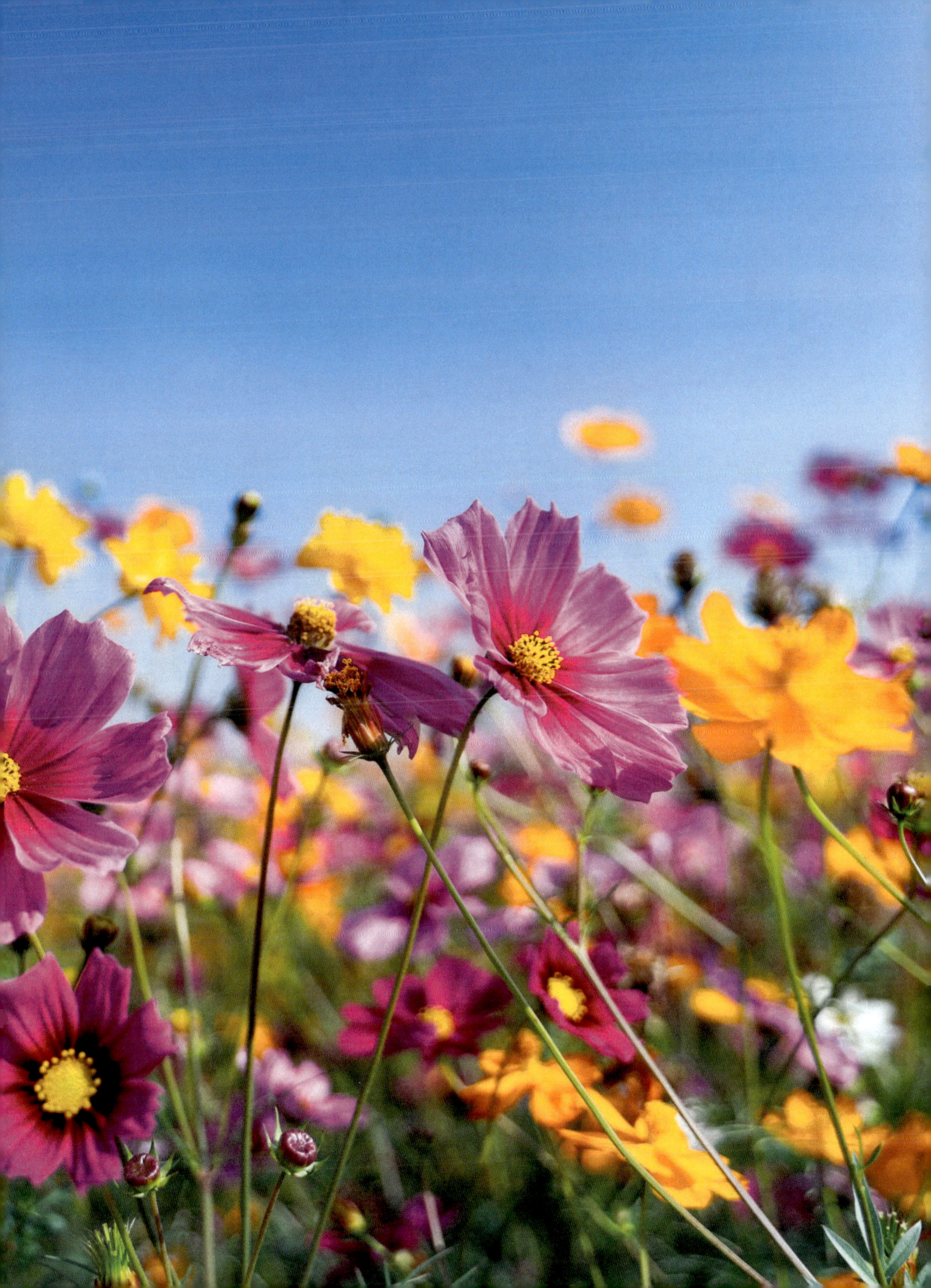

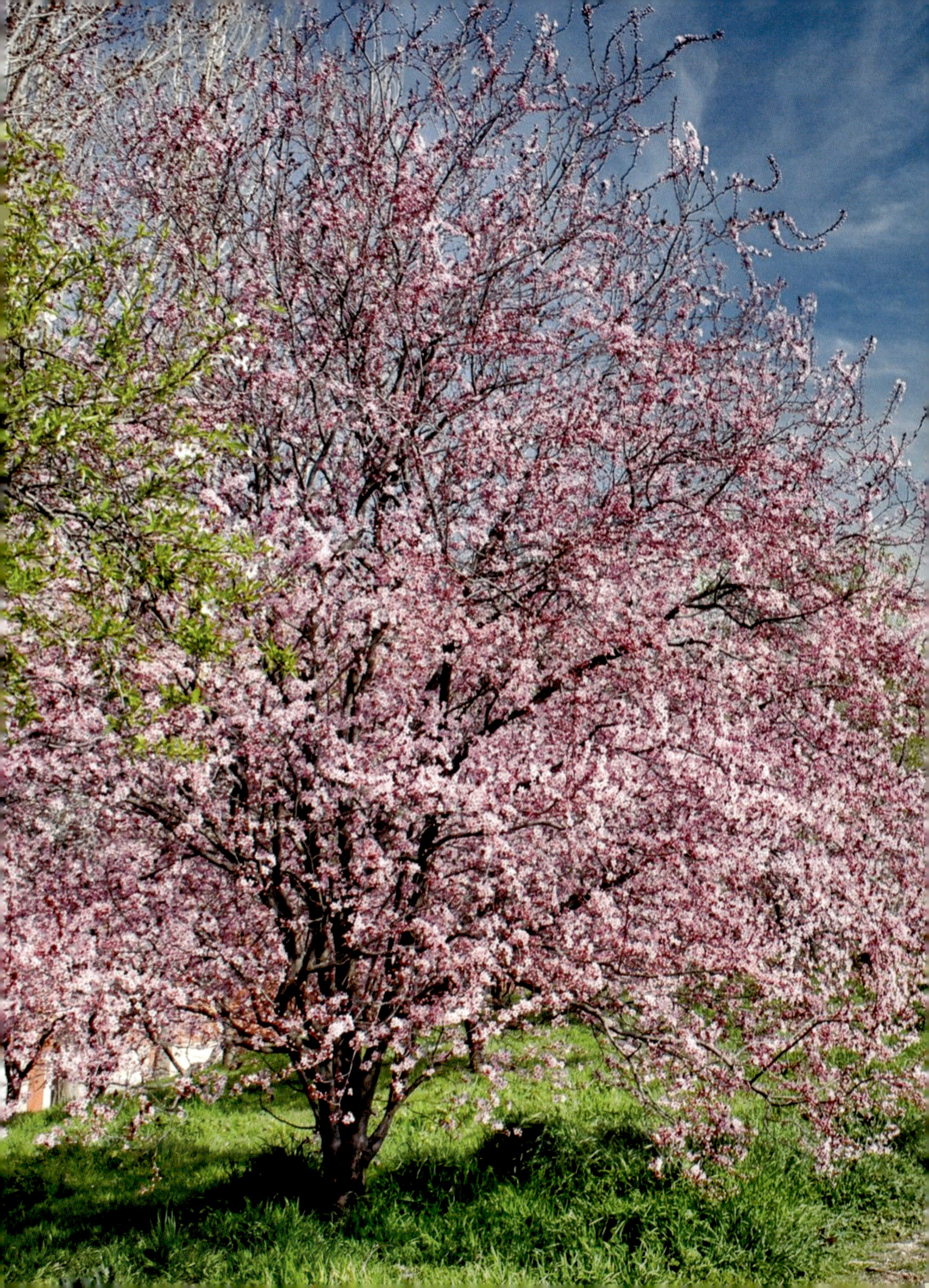

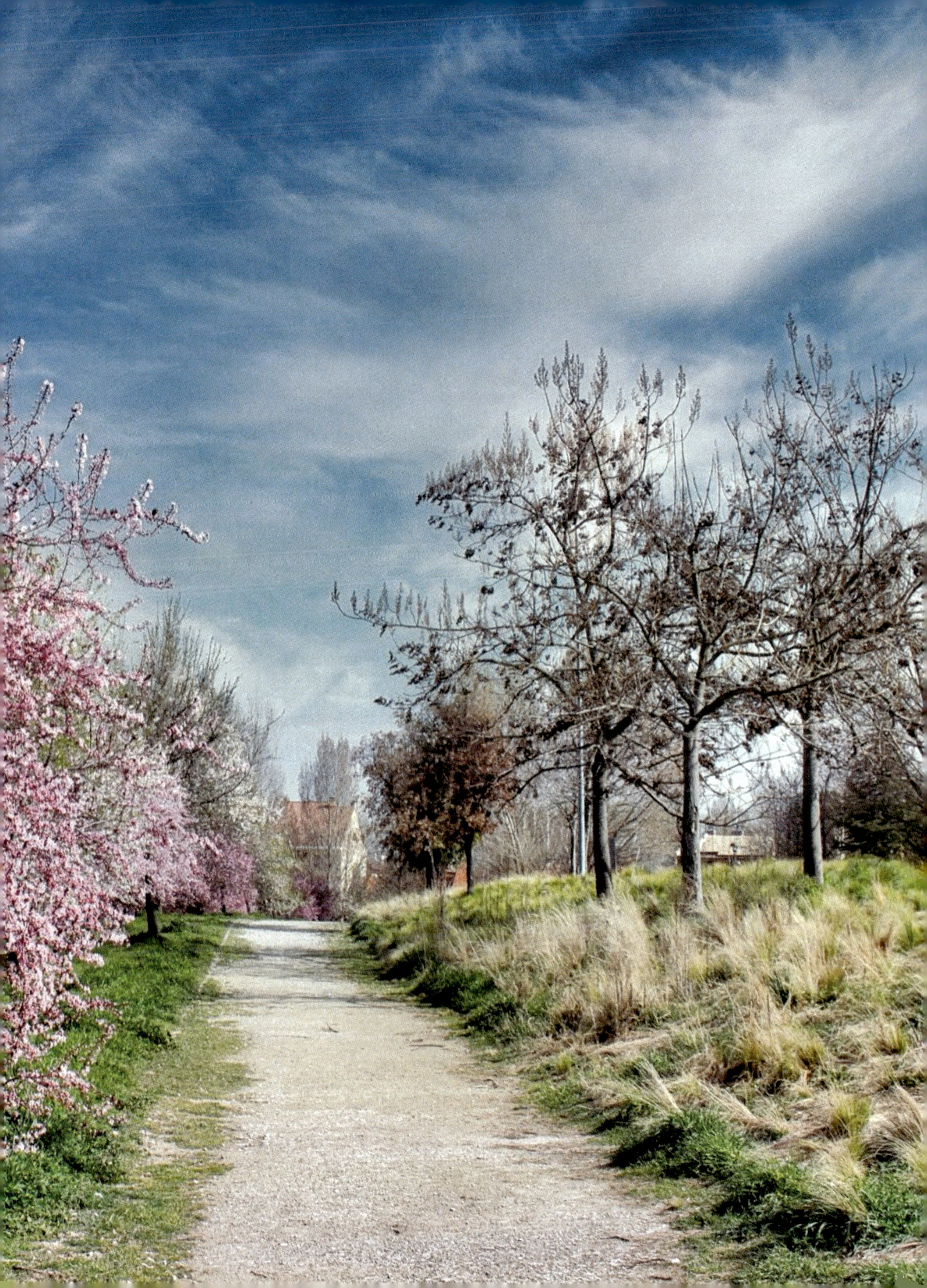

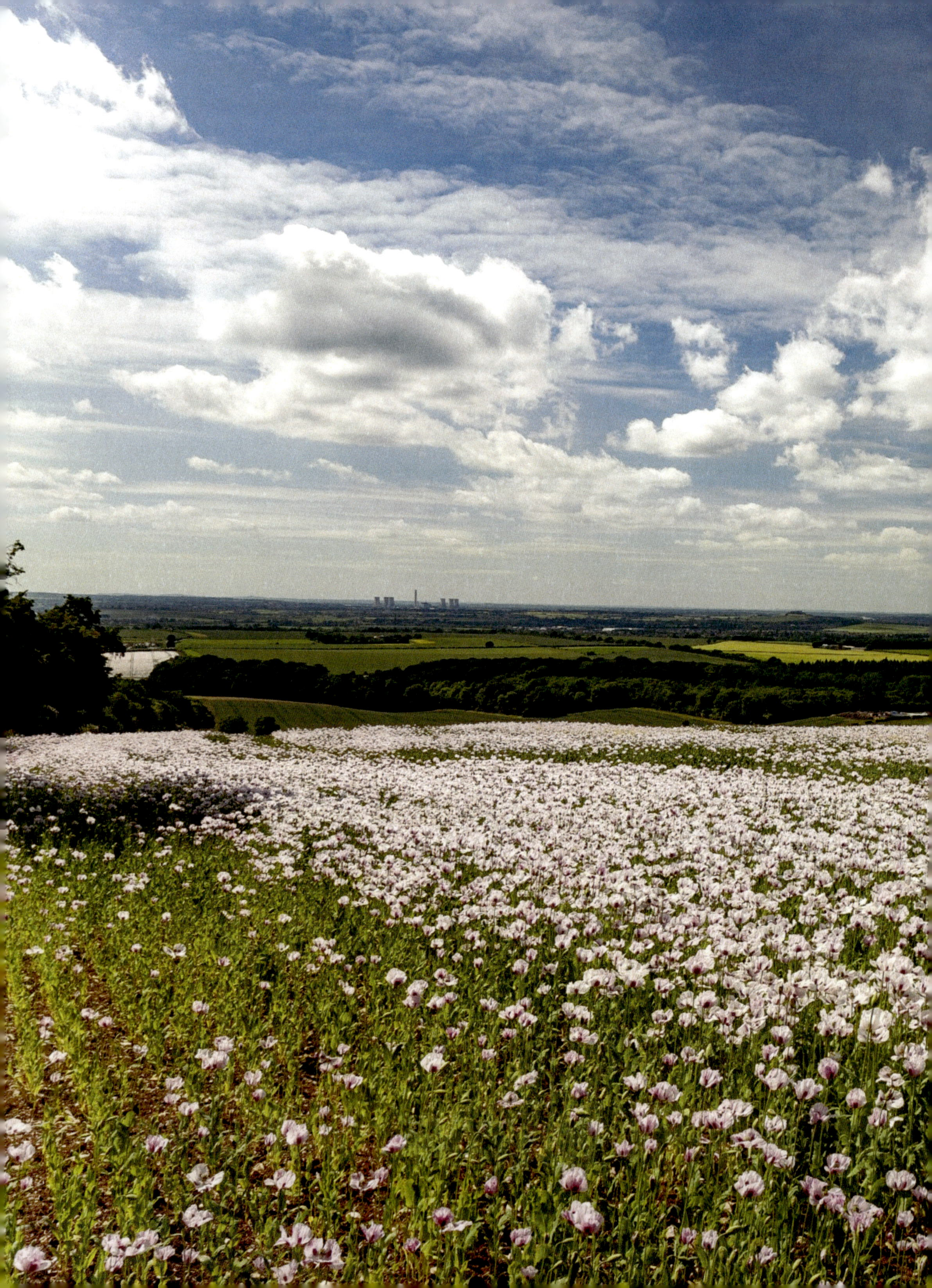

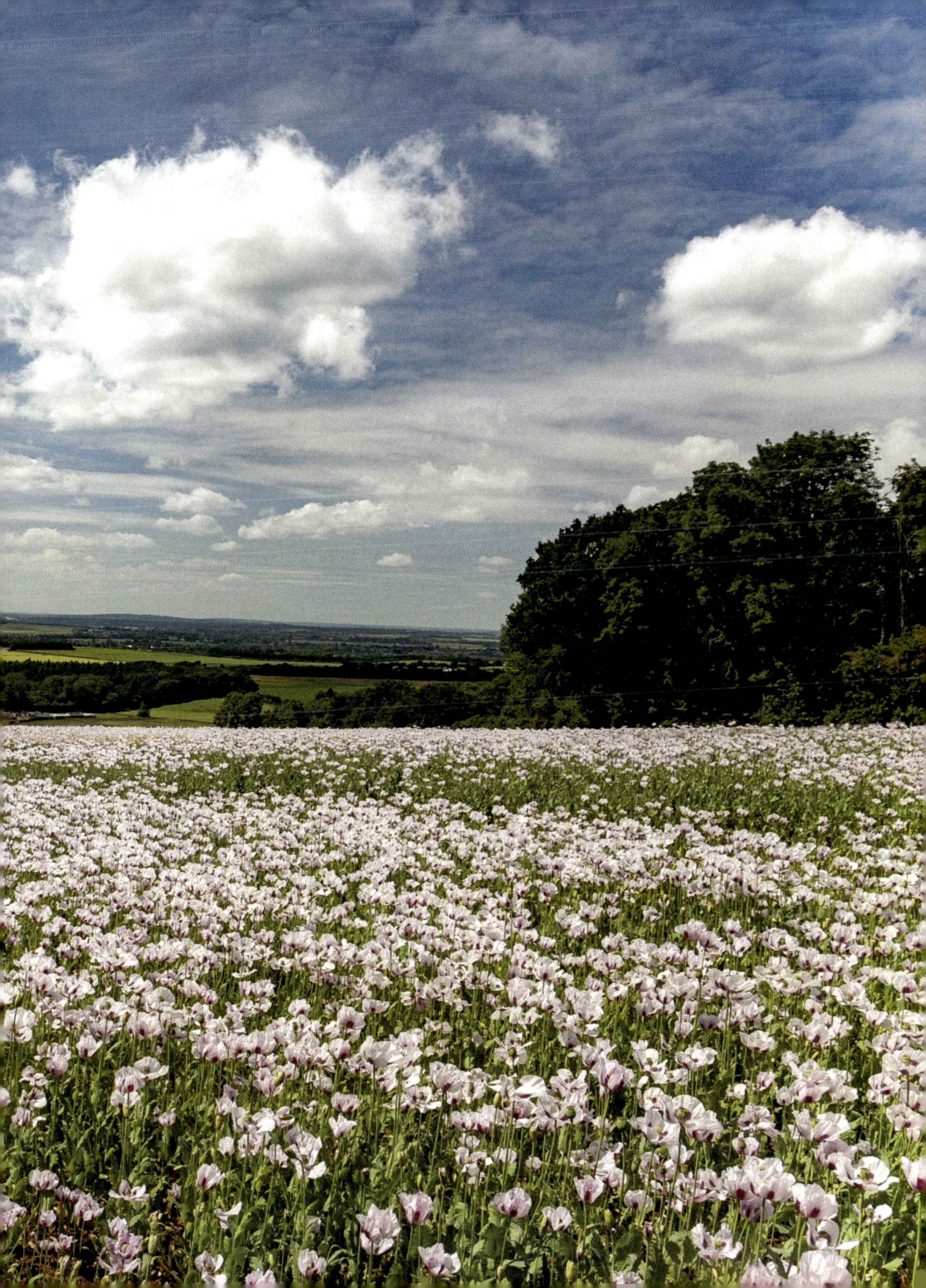

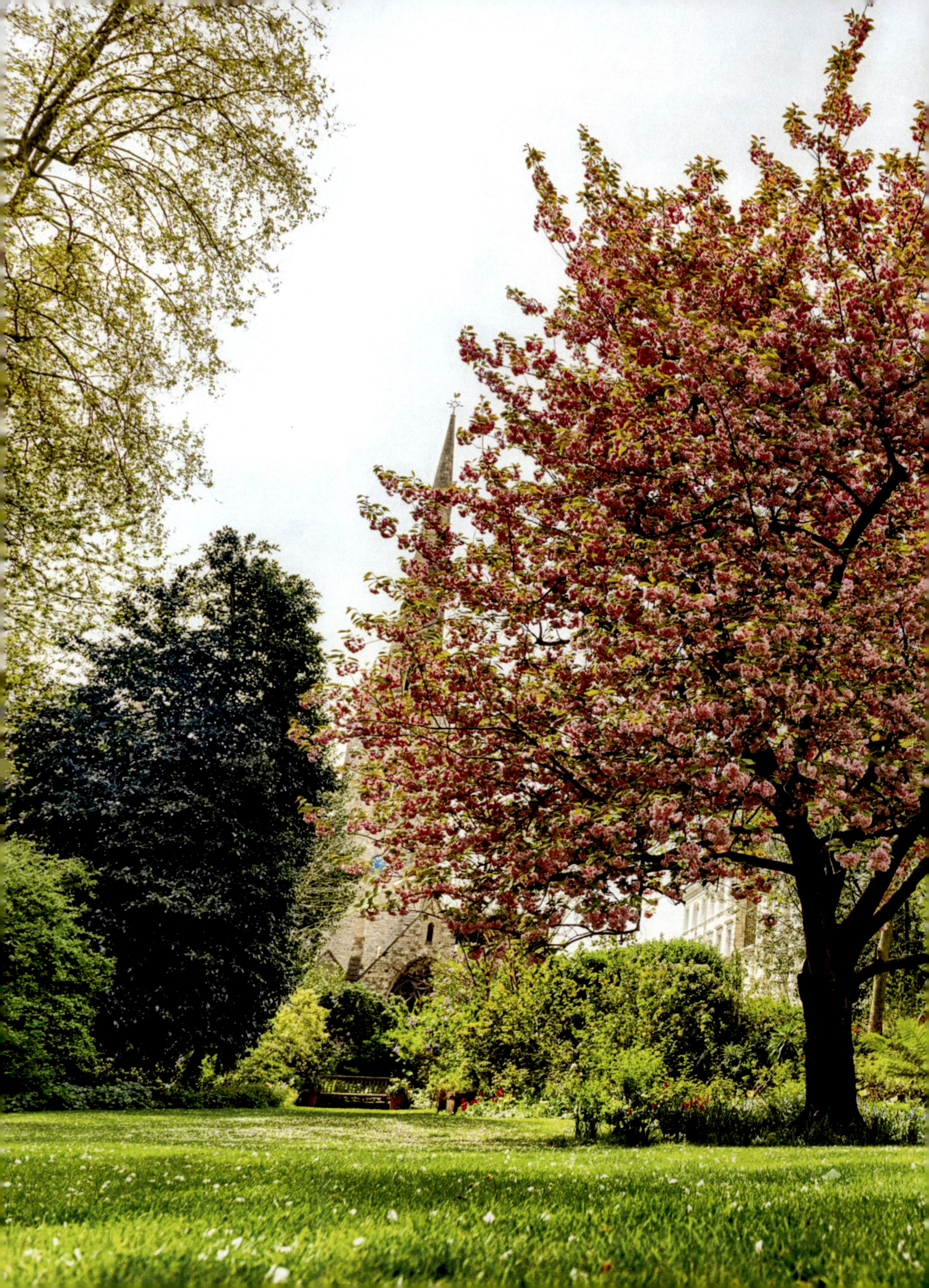

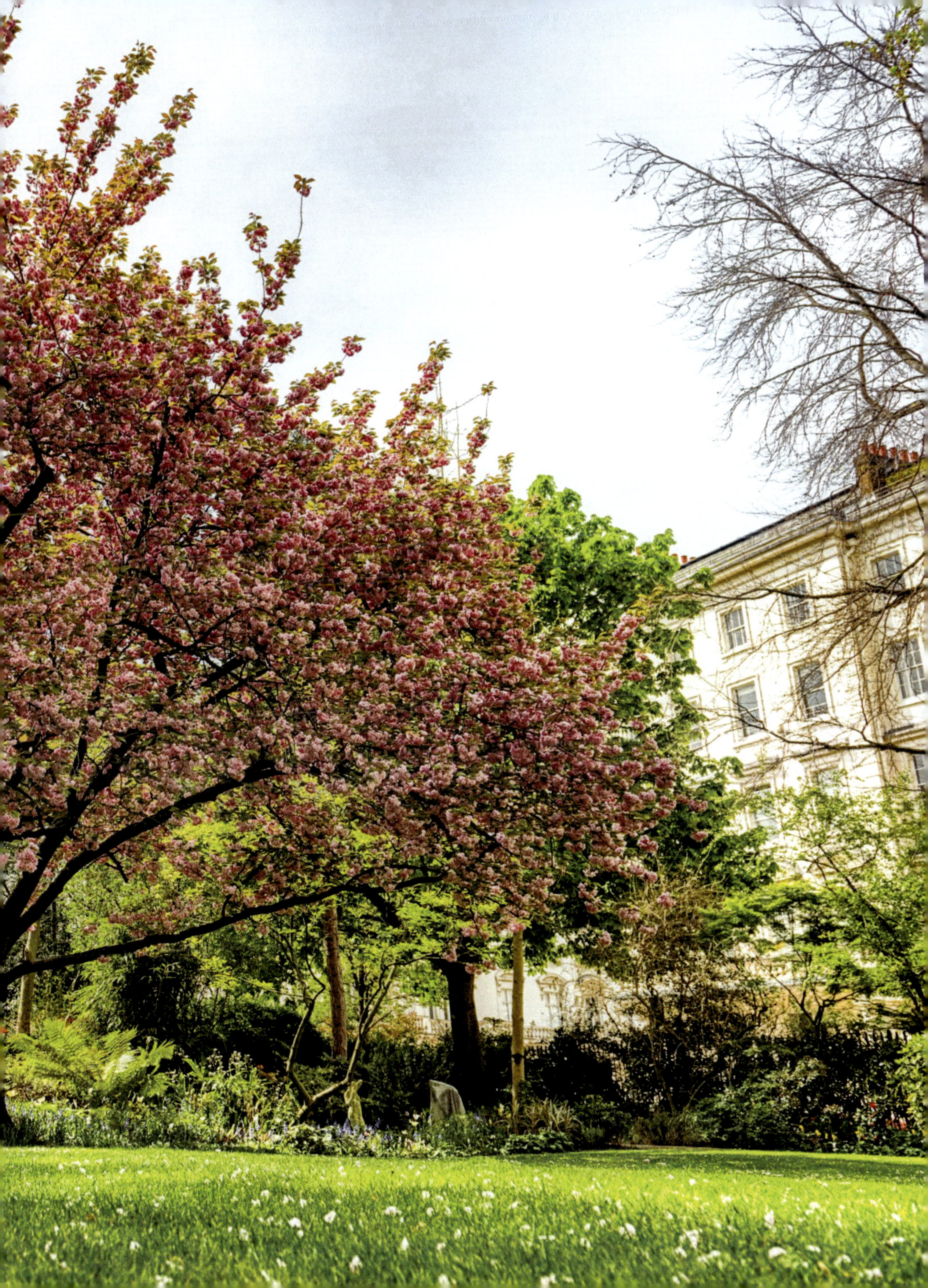

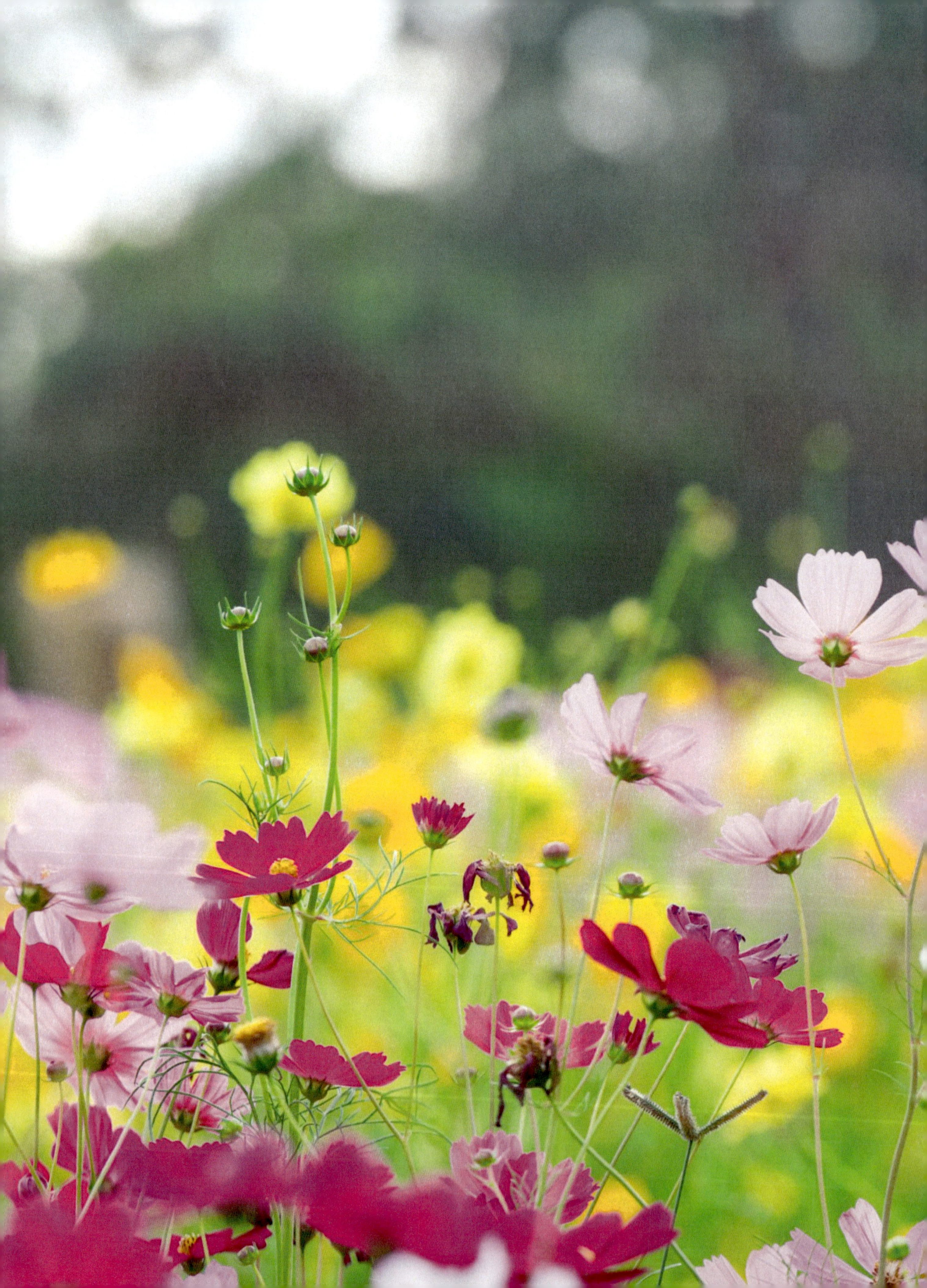

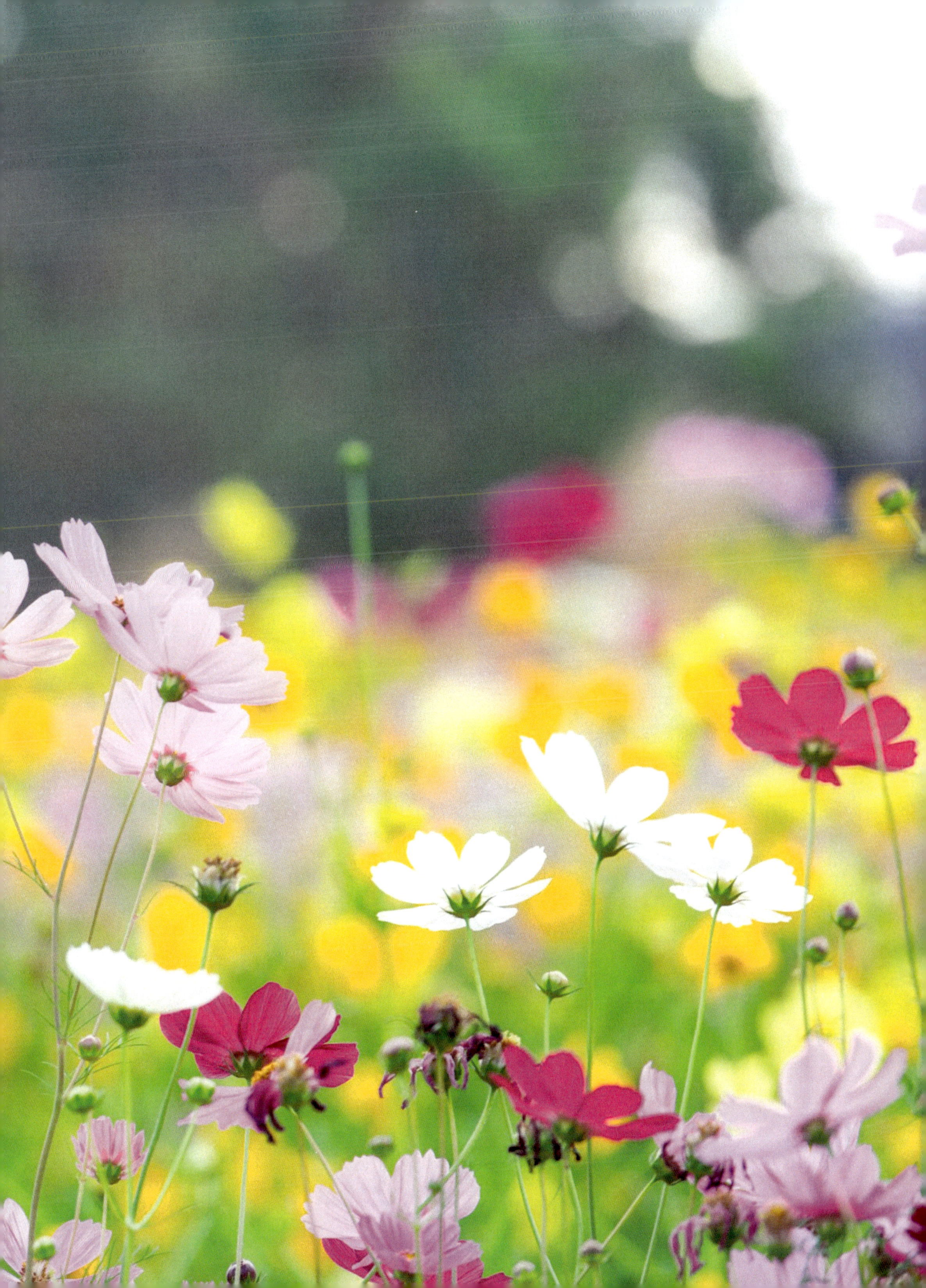

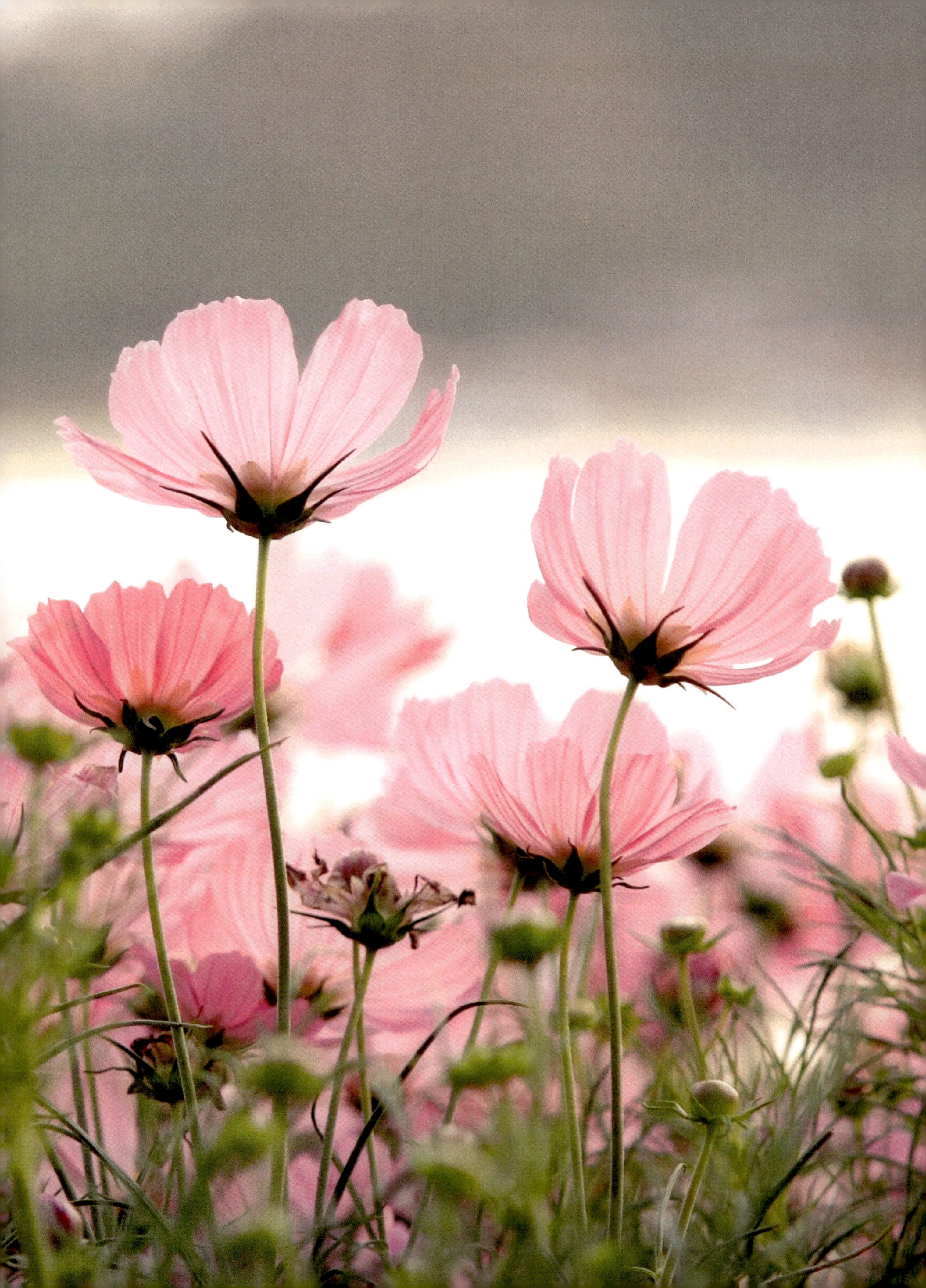

During springtime, nature is lush, with greenery and the vibrant colors of the beautiful flowers come back to life.

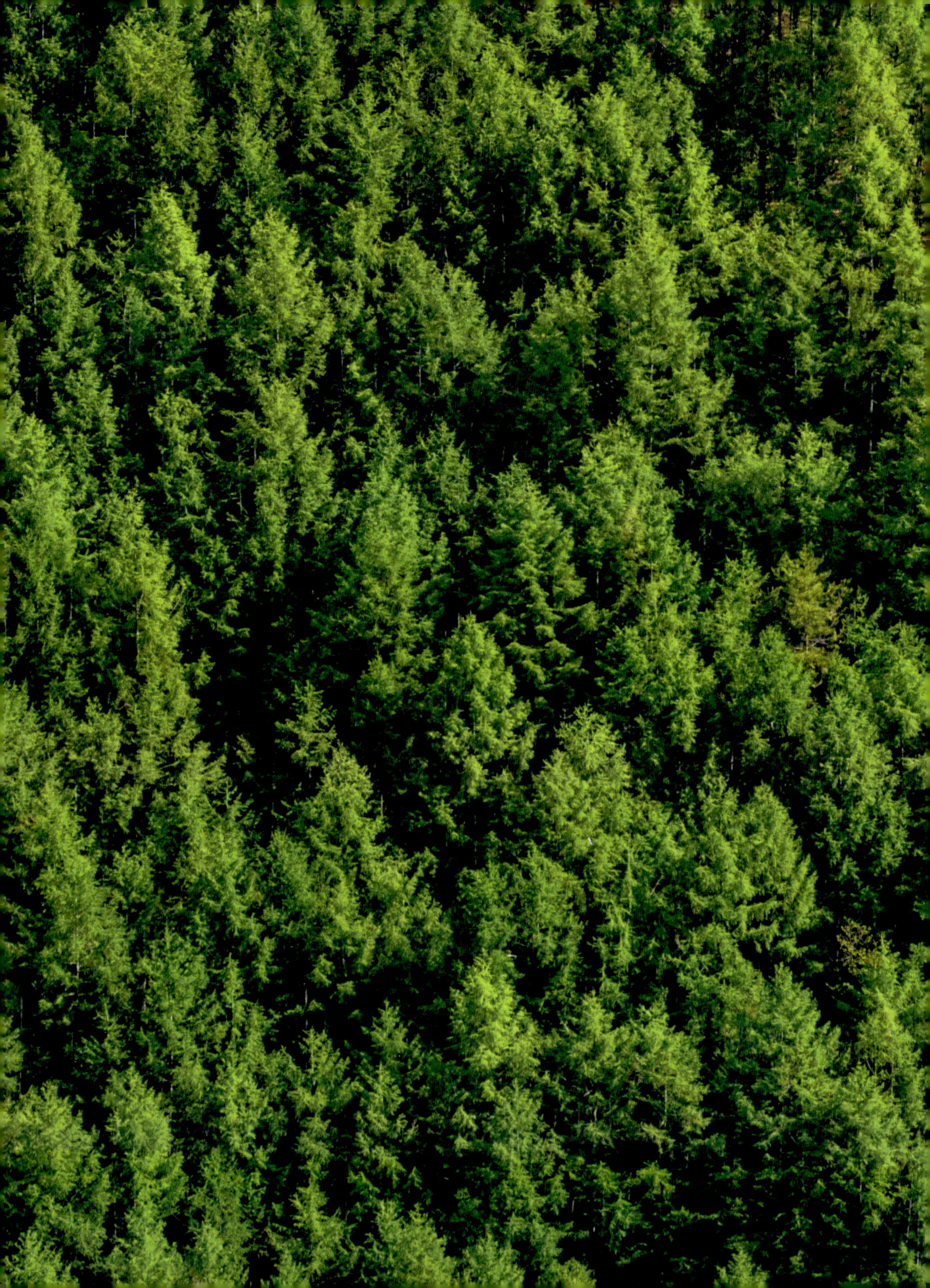

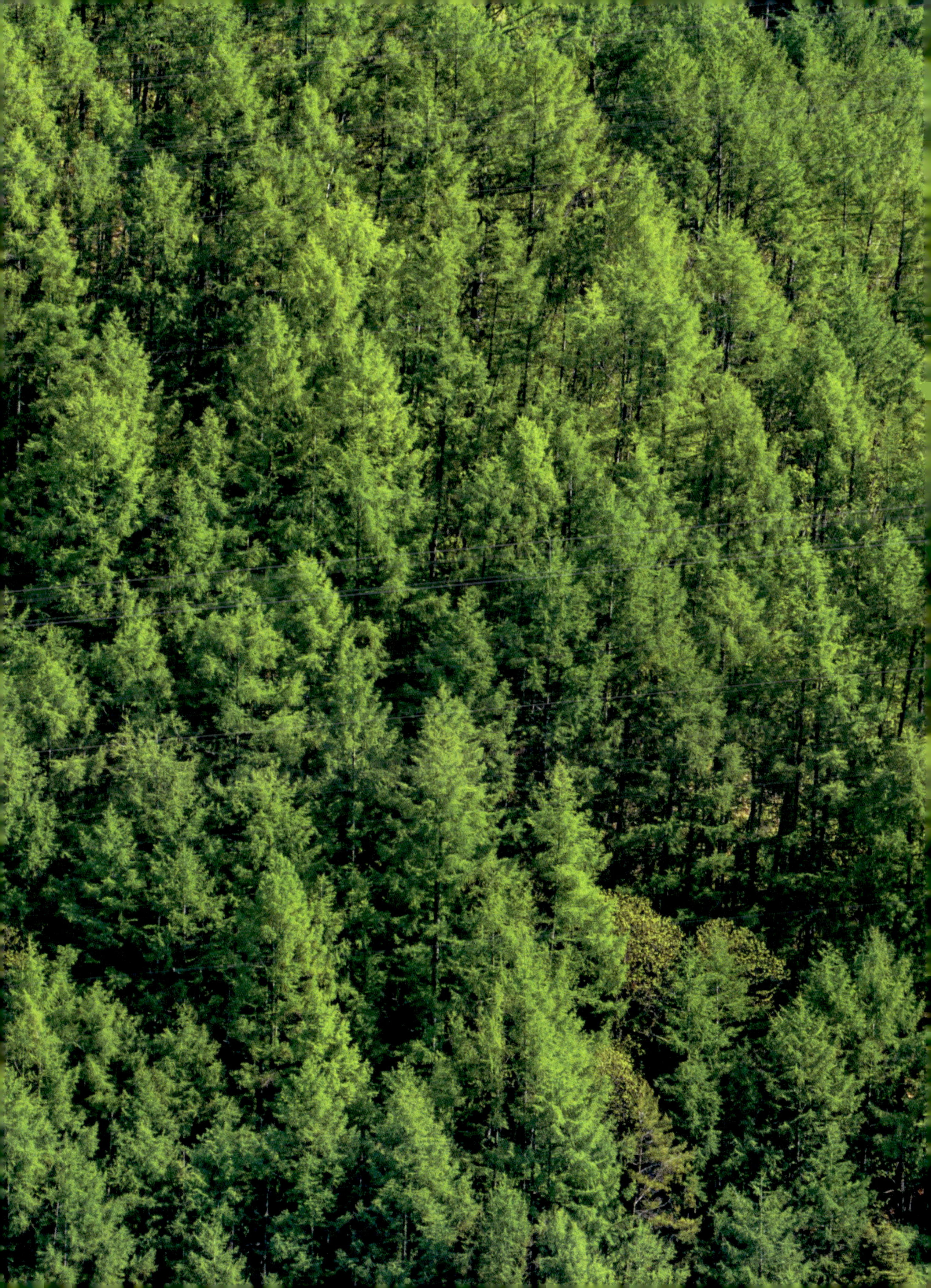

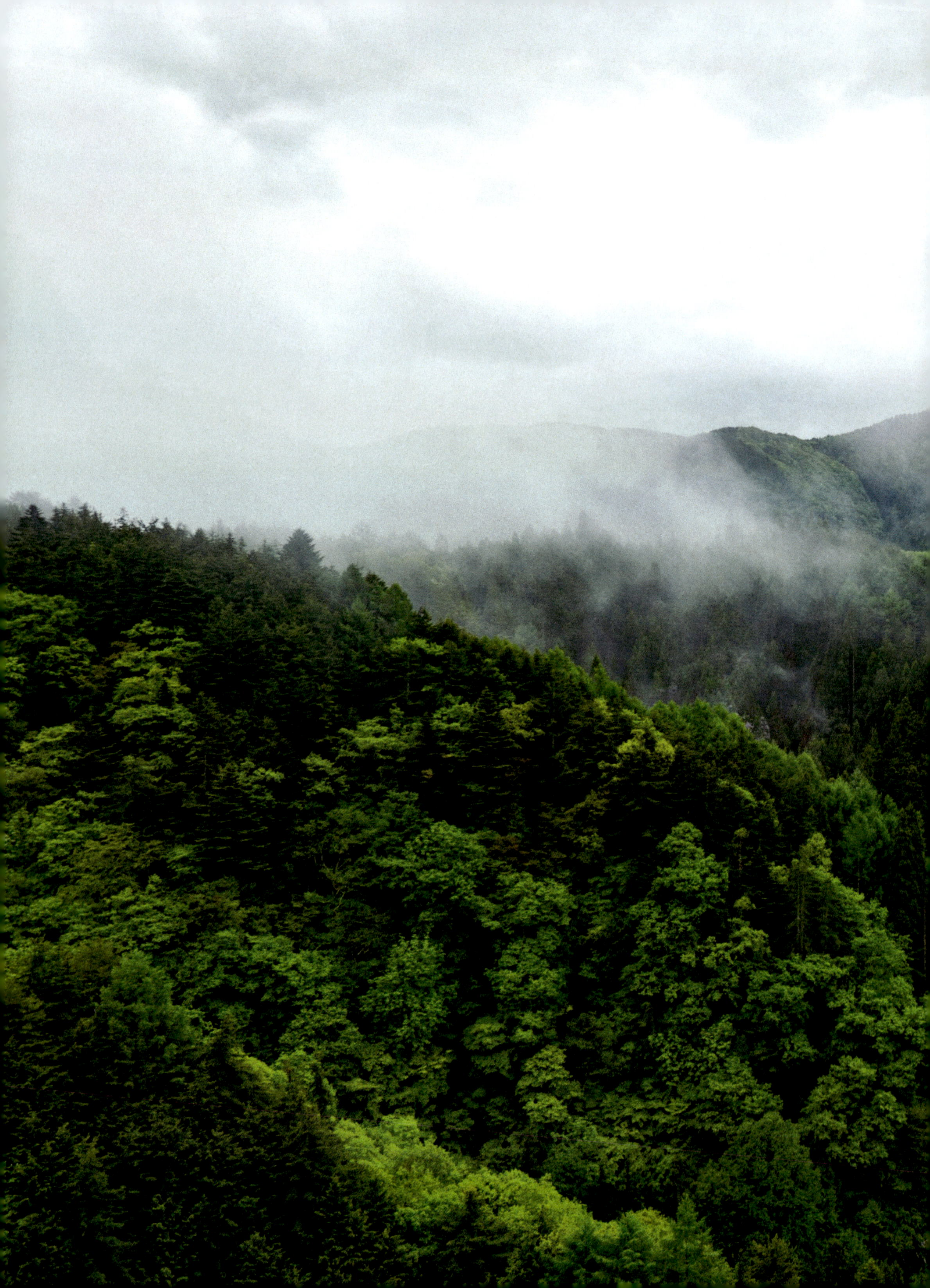

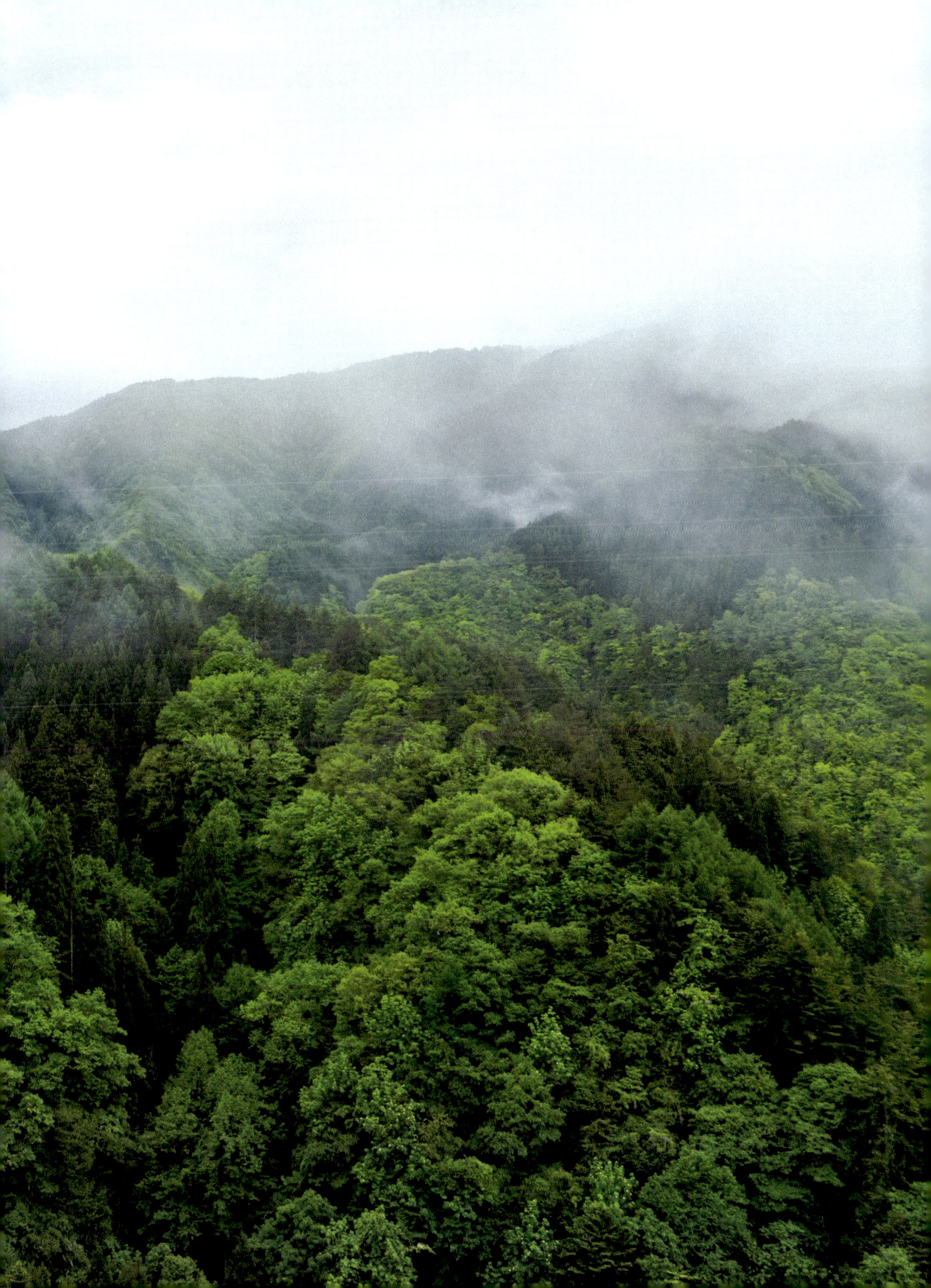

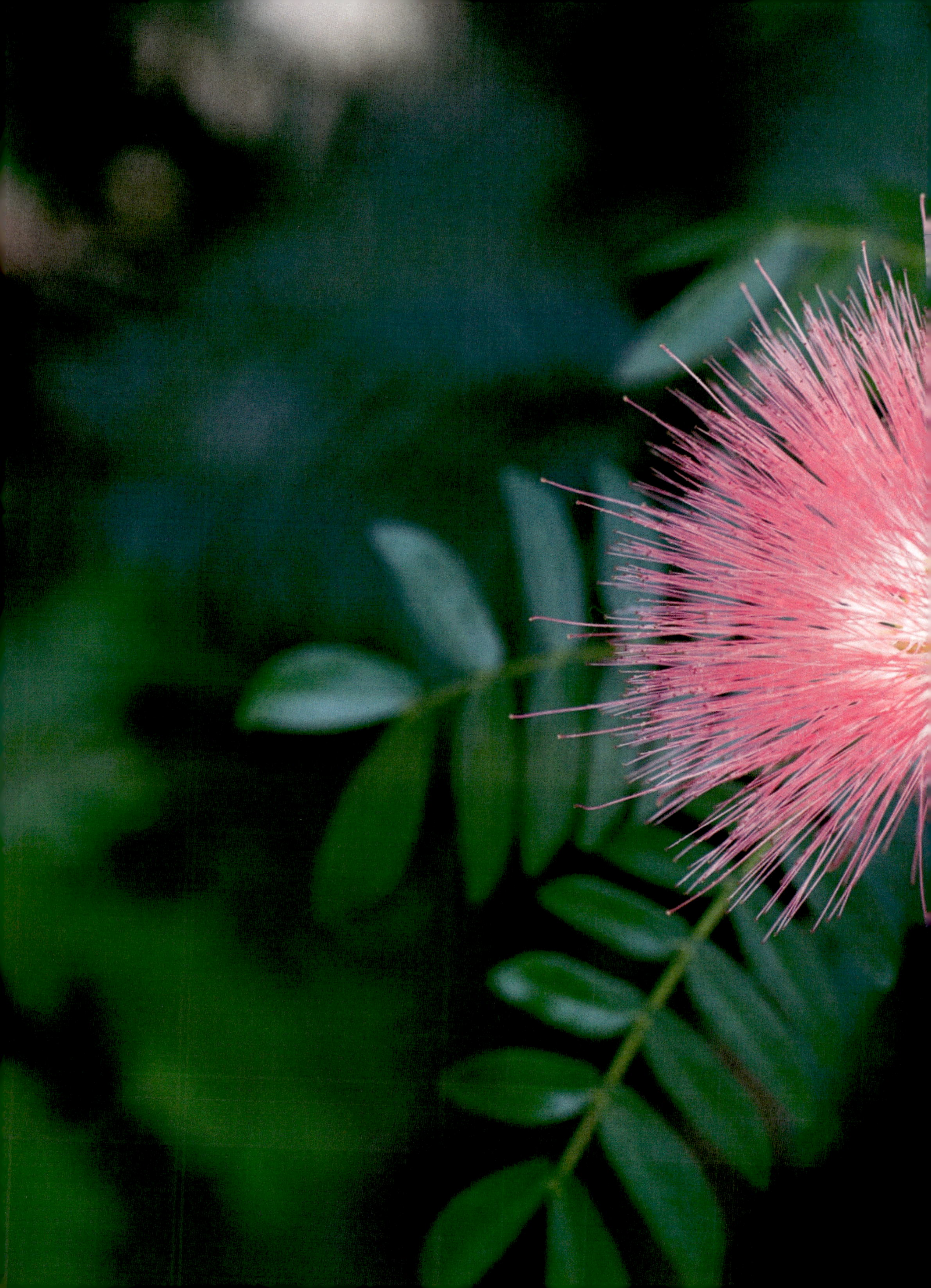

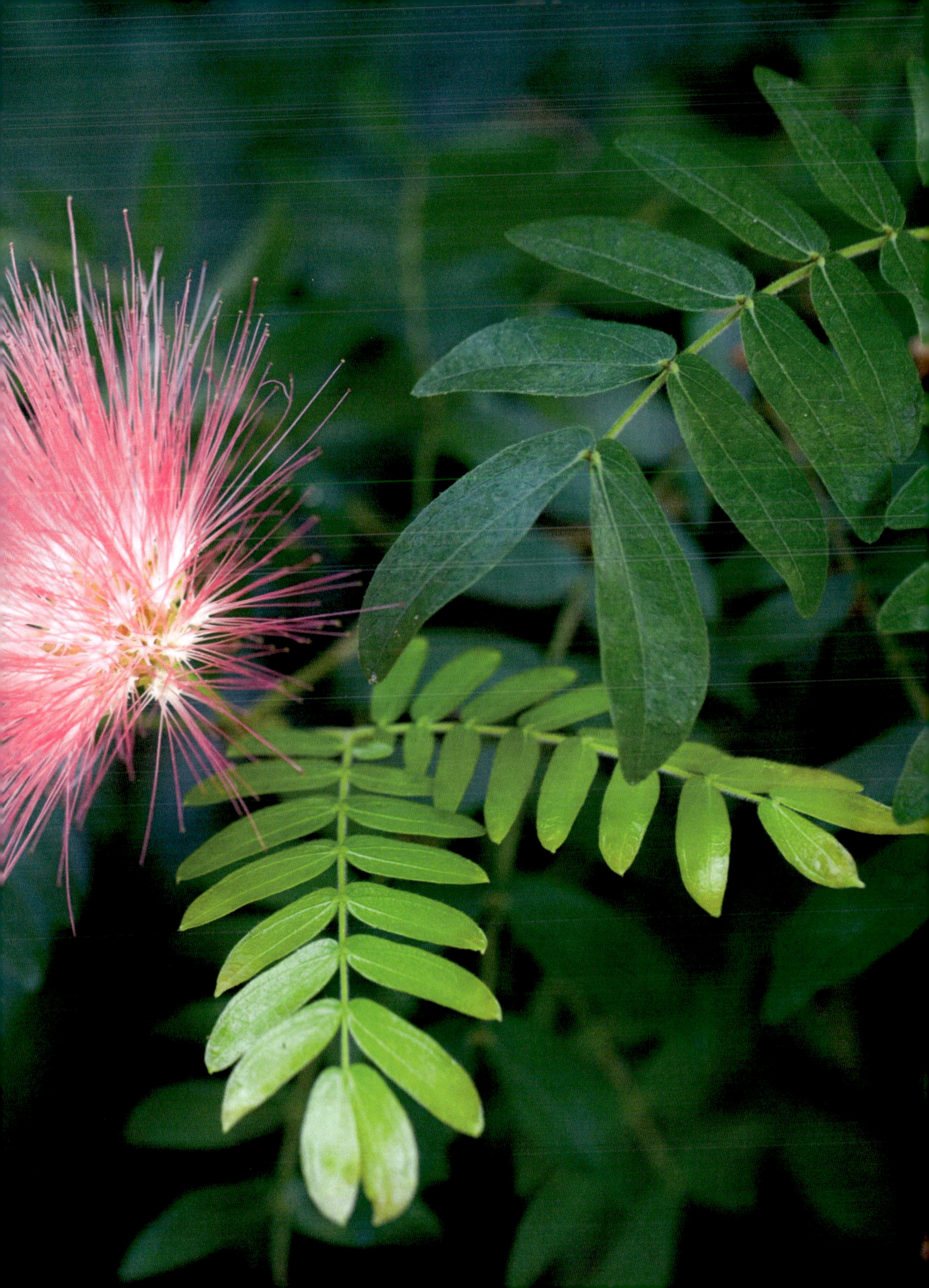

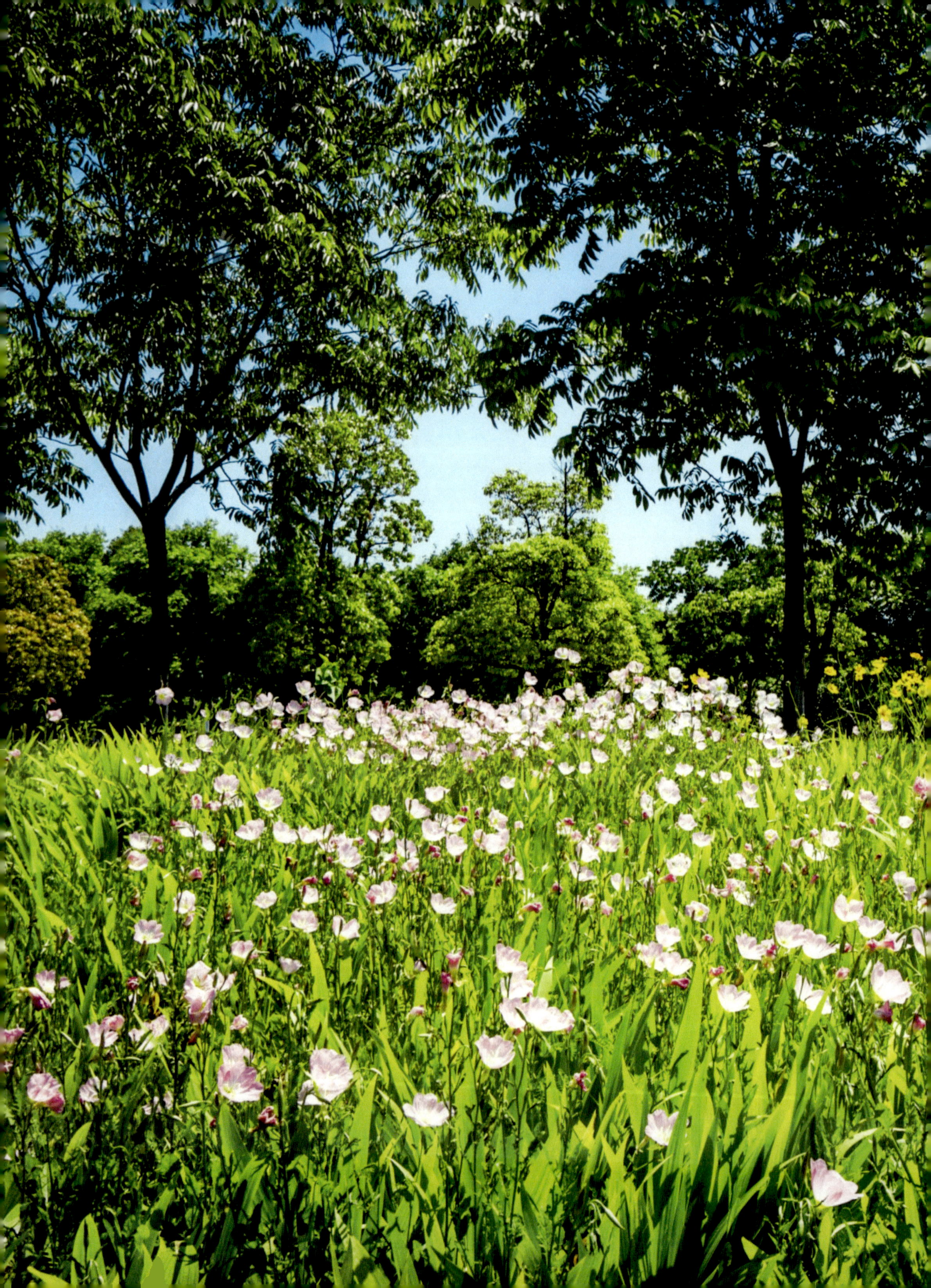

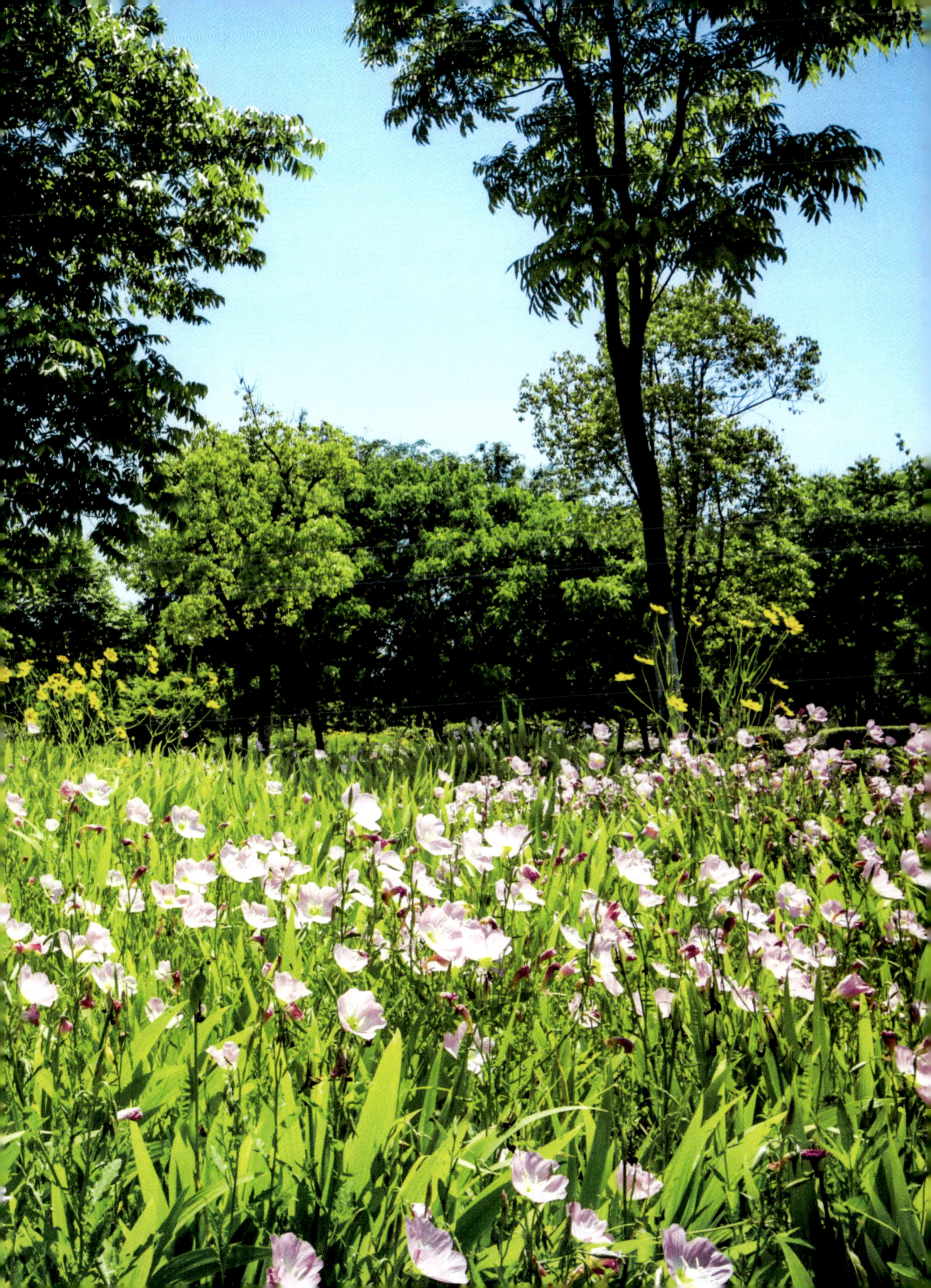

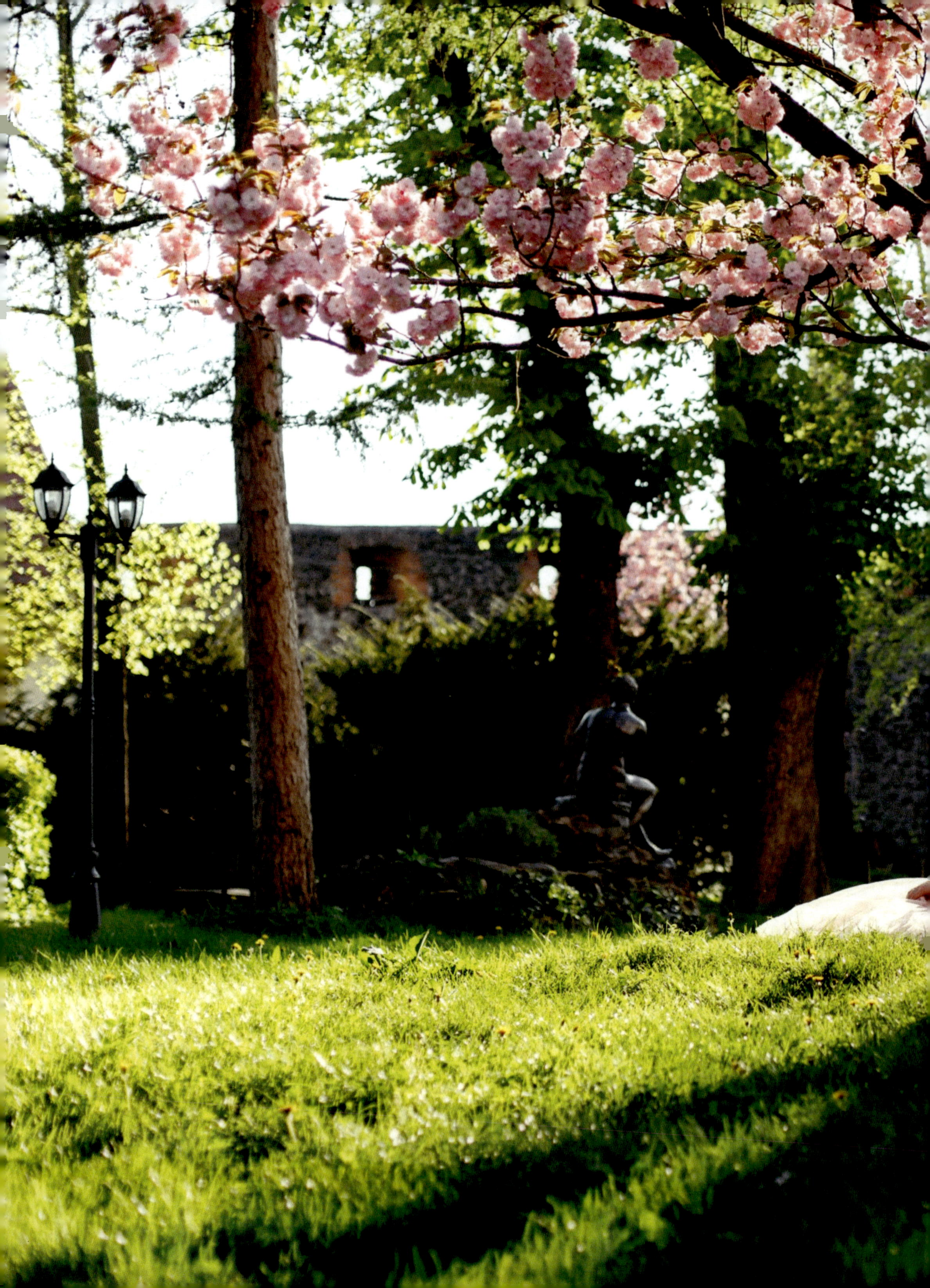

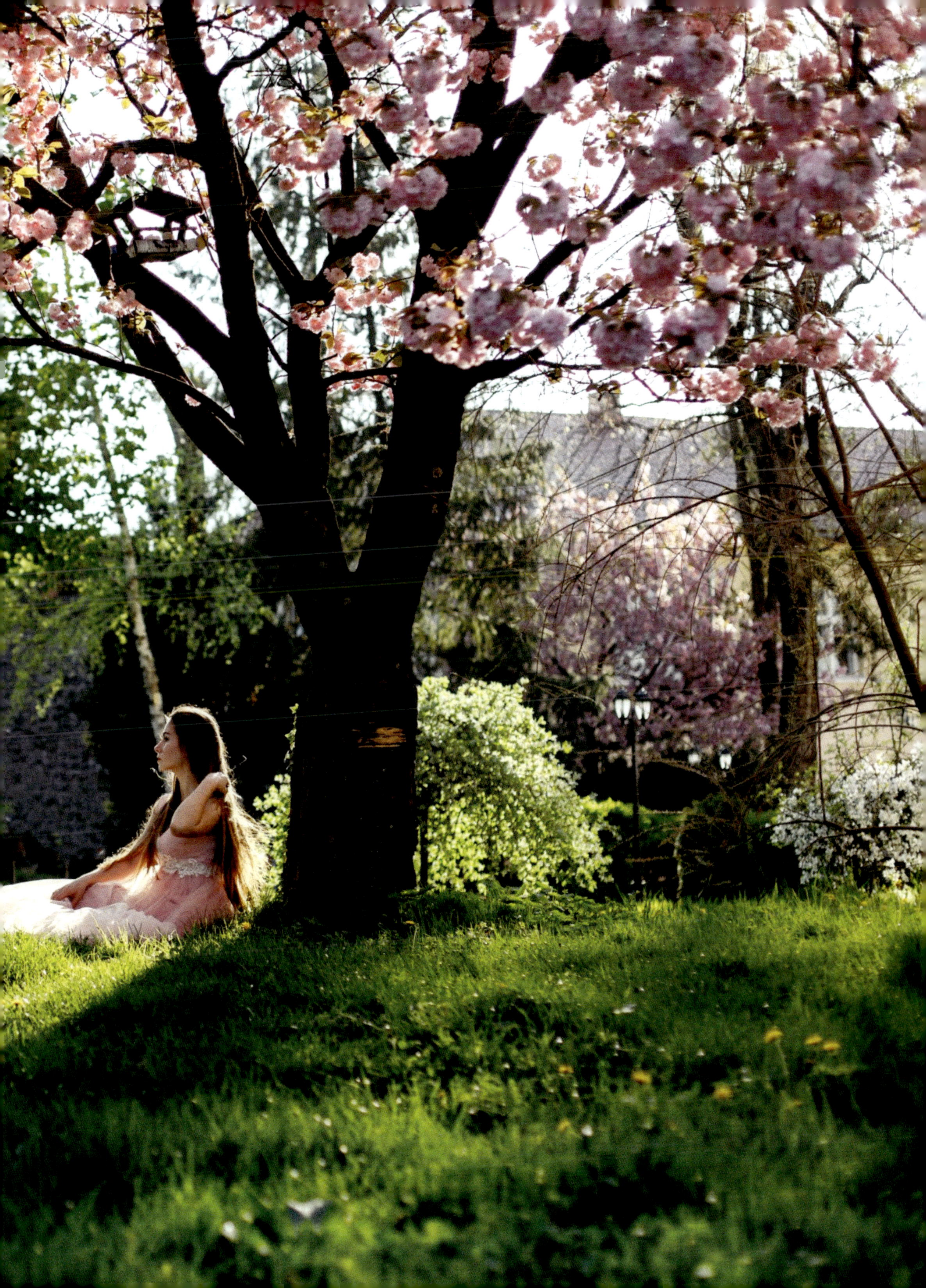

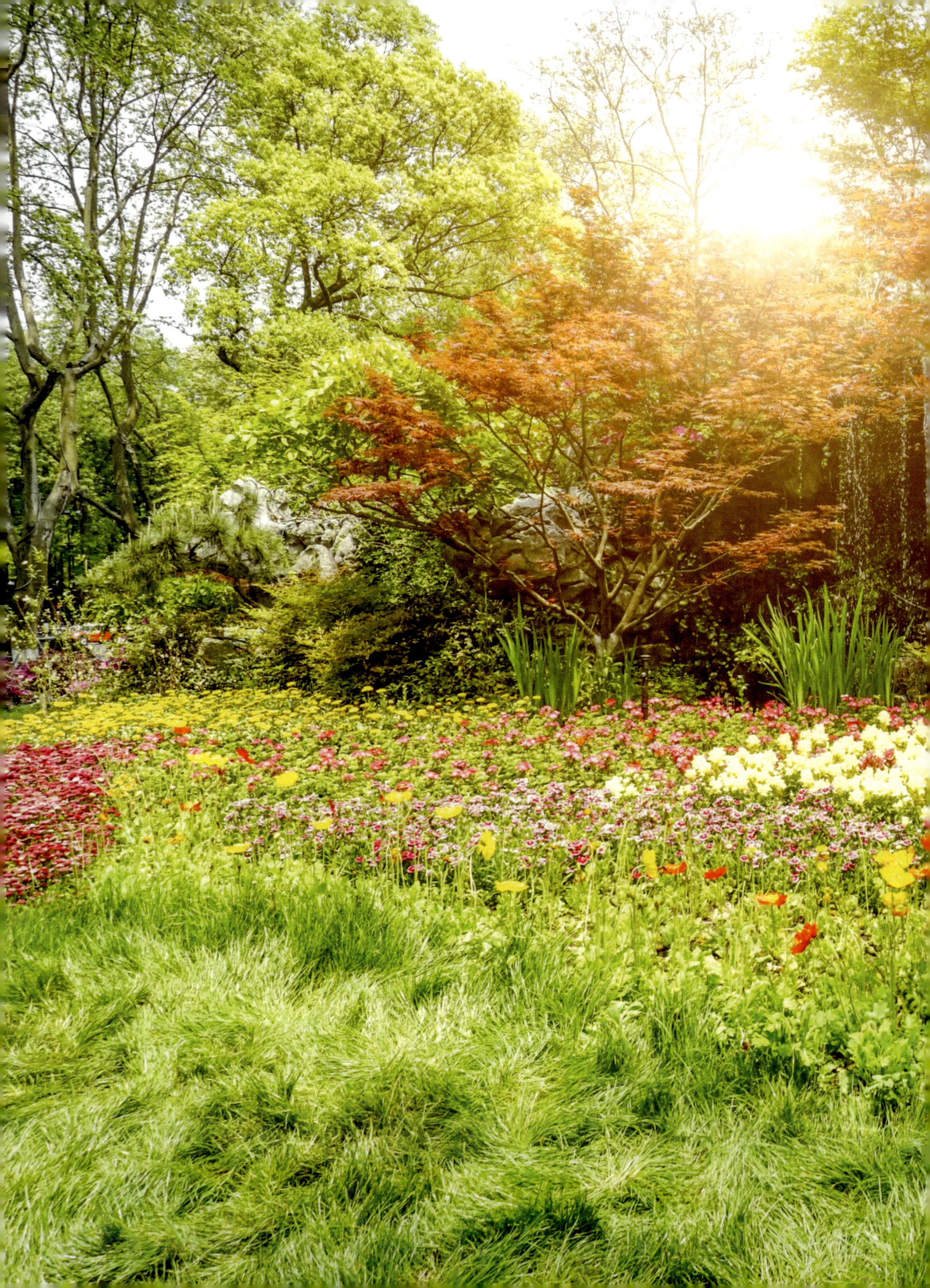

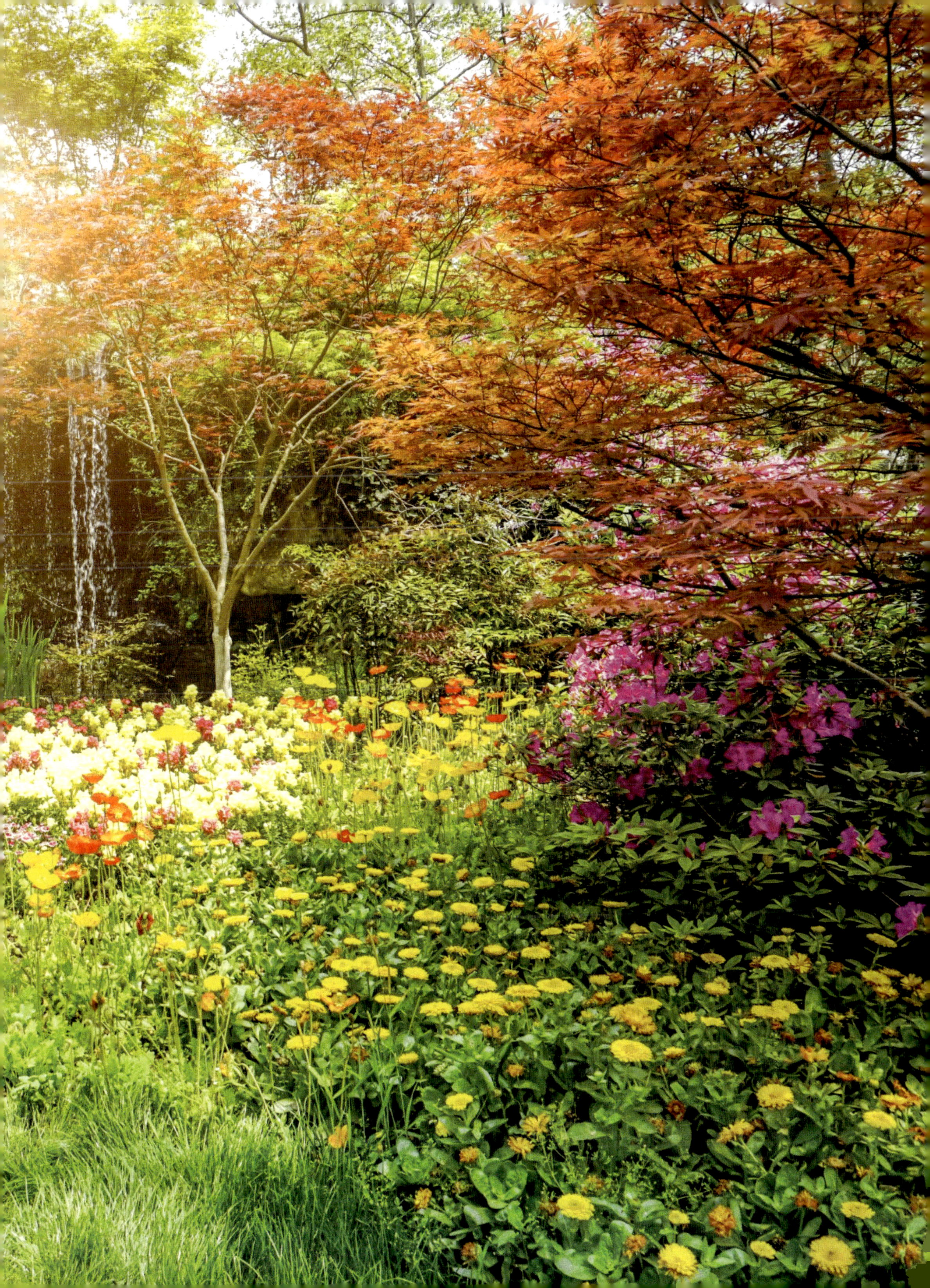

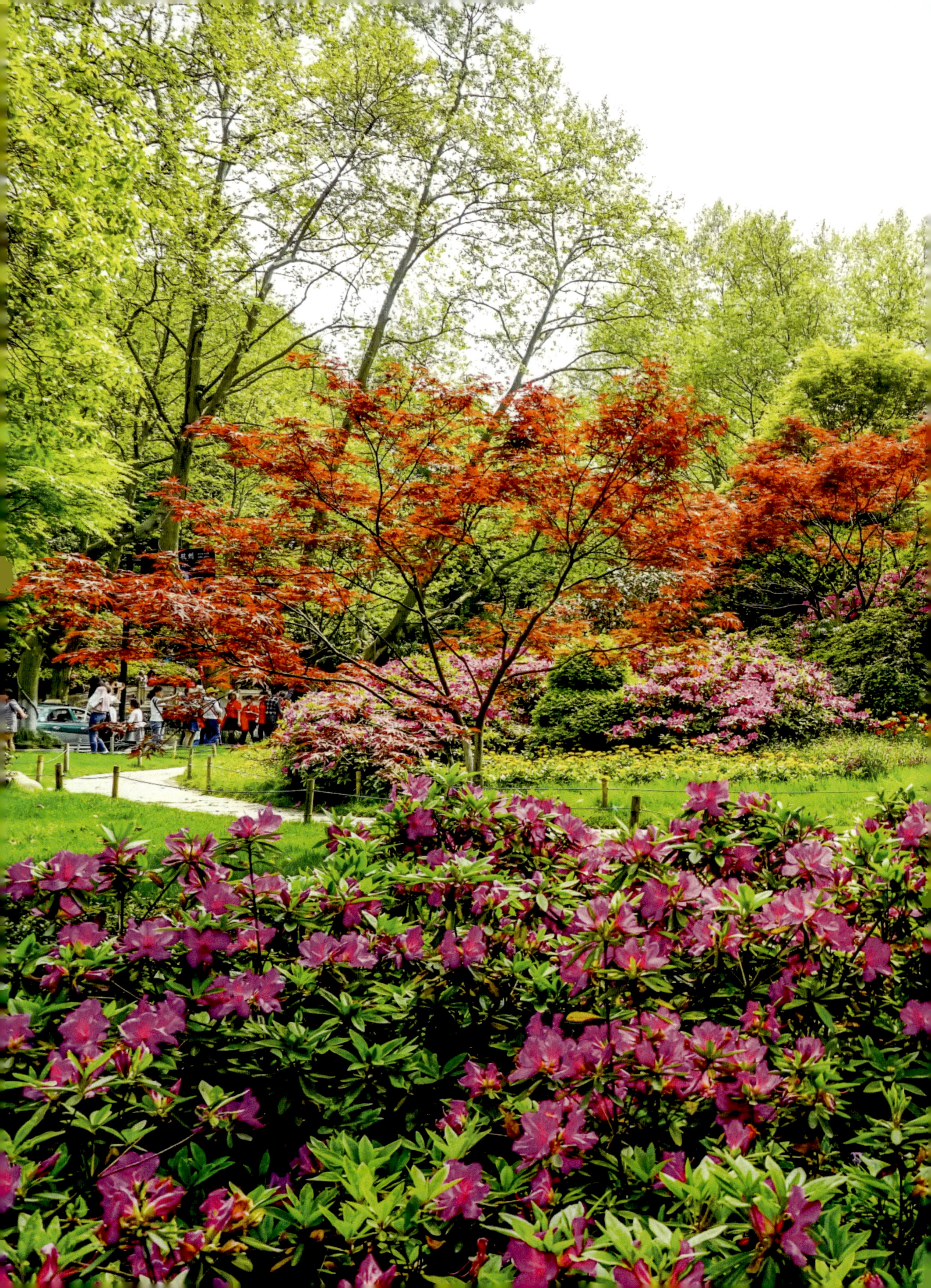

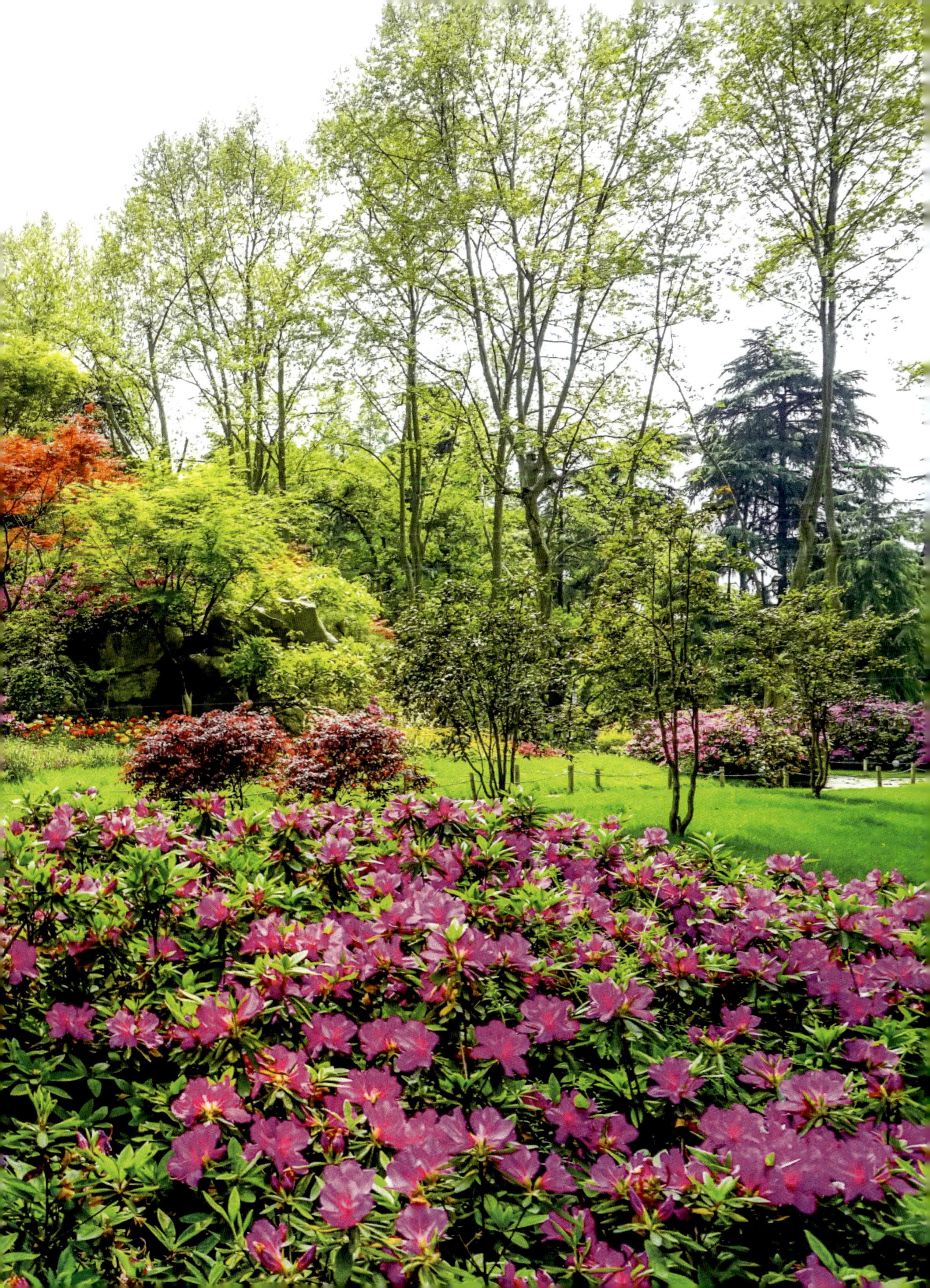

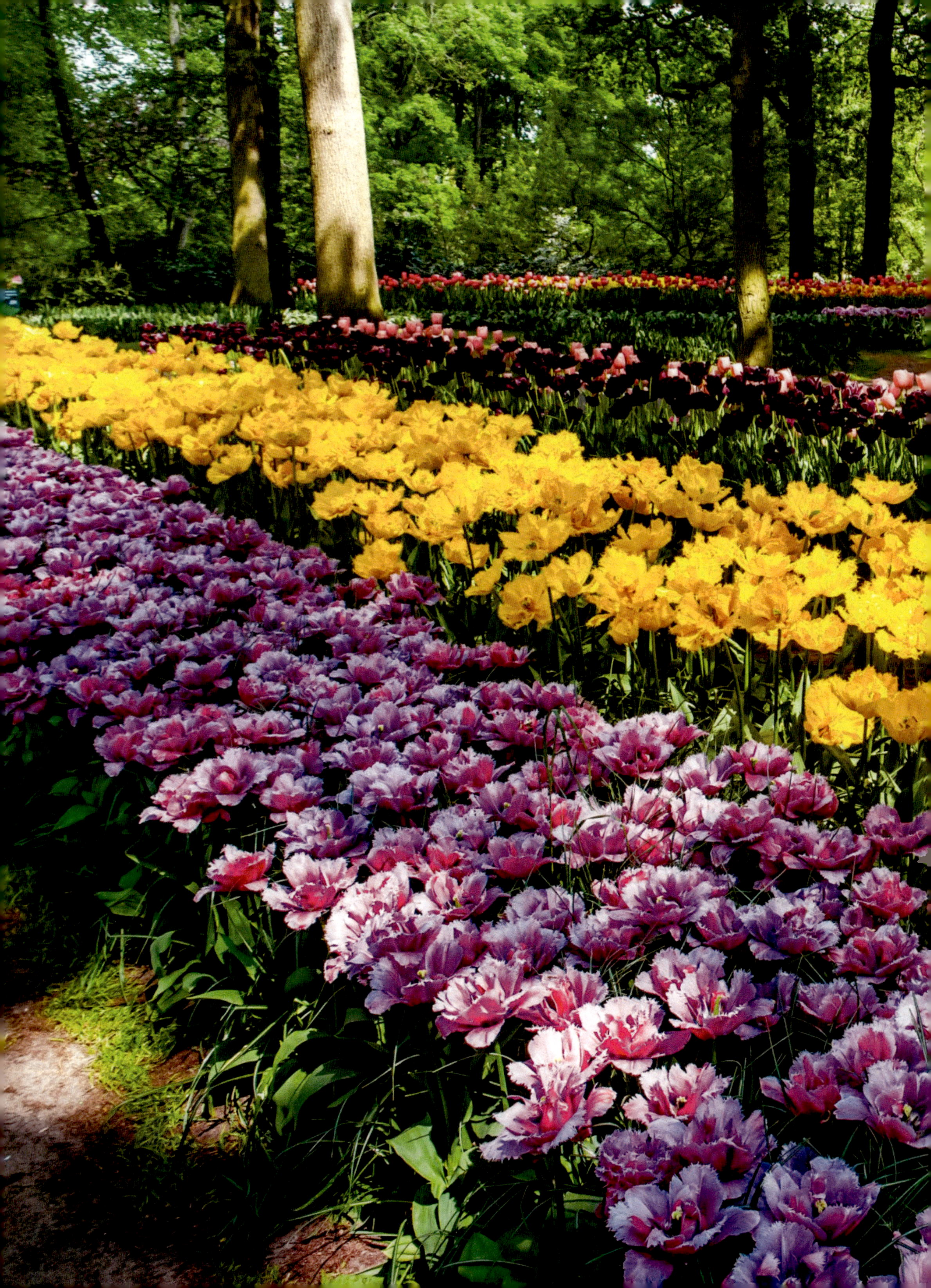

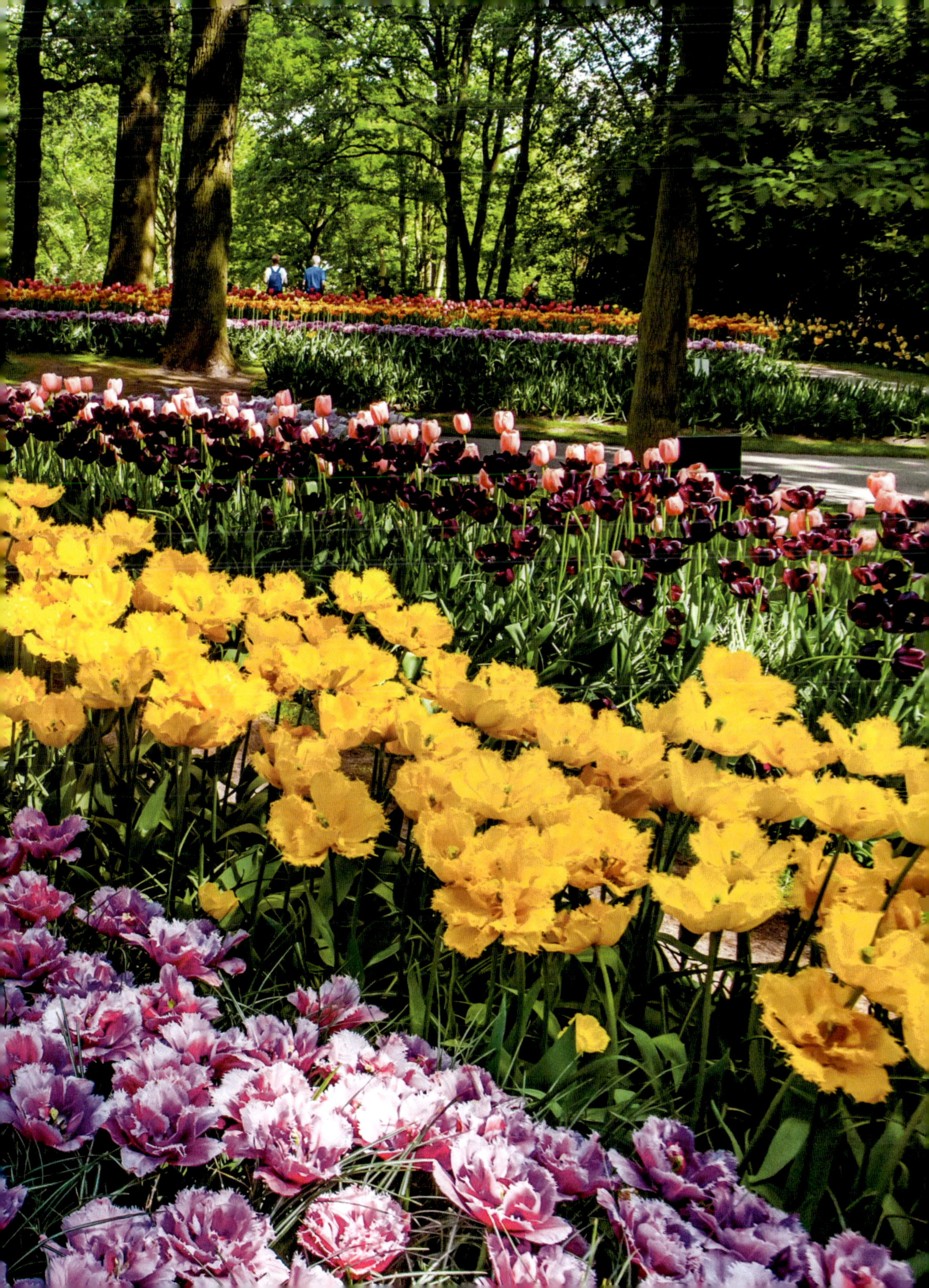

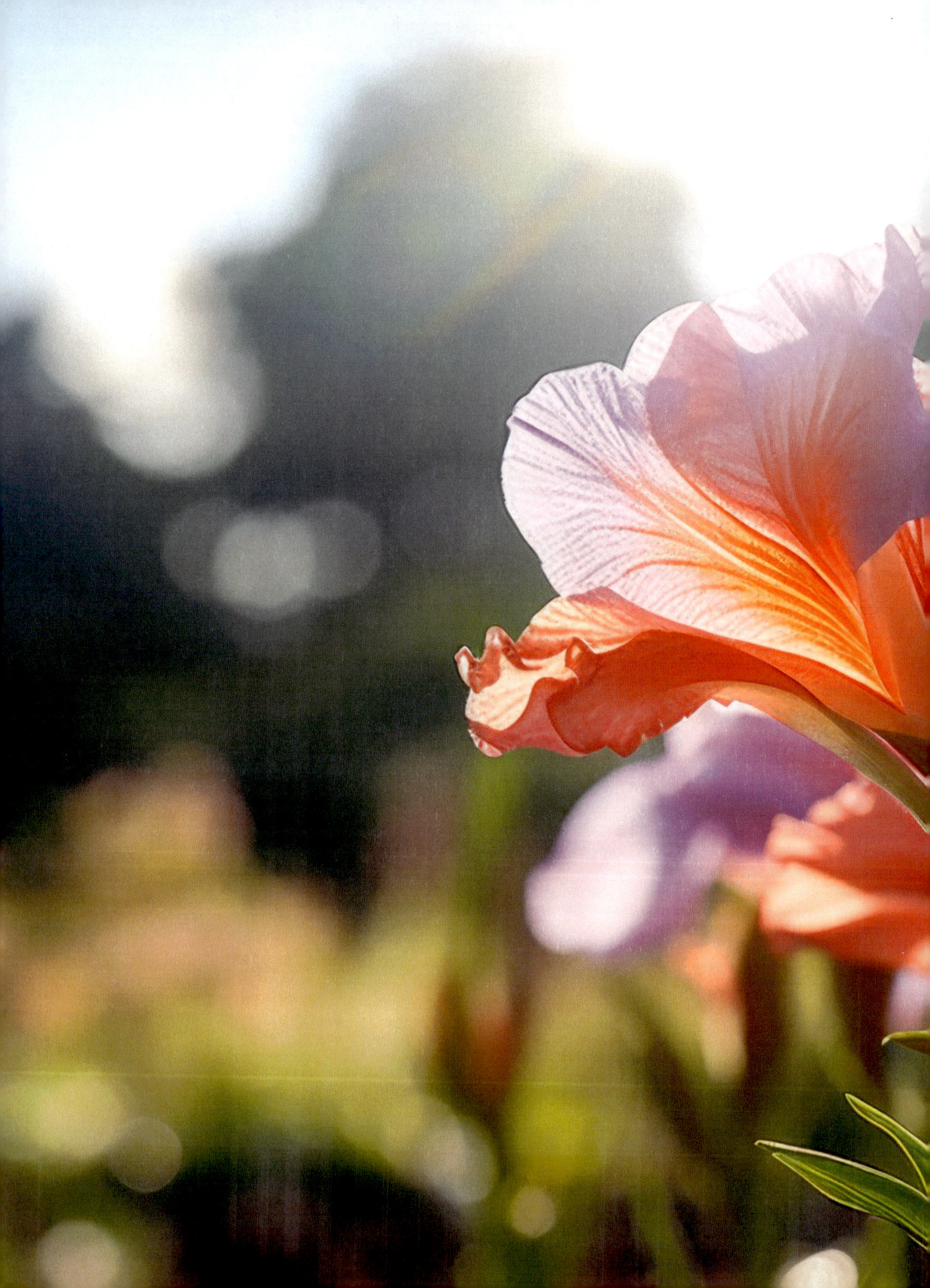

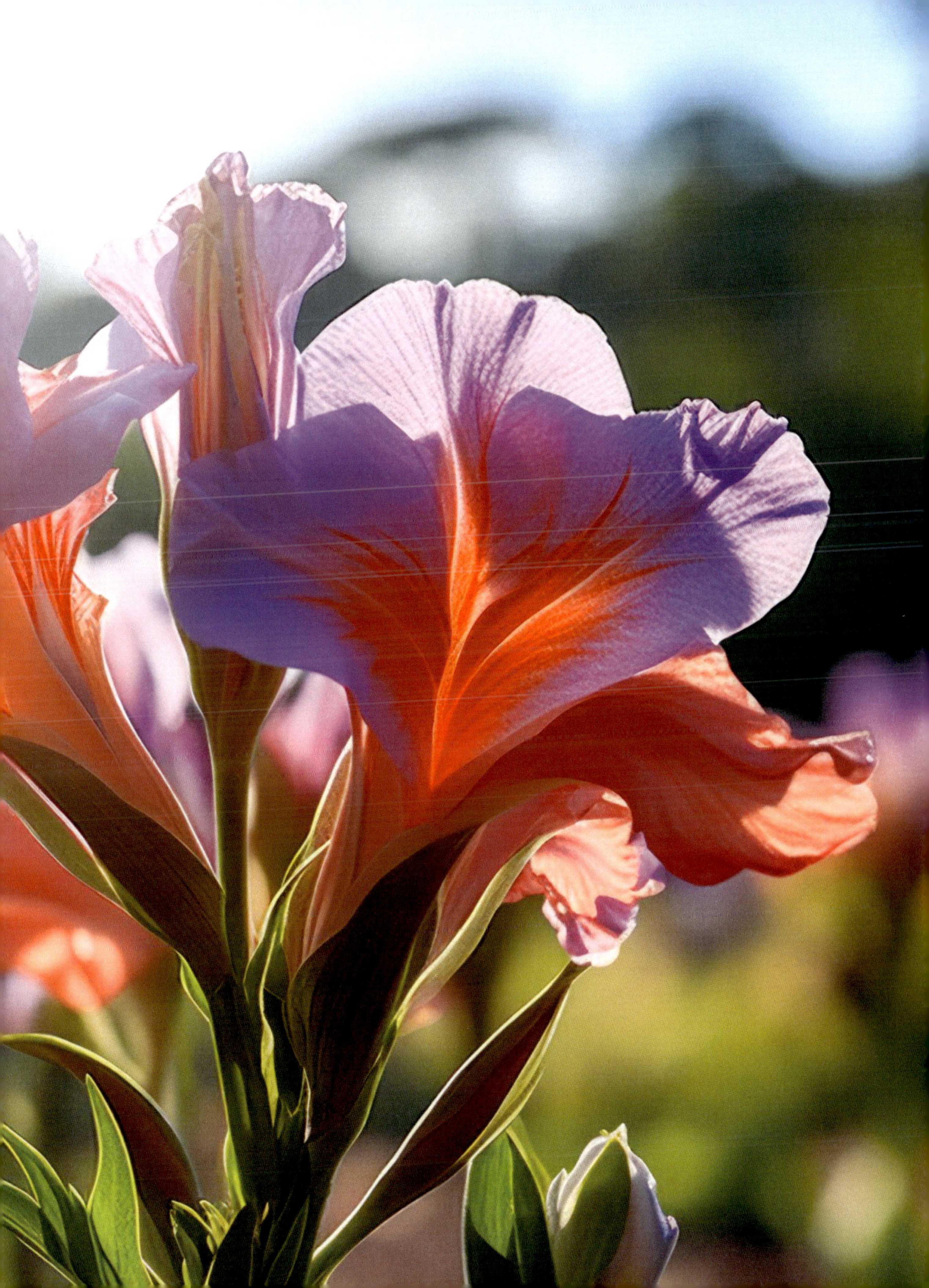

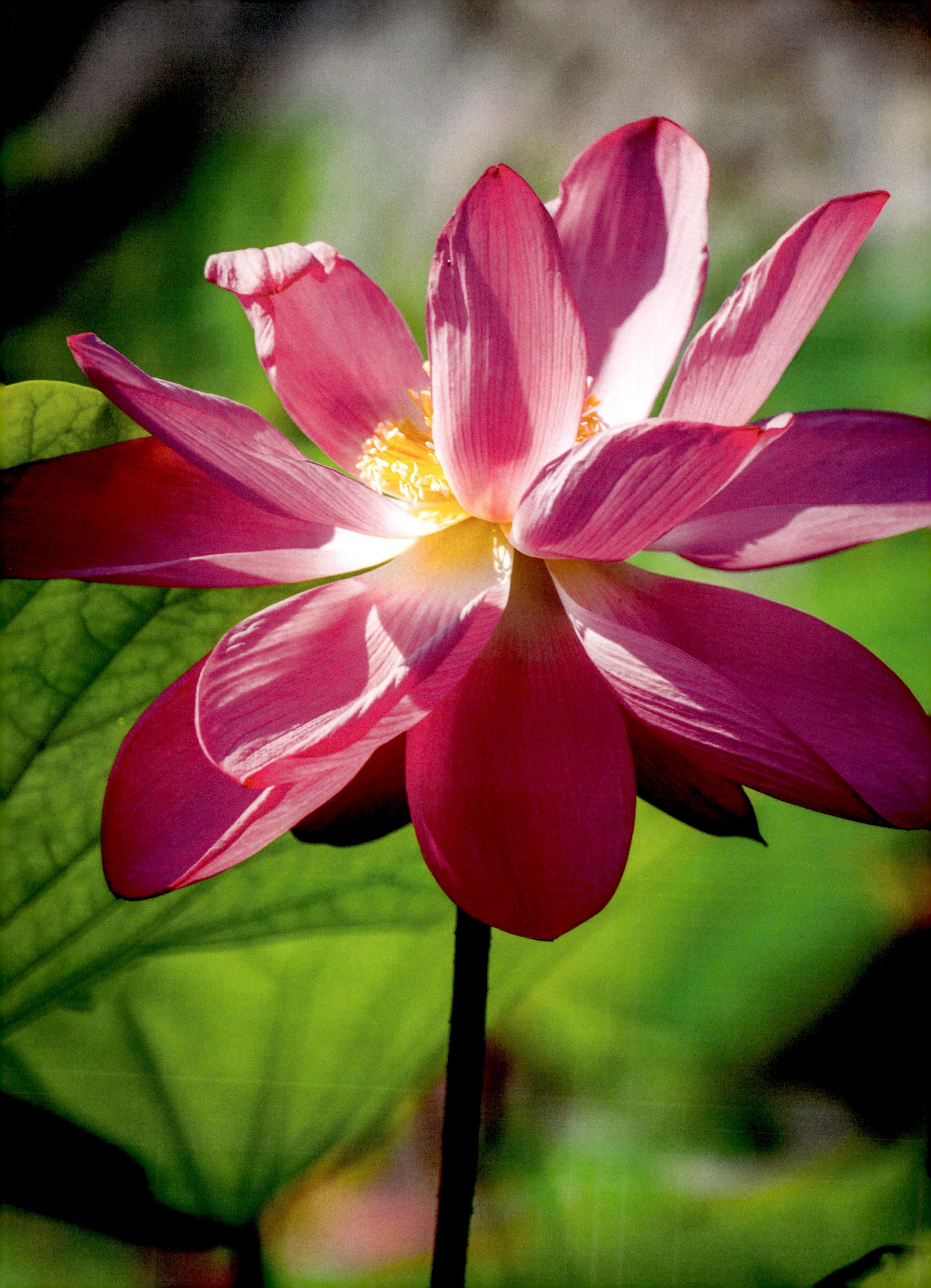

It's a time of beginnings and rejuvenation as plants, flowers, and animals awaken from their winter slumber and thrive more.

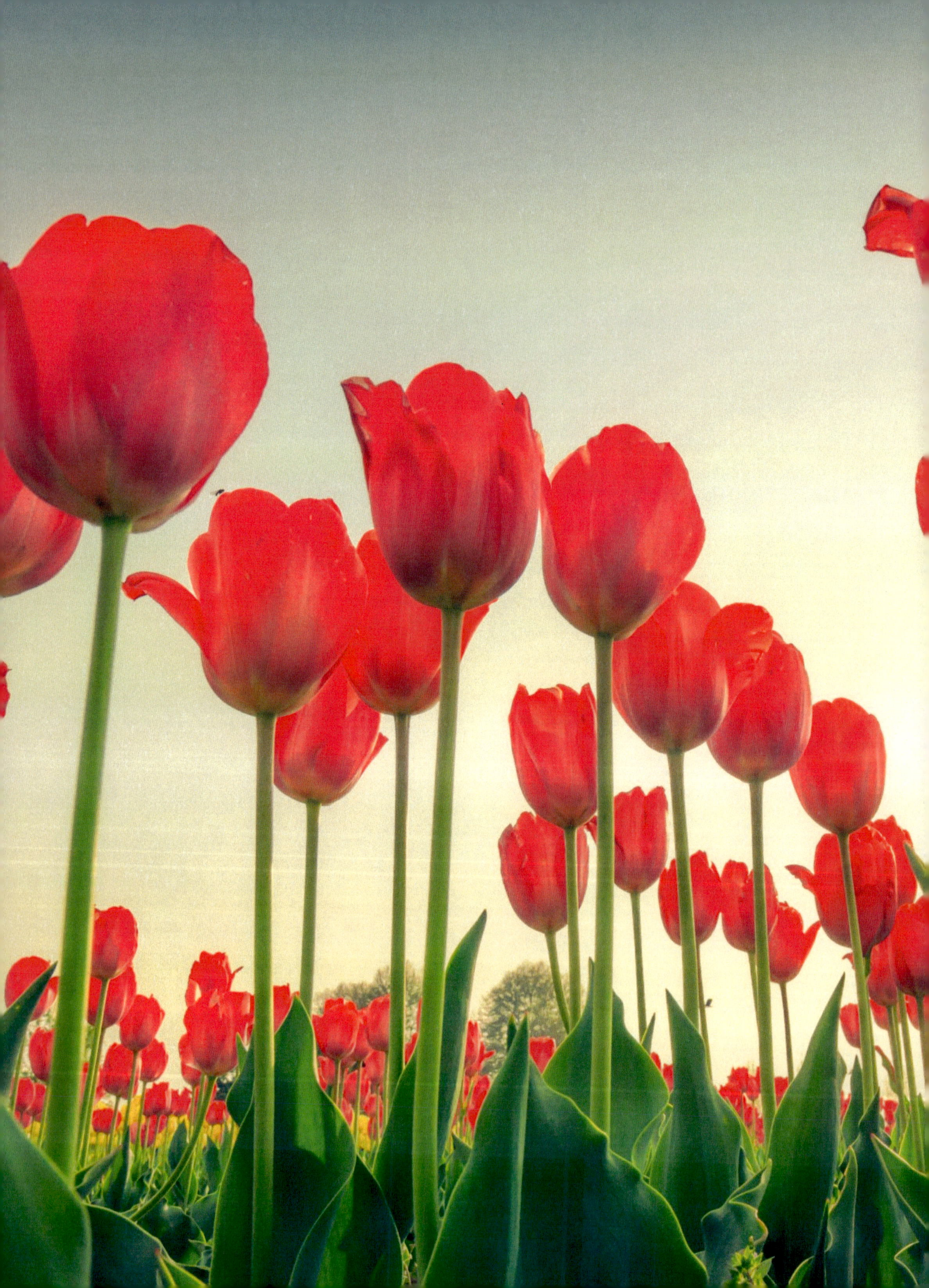

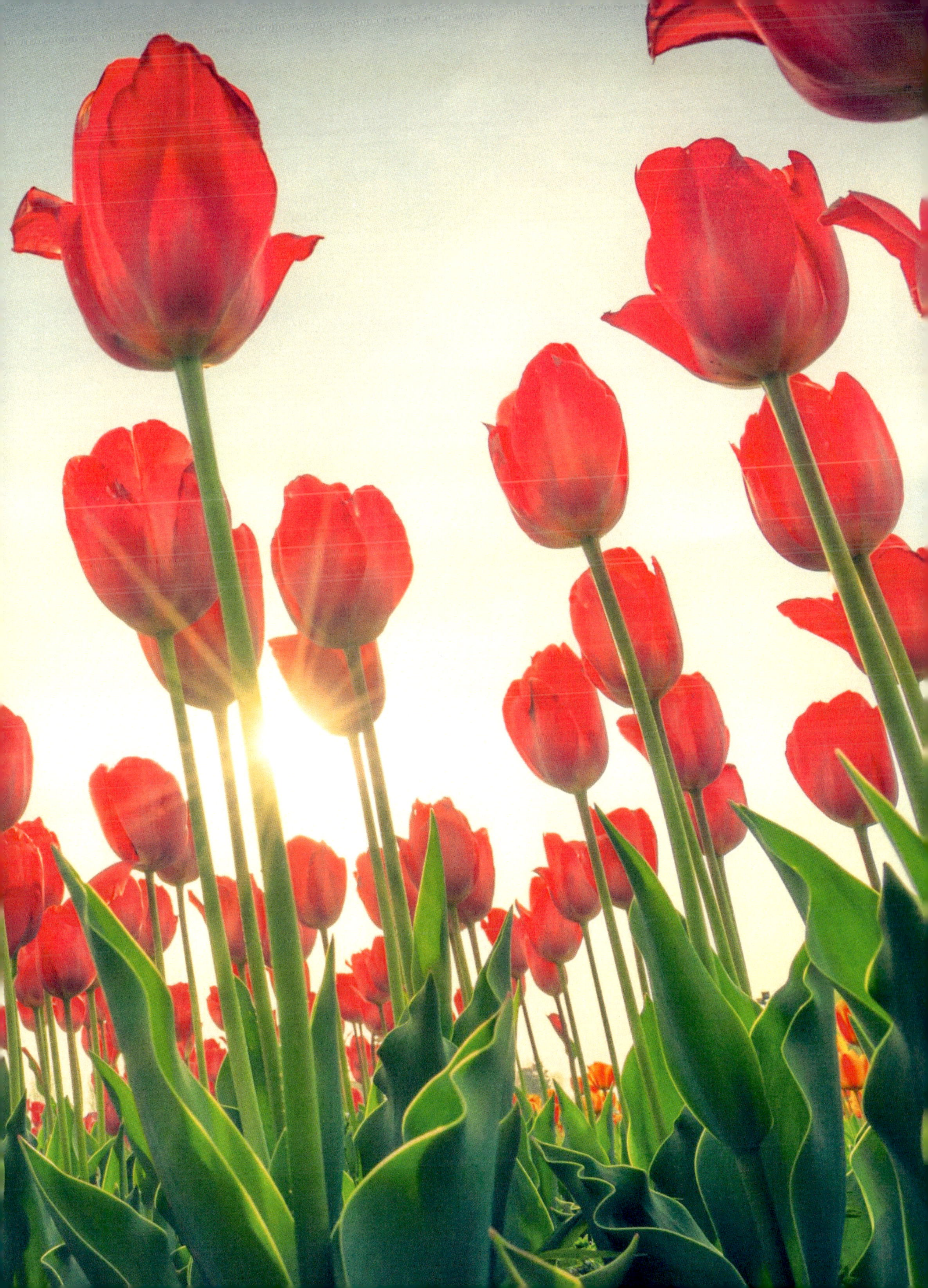

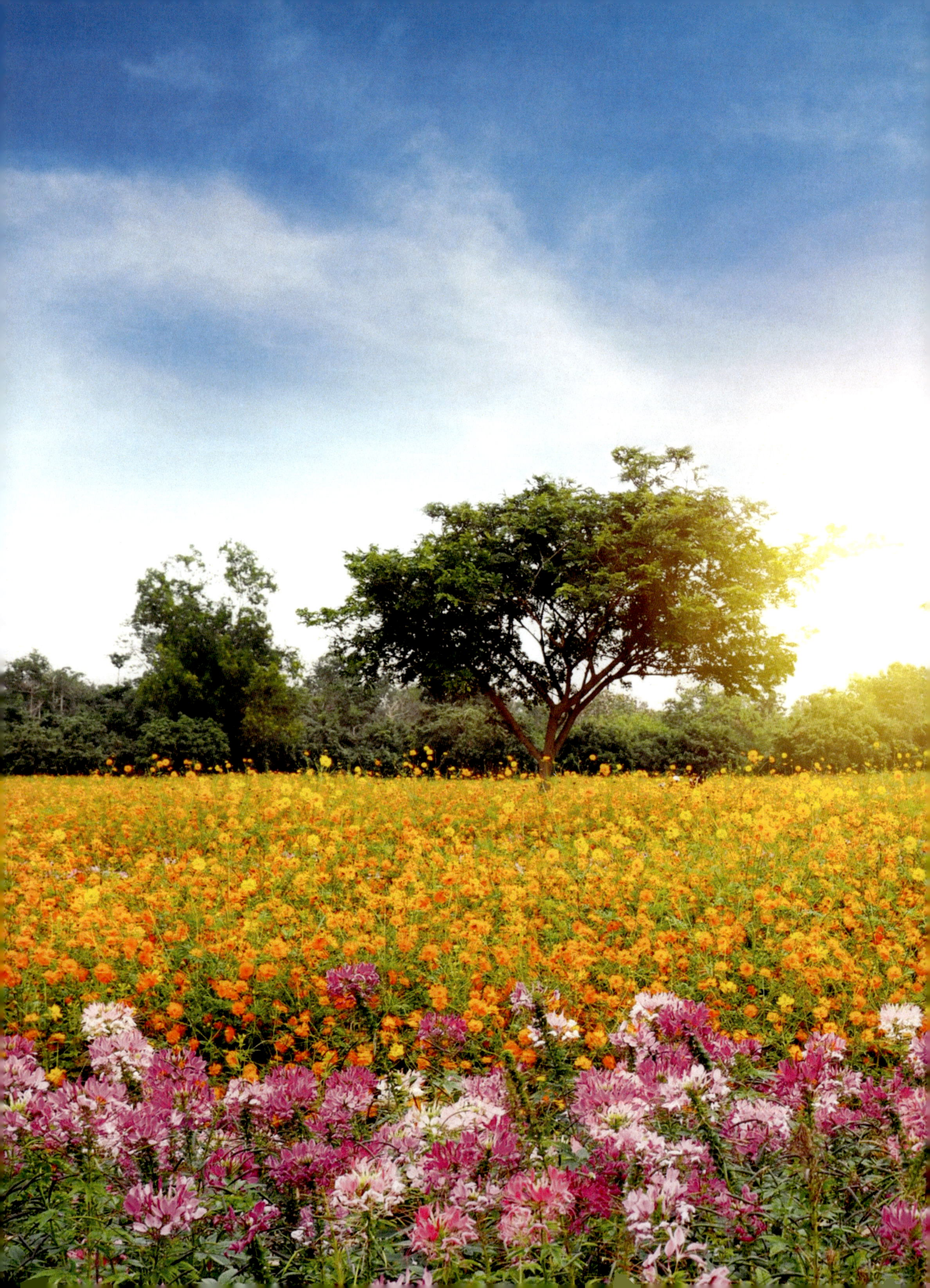

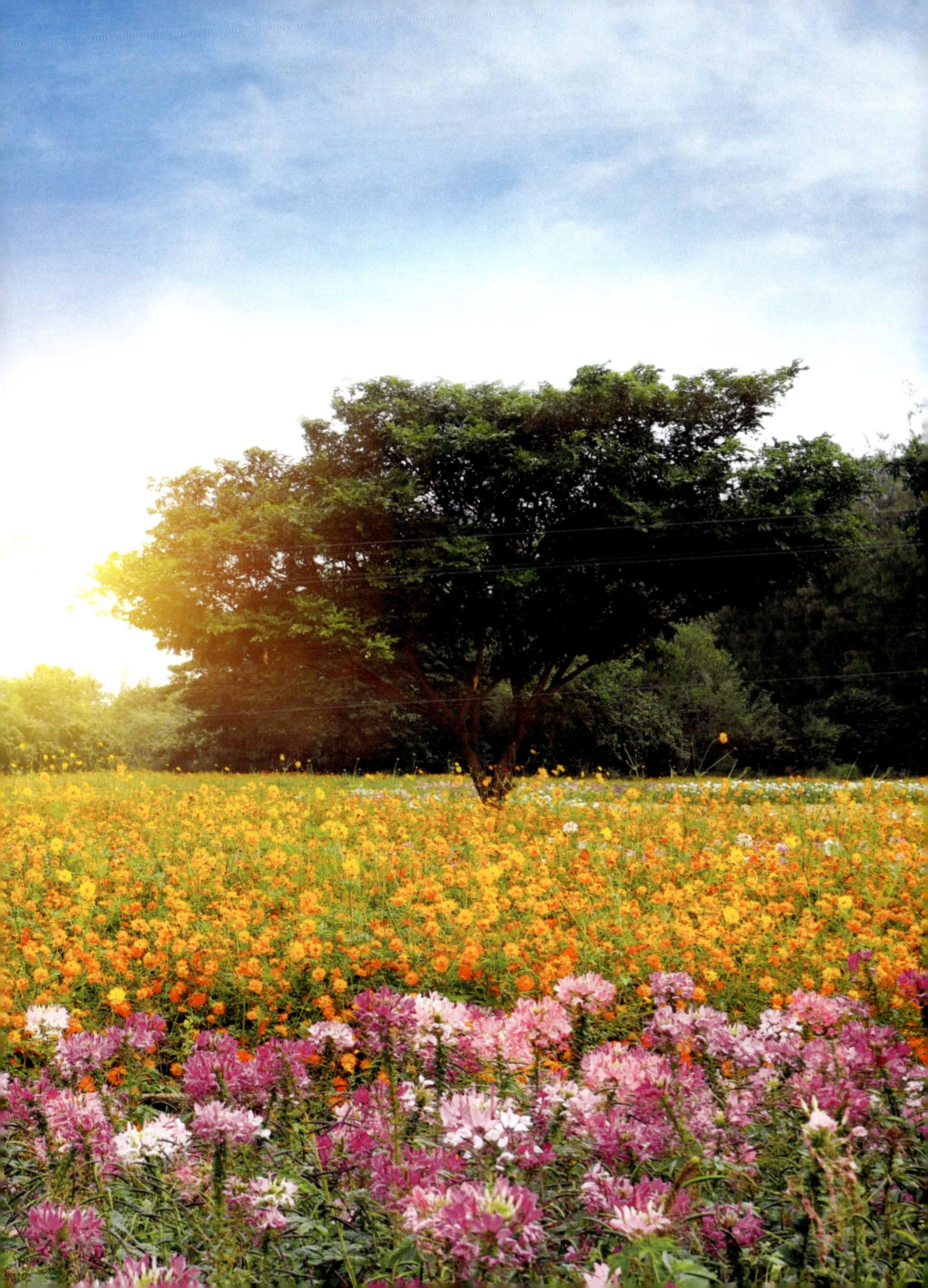

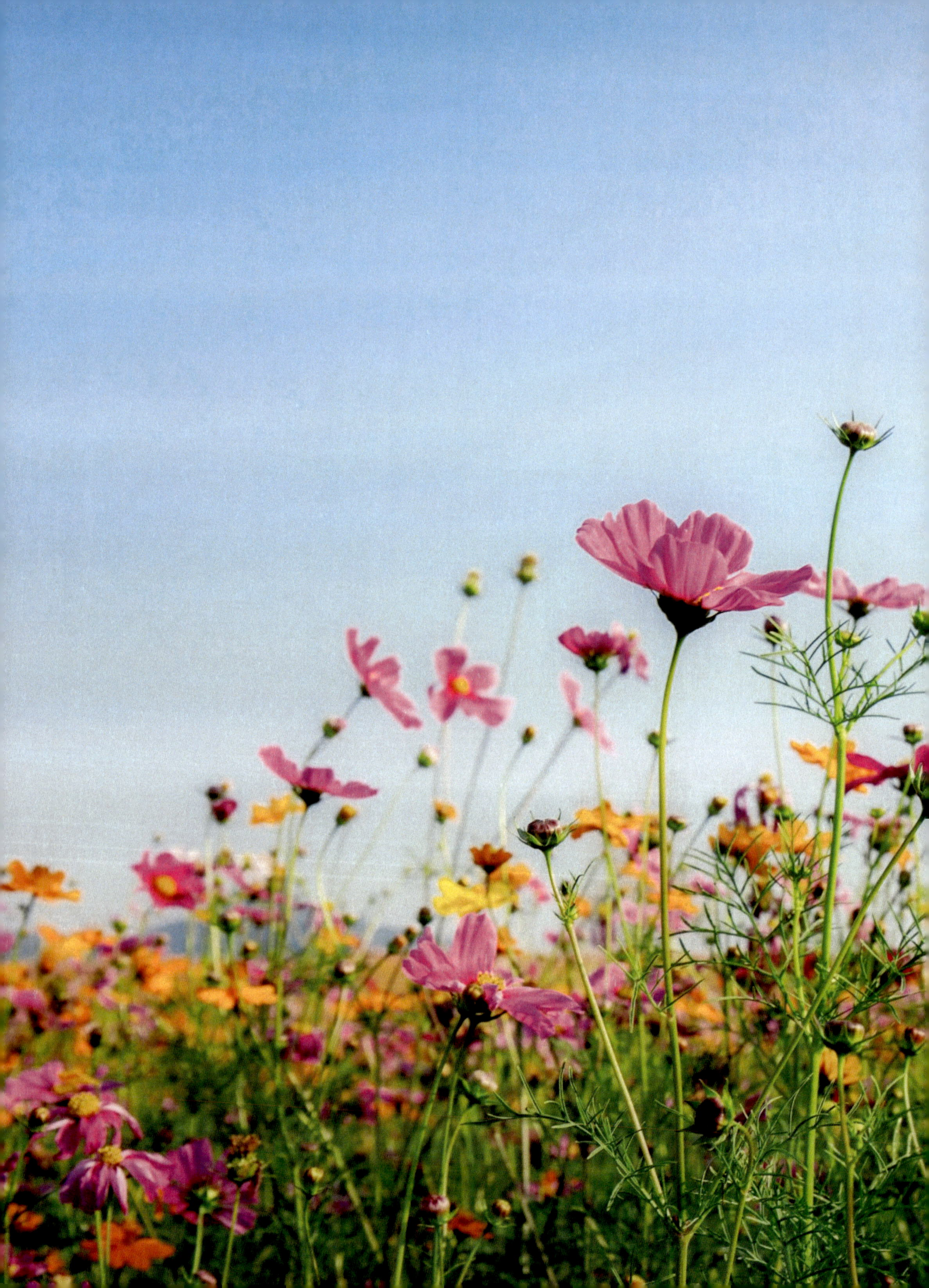

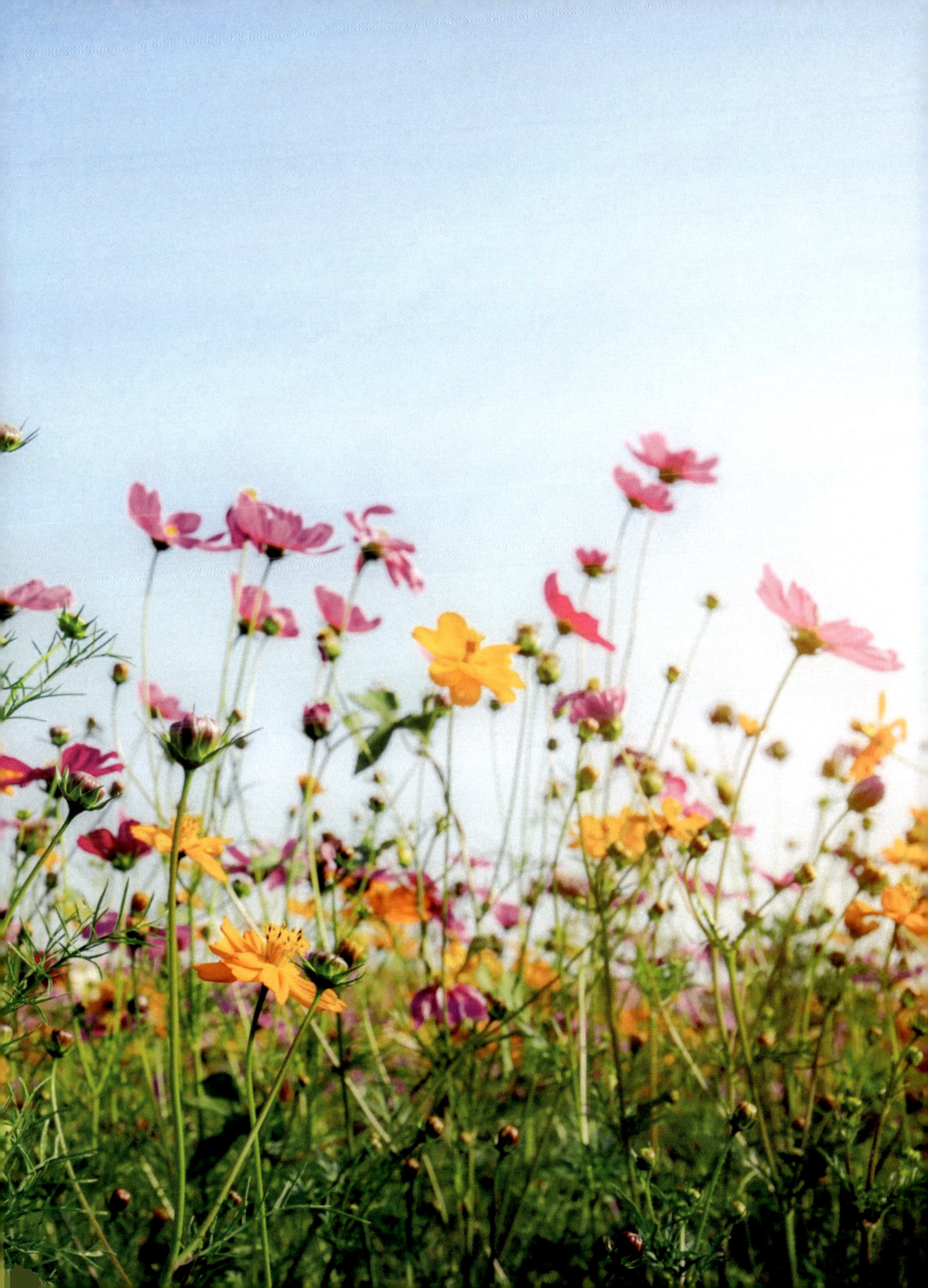

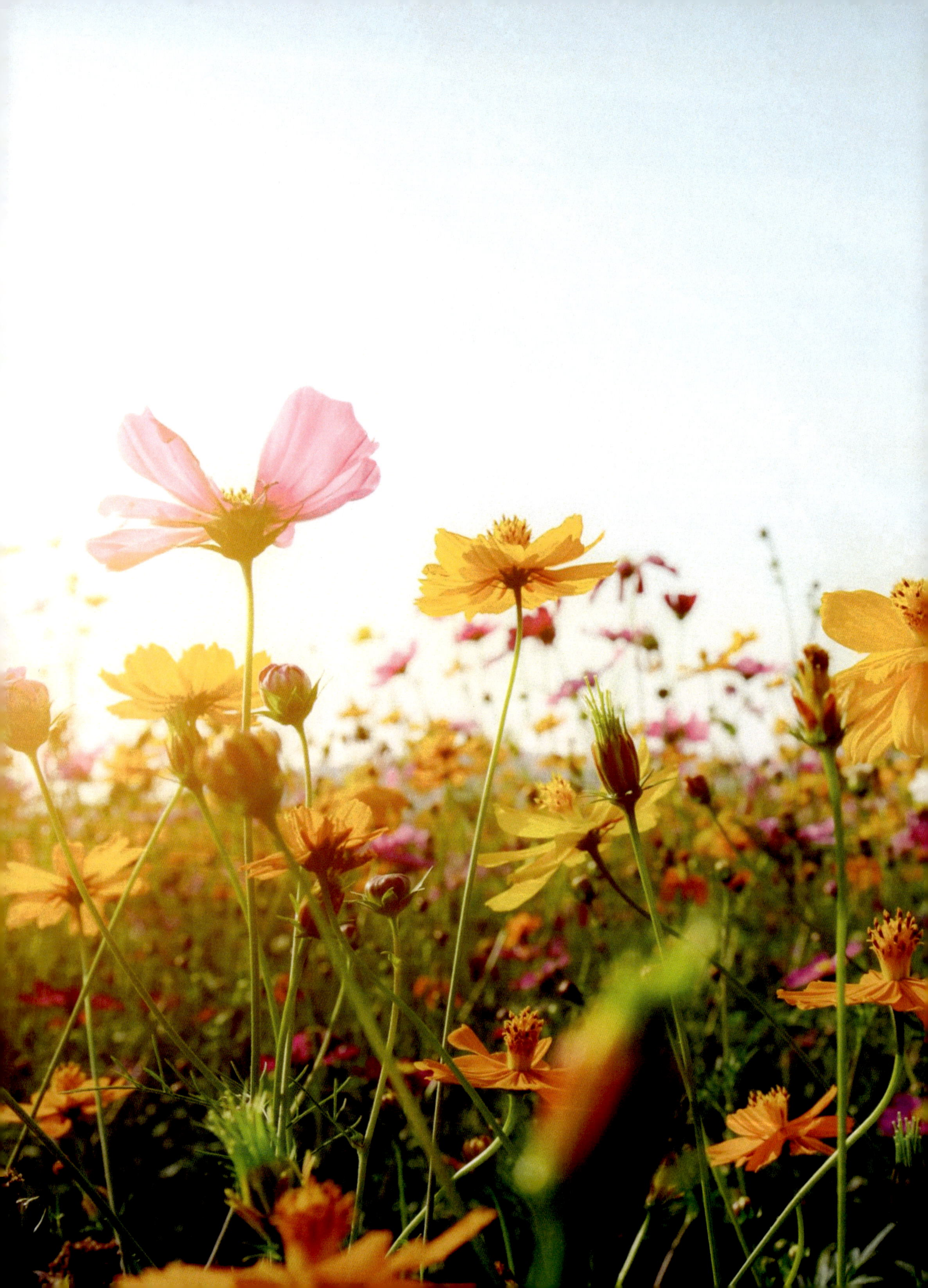

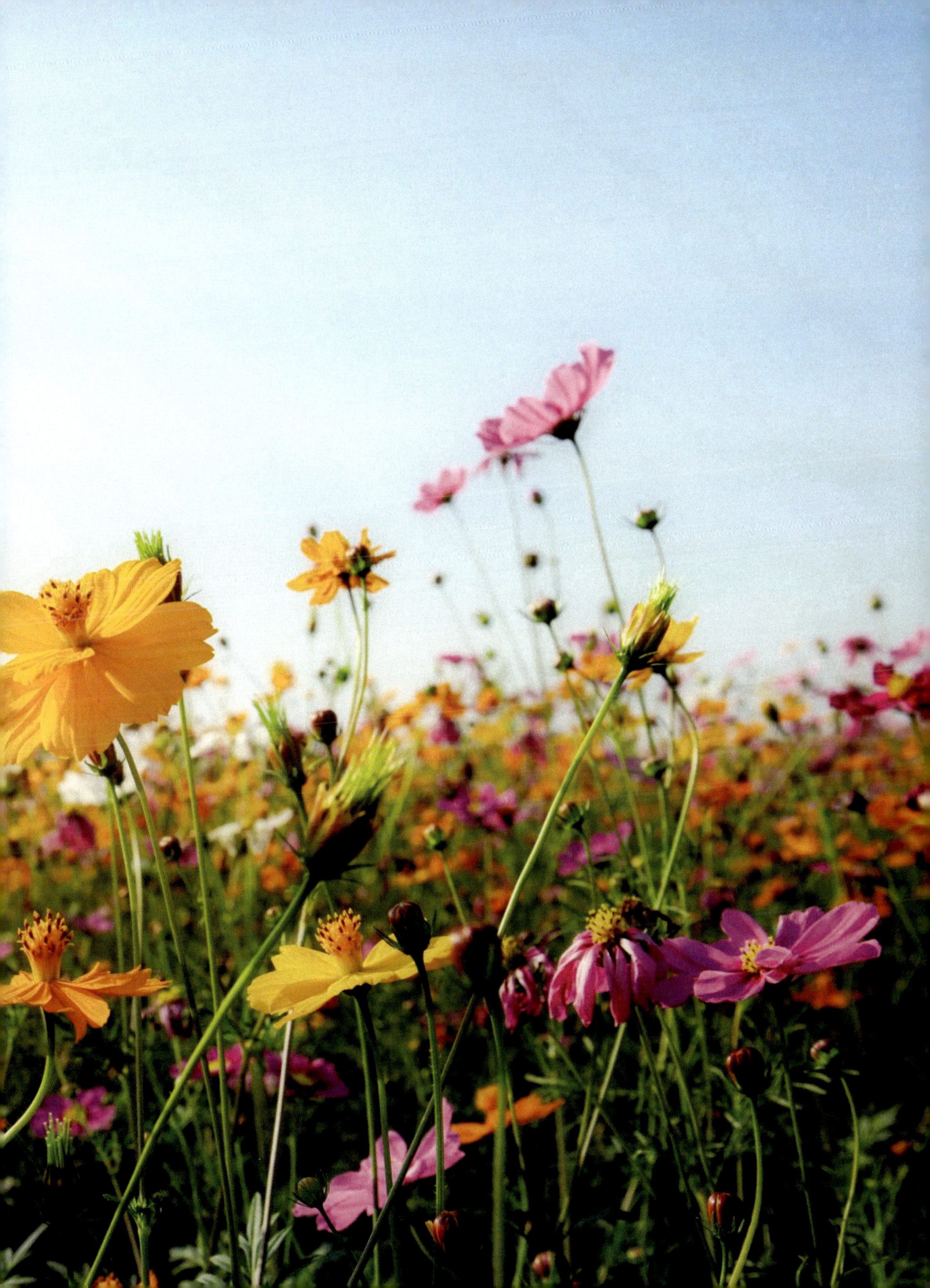

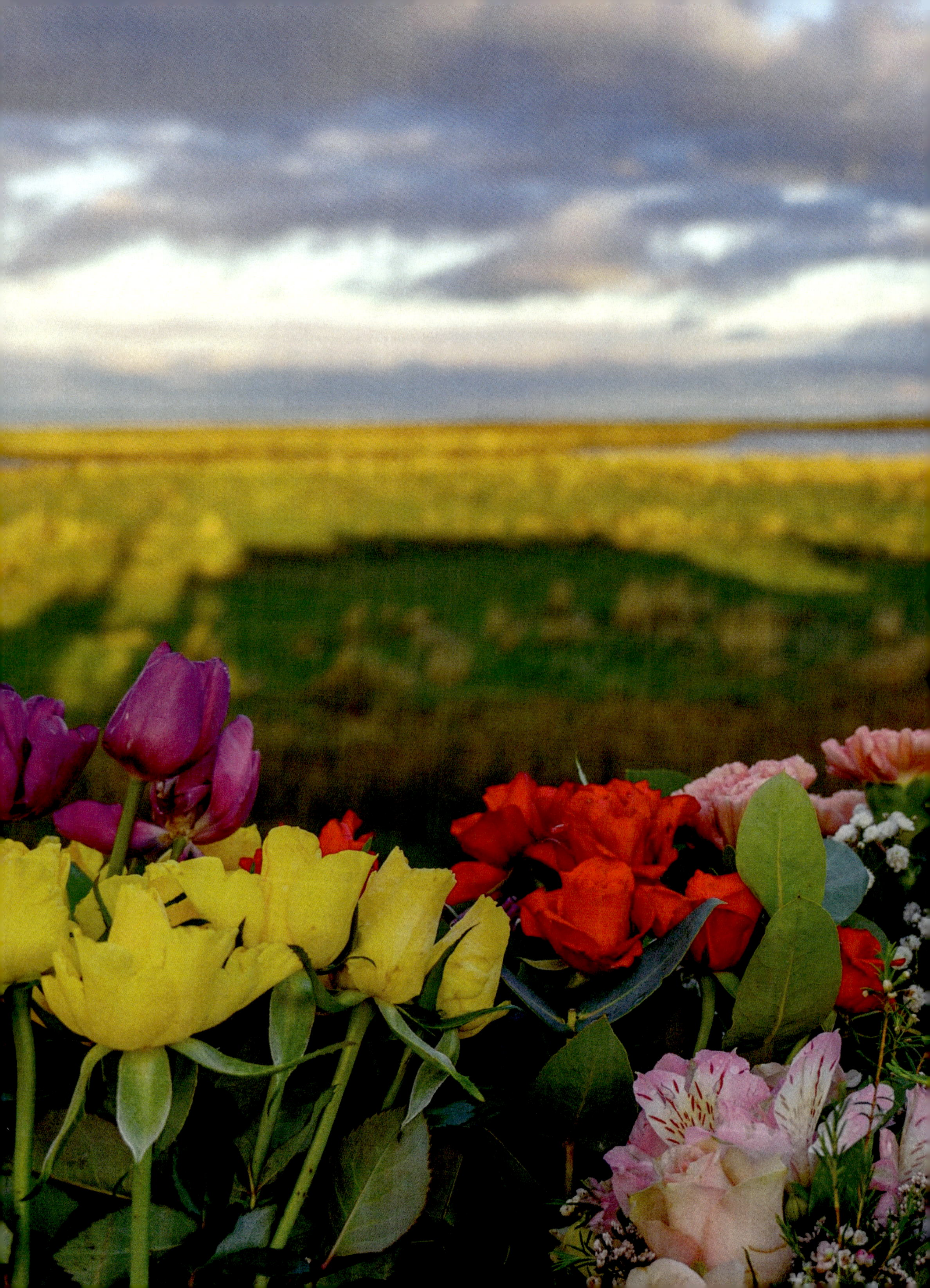

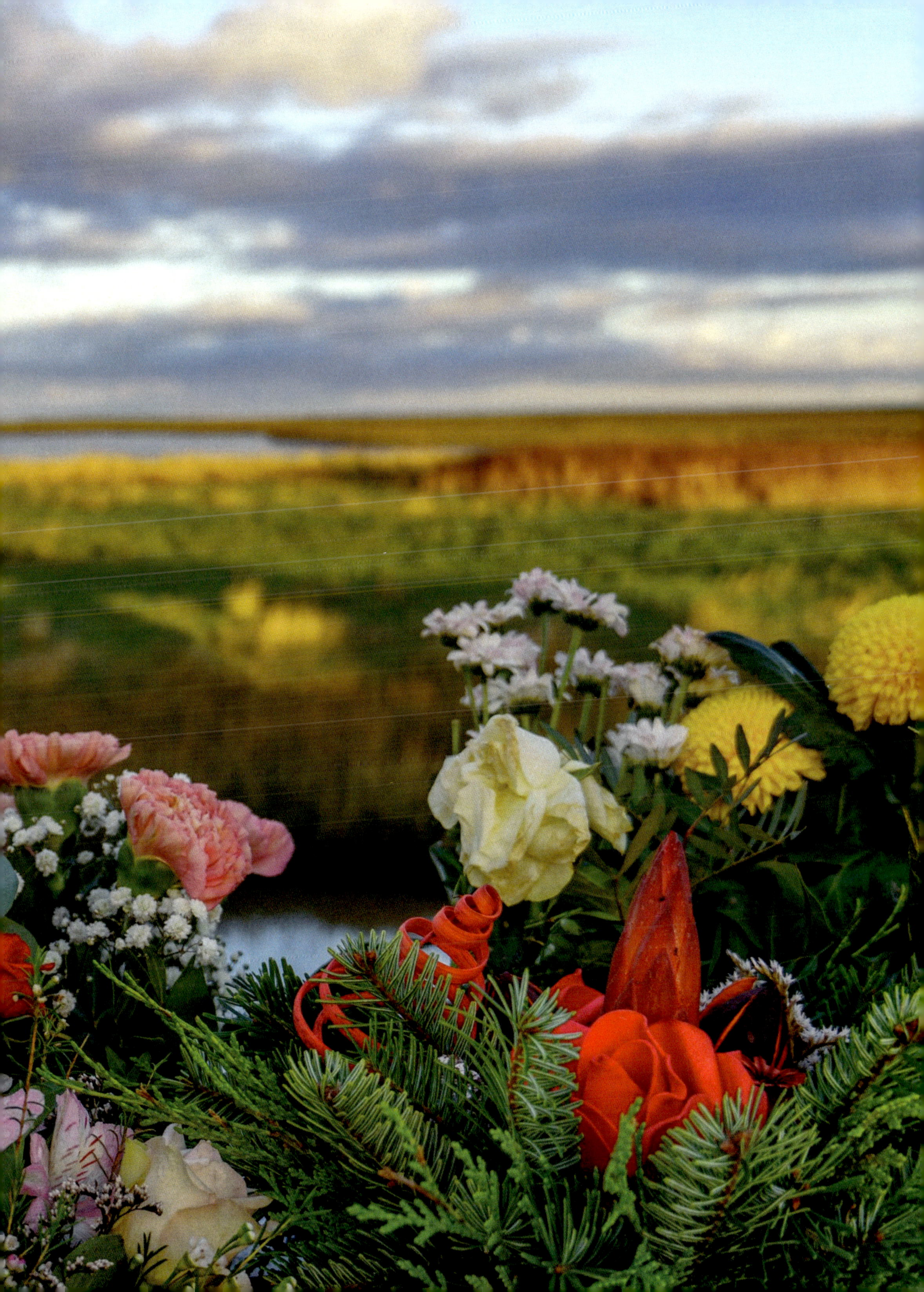

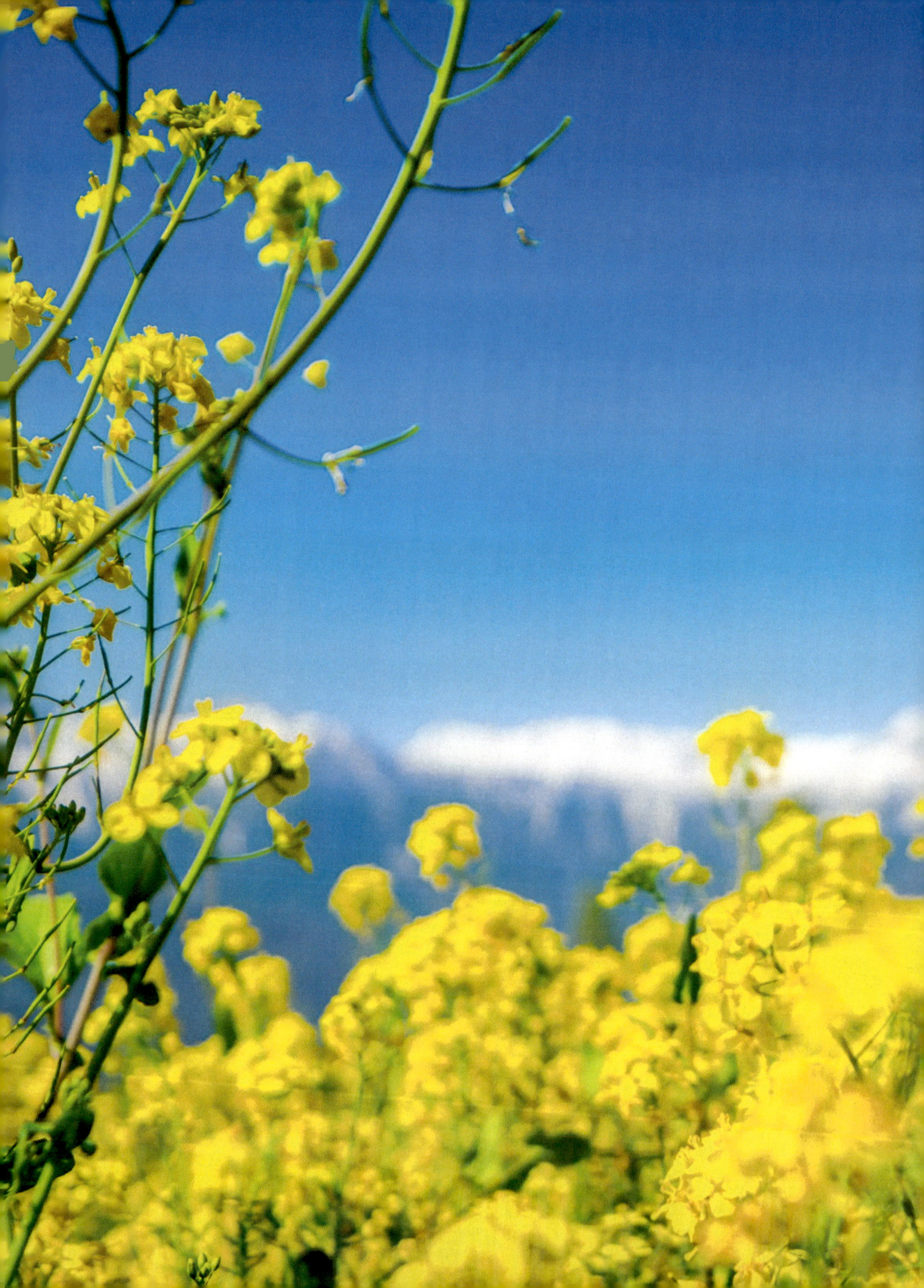

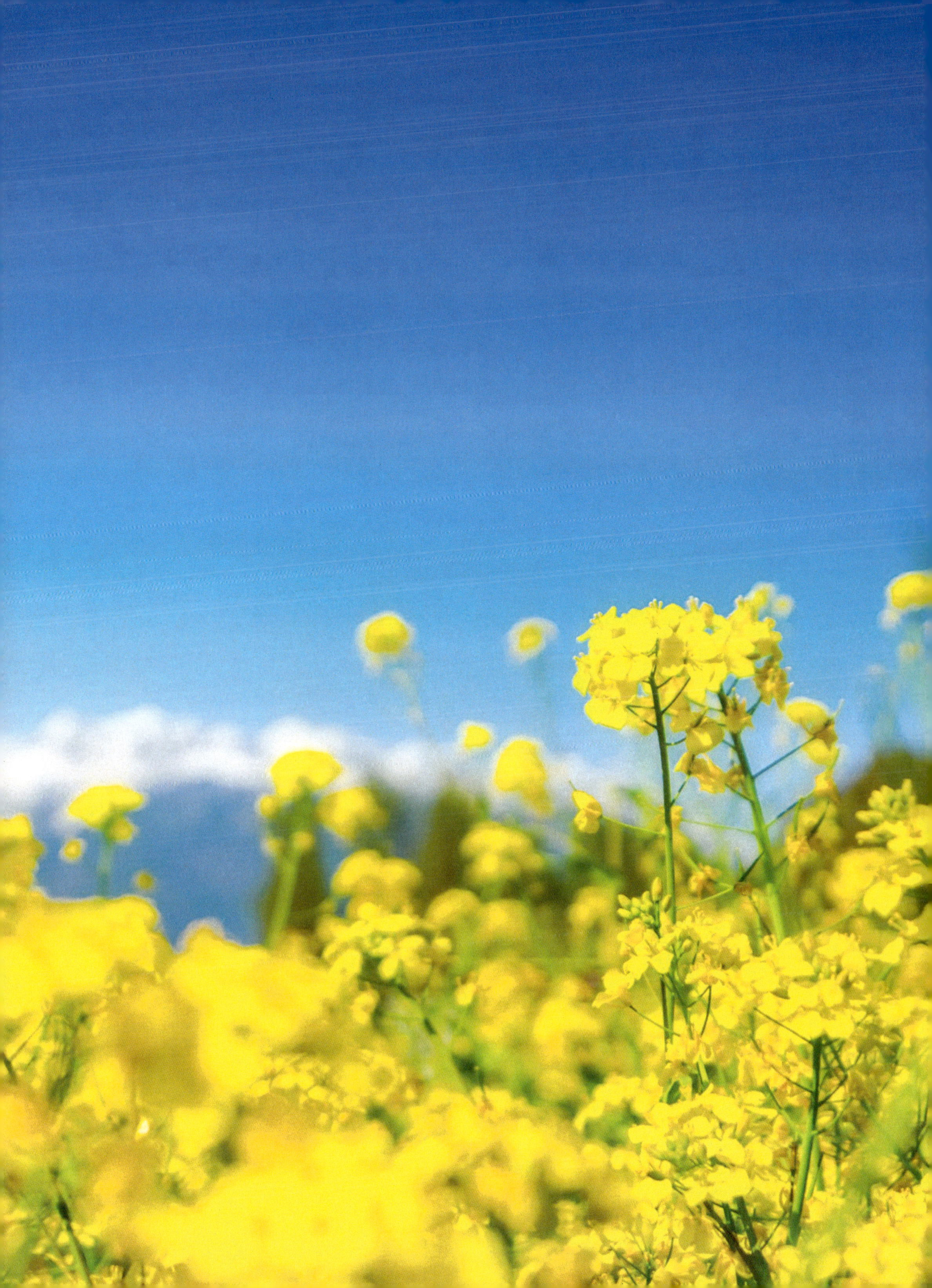

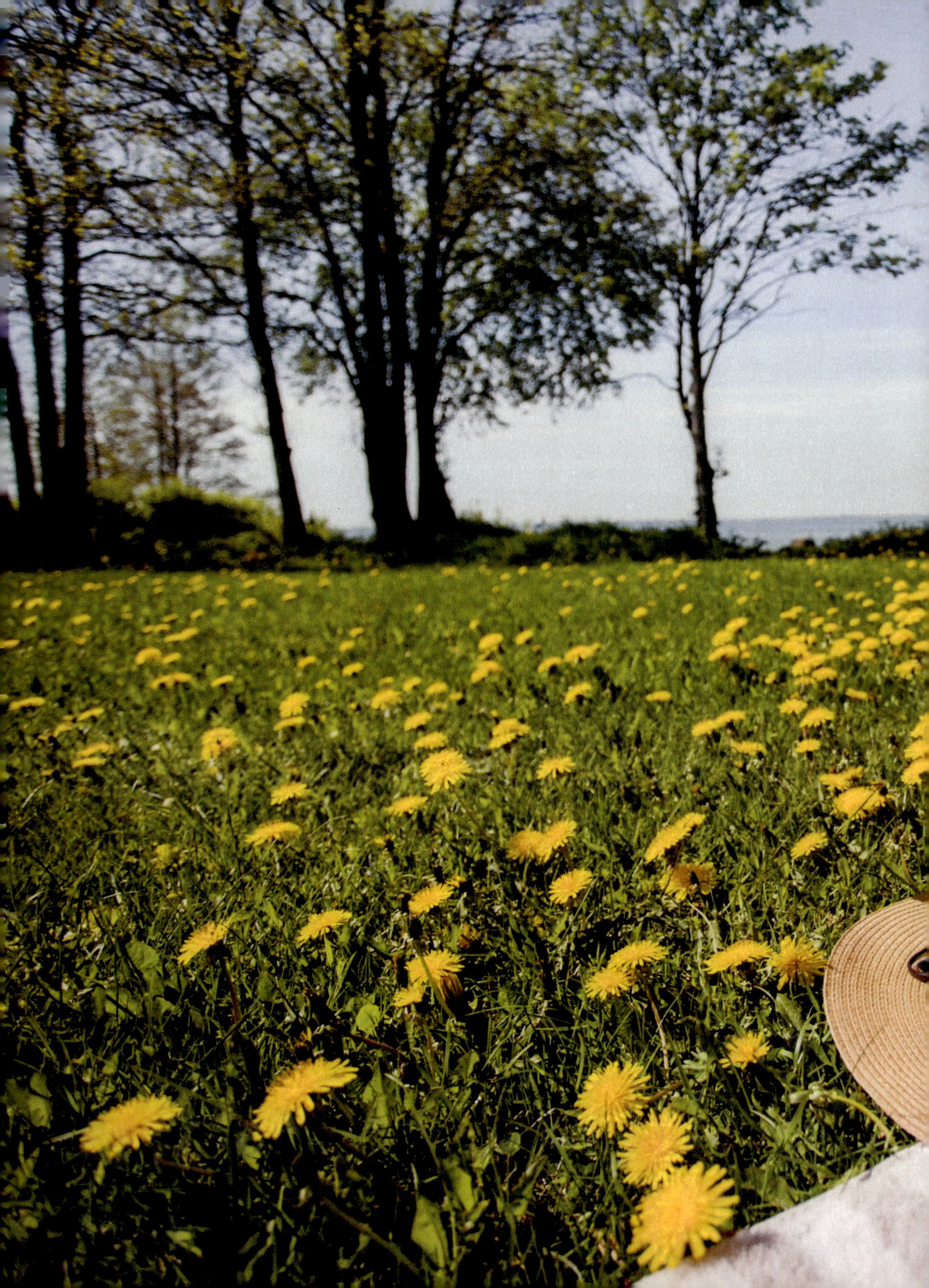

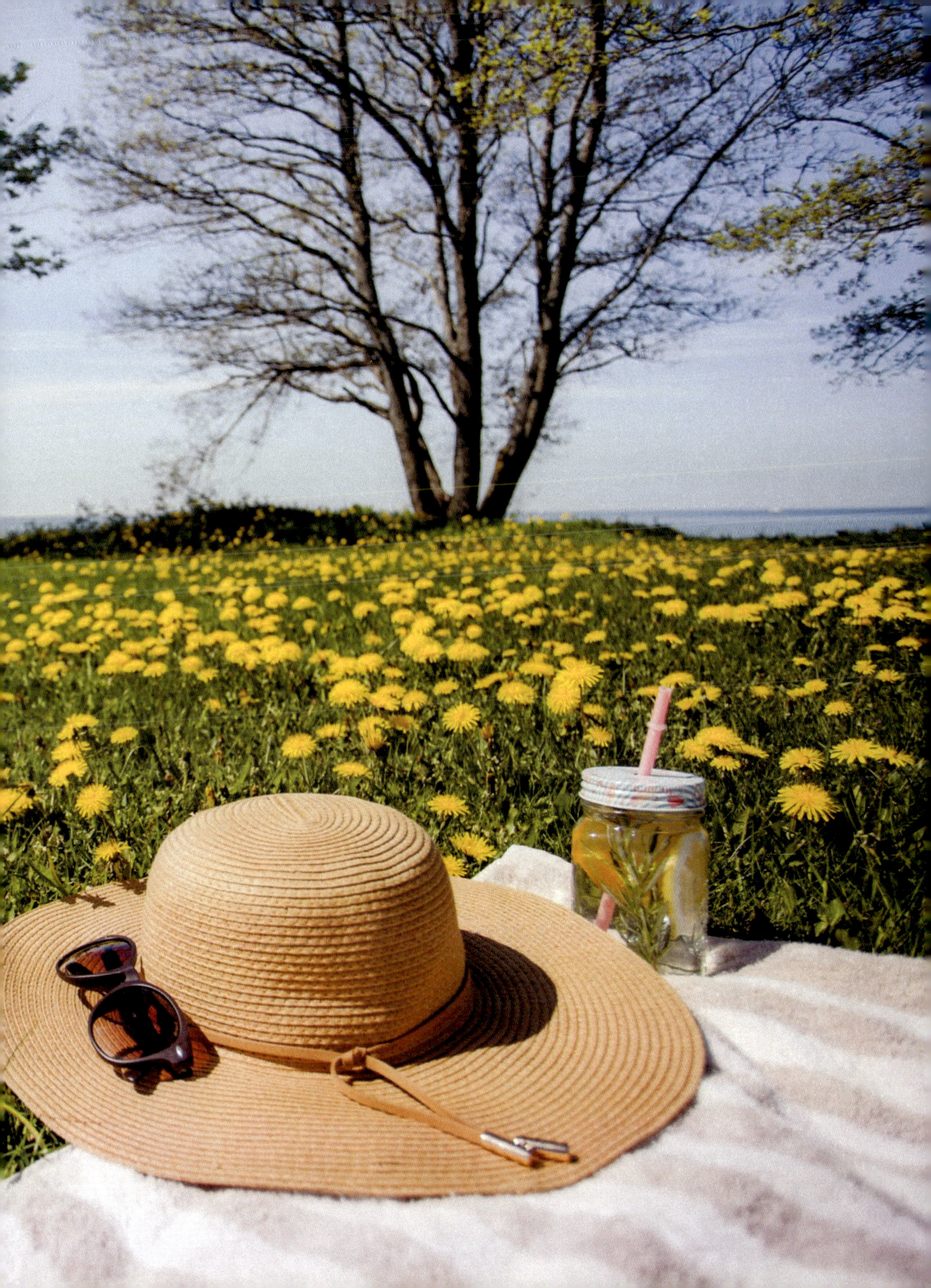

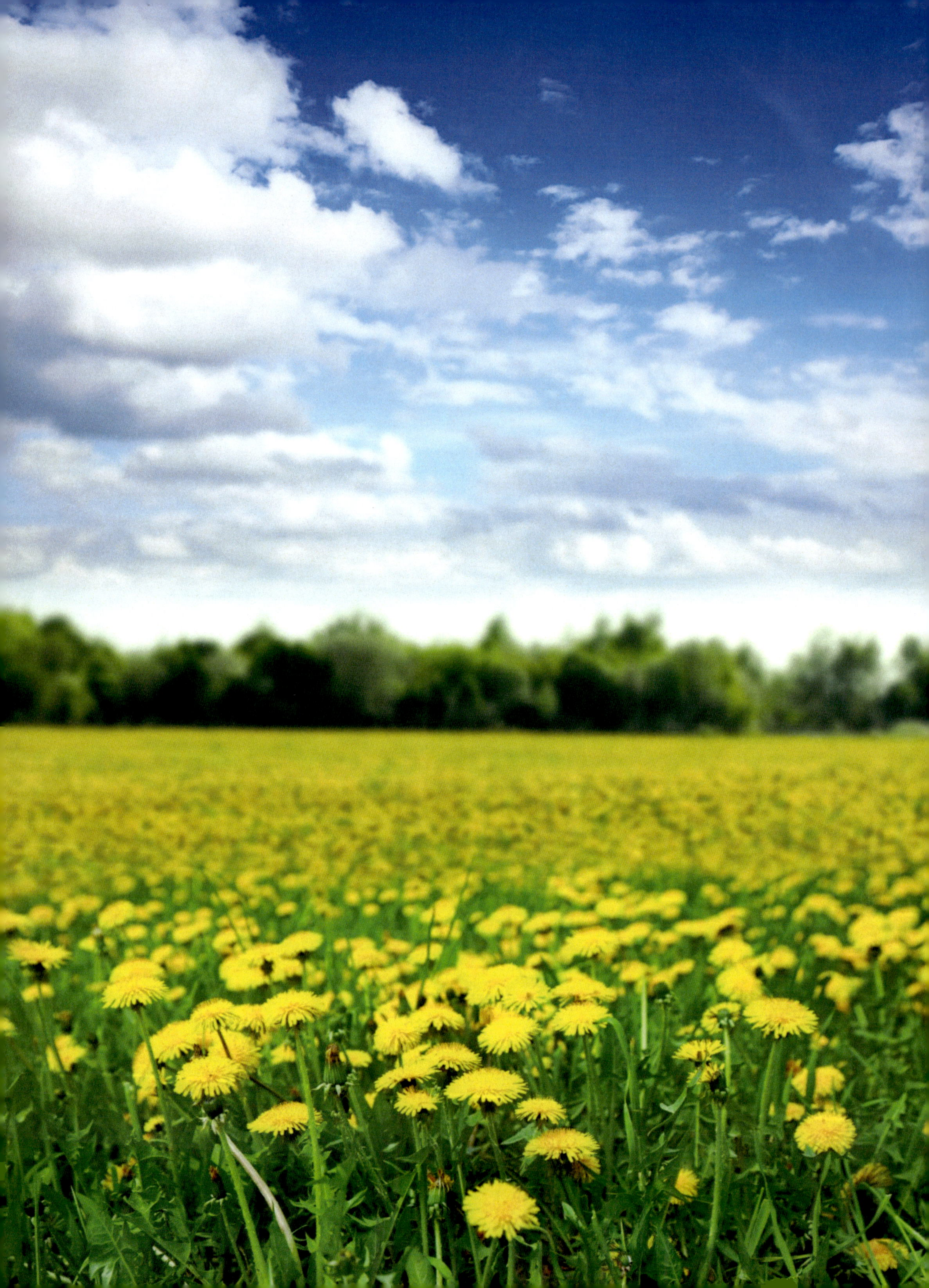

Spring symbolizes themes of renewal, revival, regeneration, rejuvenation, resurrection, and growth for every place on the planet.

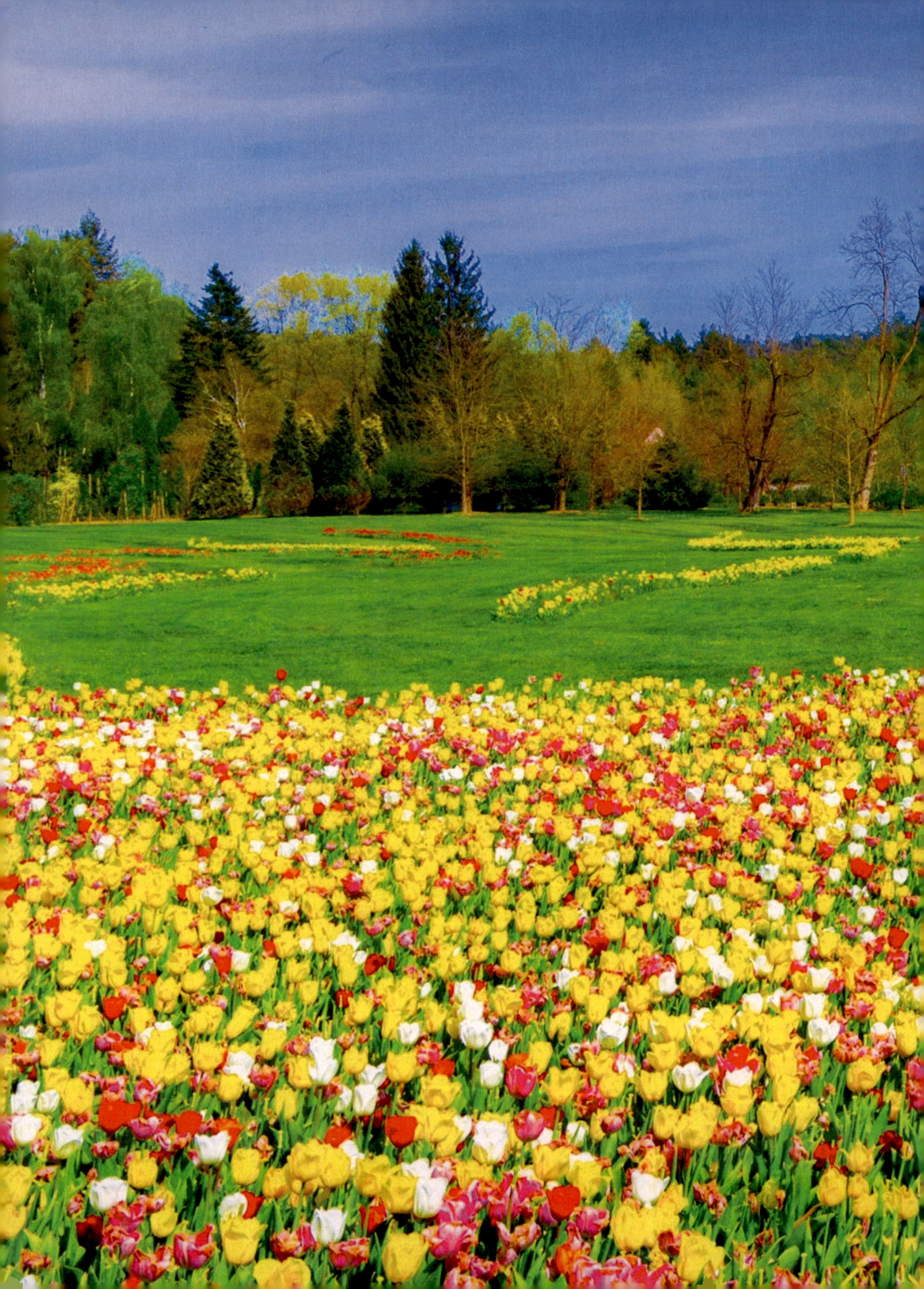

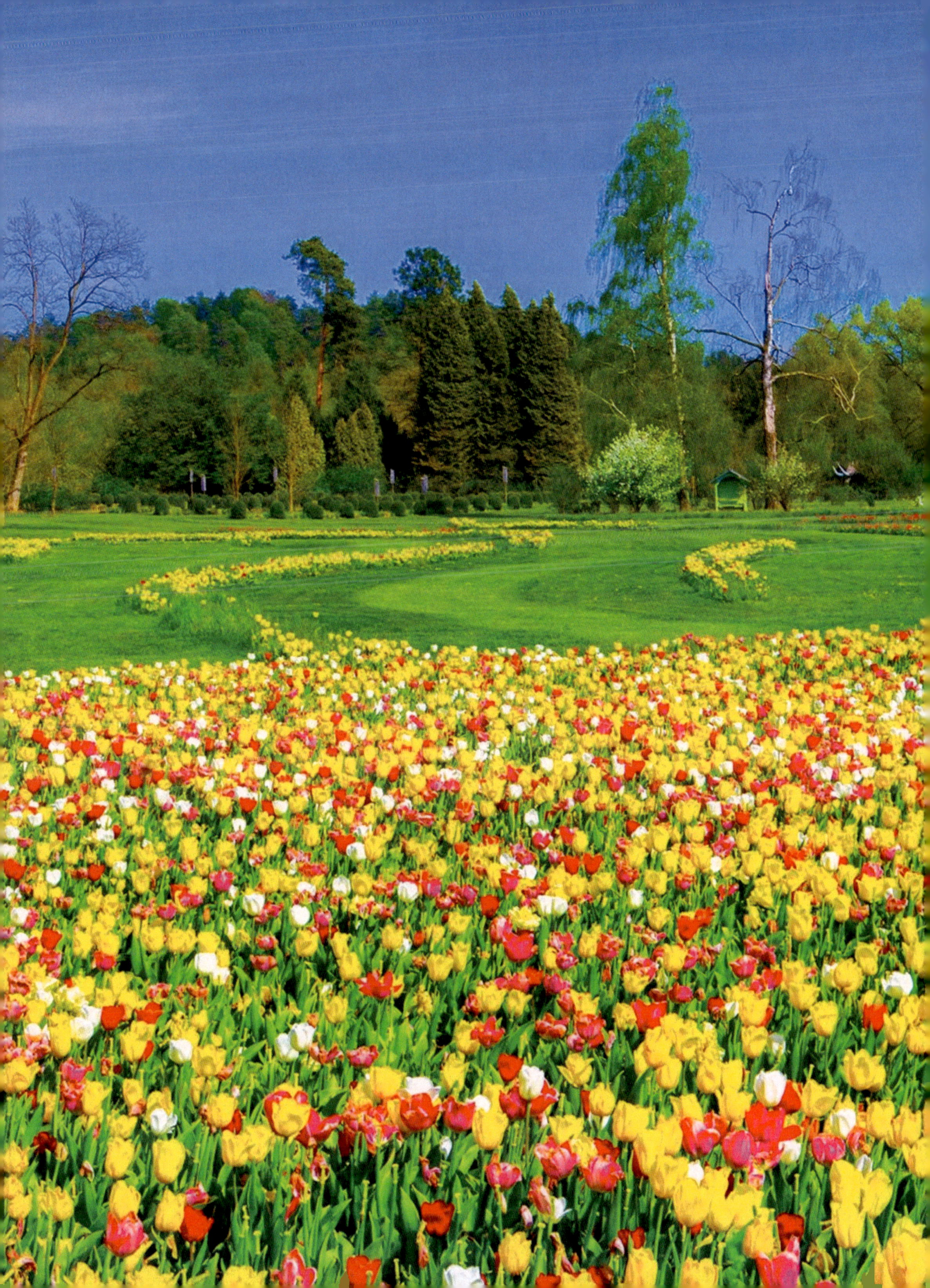

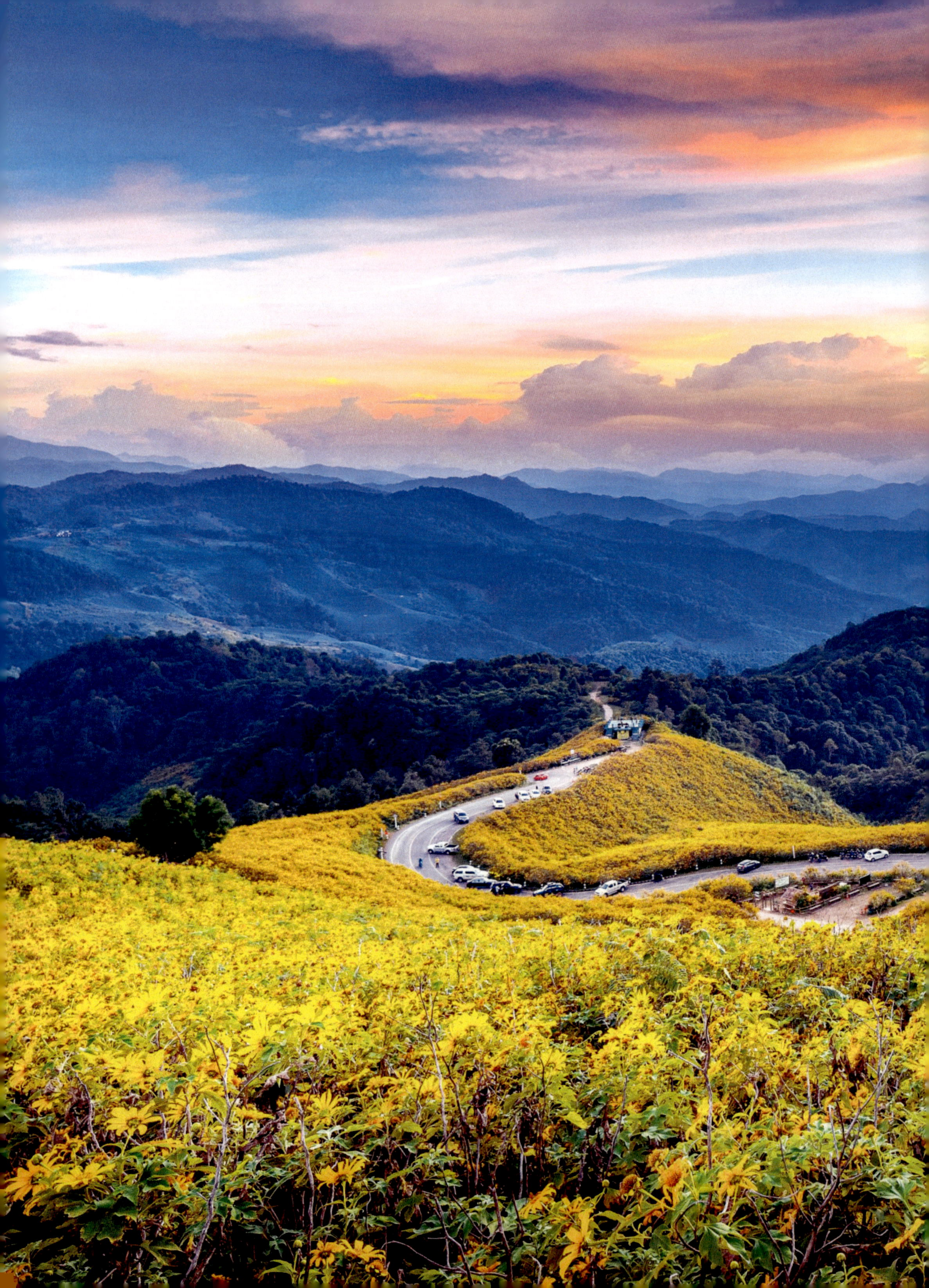

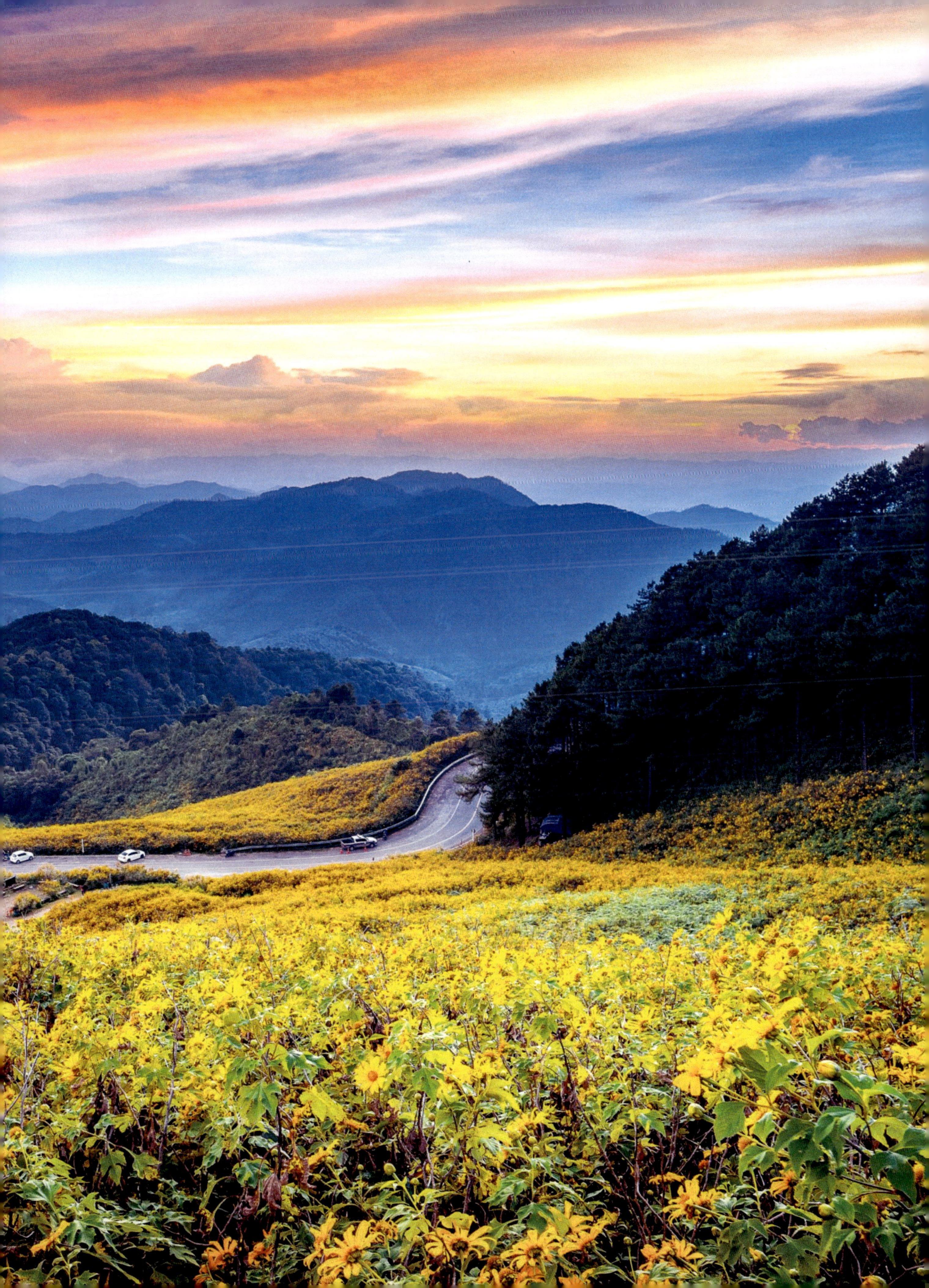

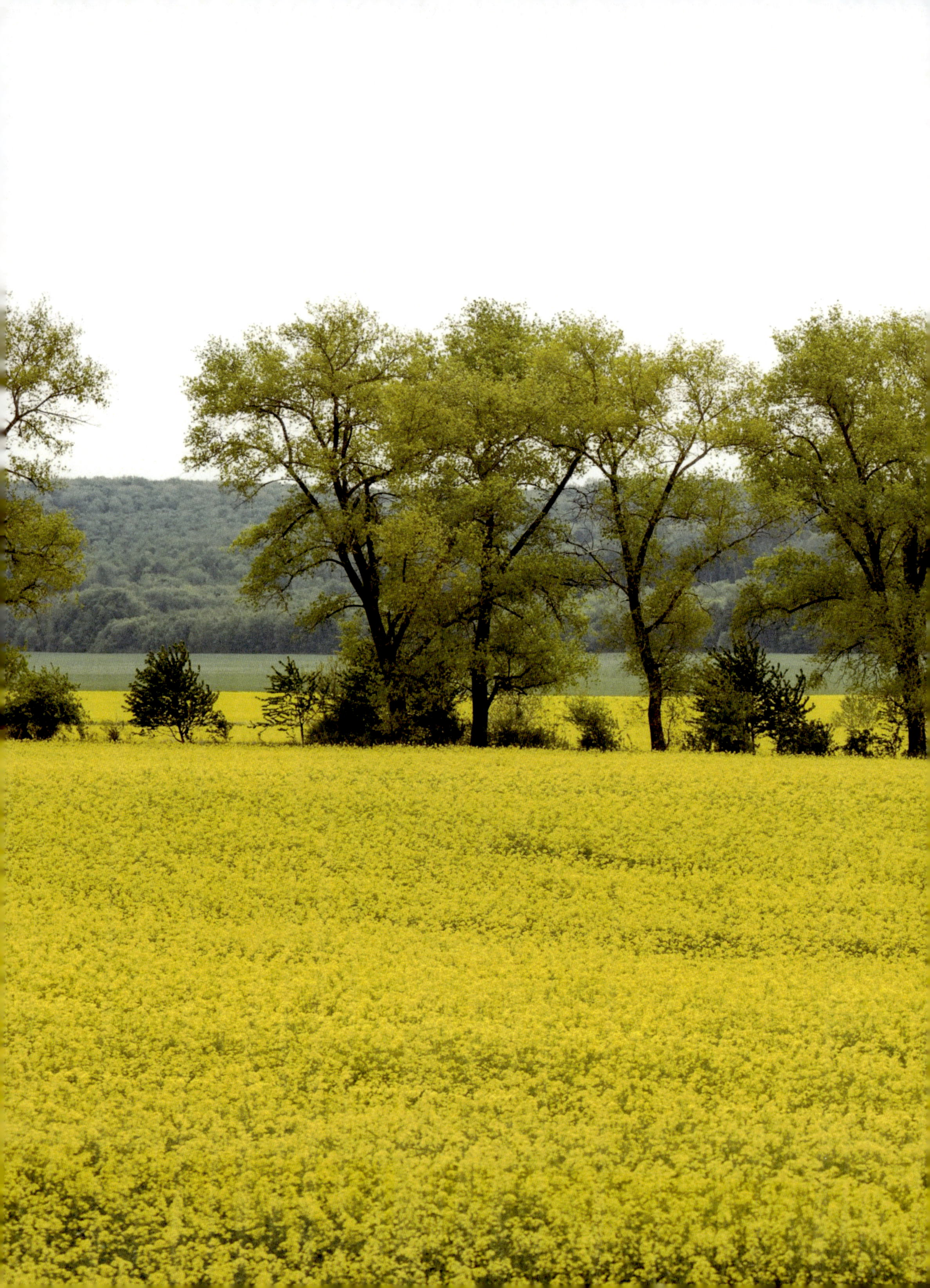

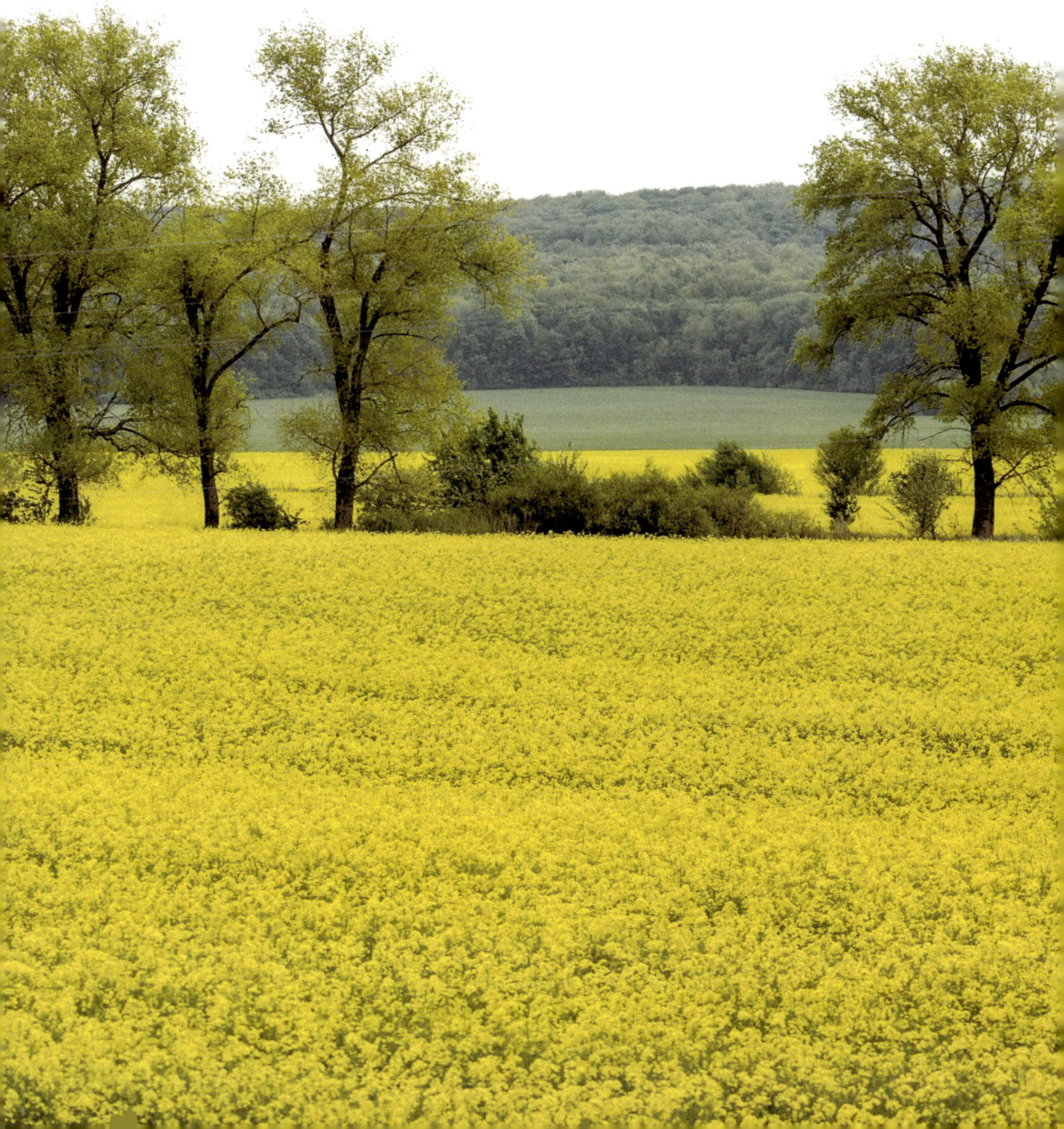

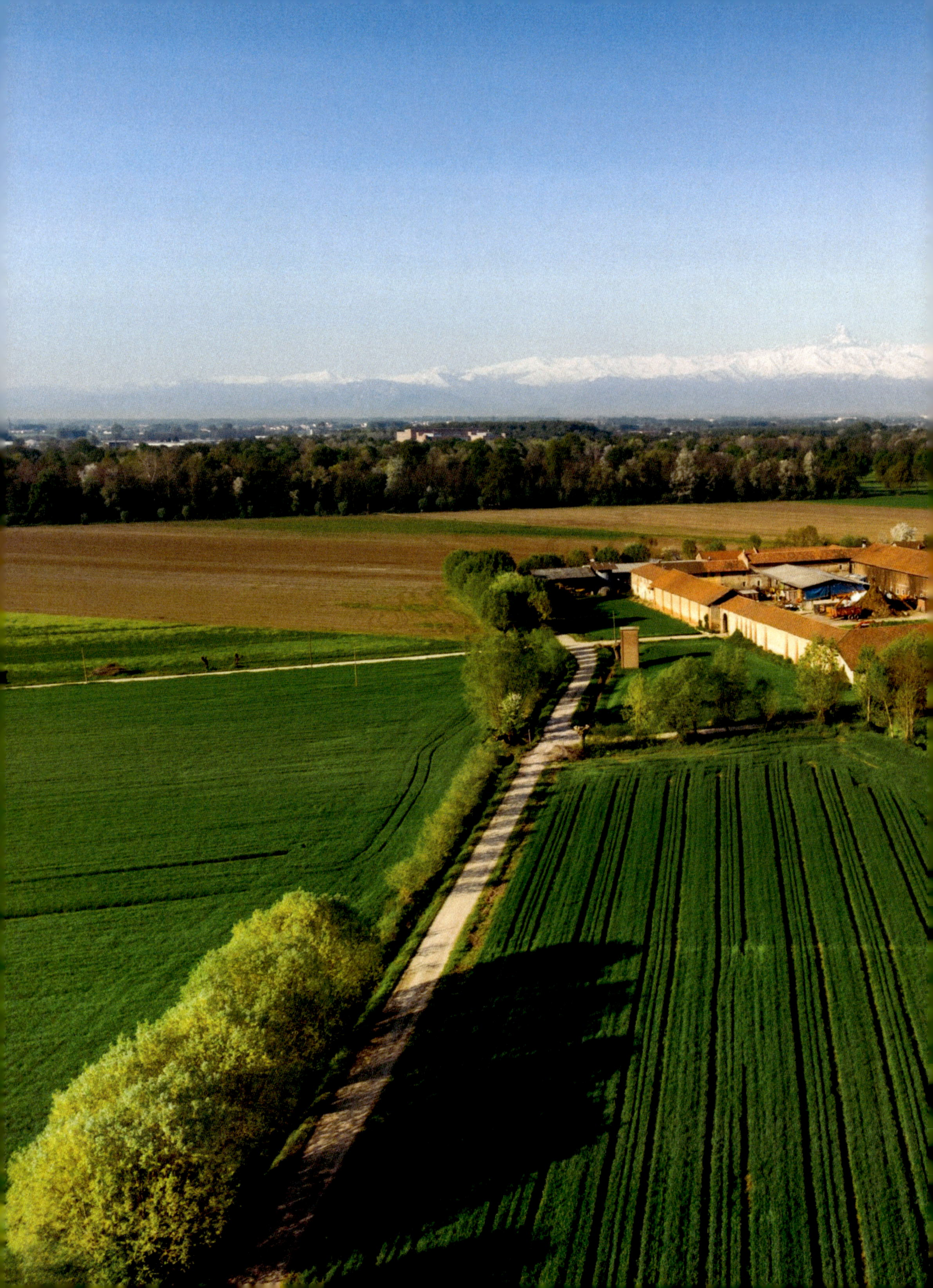

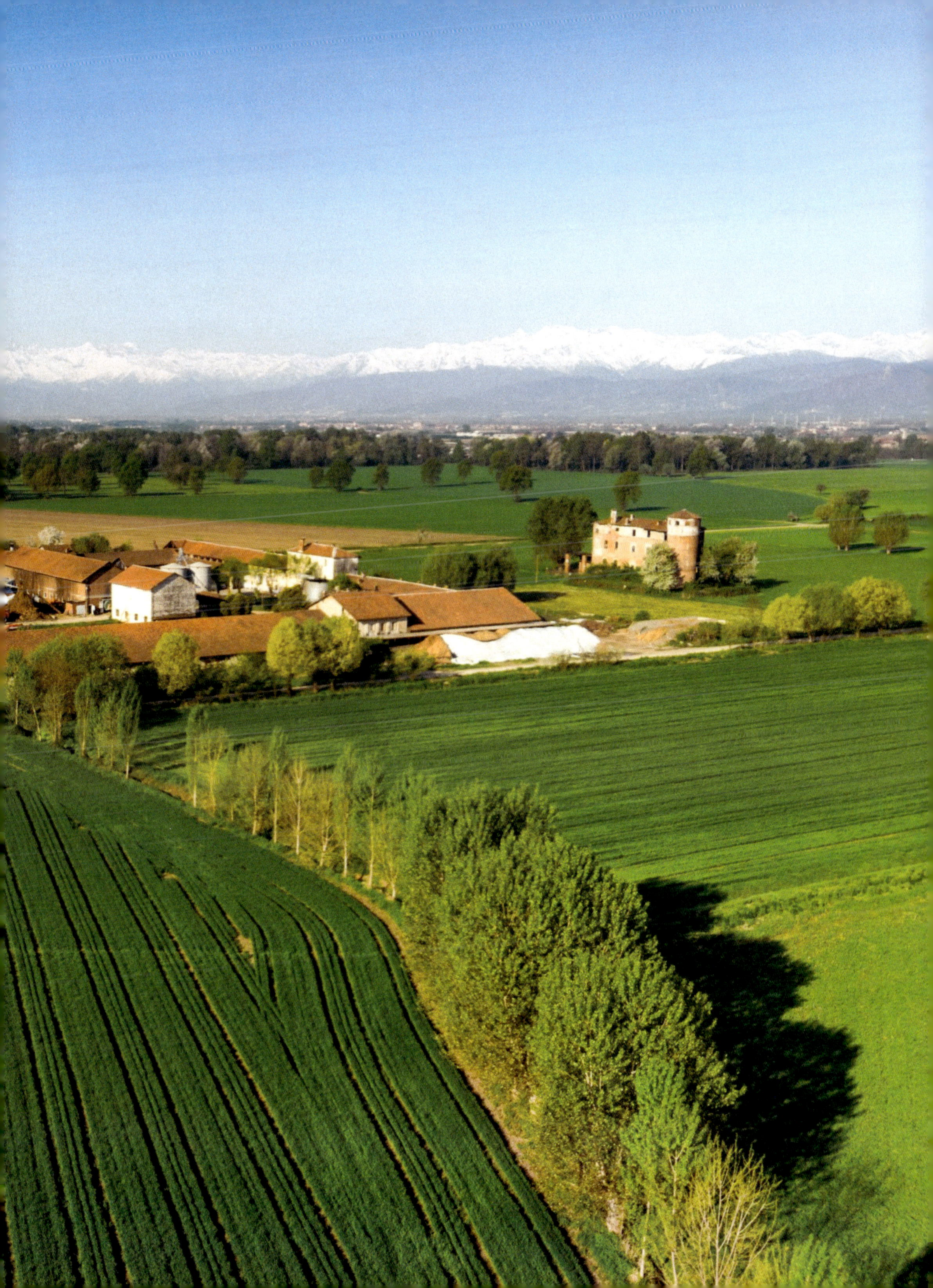

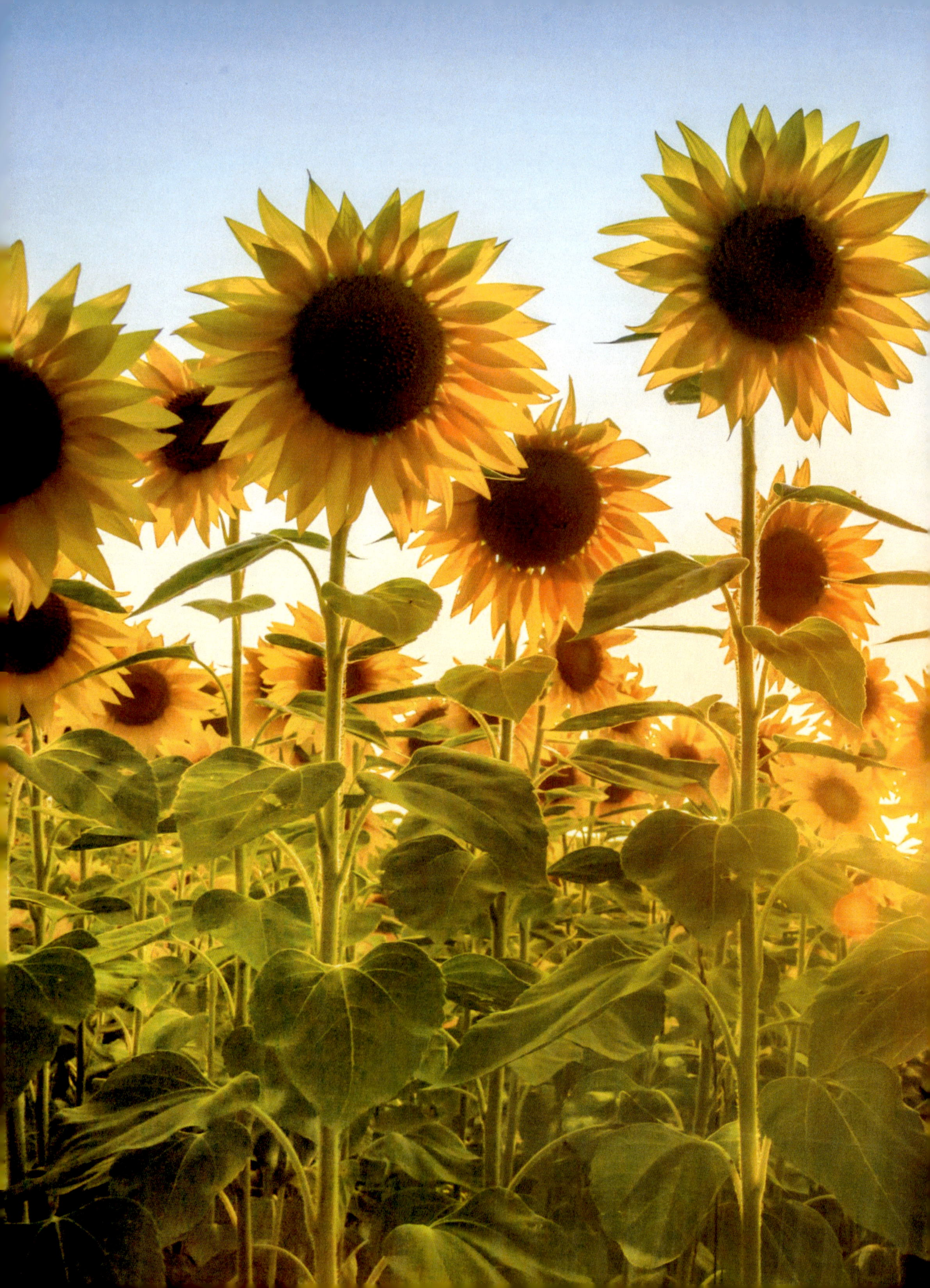

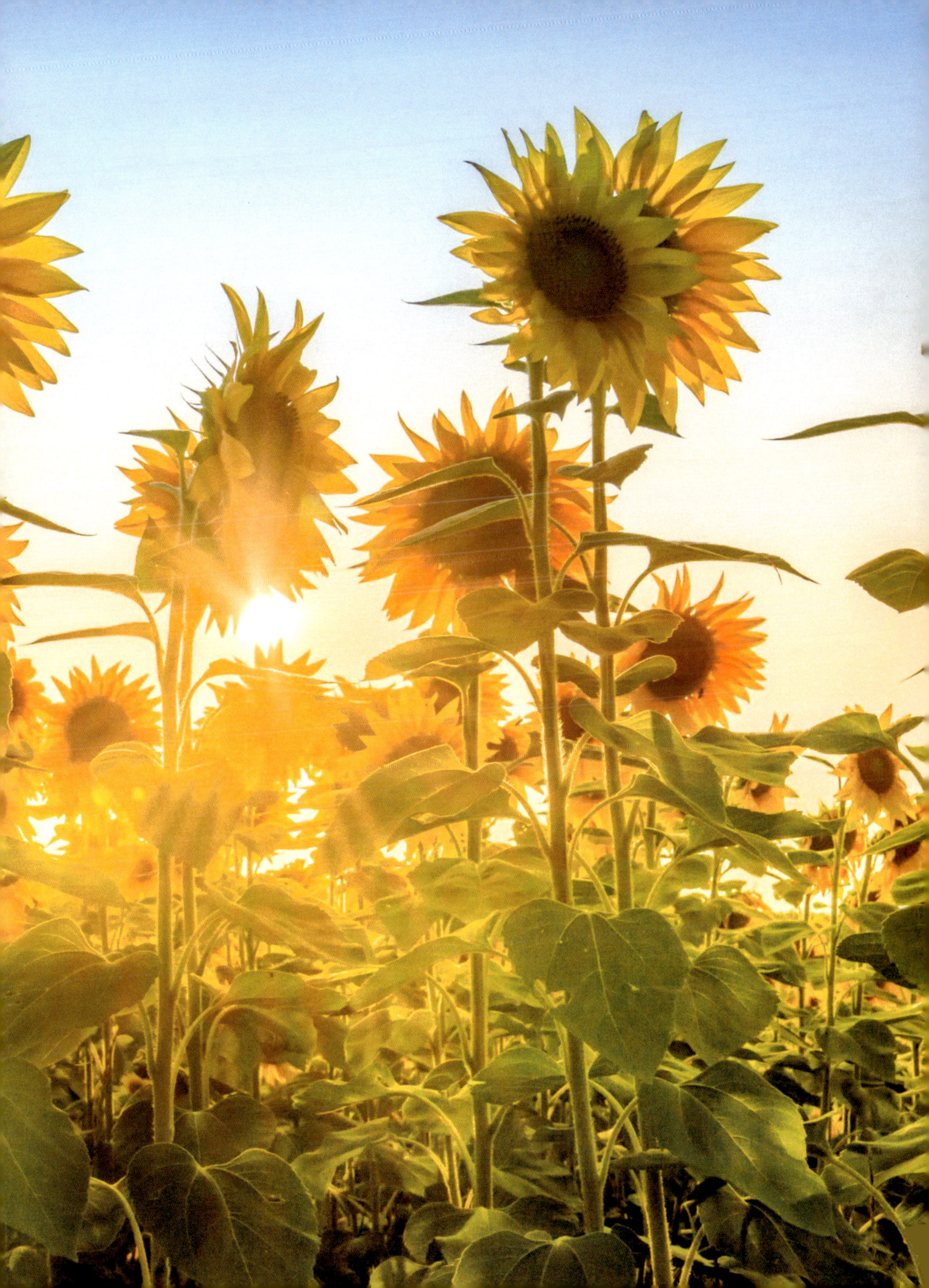

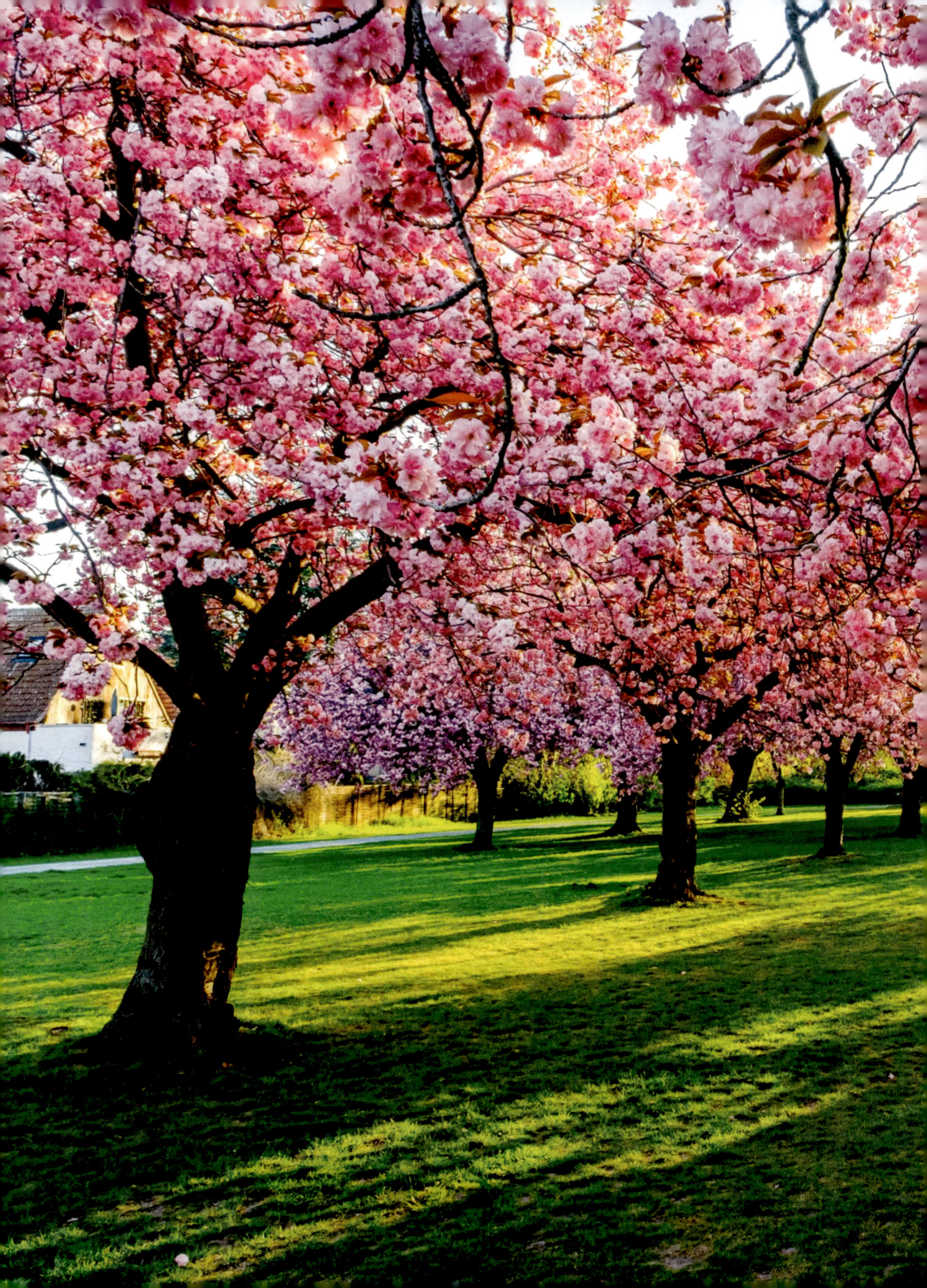

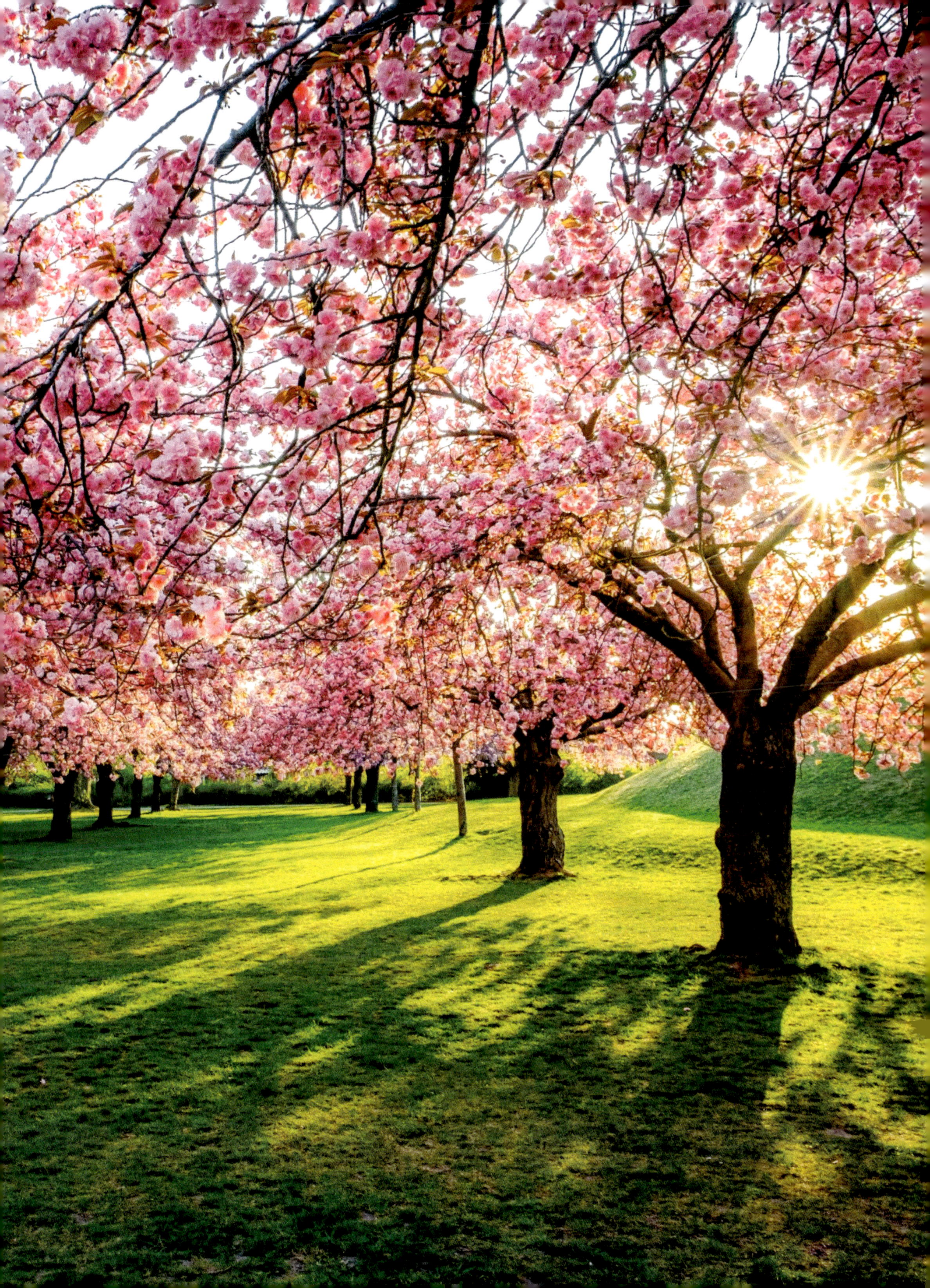

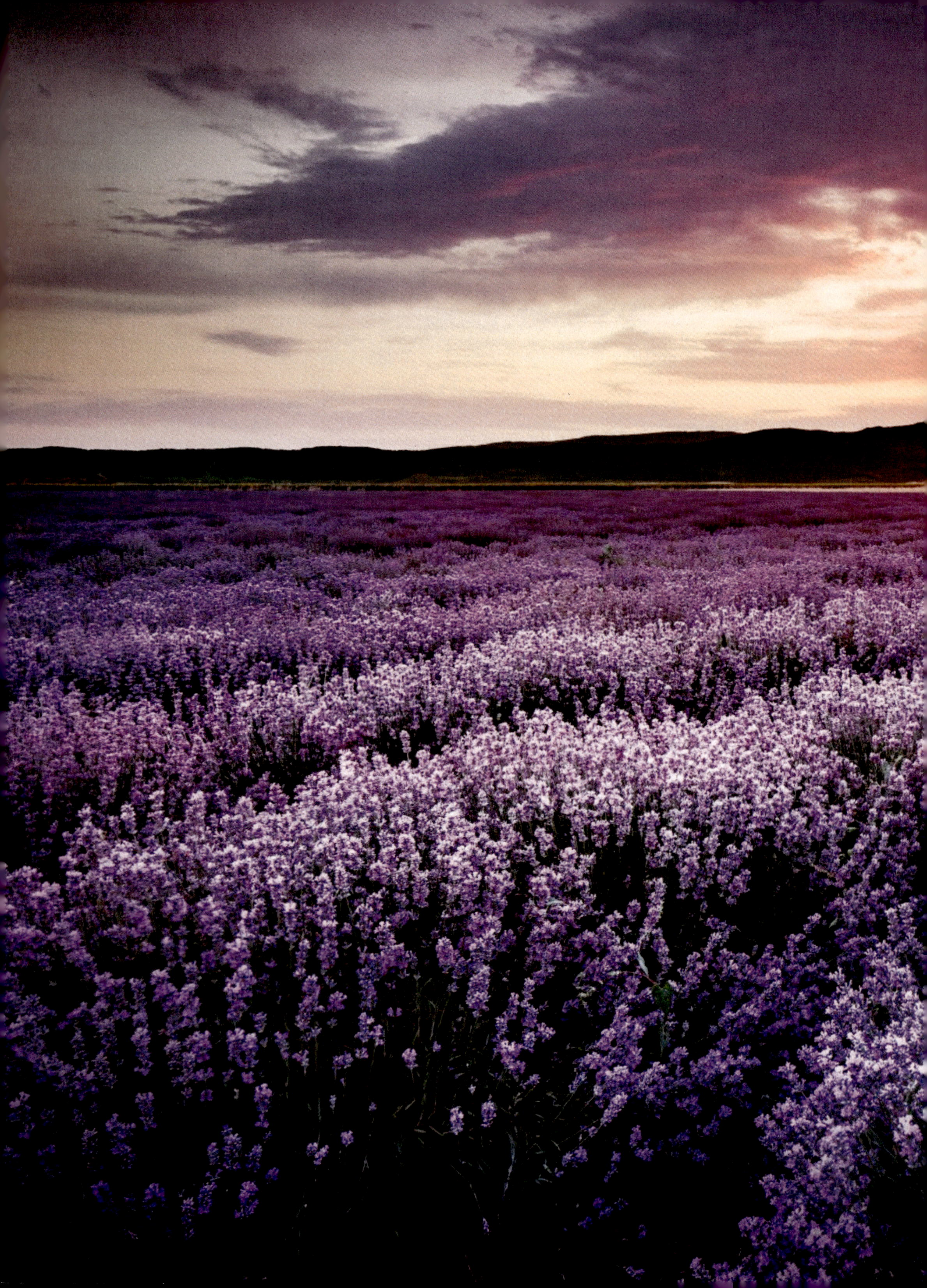

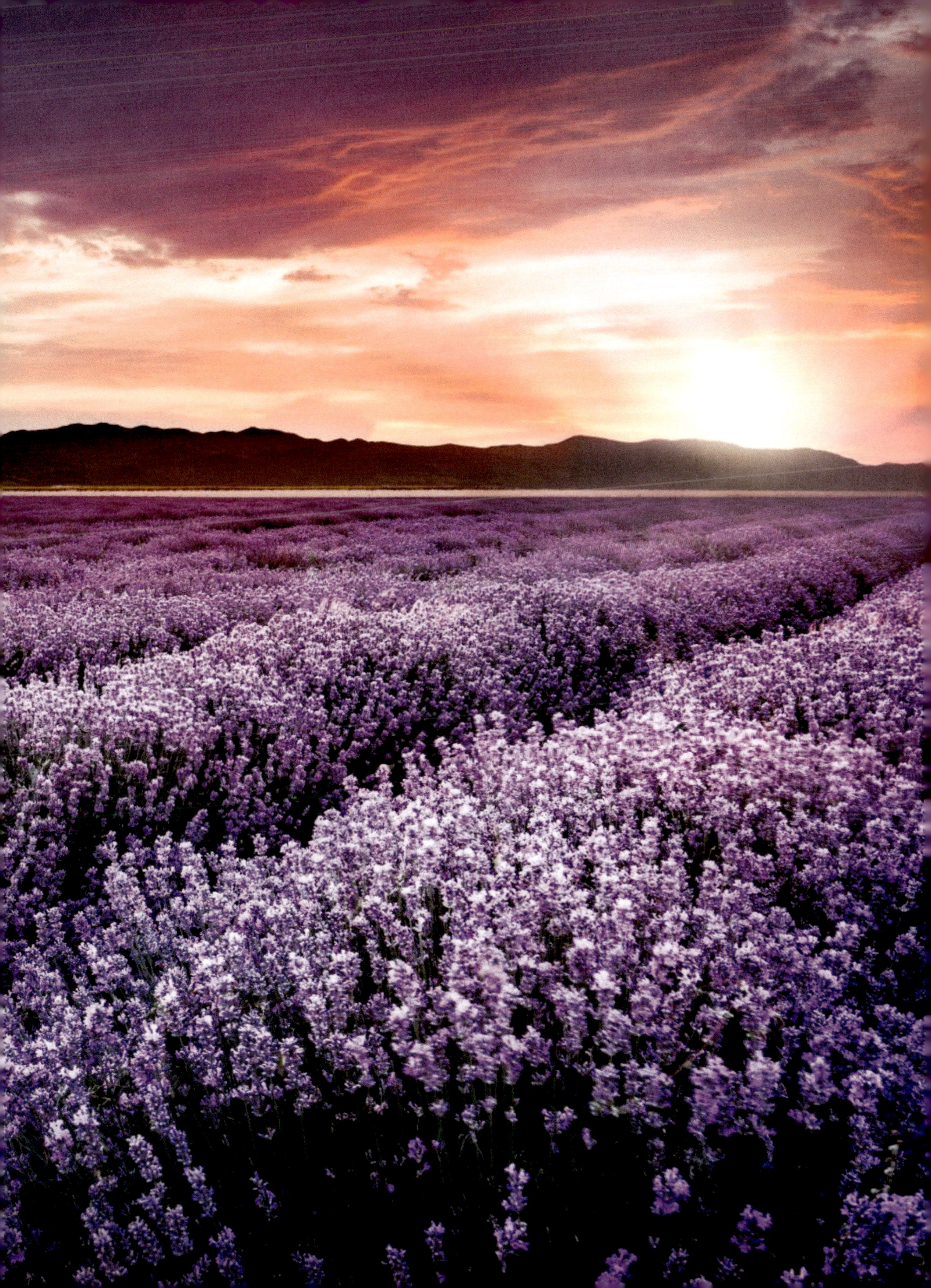

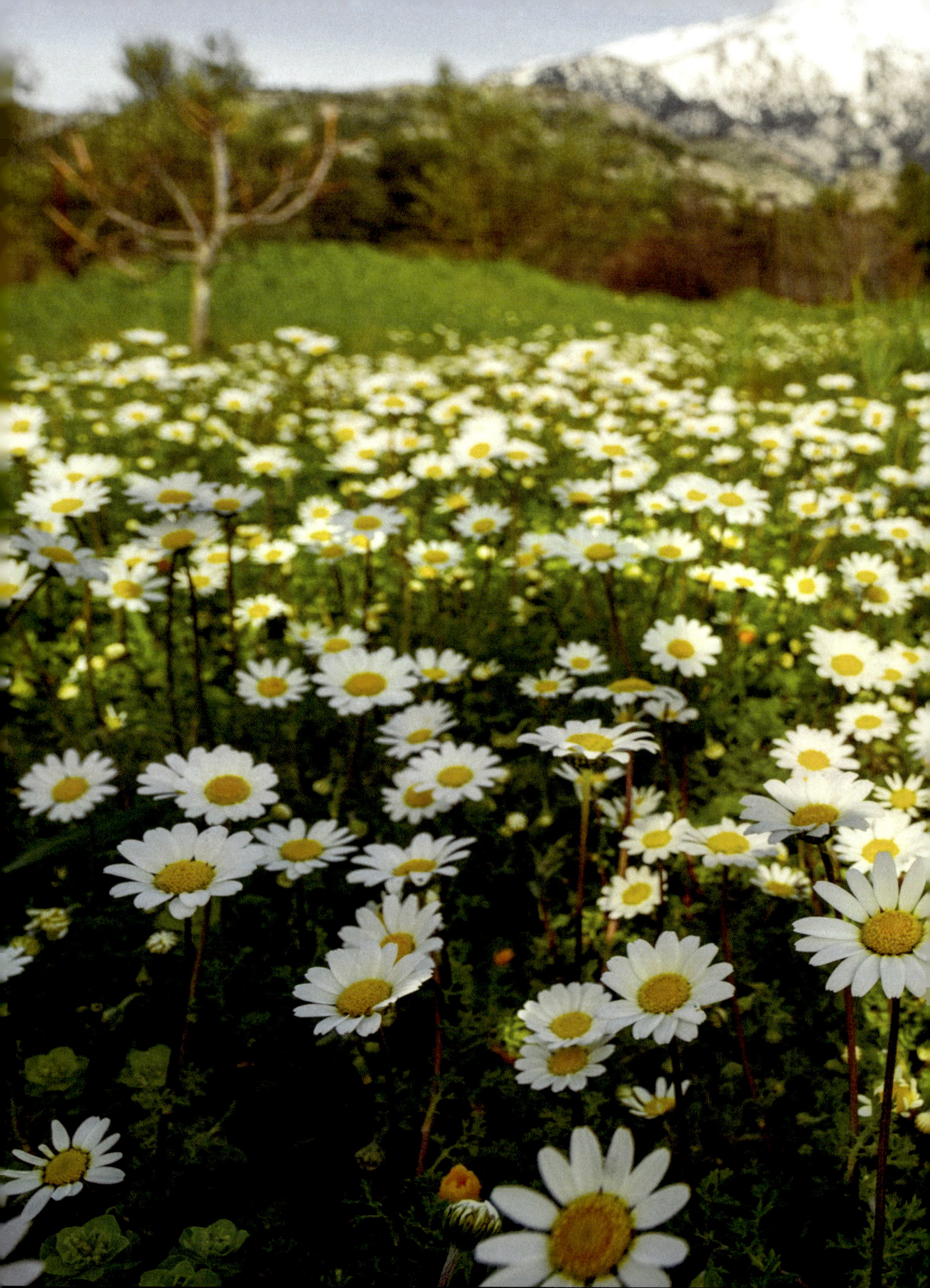

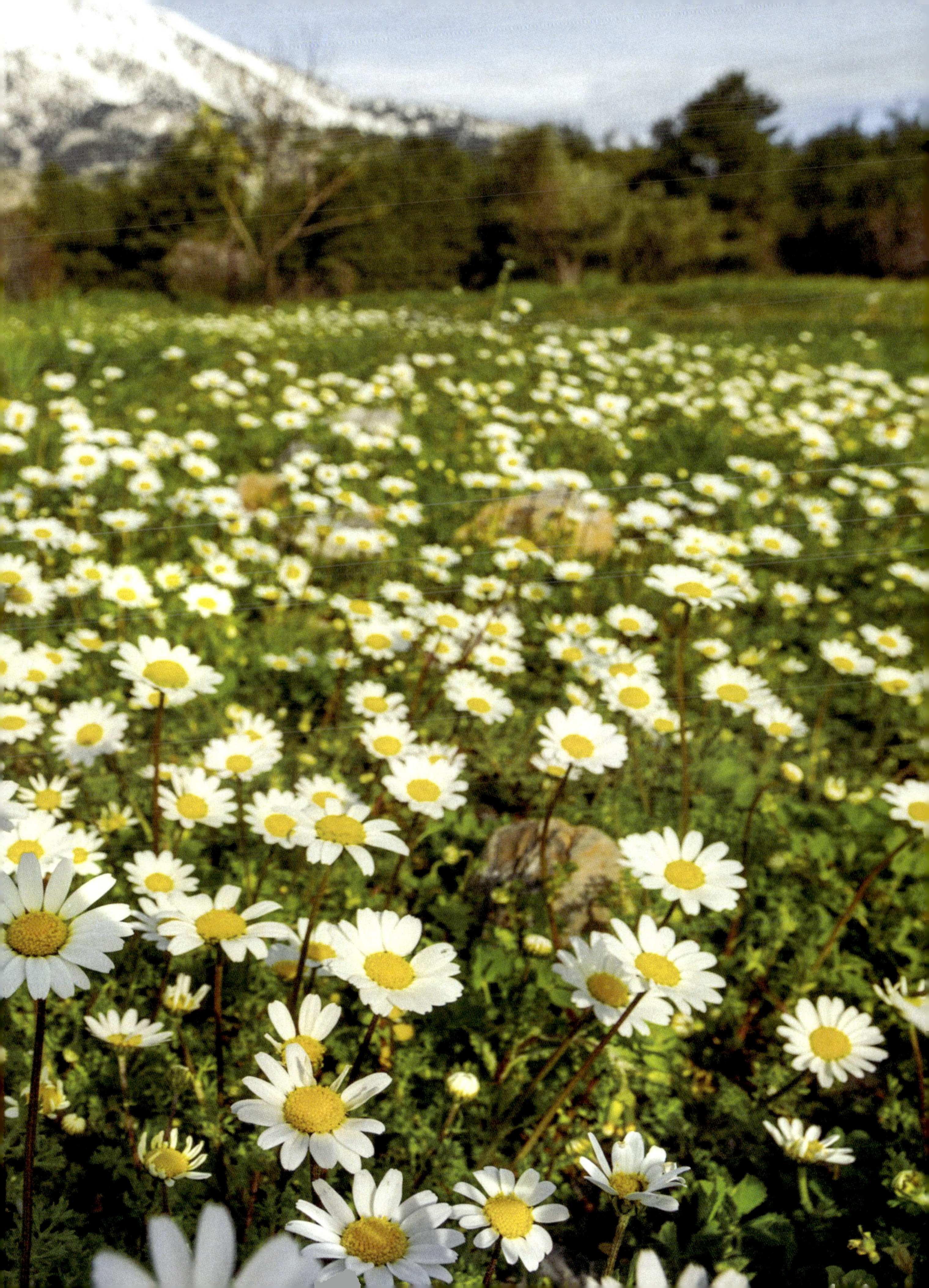

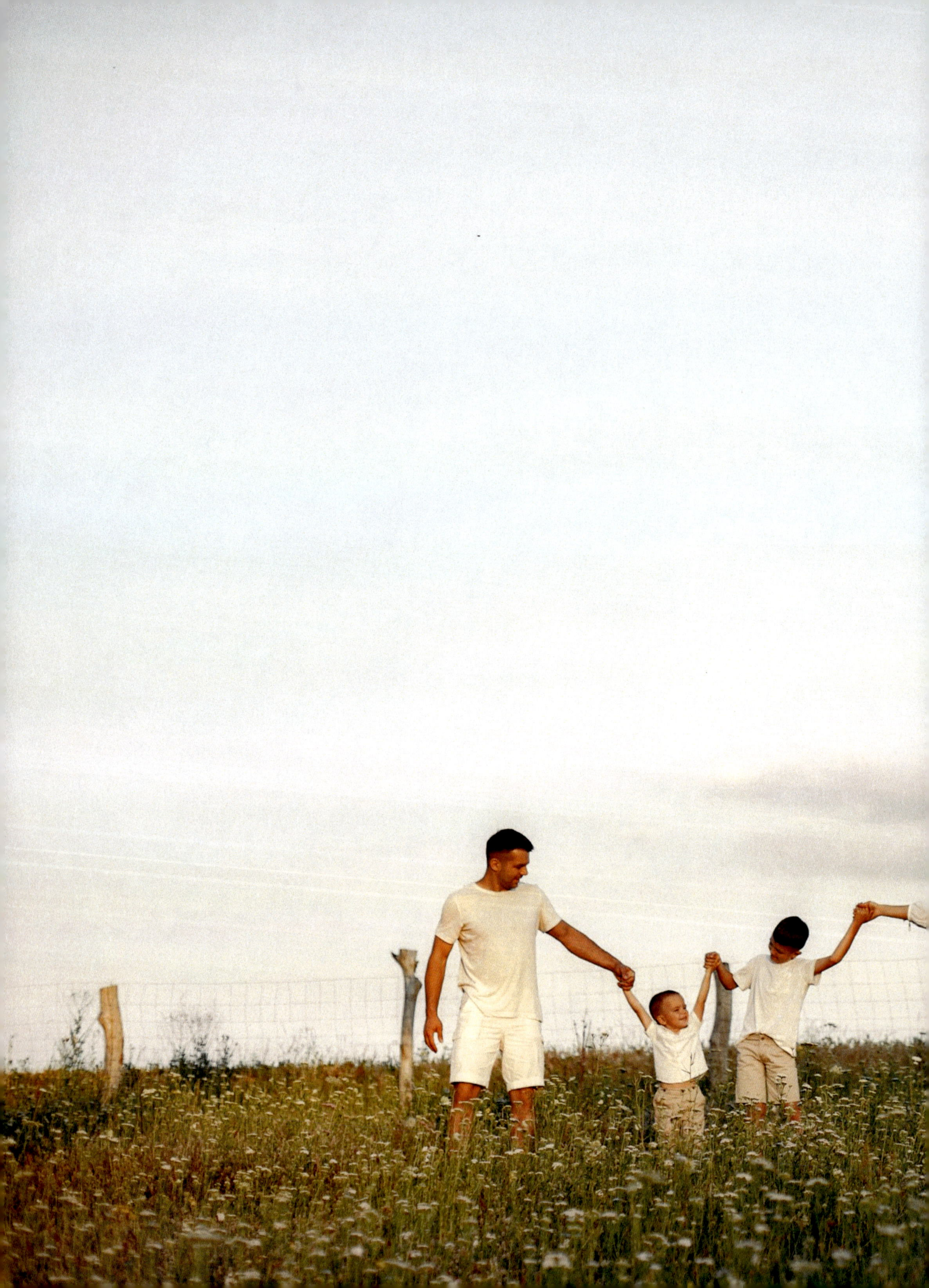

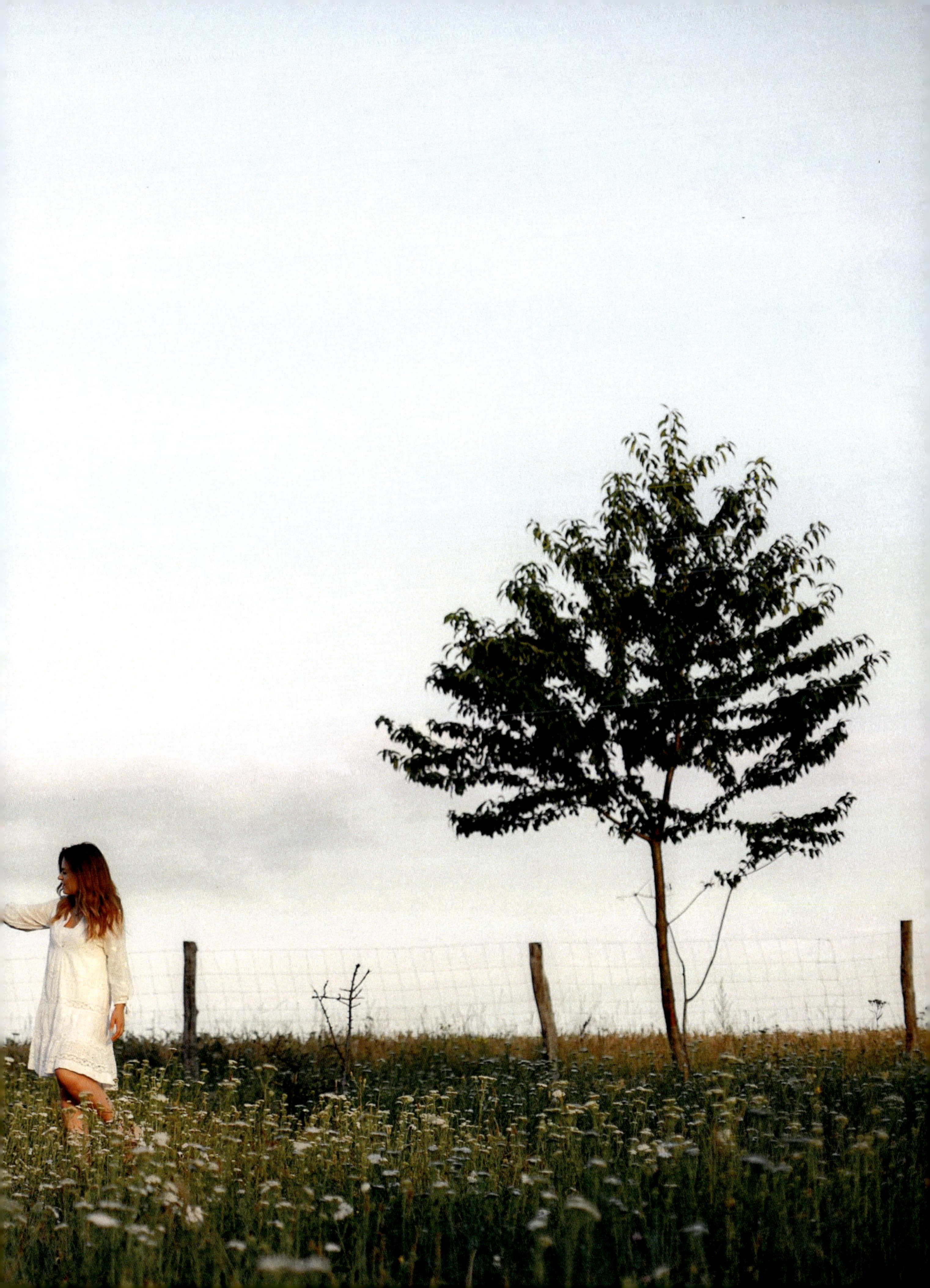

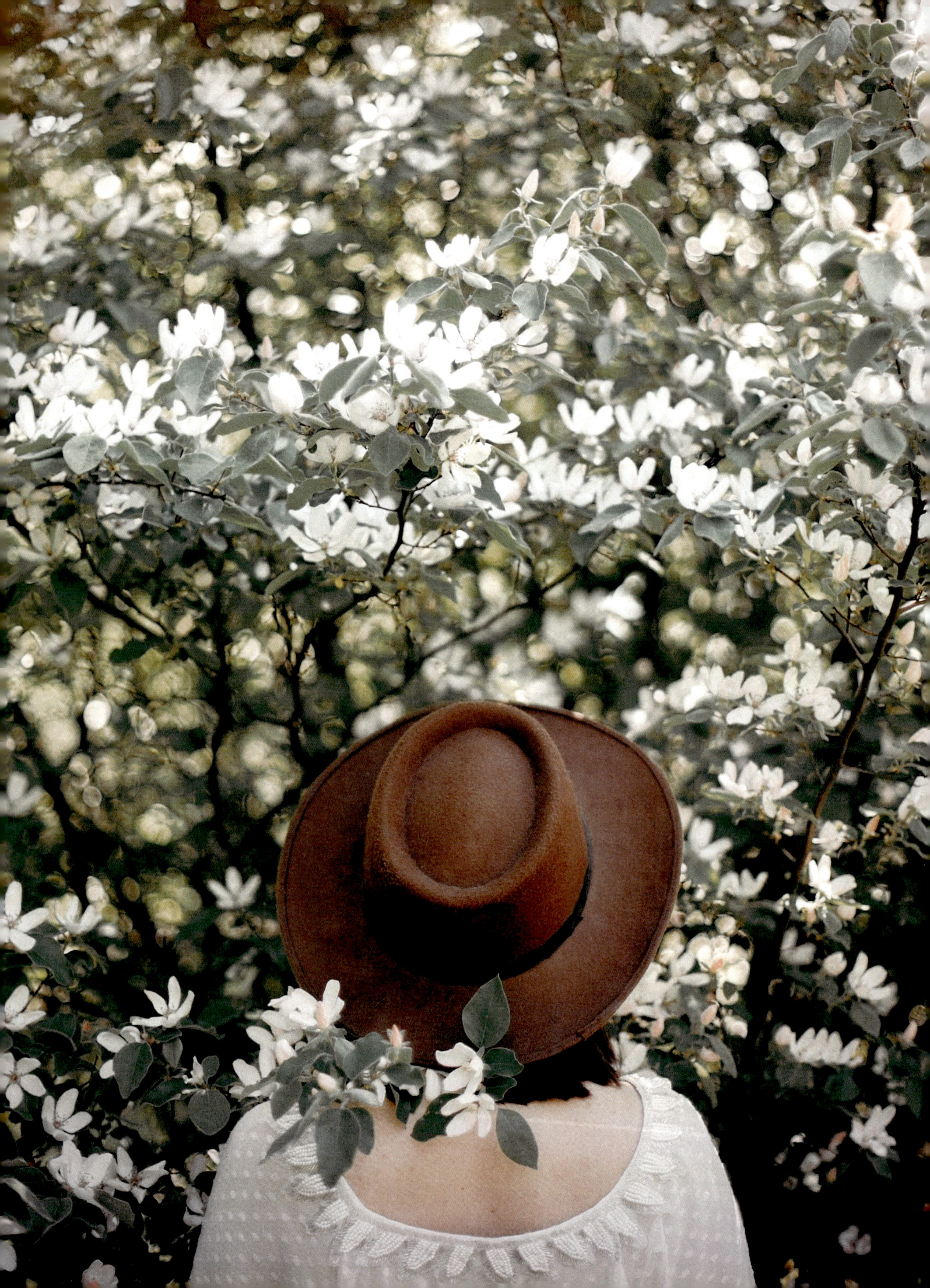

The spring equinox
is the perfect time of
balance and renewal,
symbolizing the start
of a new cycle of growth
and new life in the
natural world.

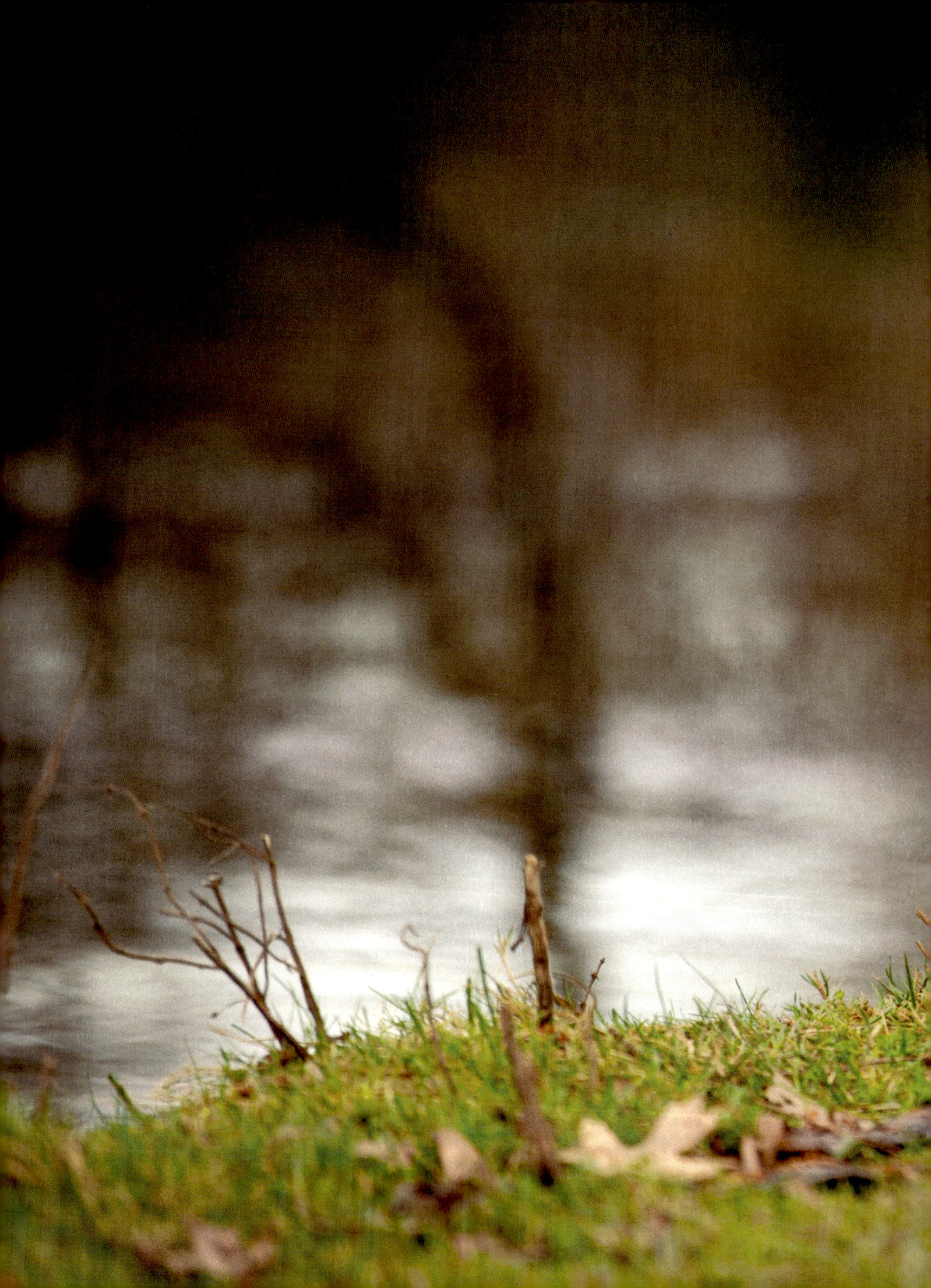

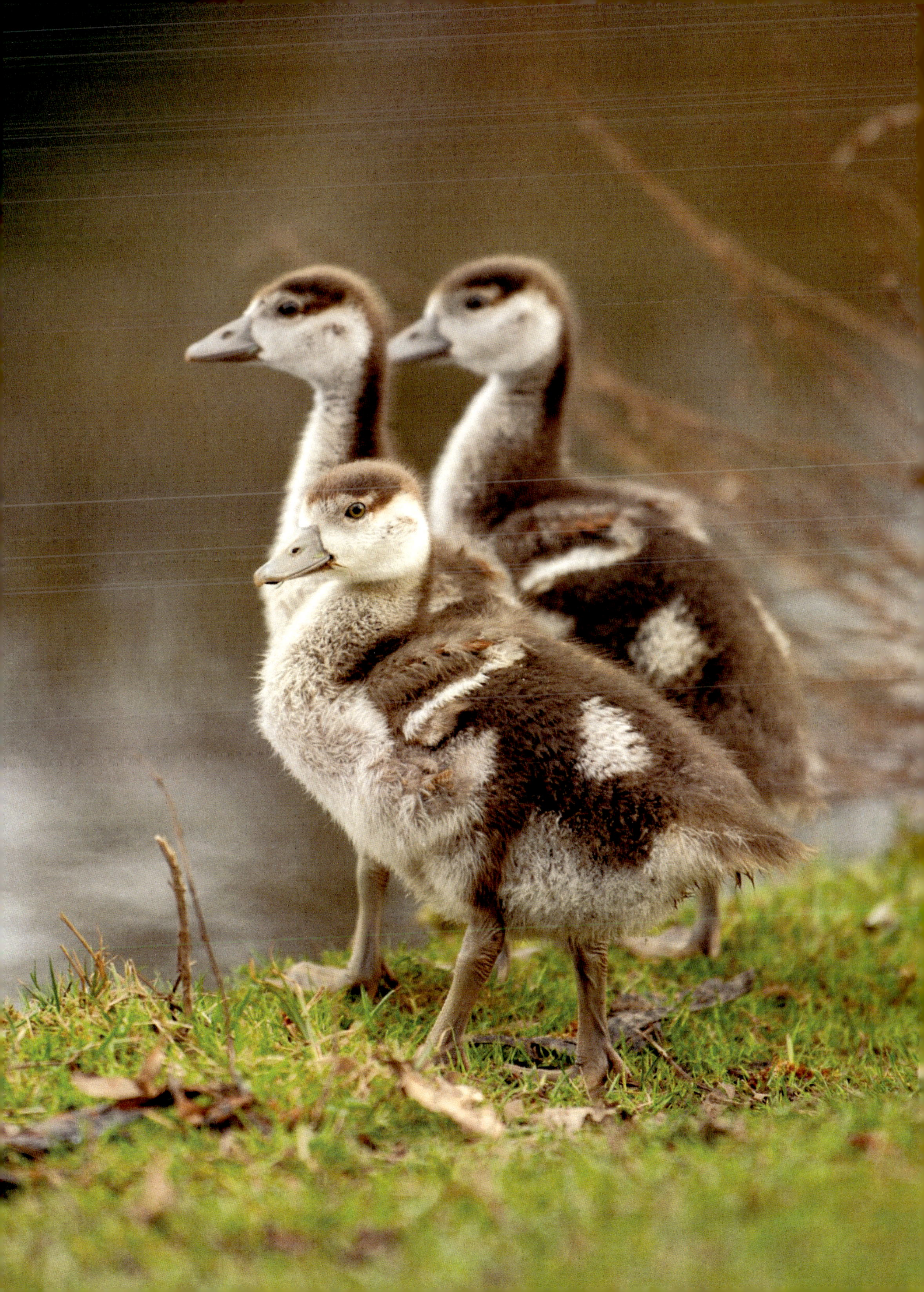

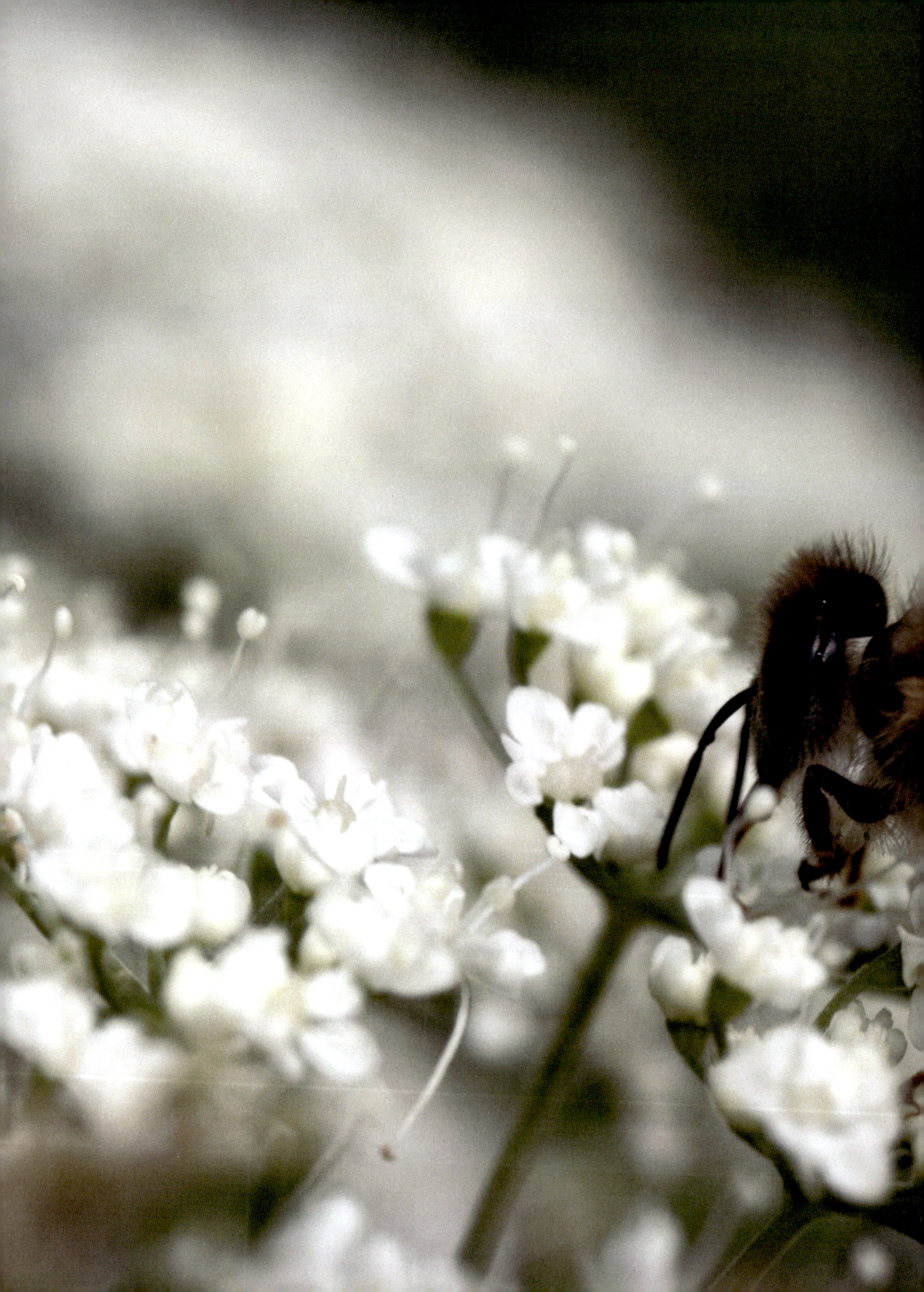

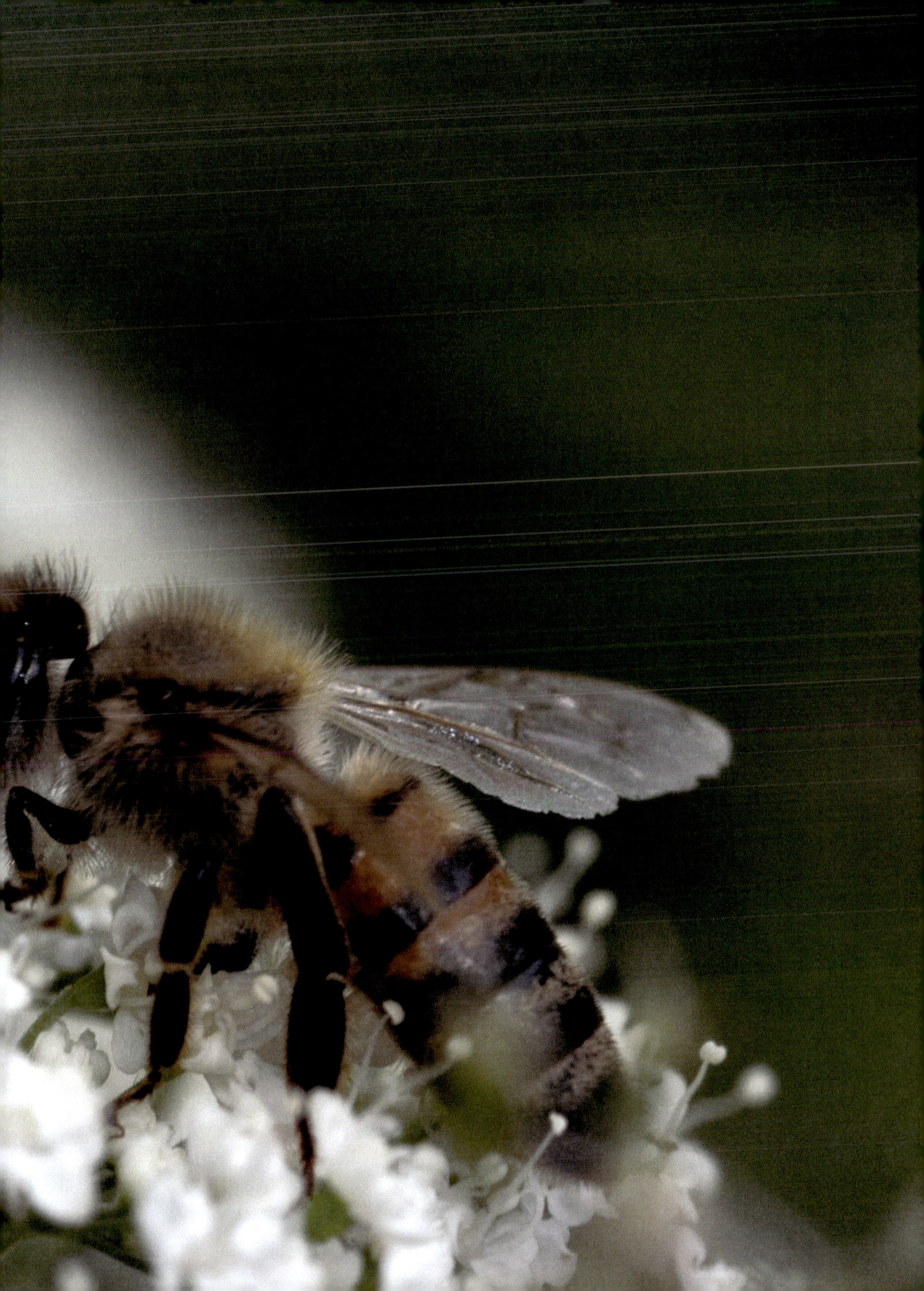

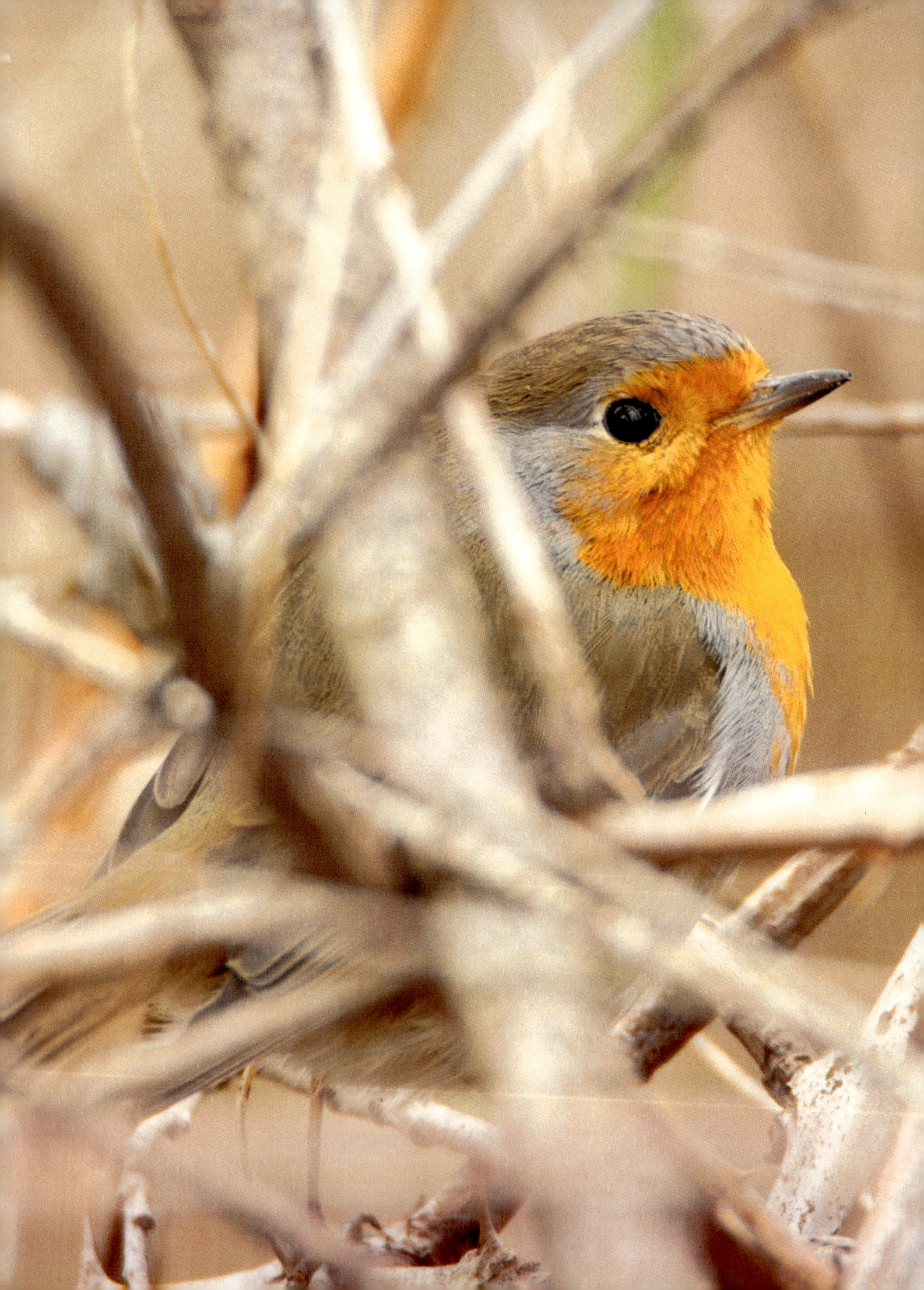

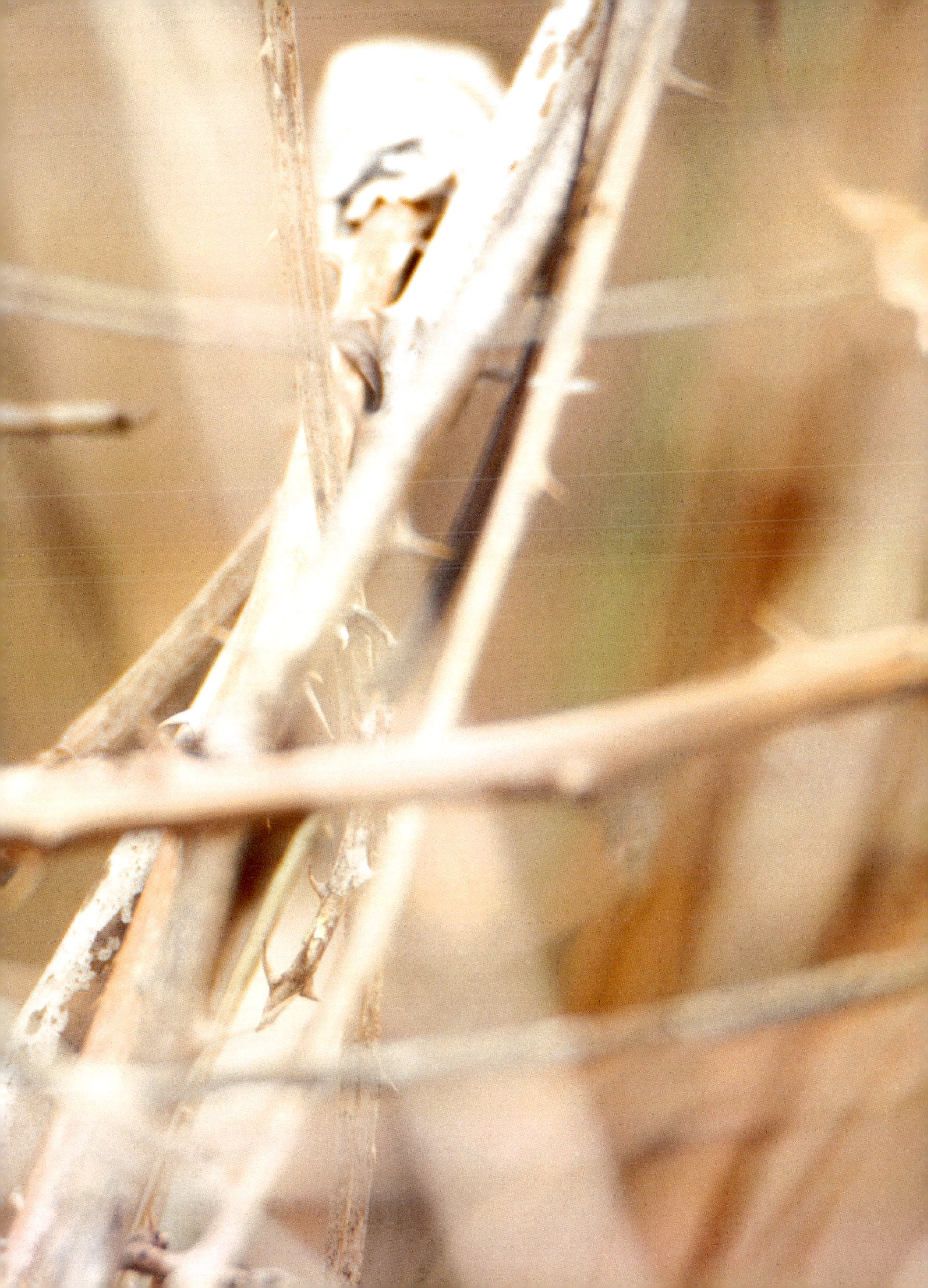

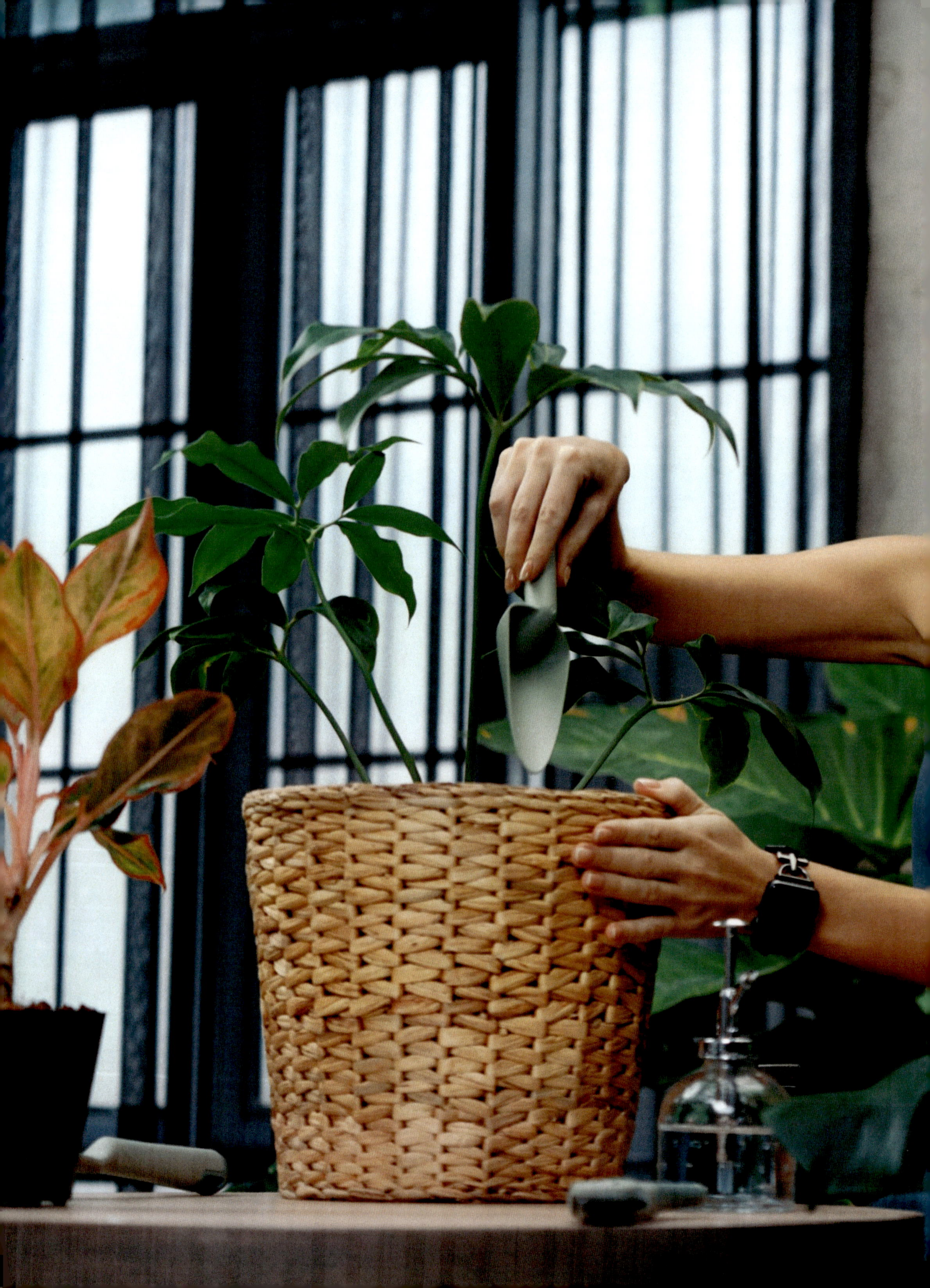

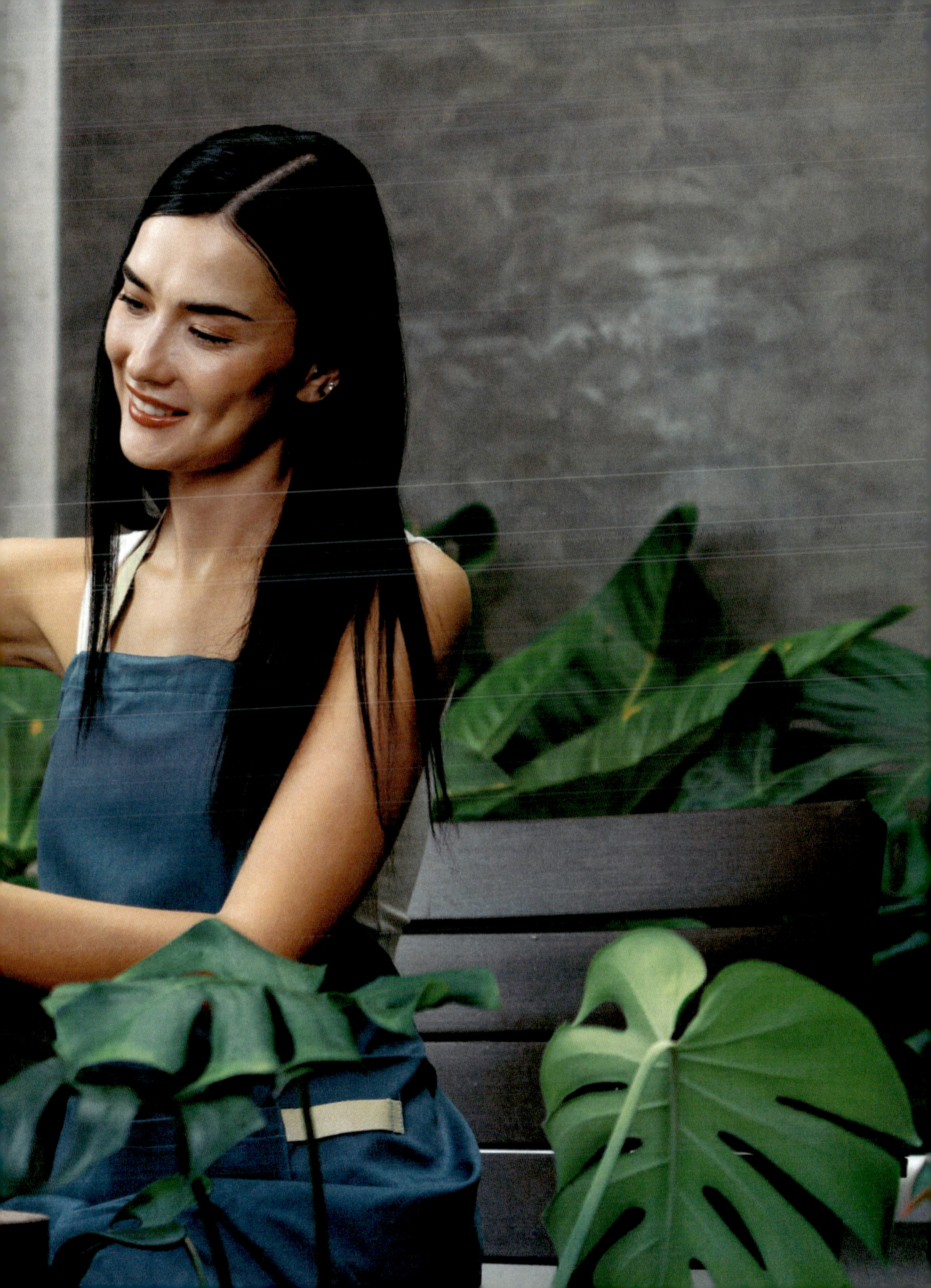

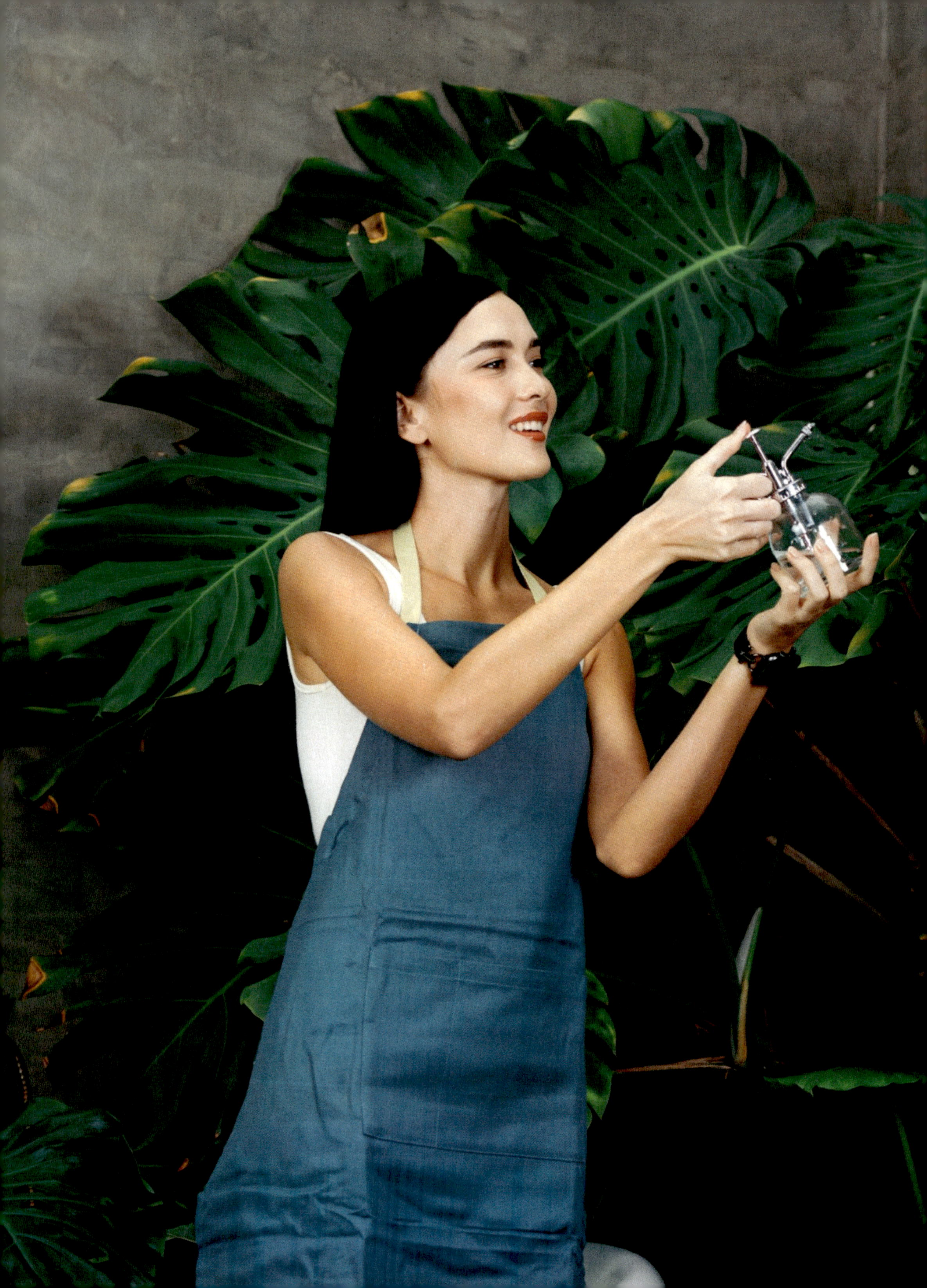

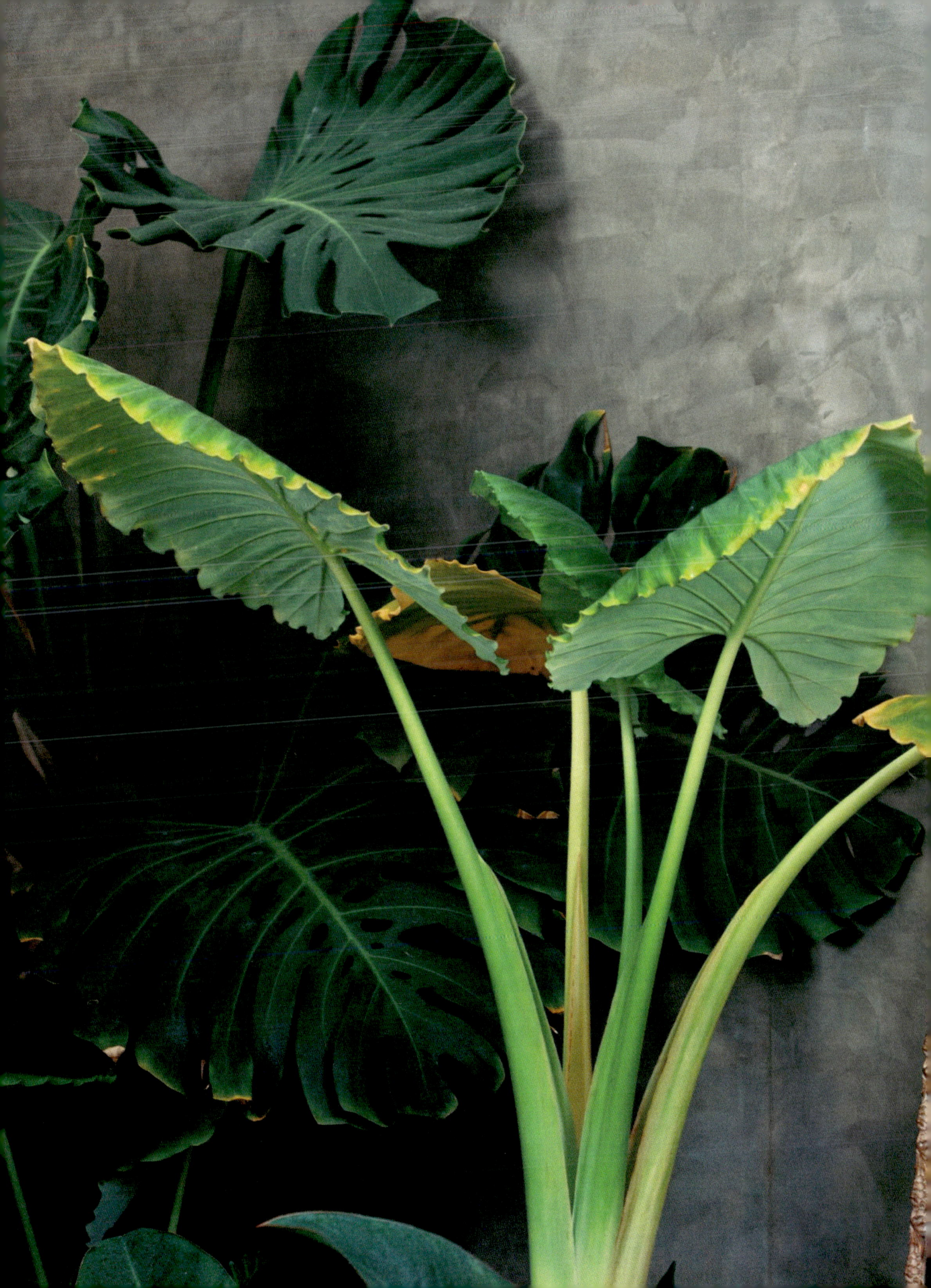

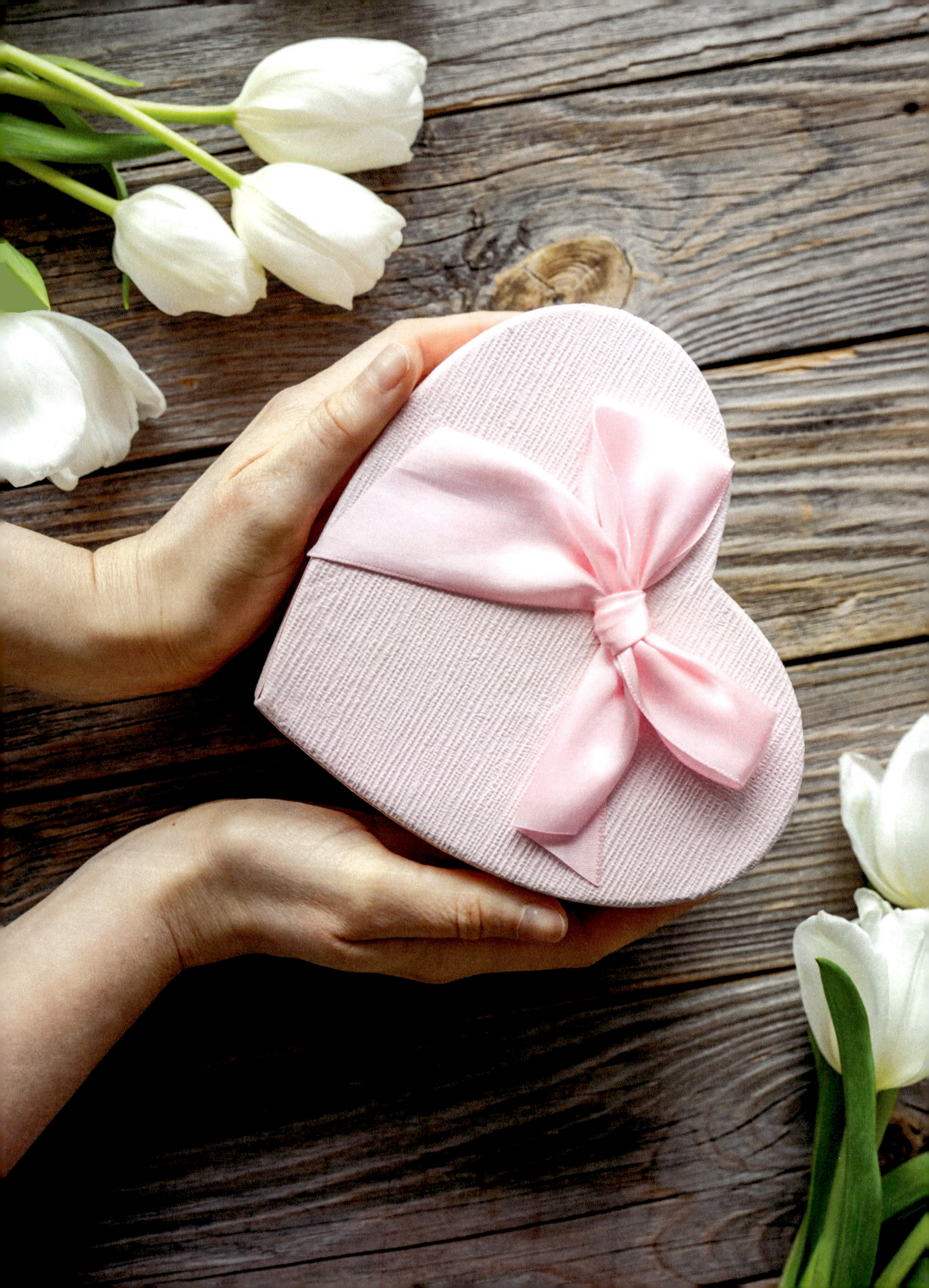

When Easter arrives,
is the time that marks
the beginning of the
spring season. This is a
time of new life and
renewal when the flowers
and the trees bloom and
the air is filled with the
sweet scent of freshness.

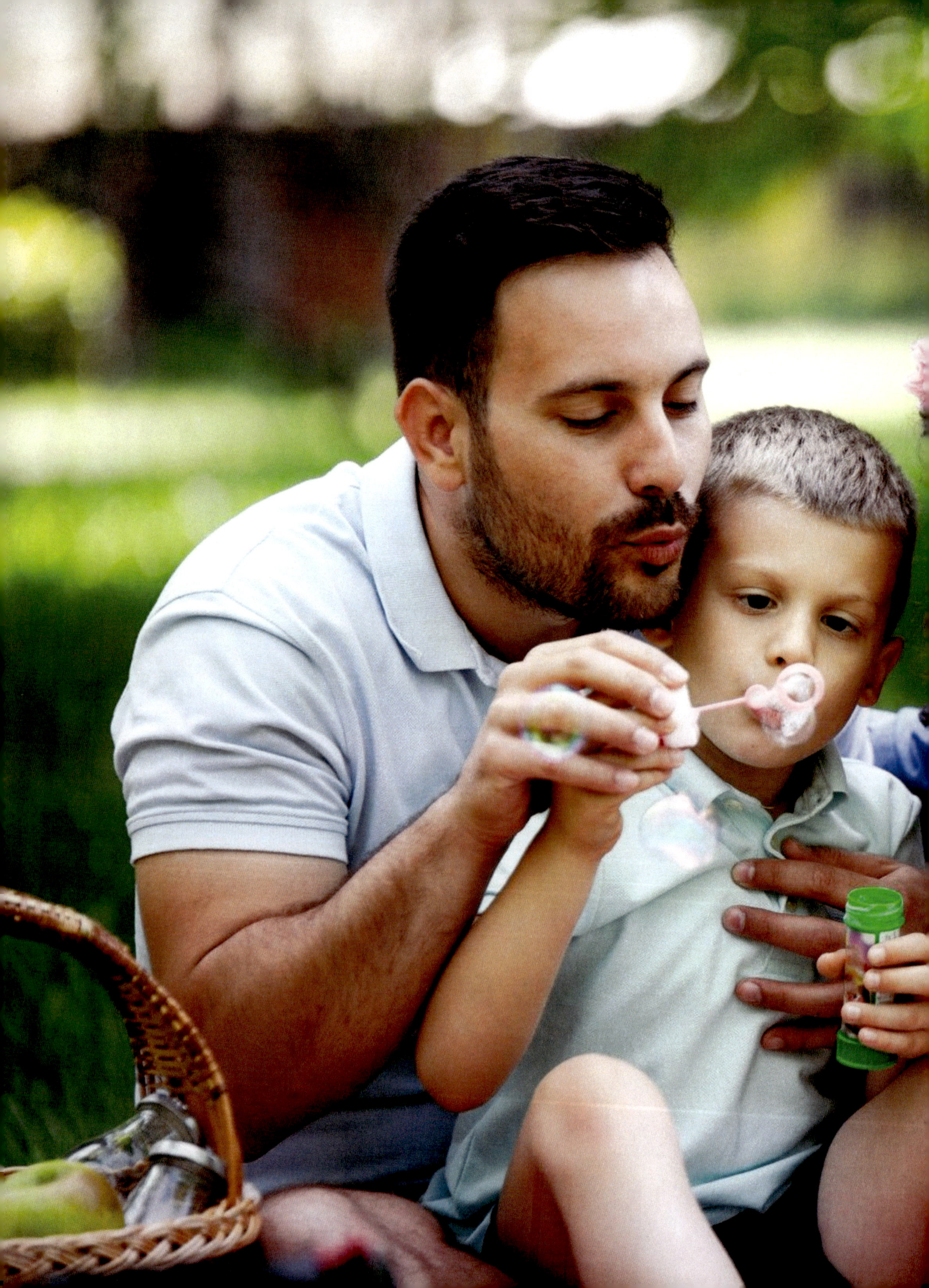

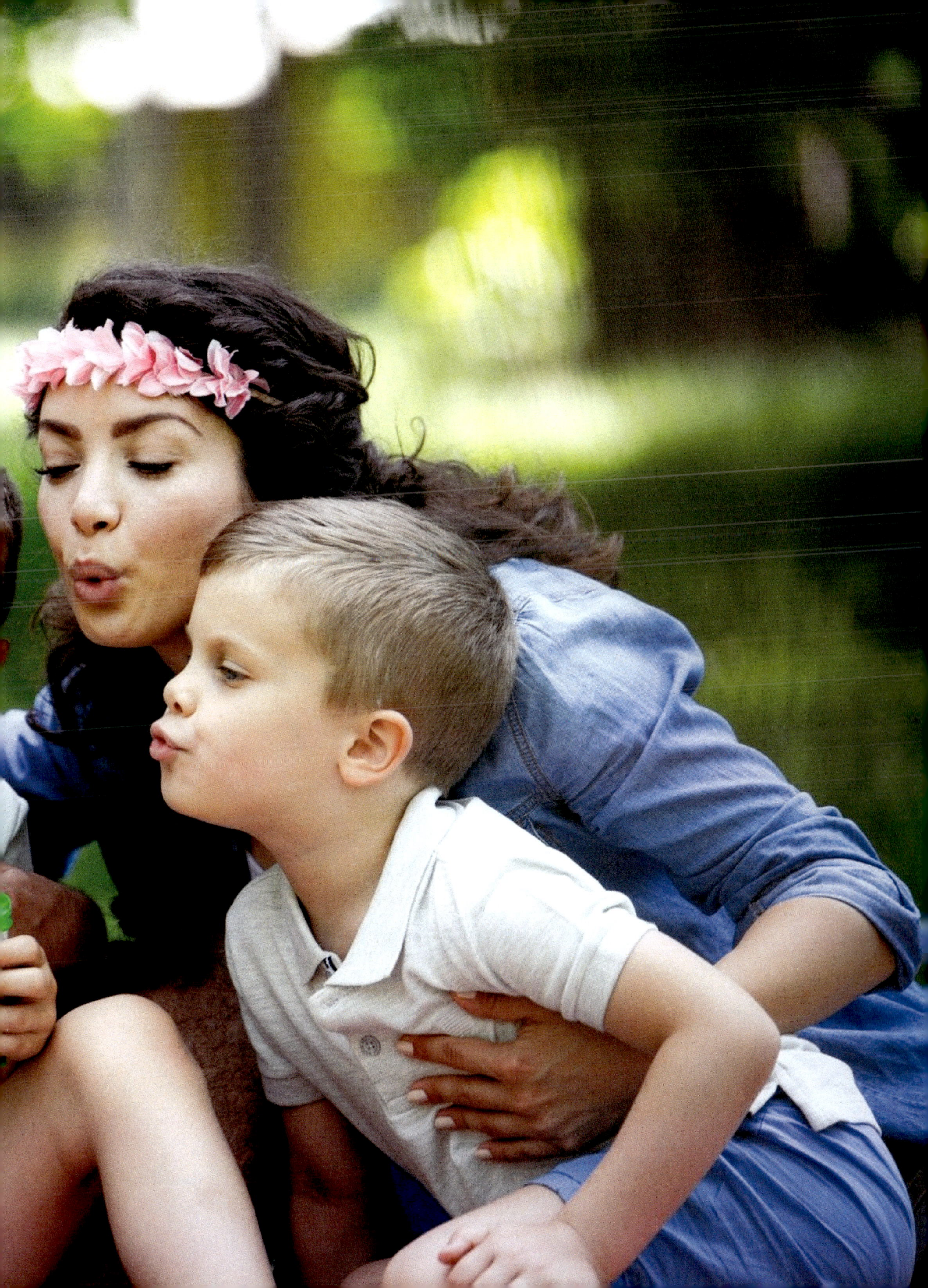

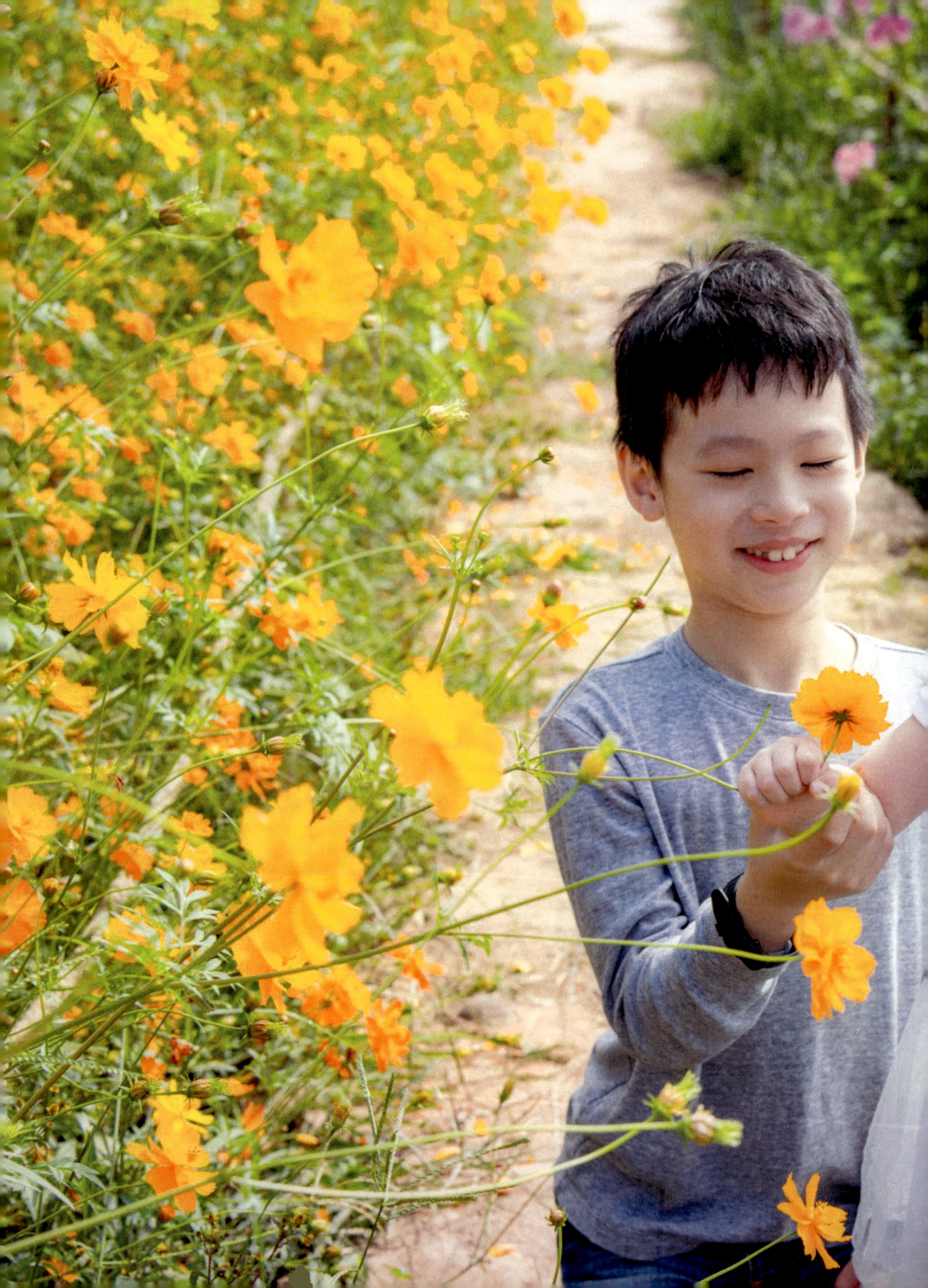

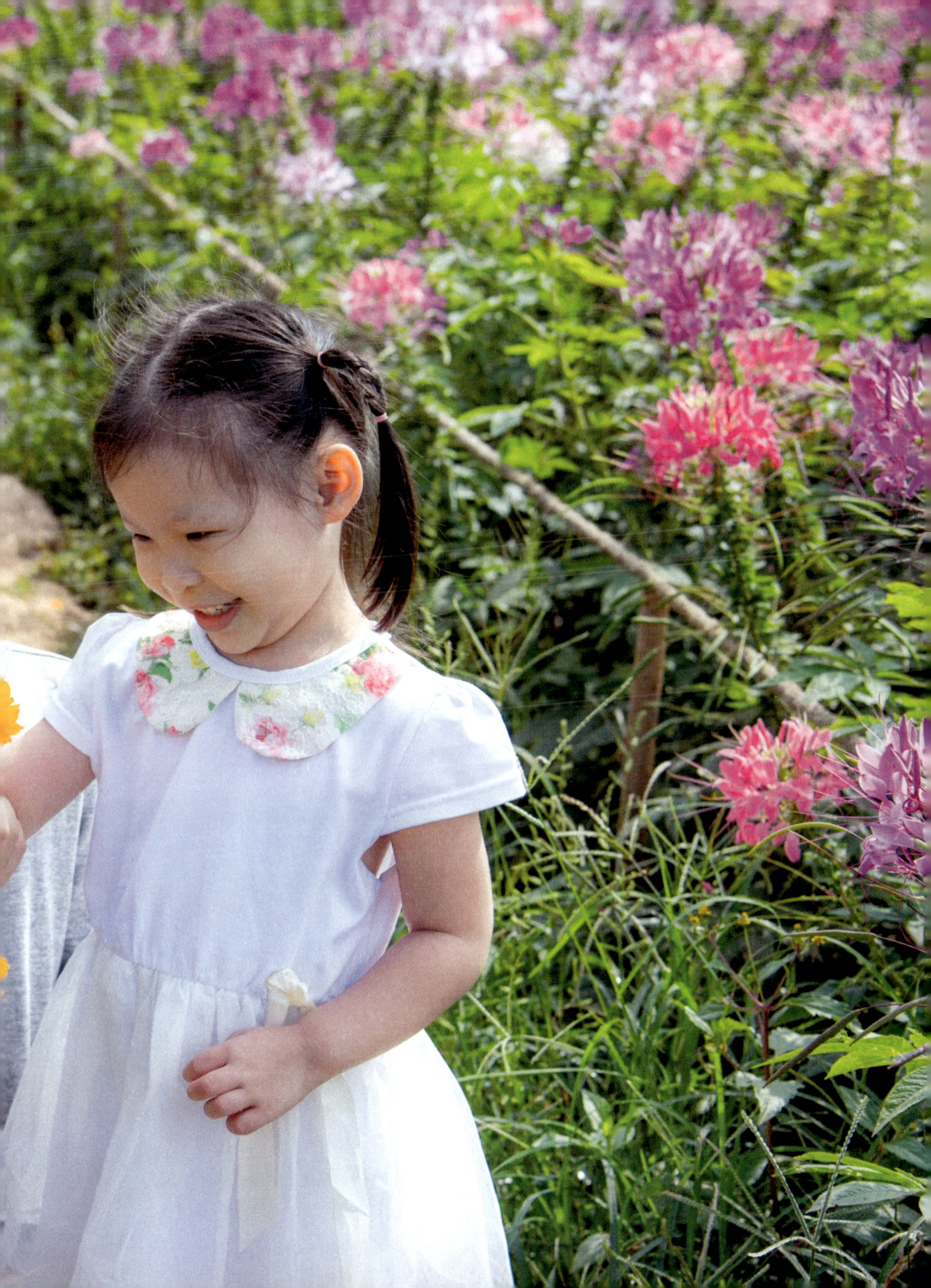

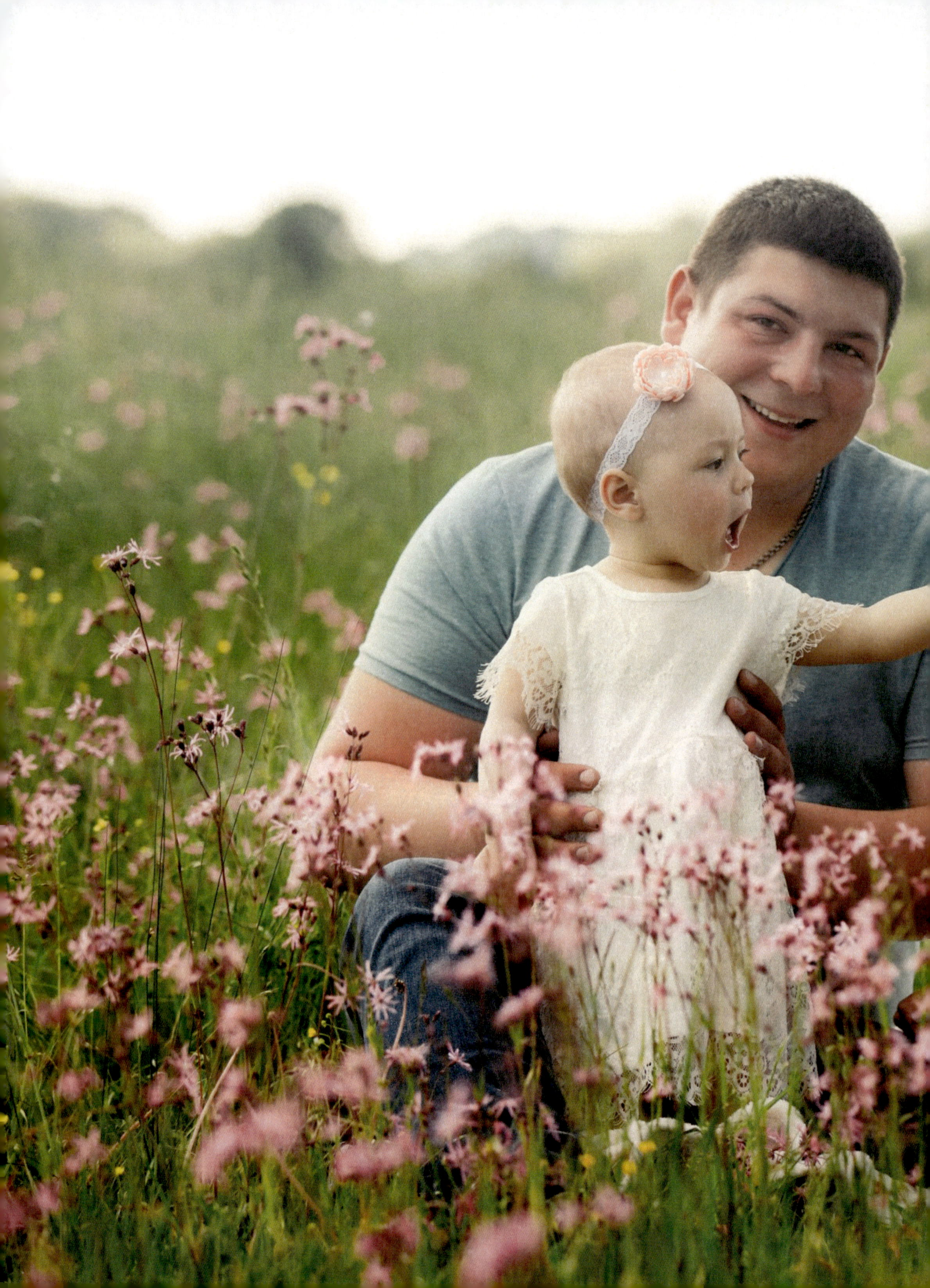

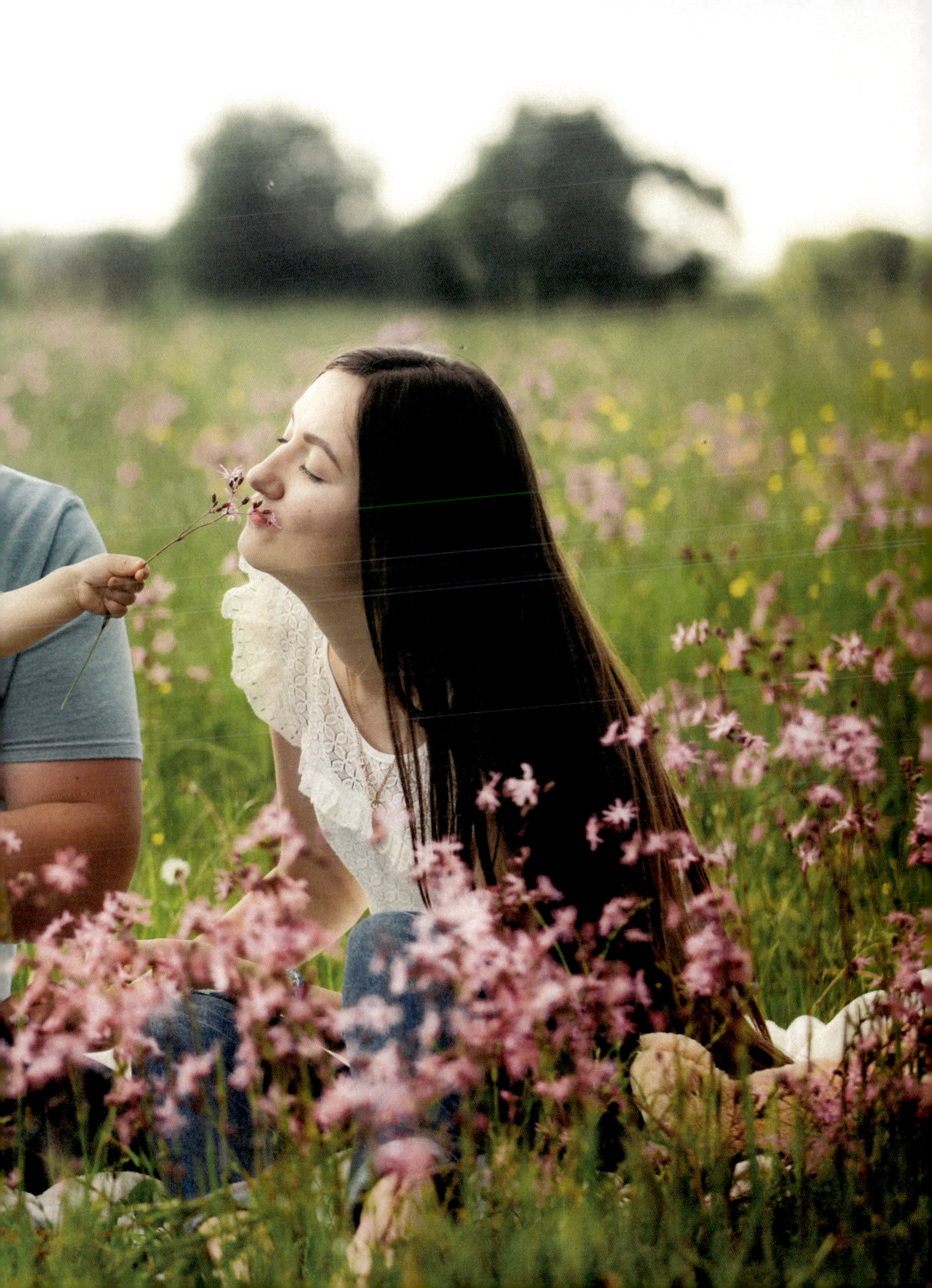

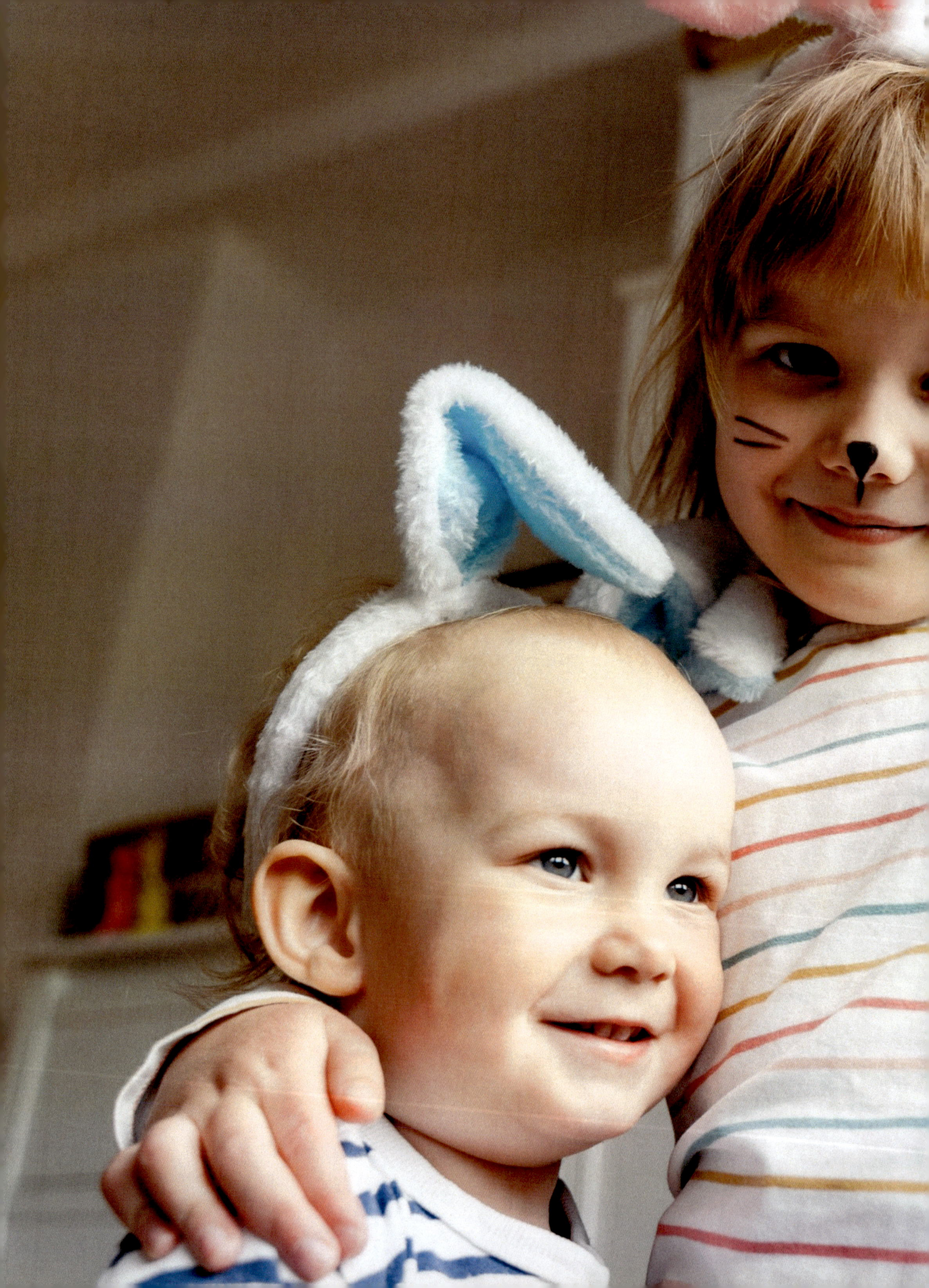

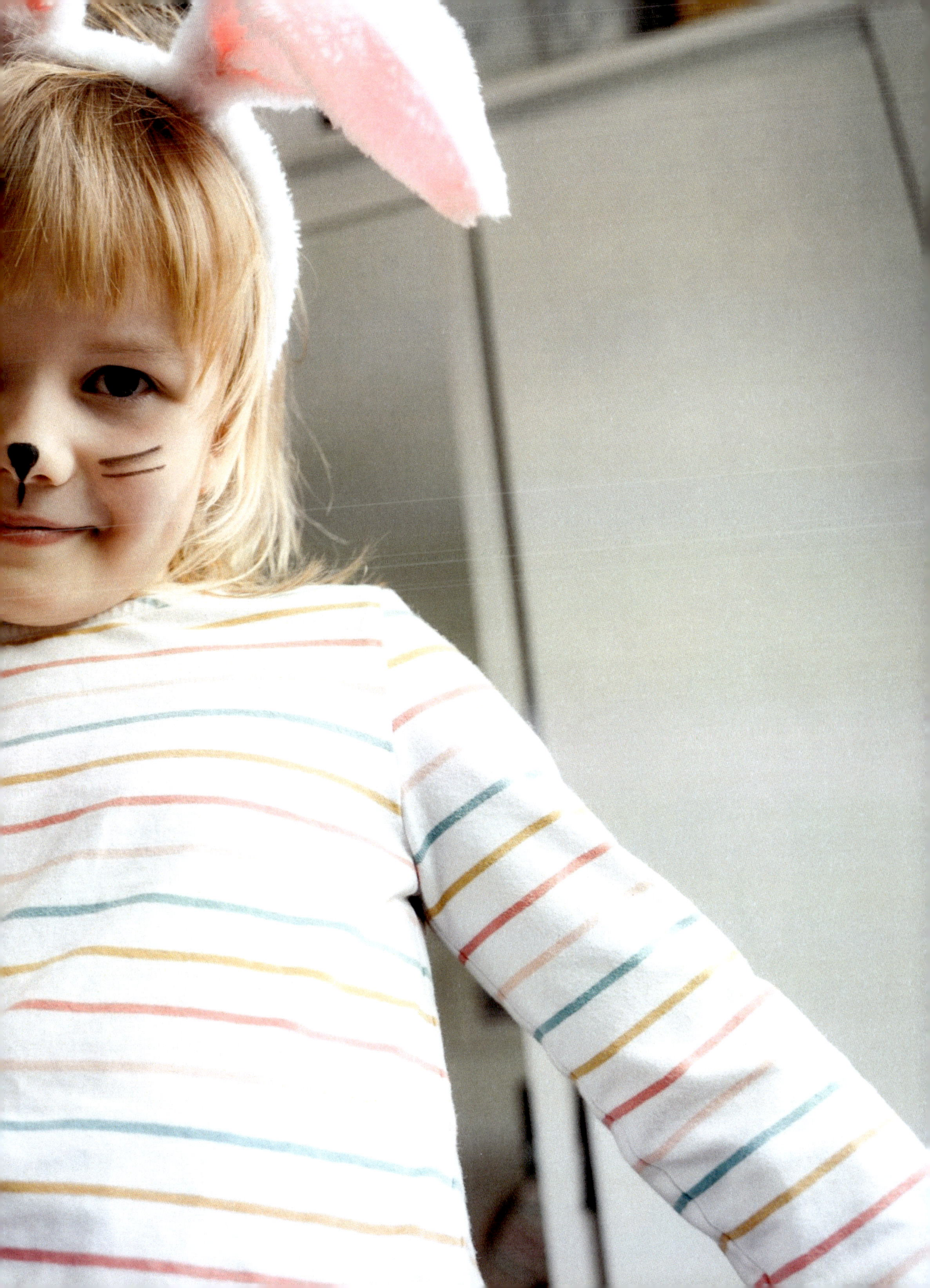

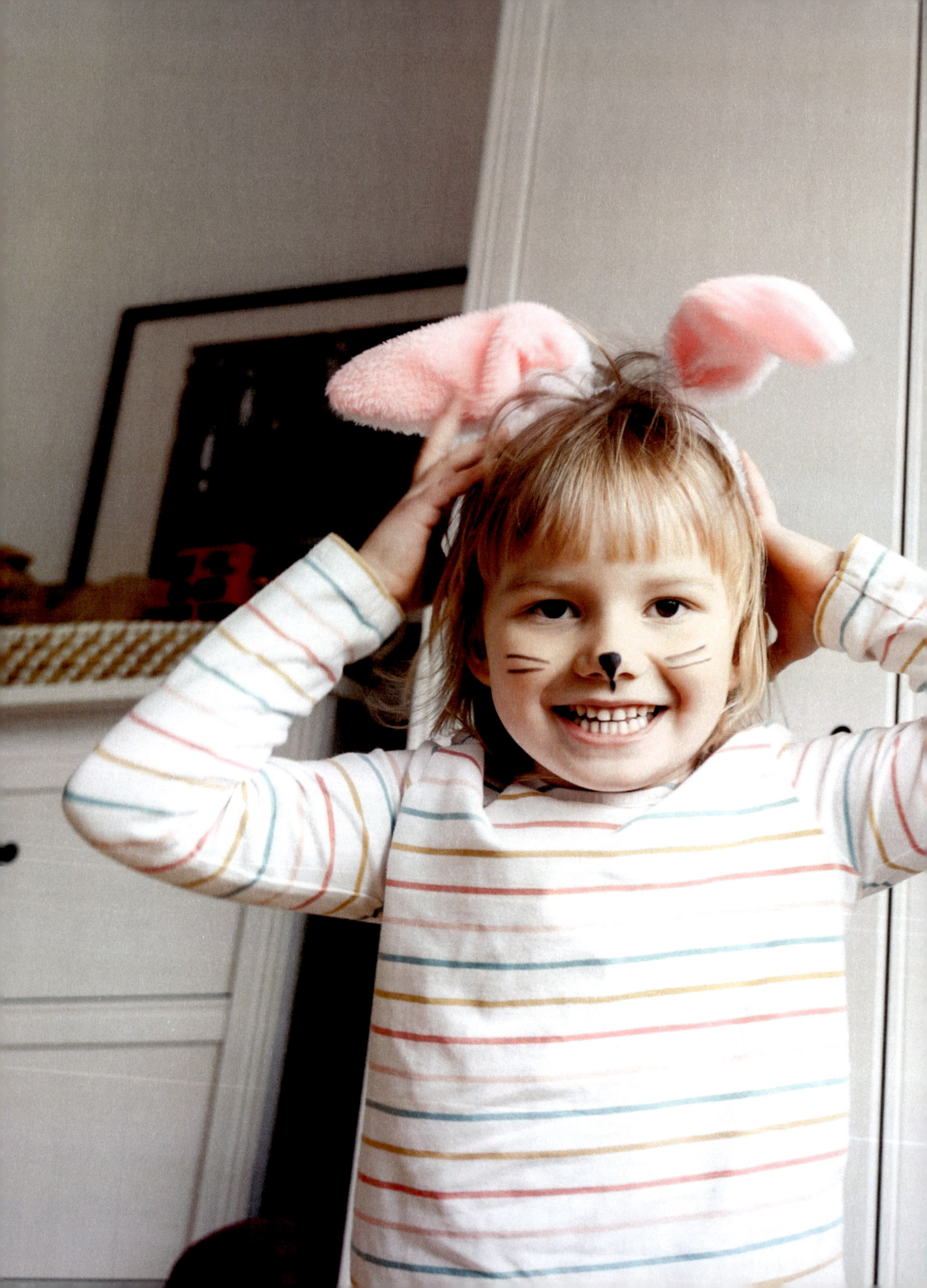

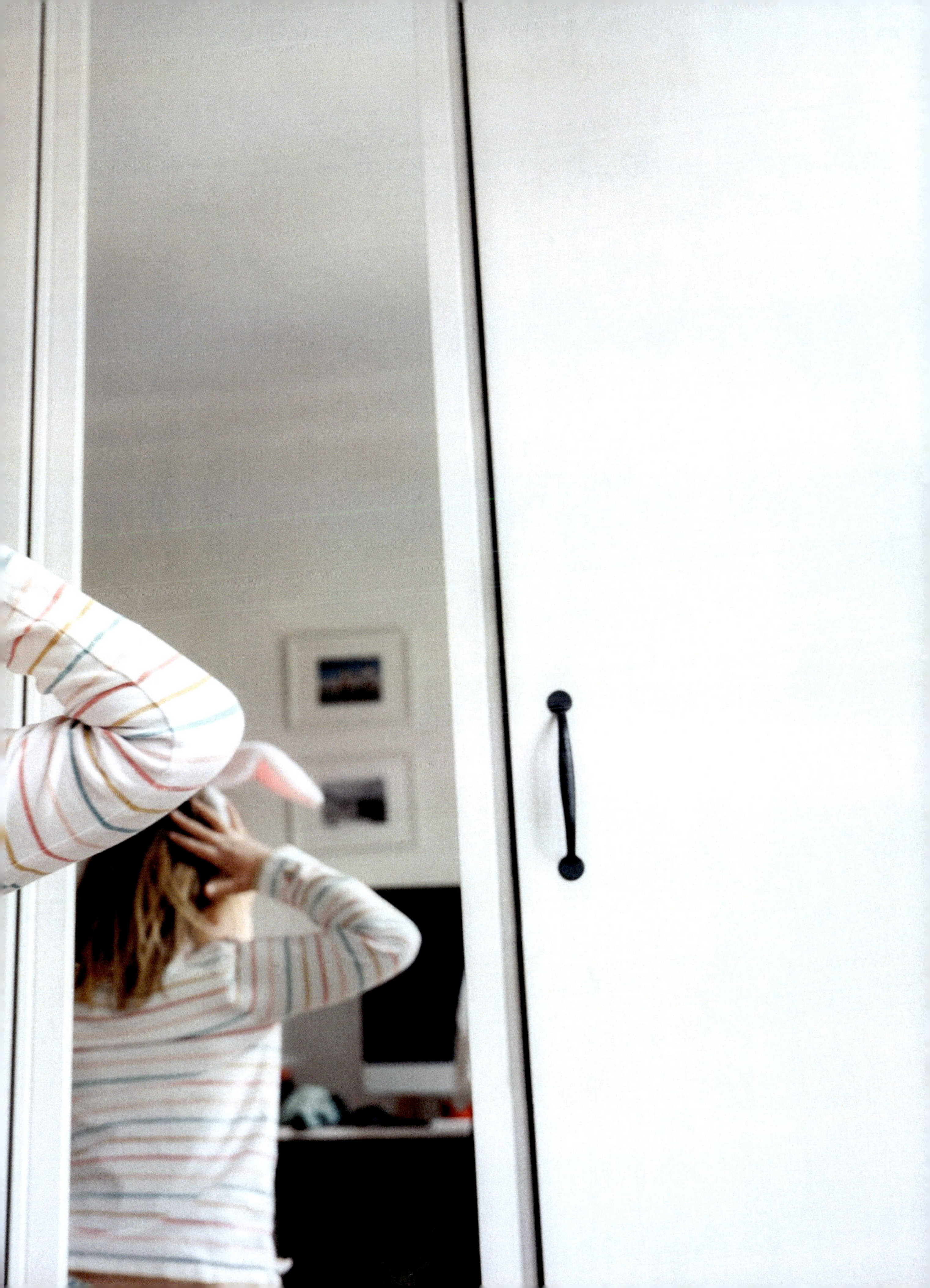

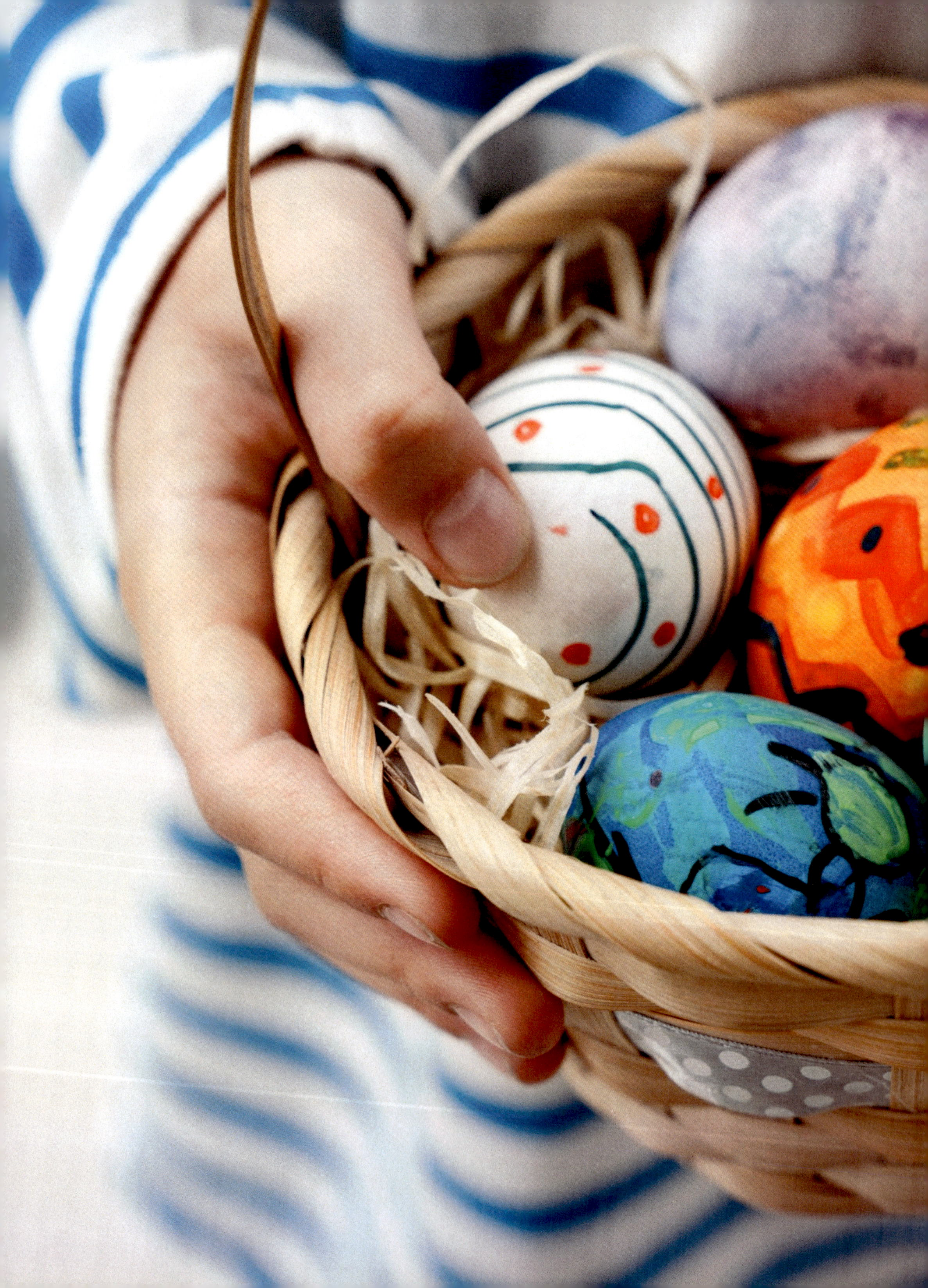

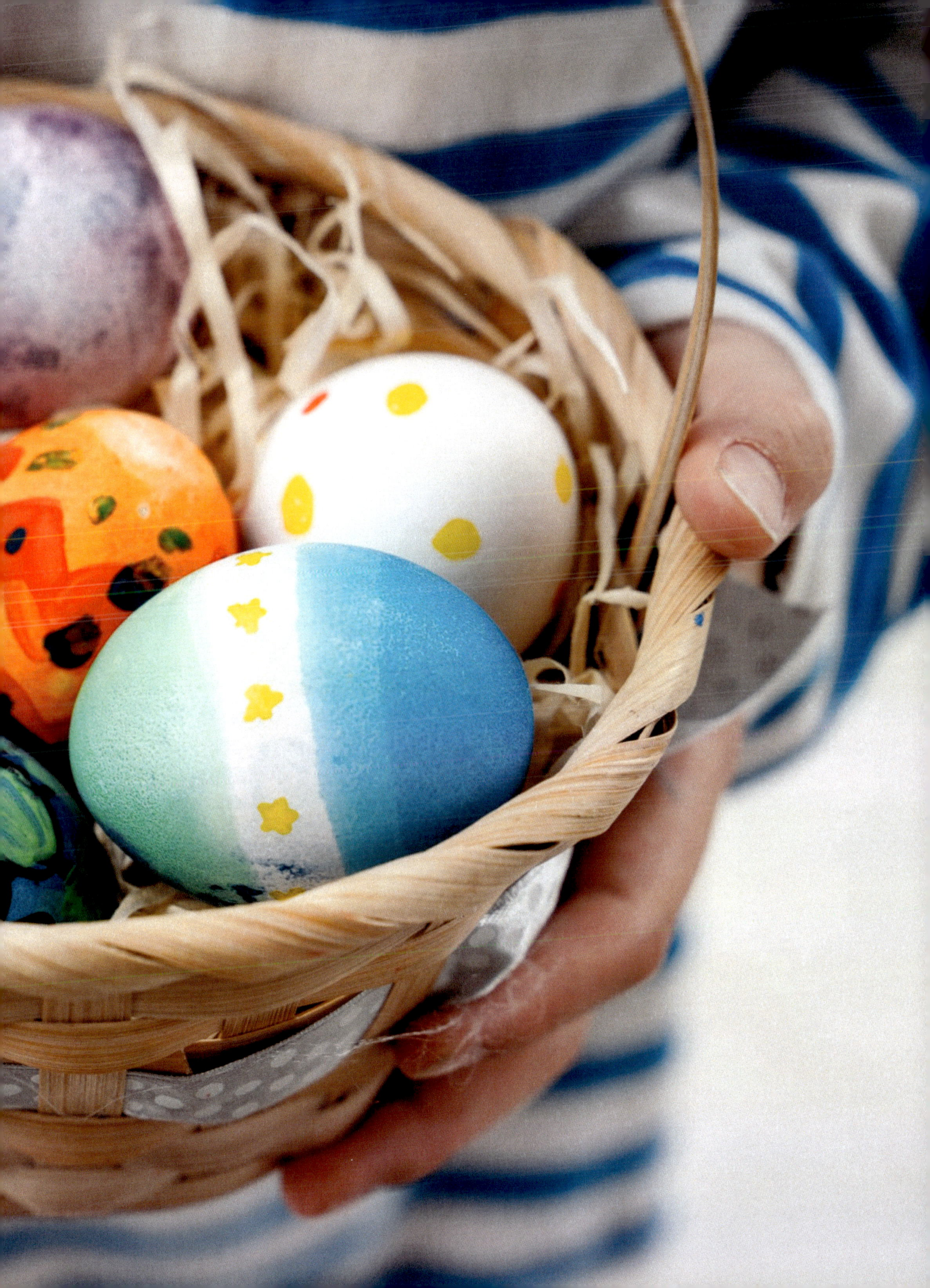

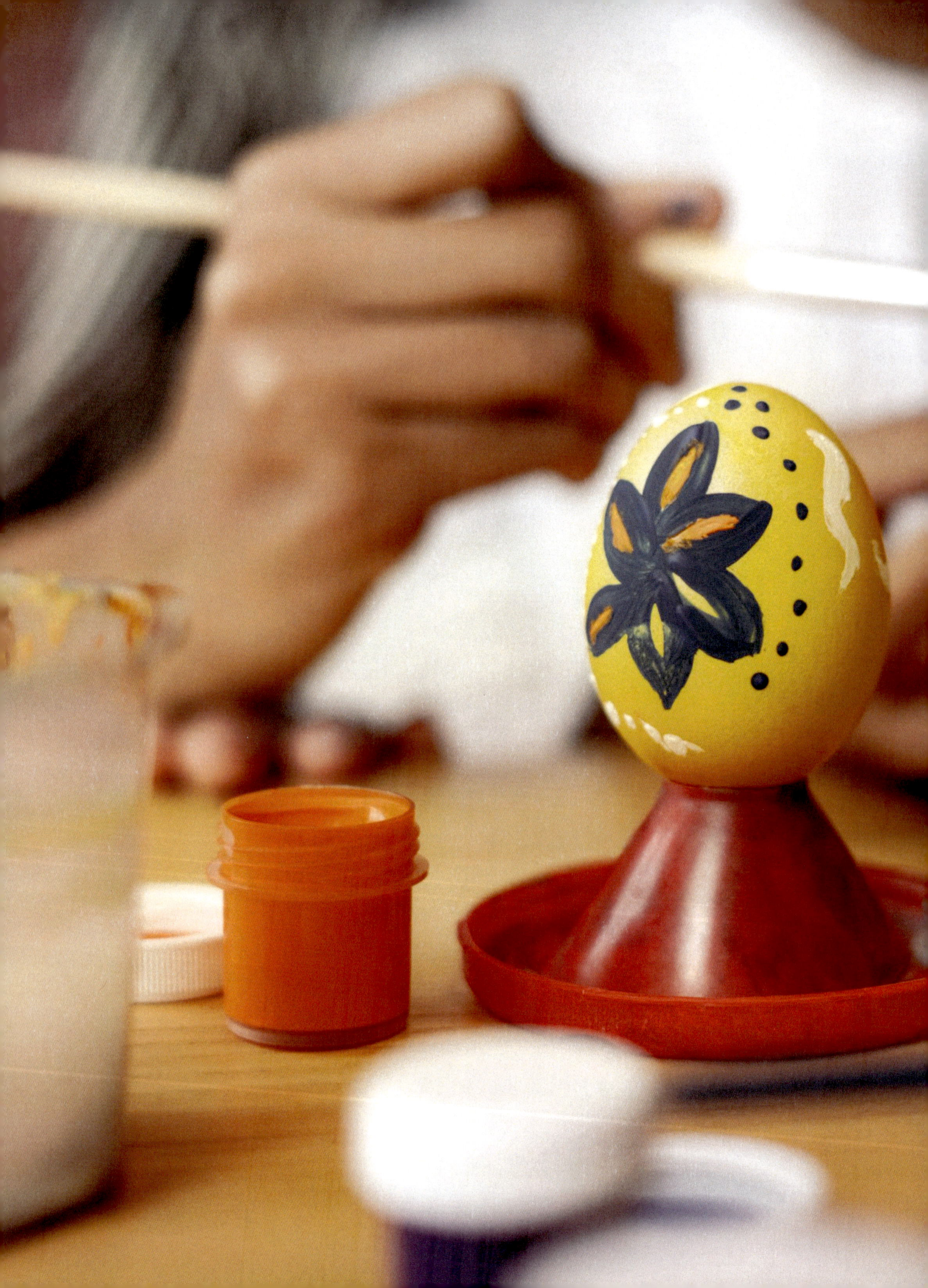

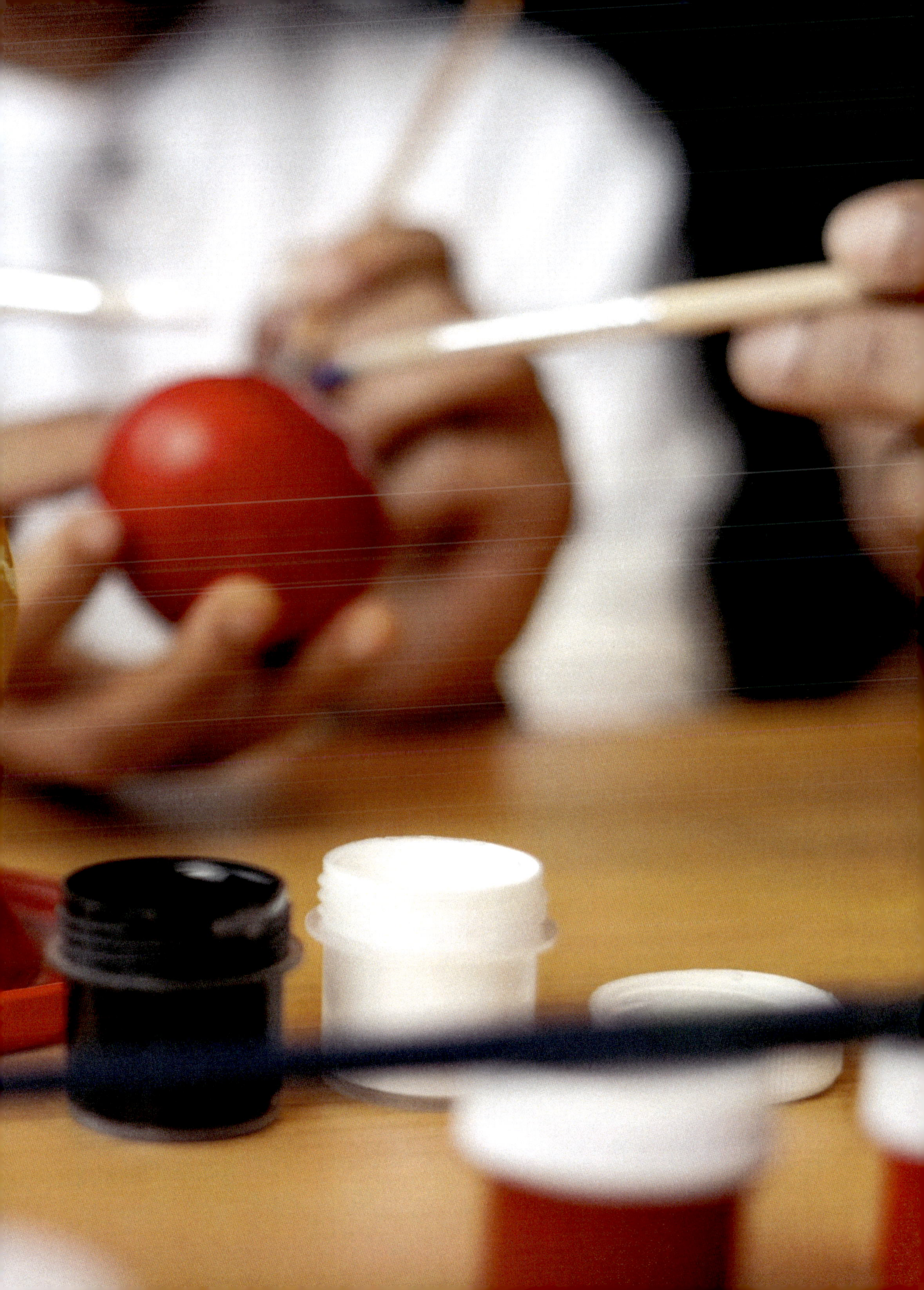

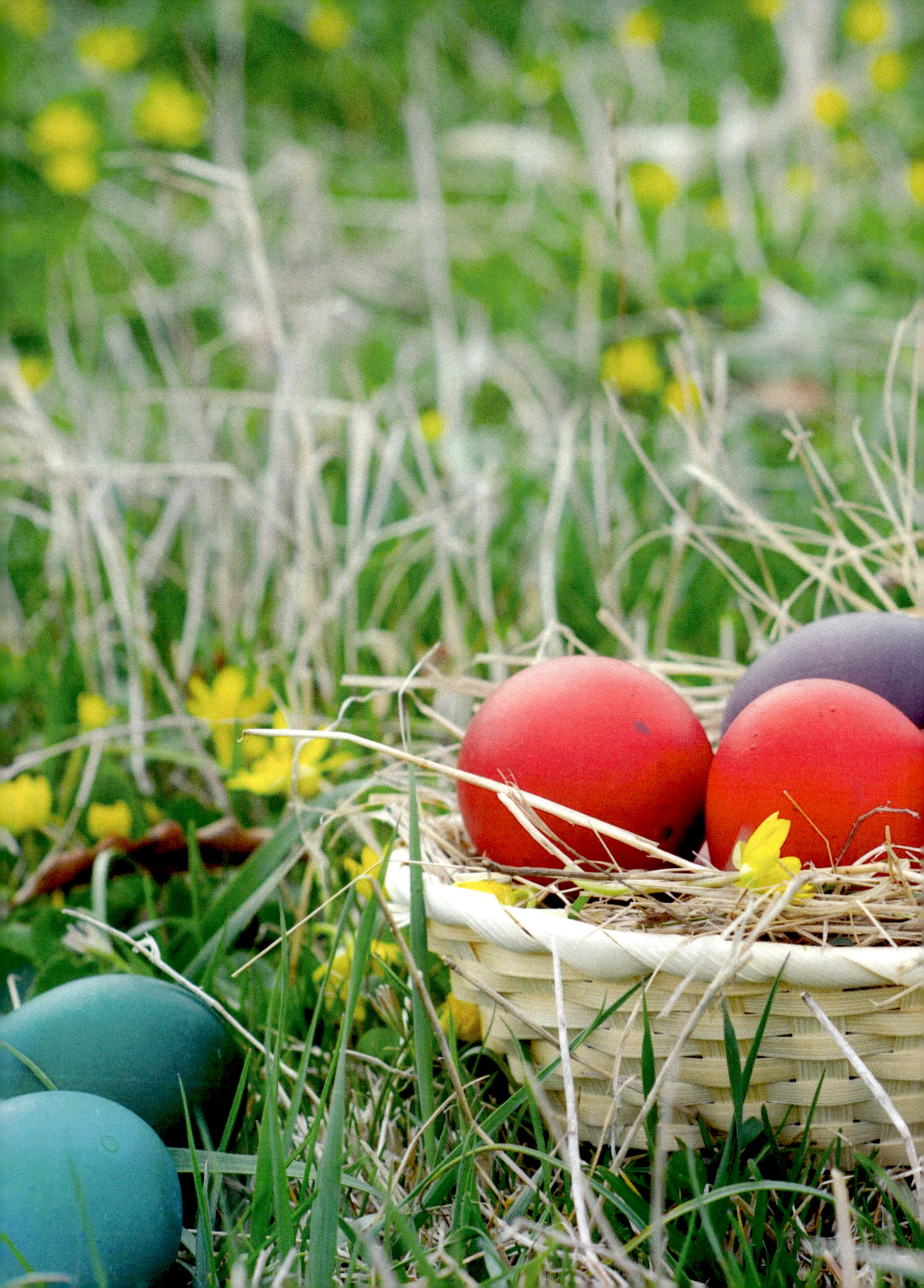

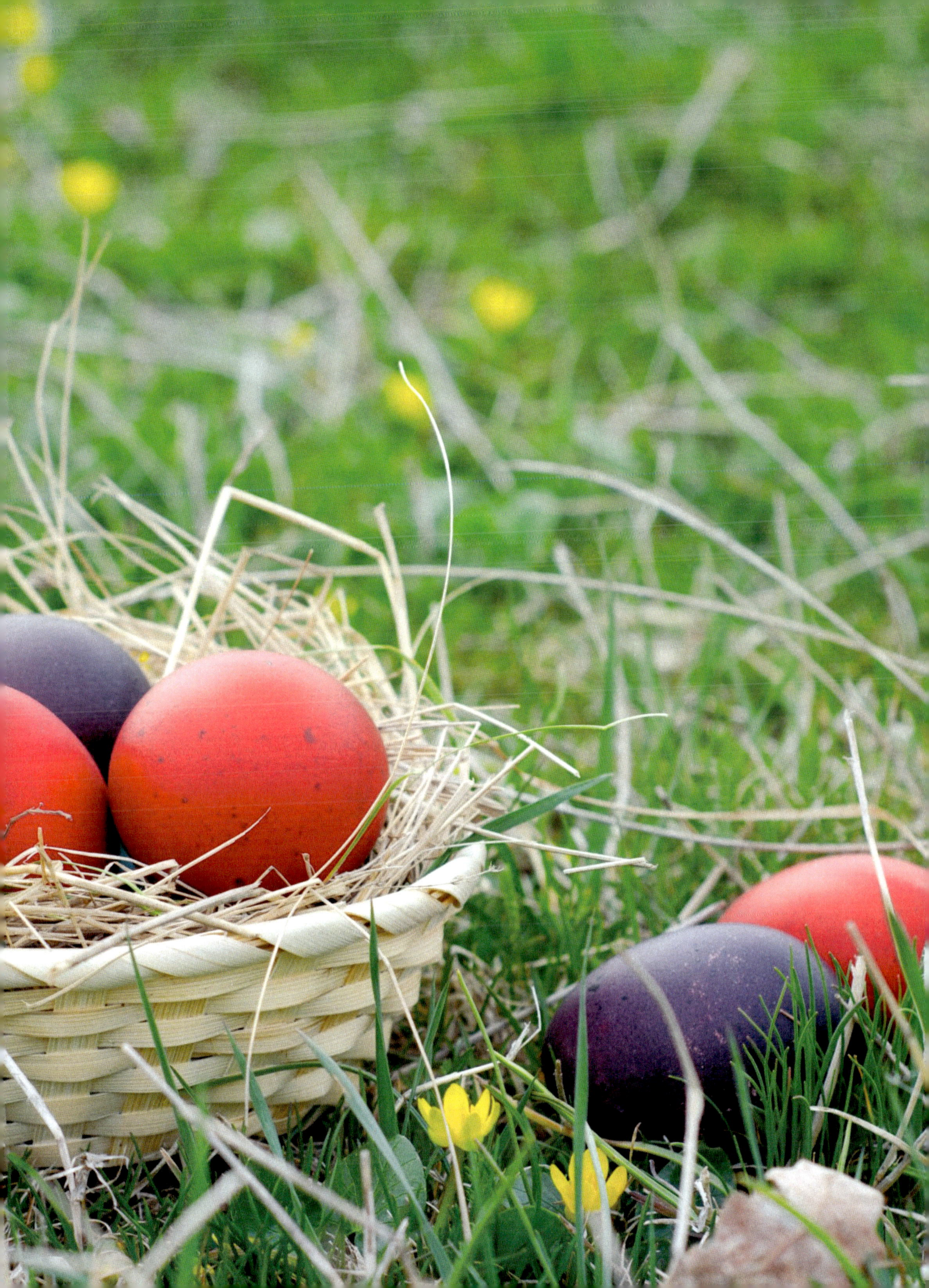

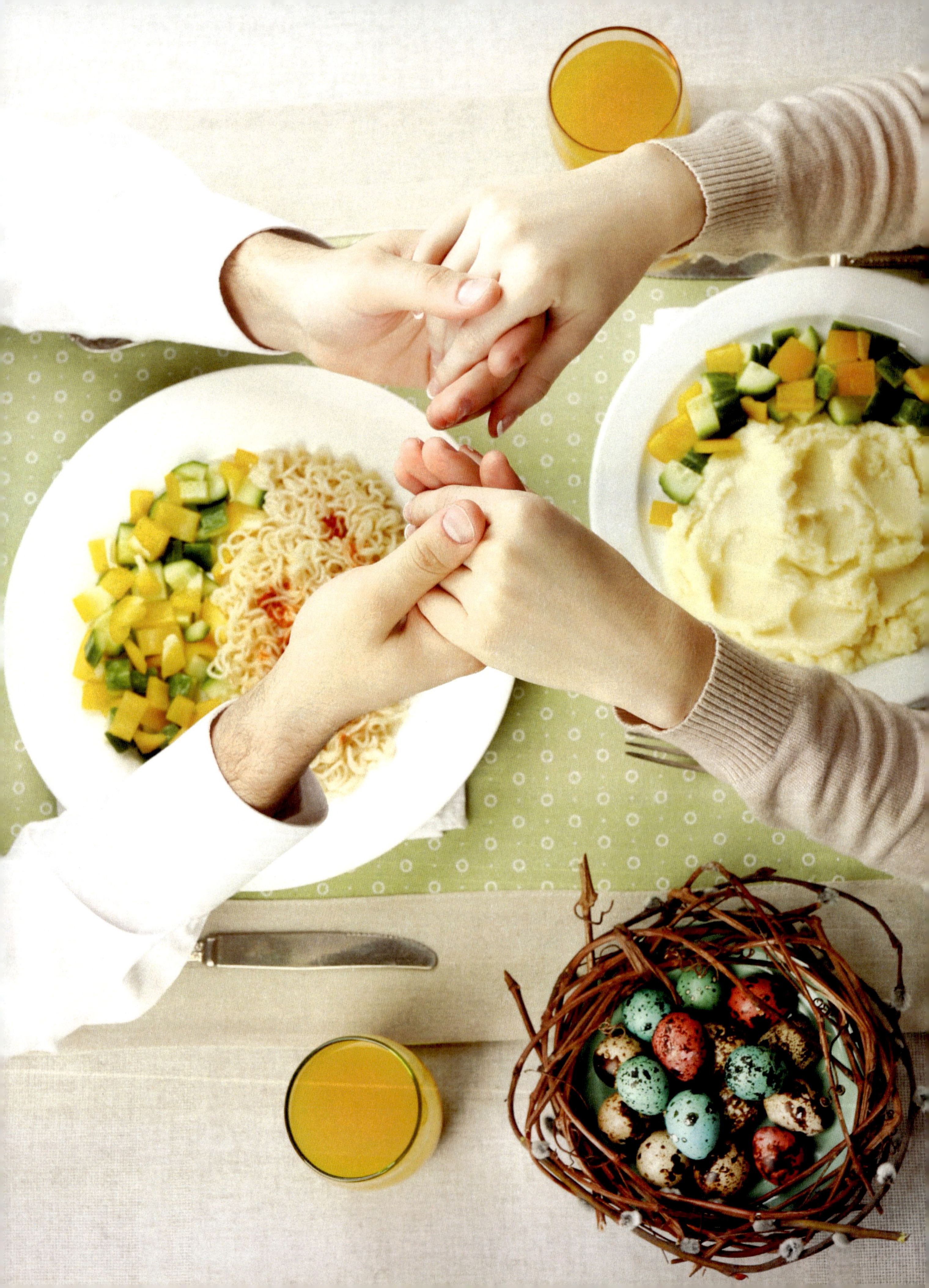

Spring is the season
of freshness and light,
bringing a lot of delicious
foods that are fresh and
good for the health, like
fruits and vegetables.
People enjoy eating fresh
and healthy food.

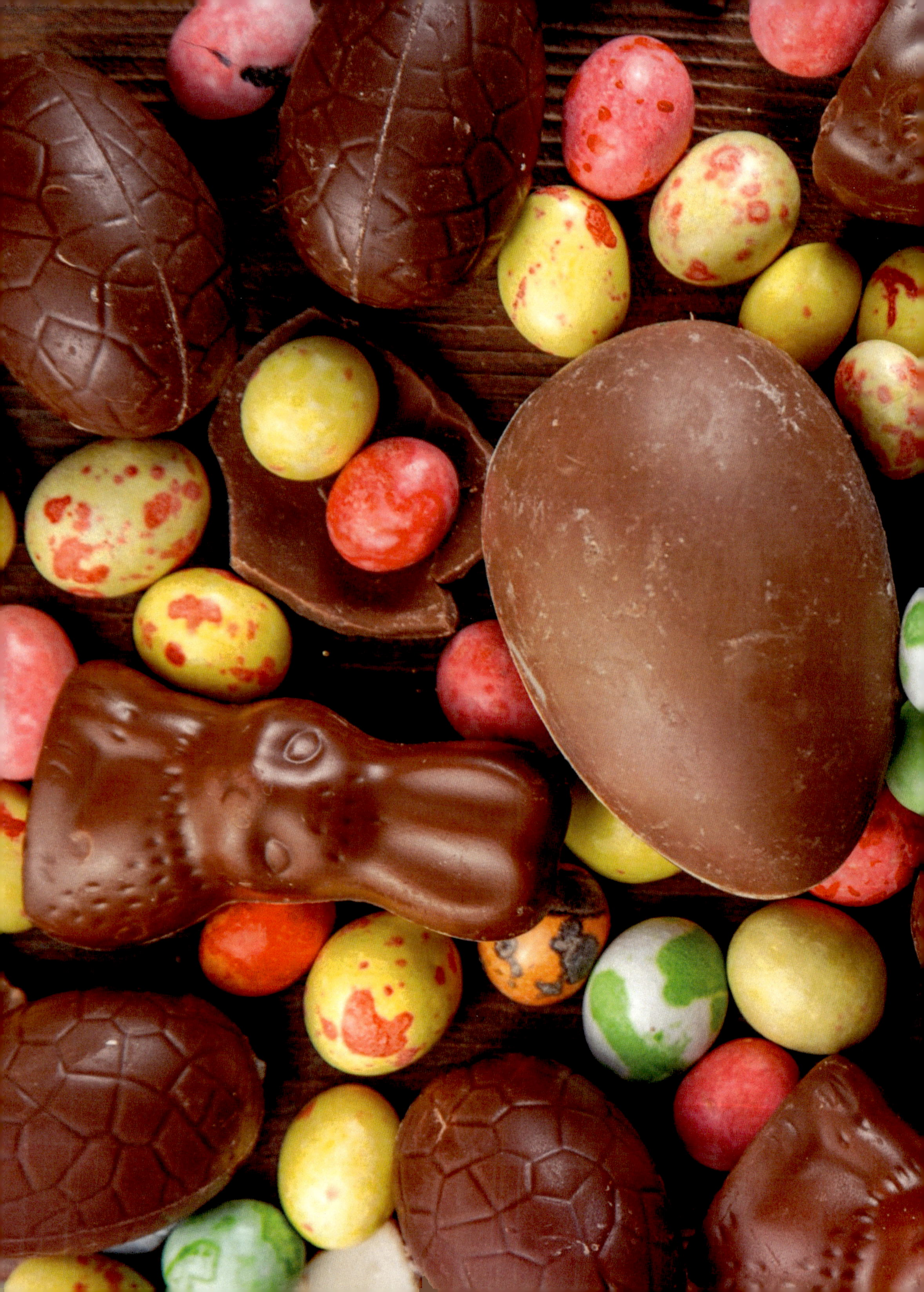

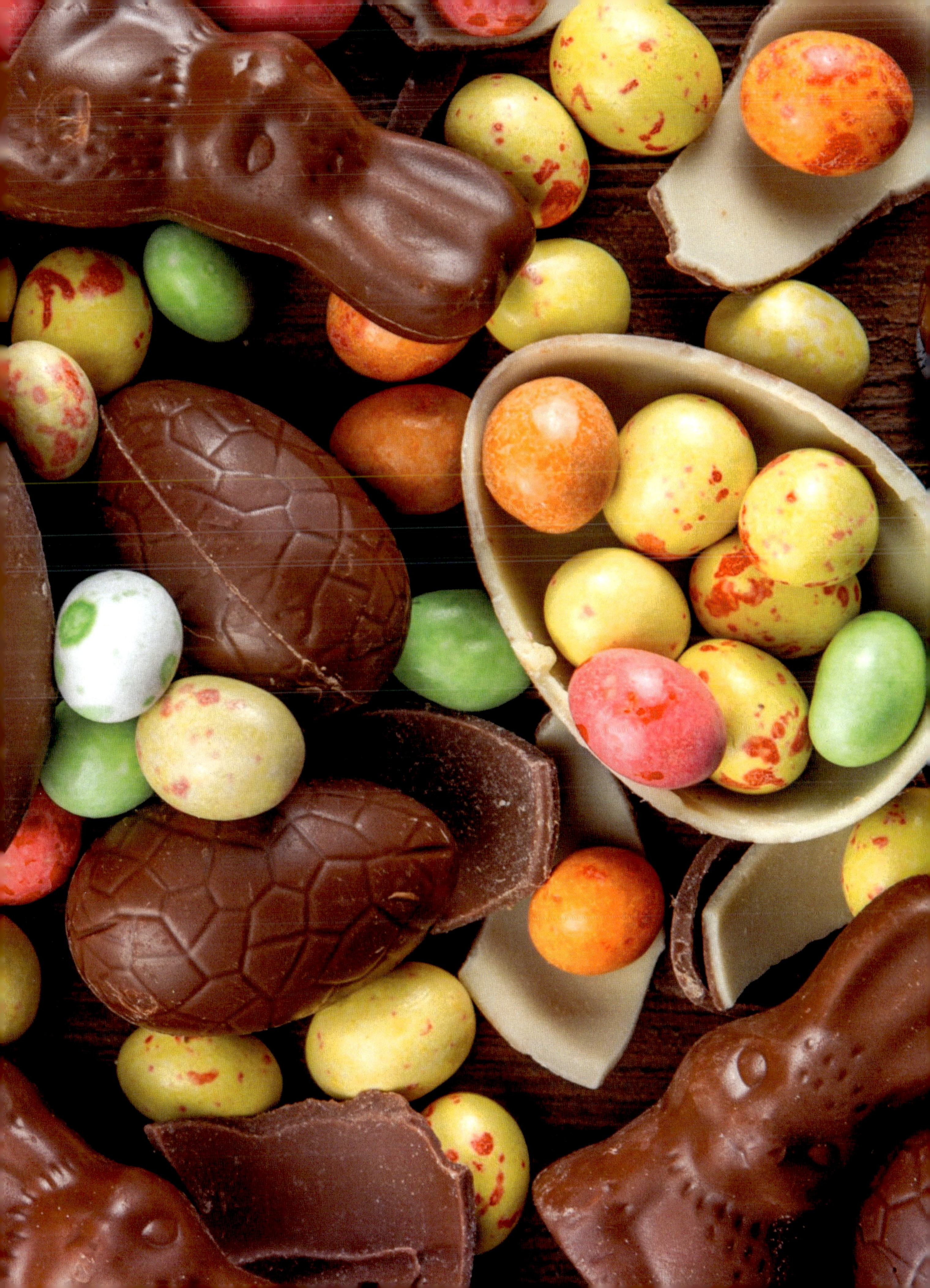

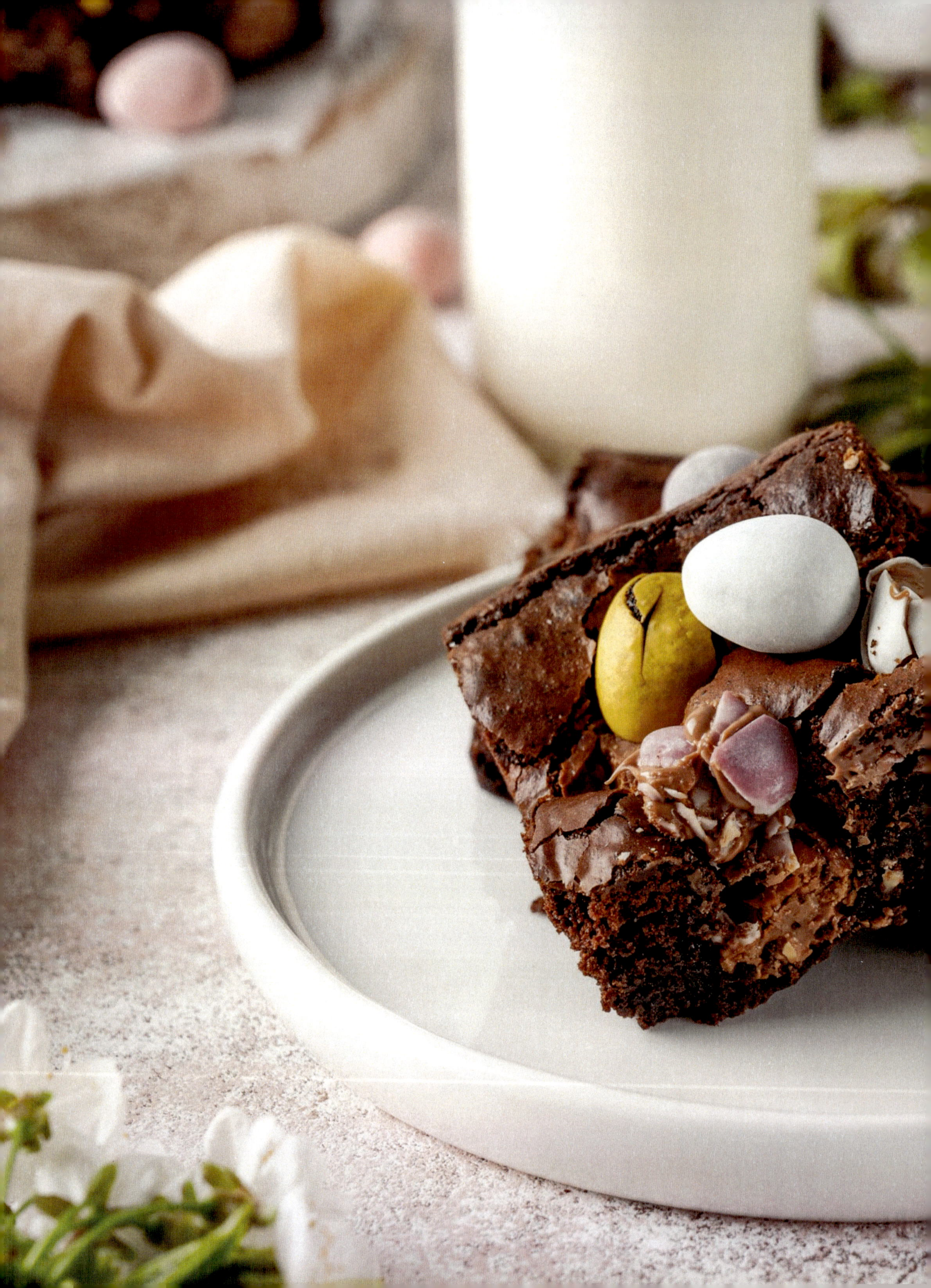

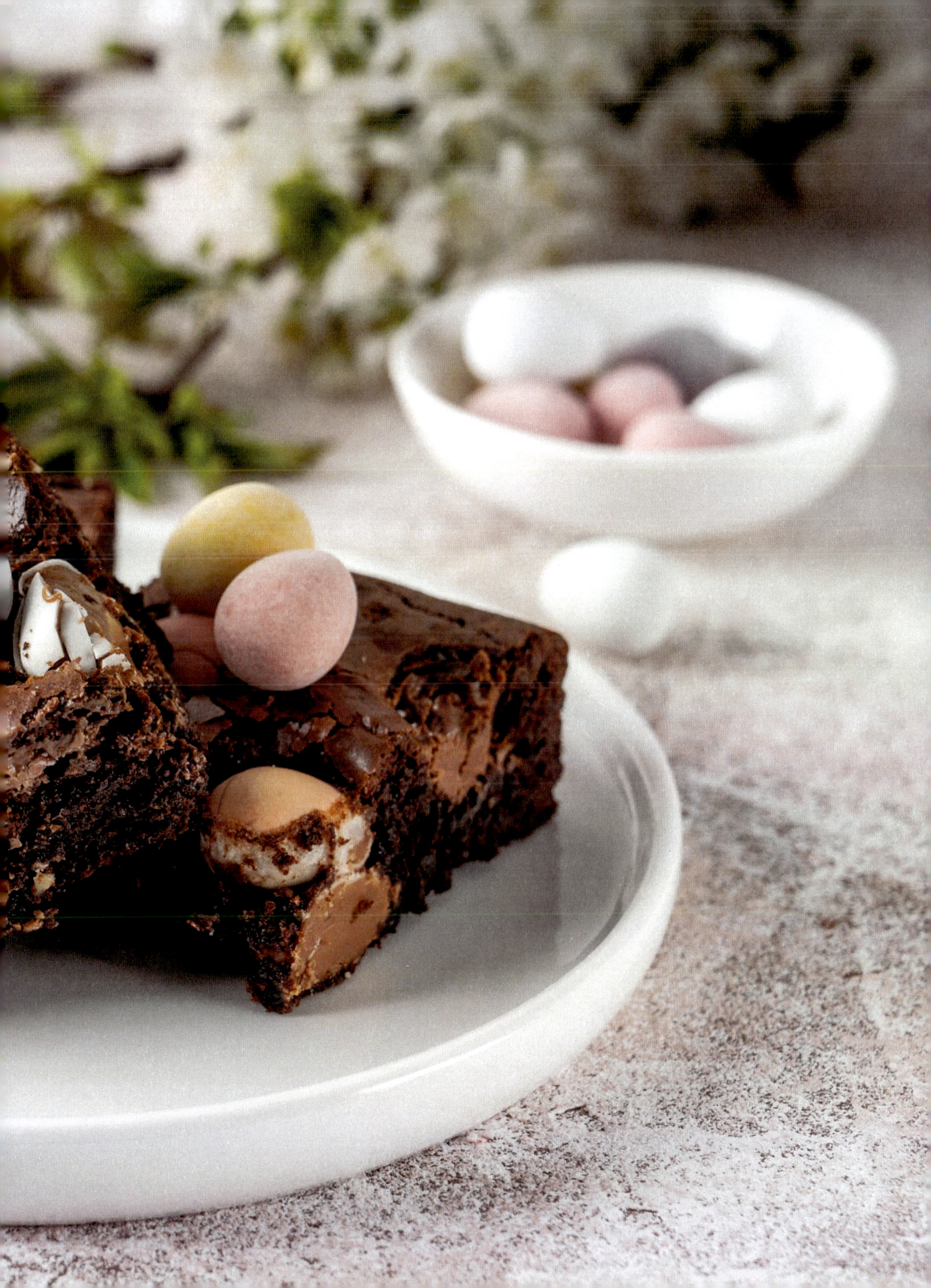

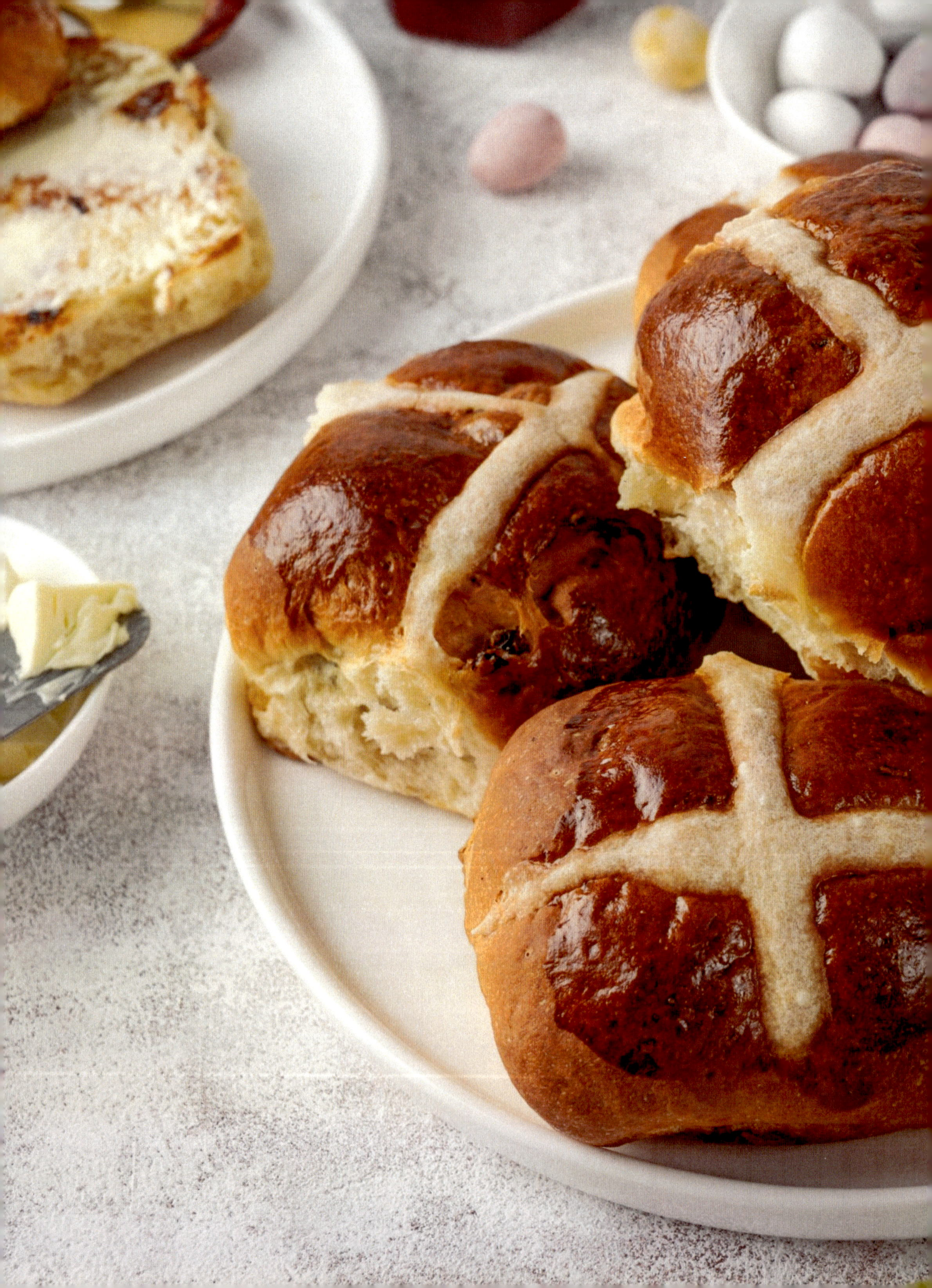

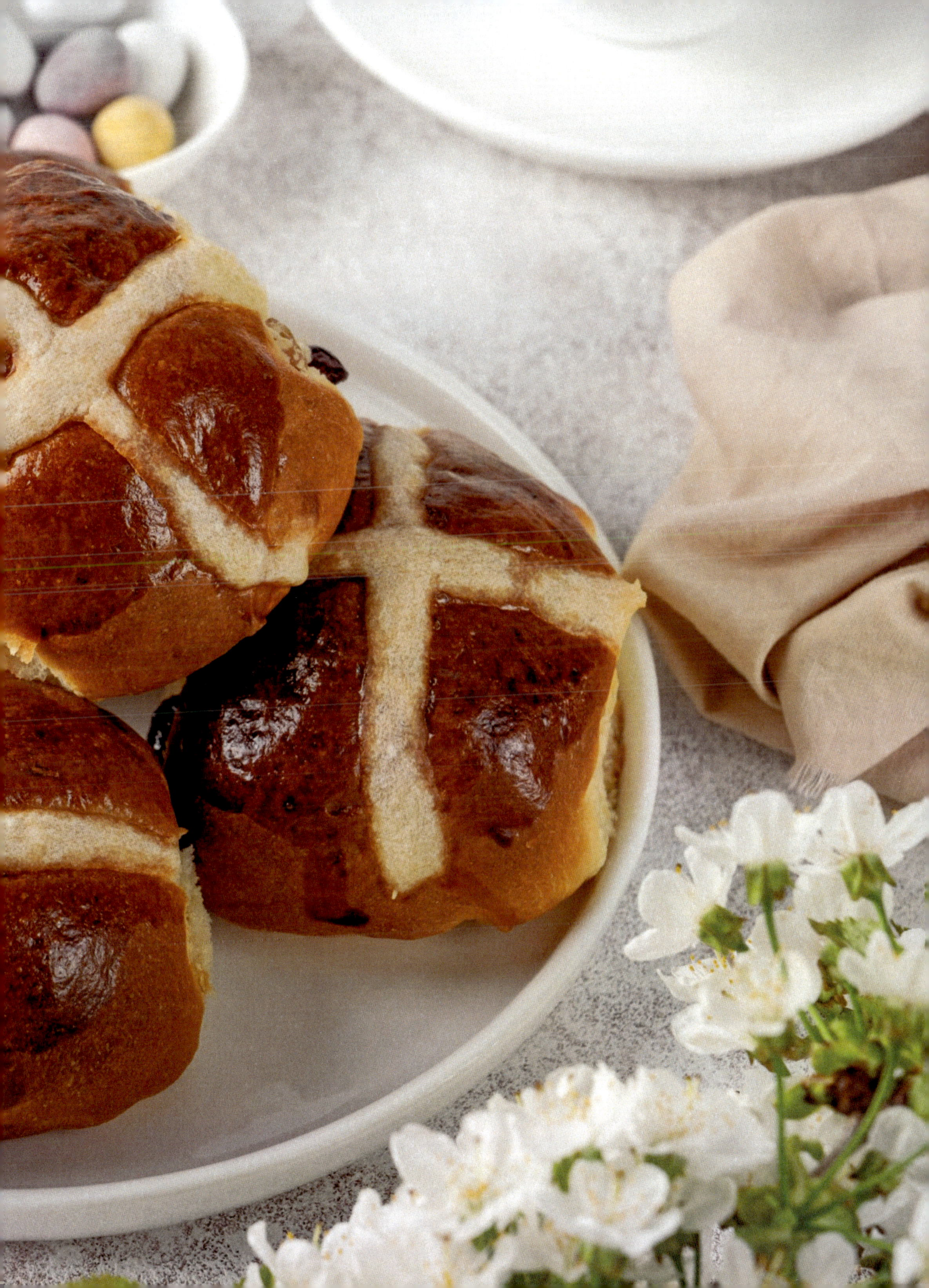

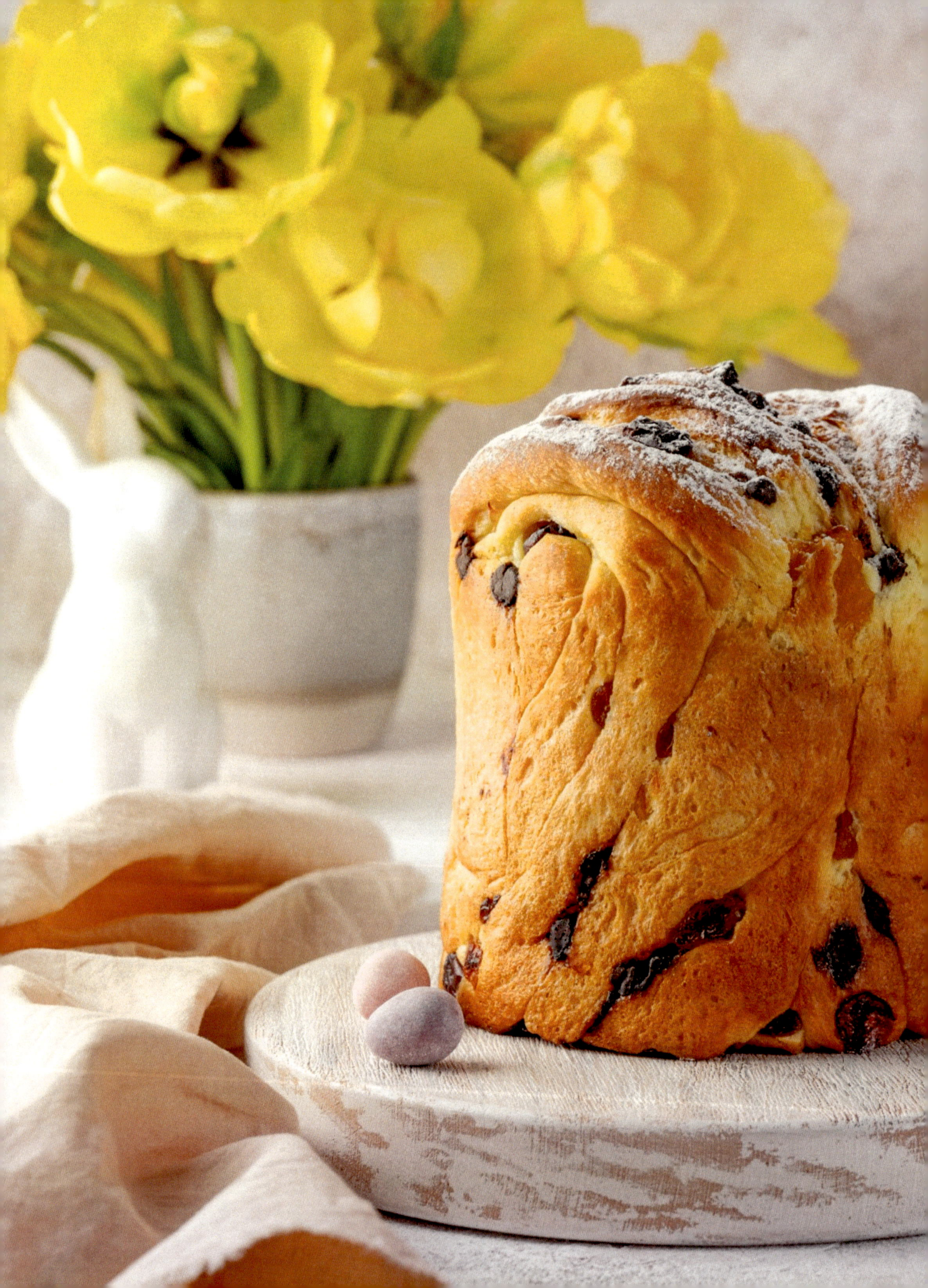

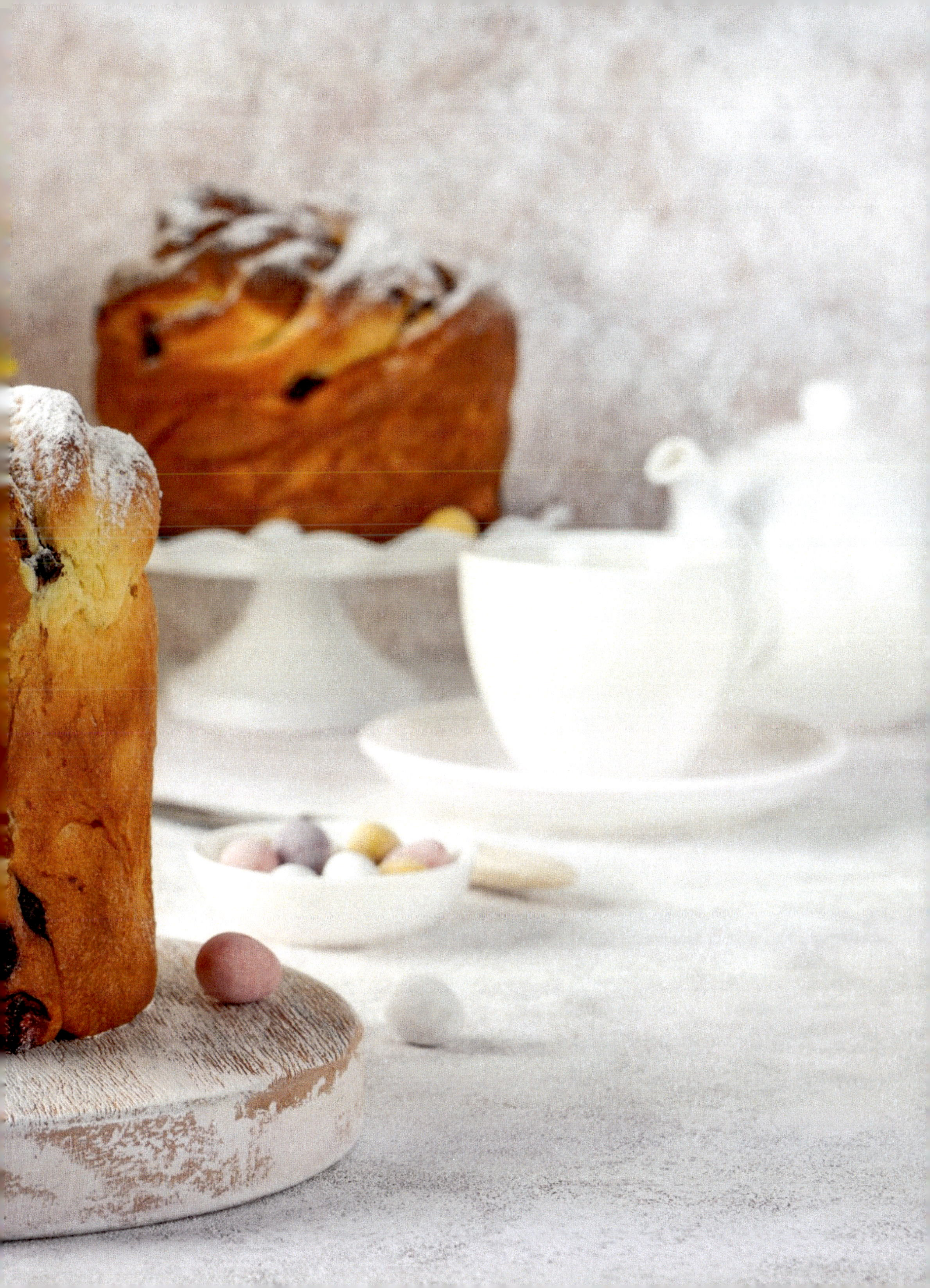

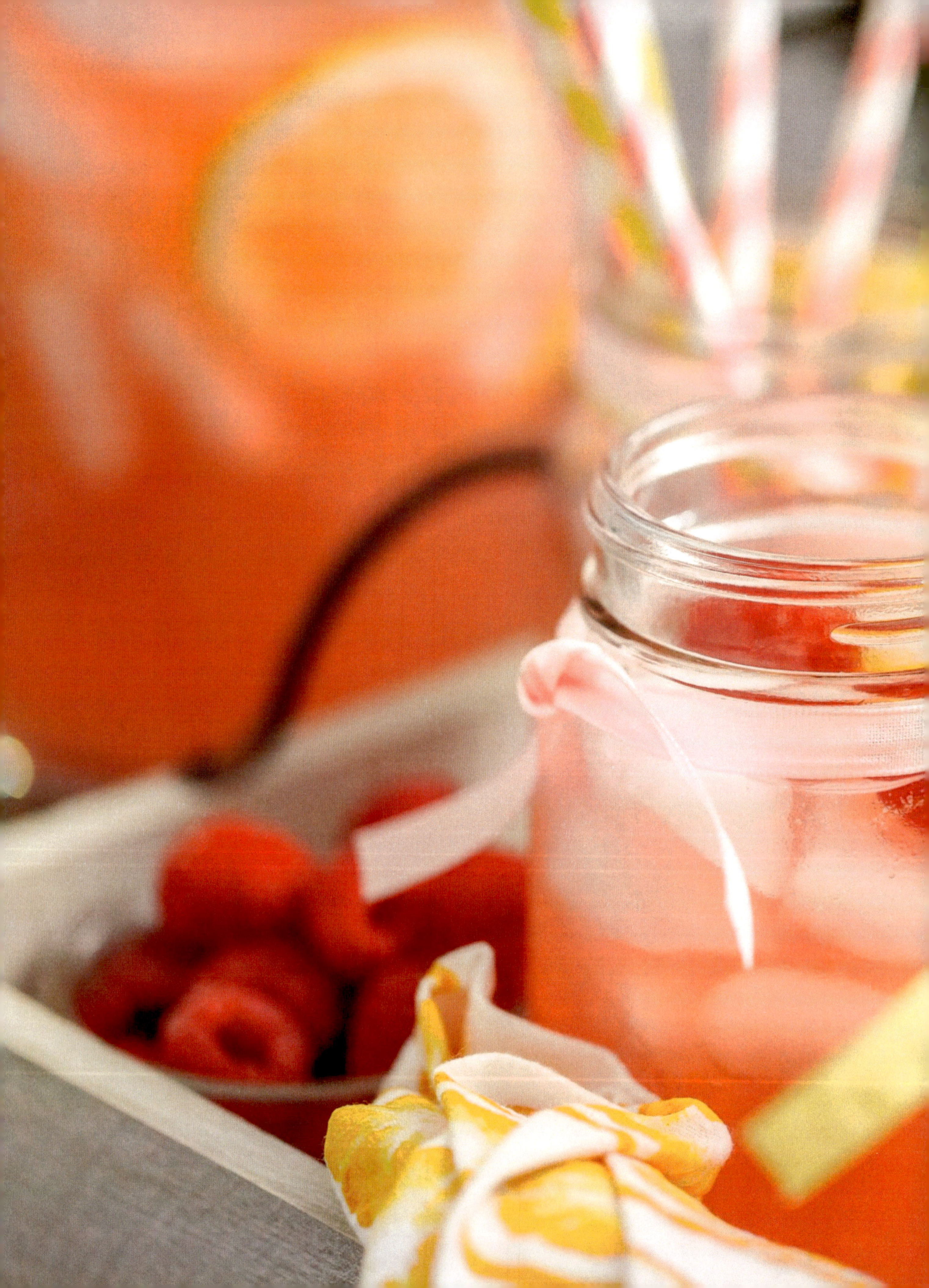

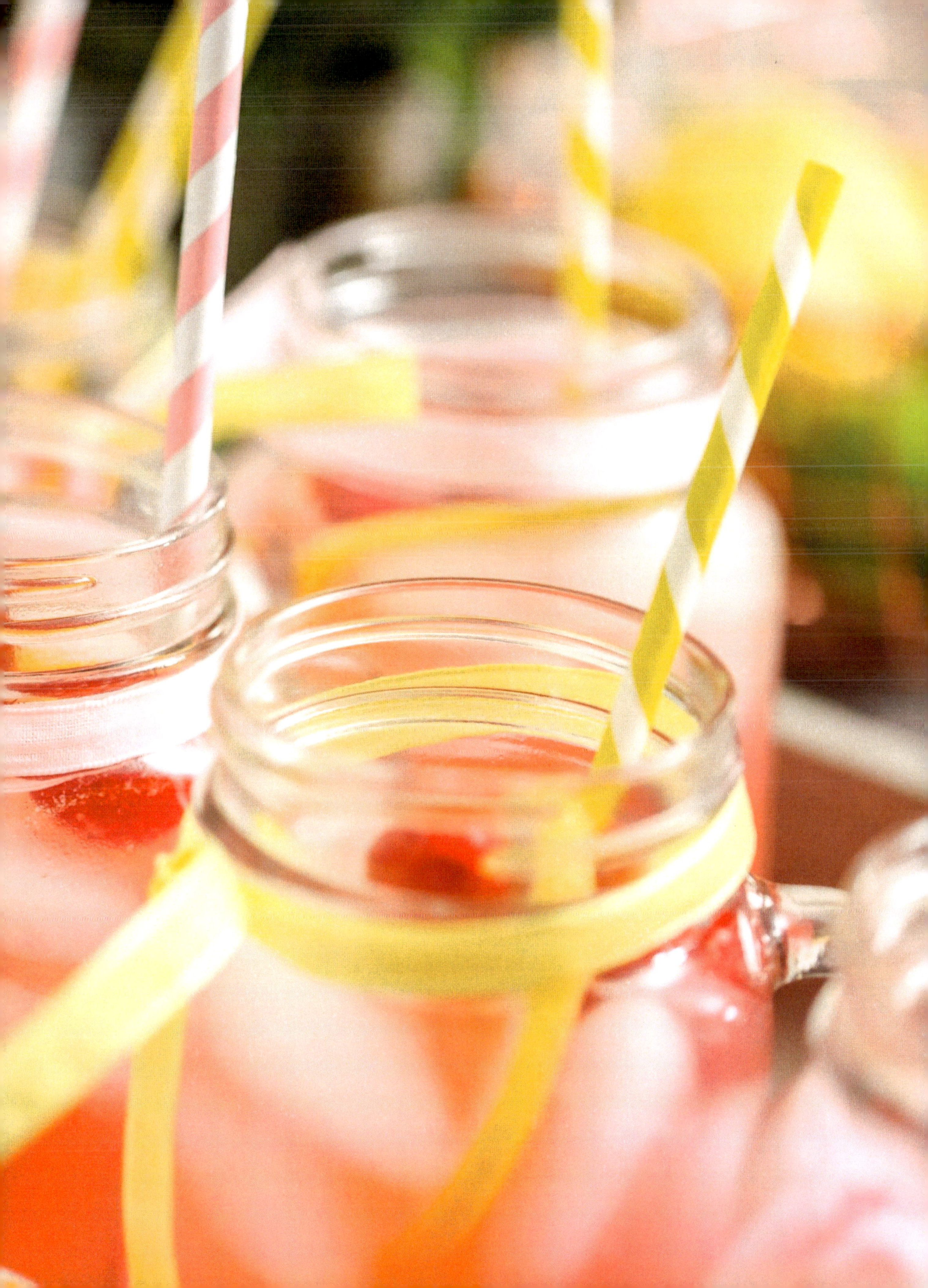

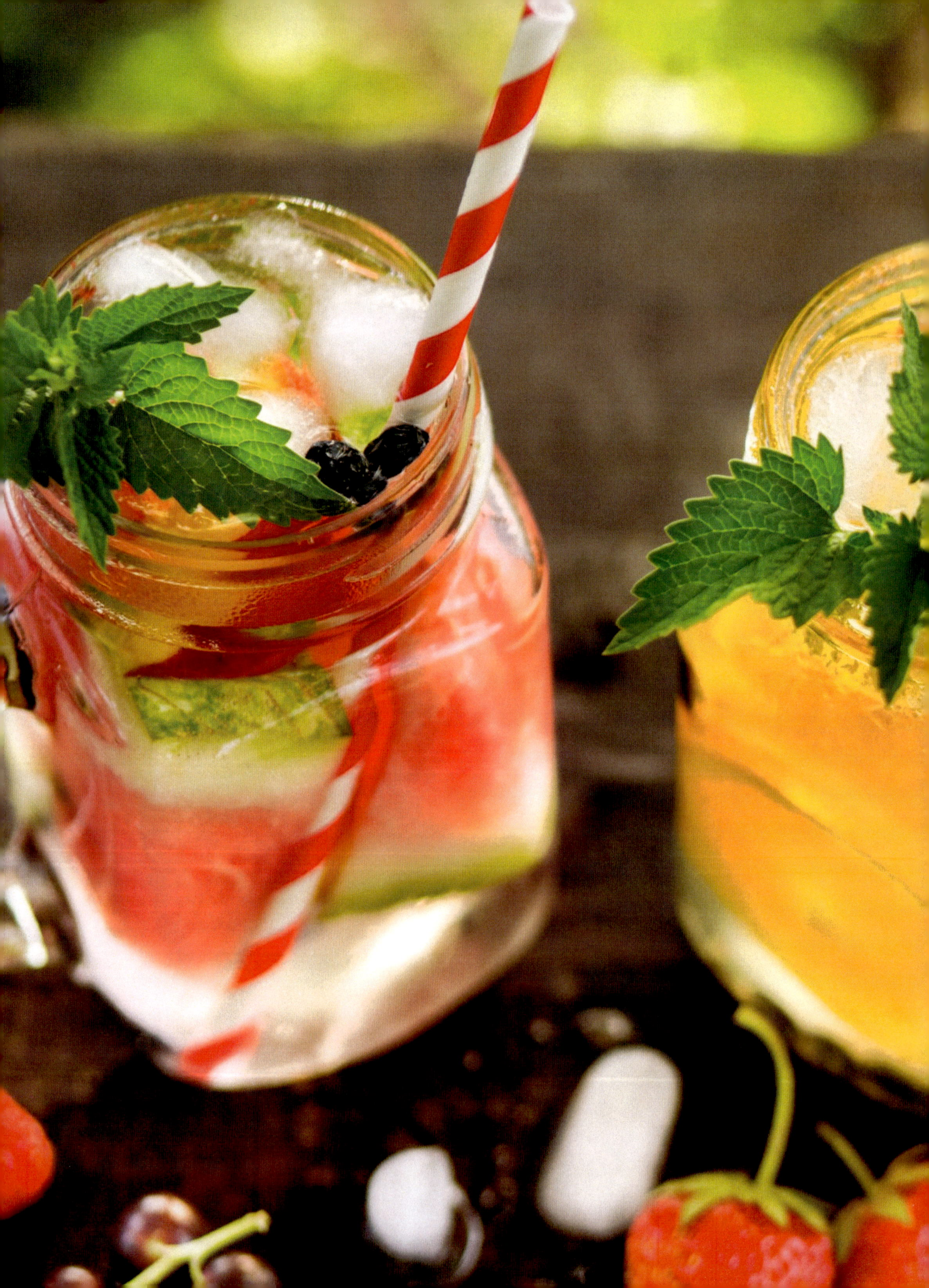

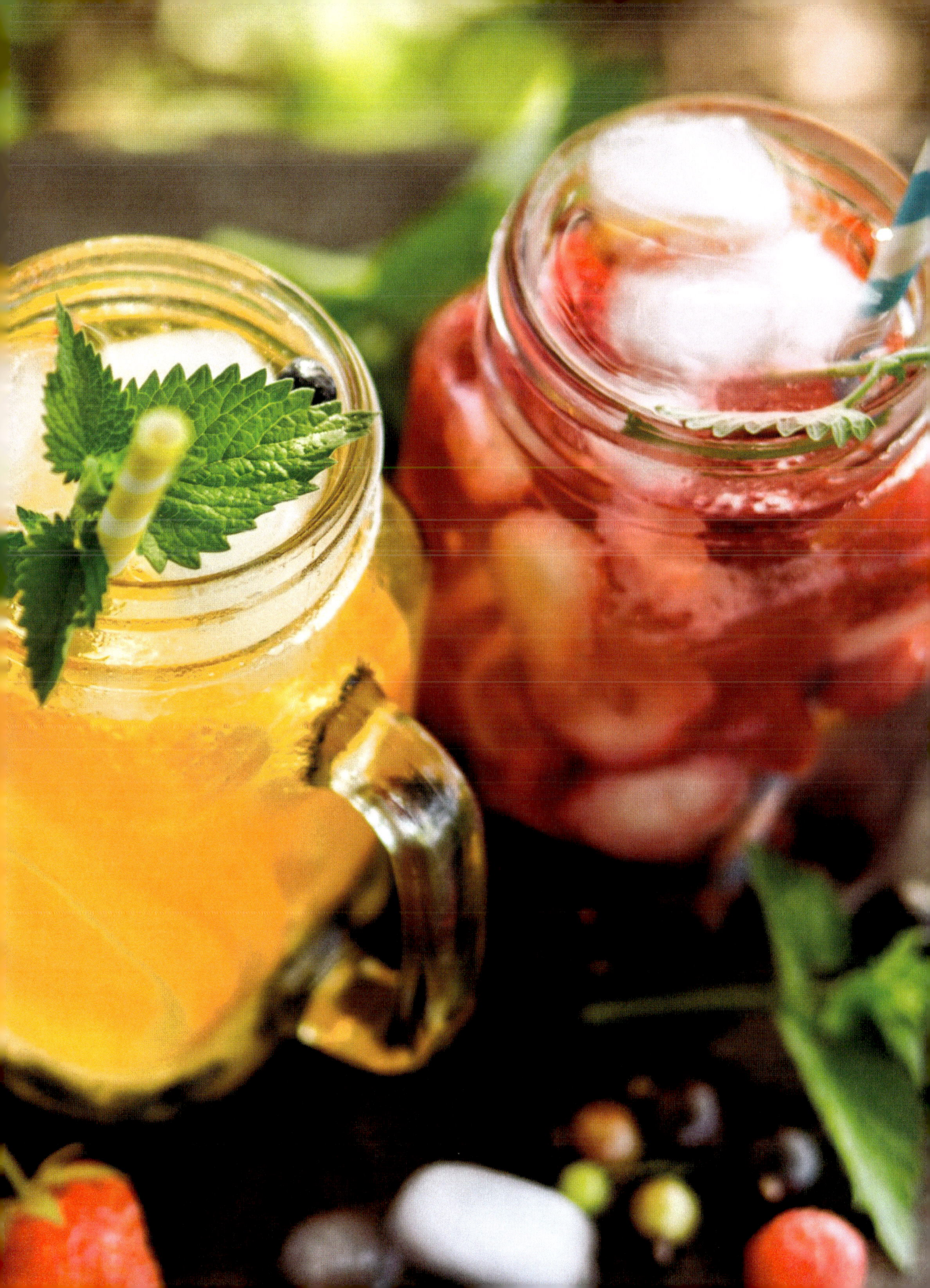

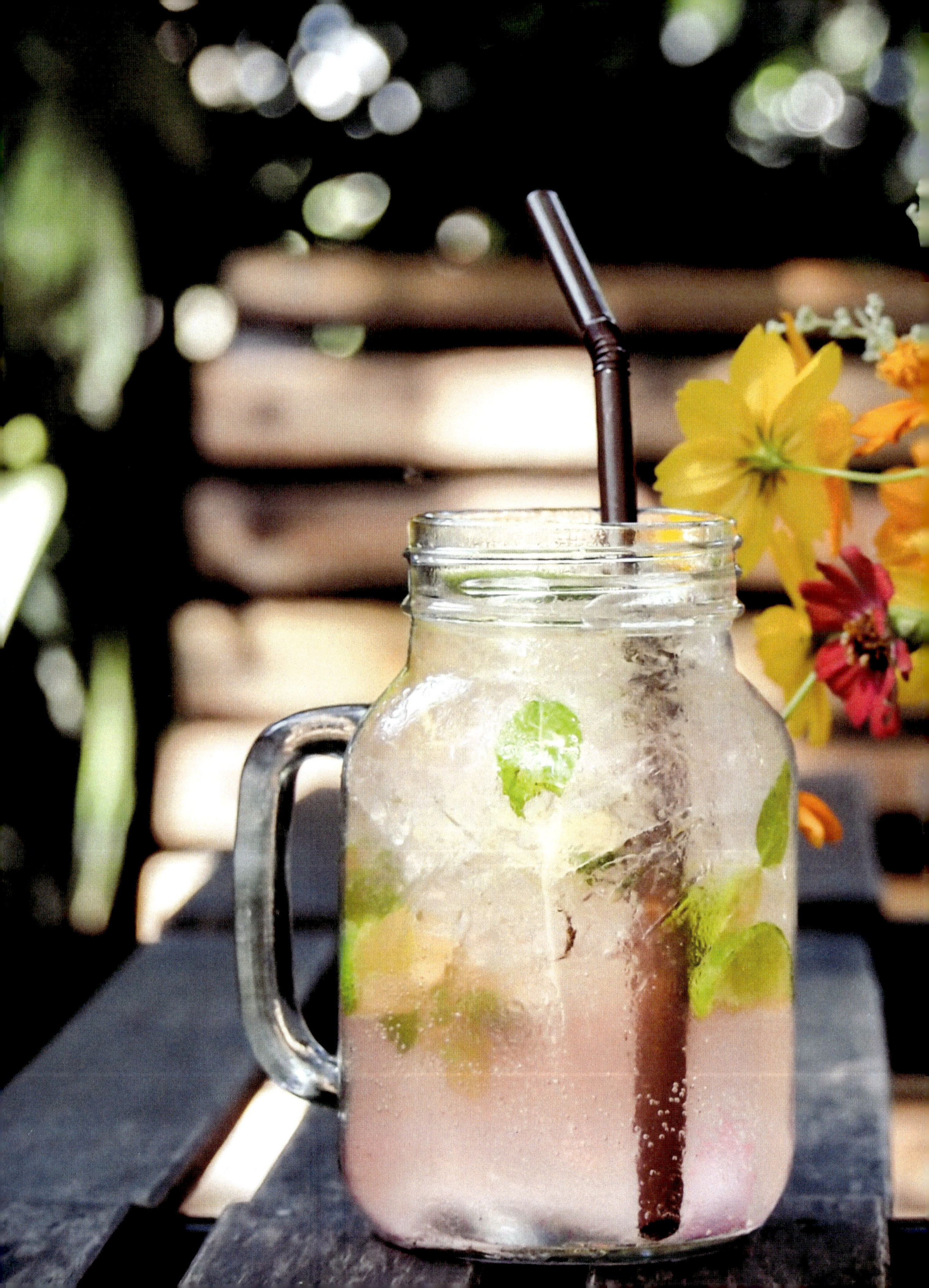

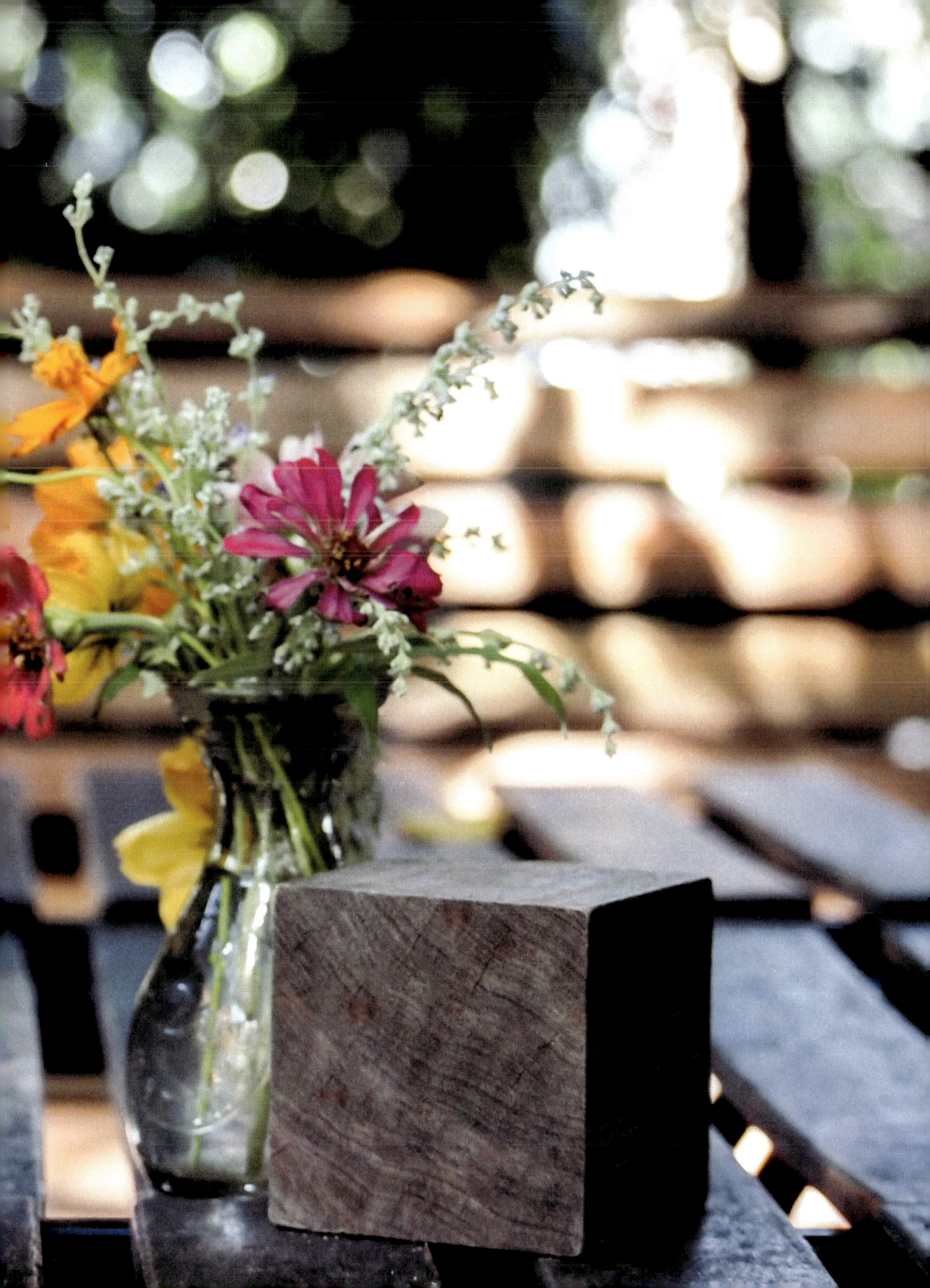

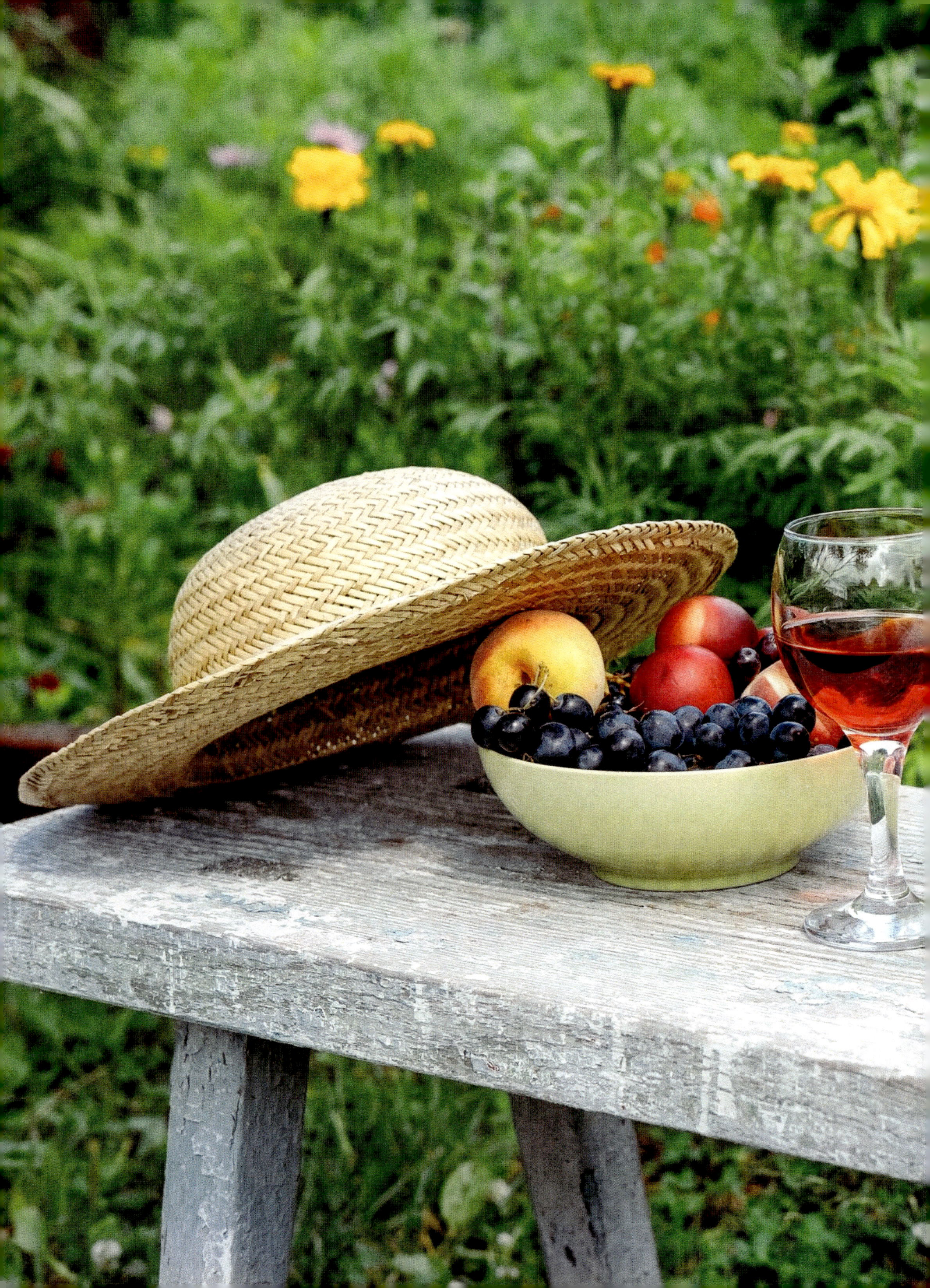

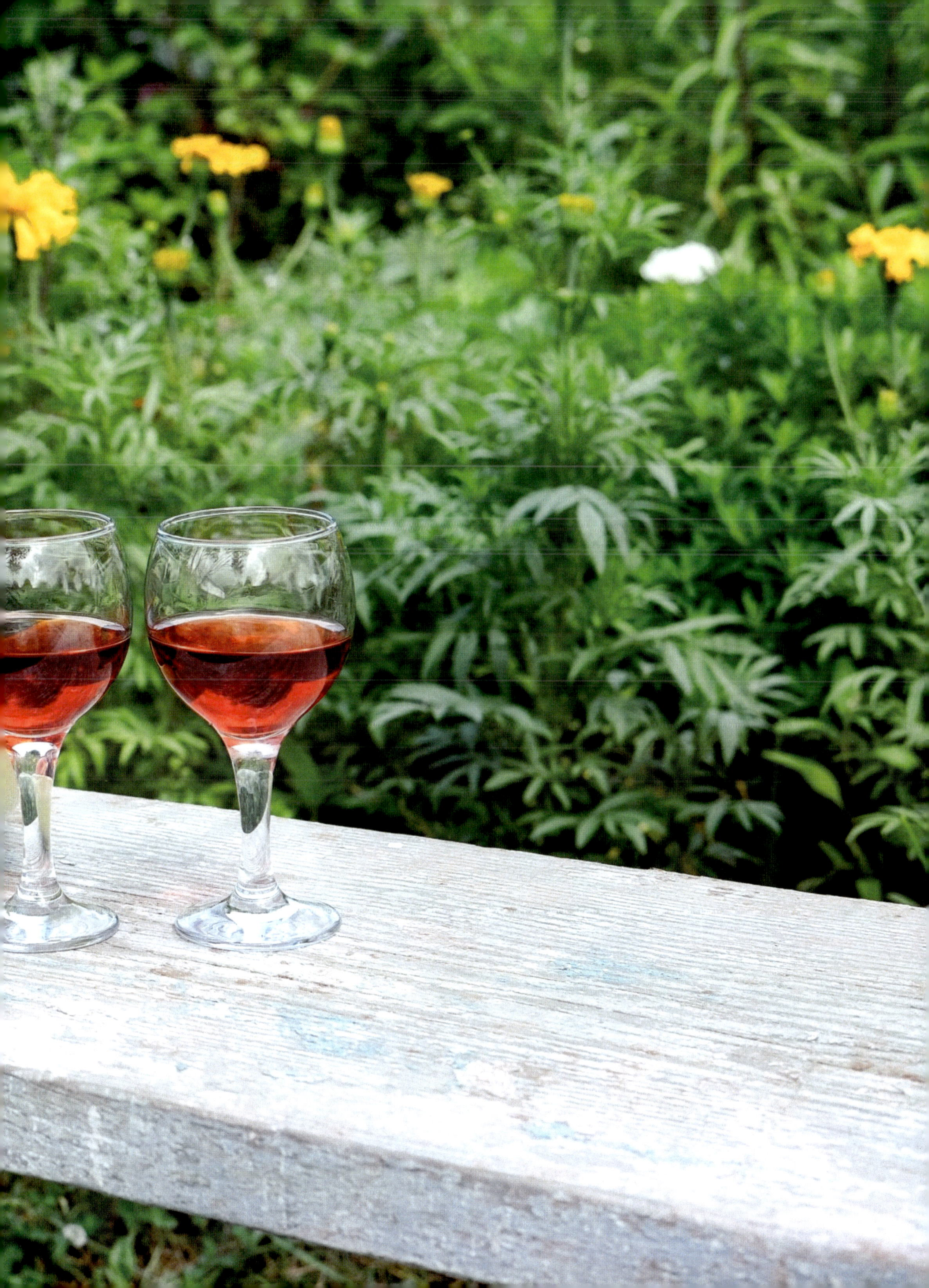

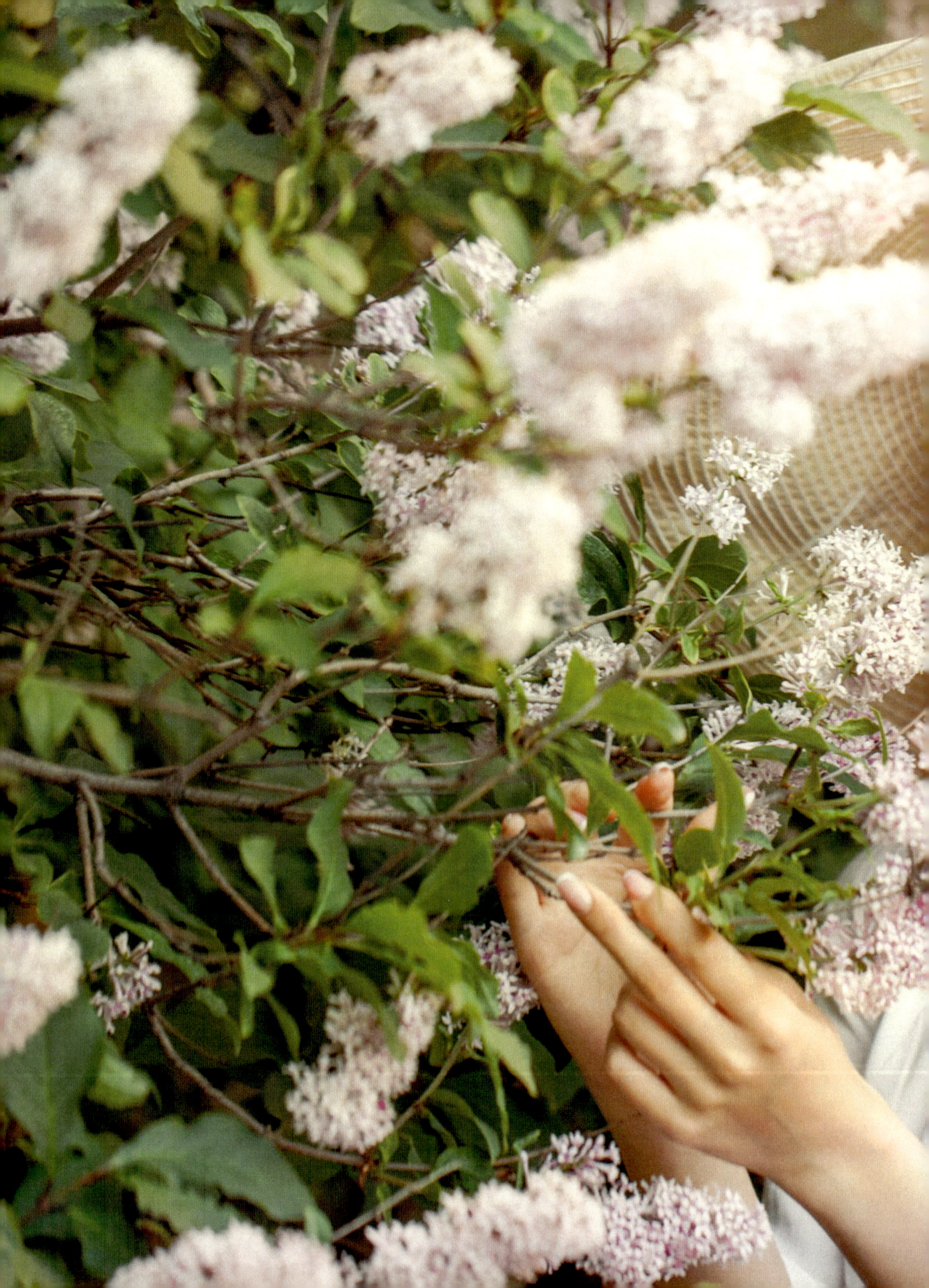

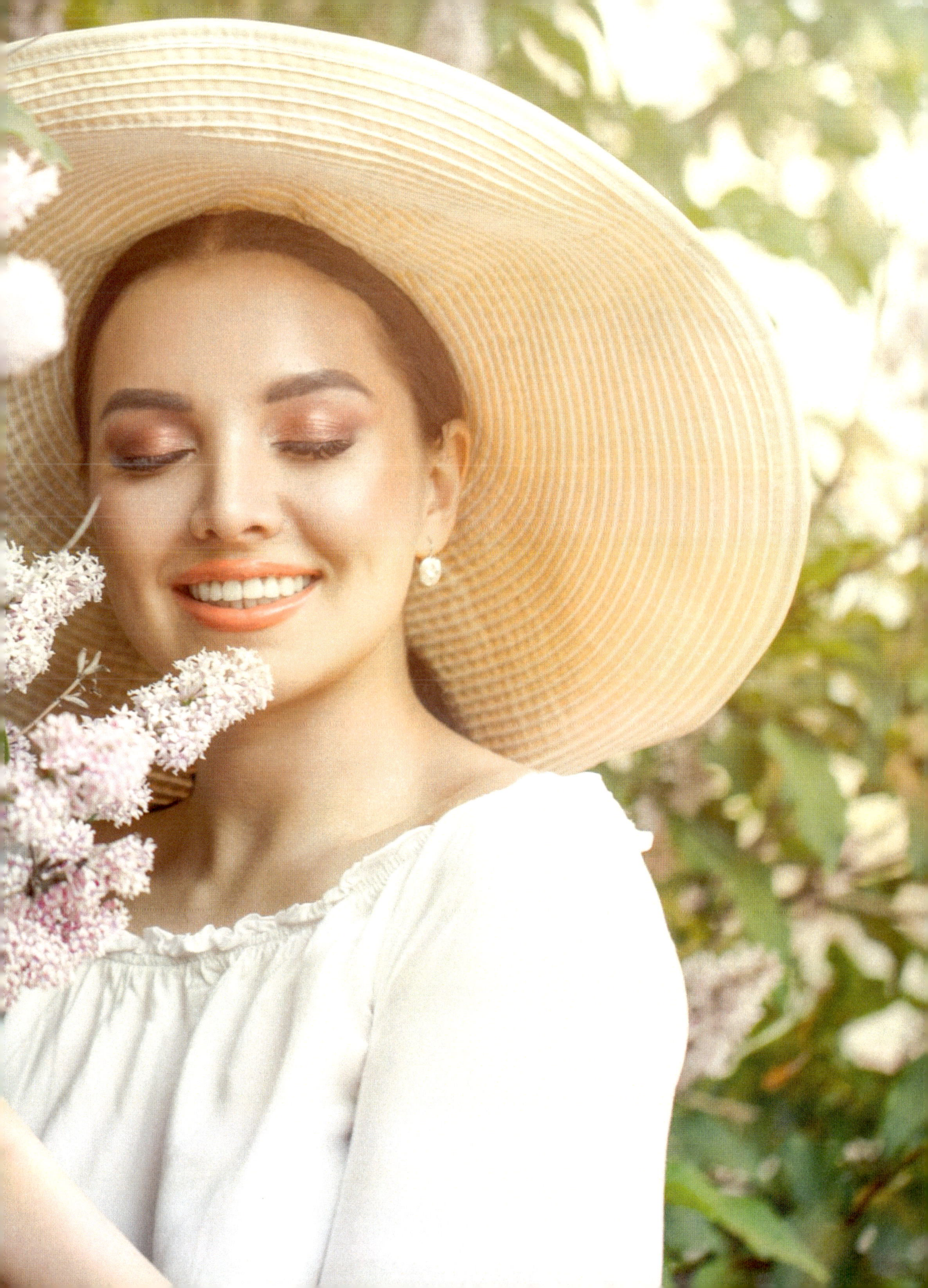

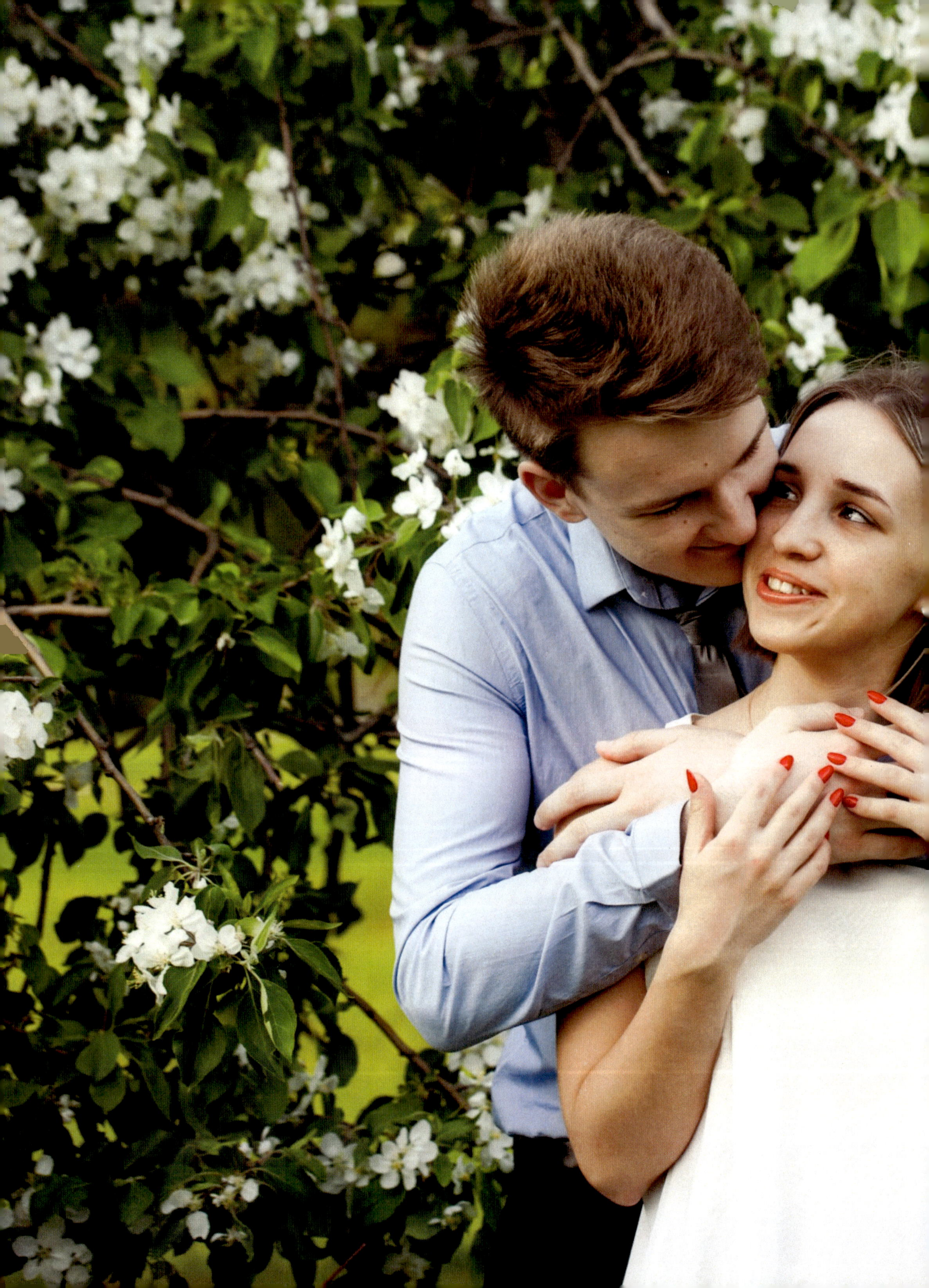

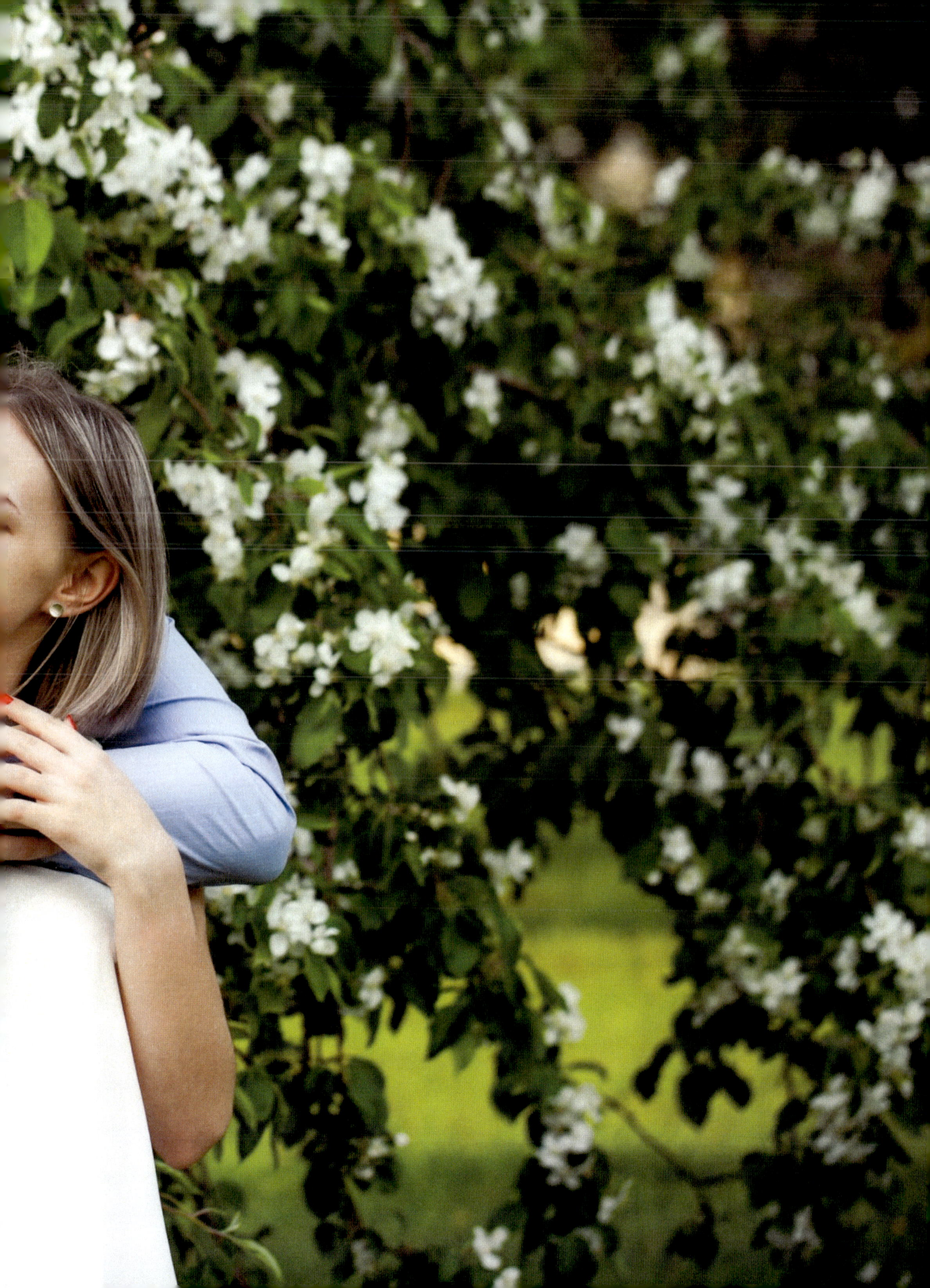

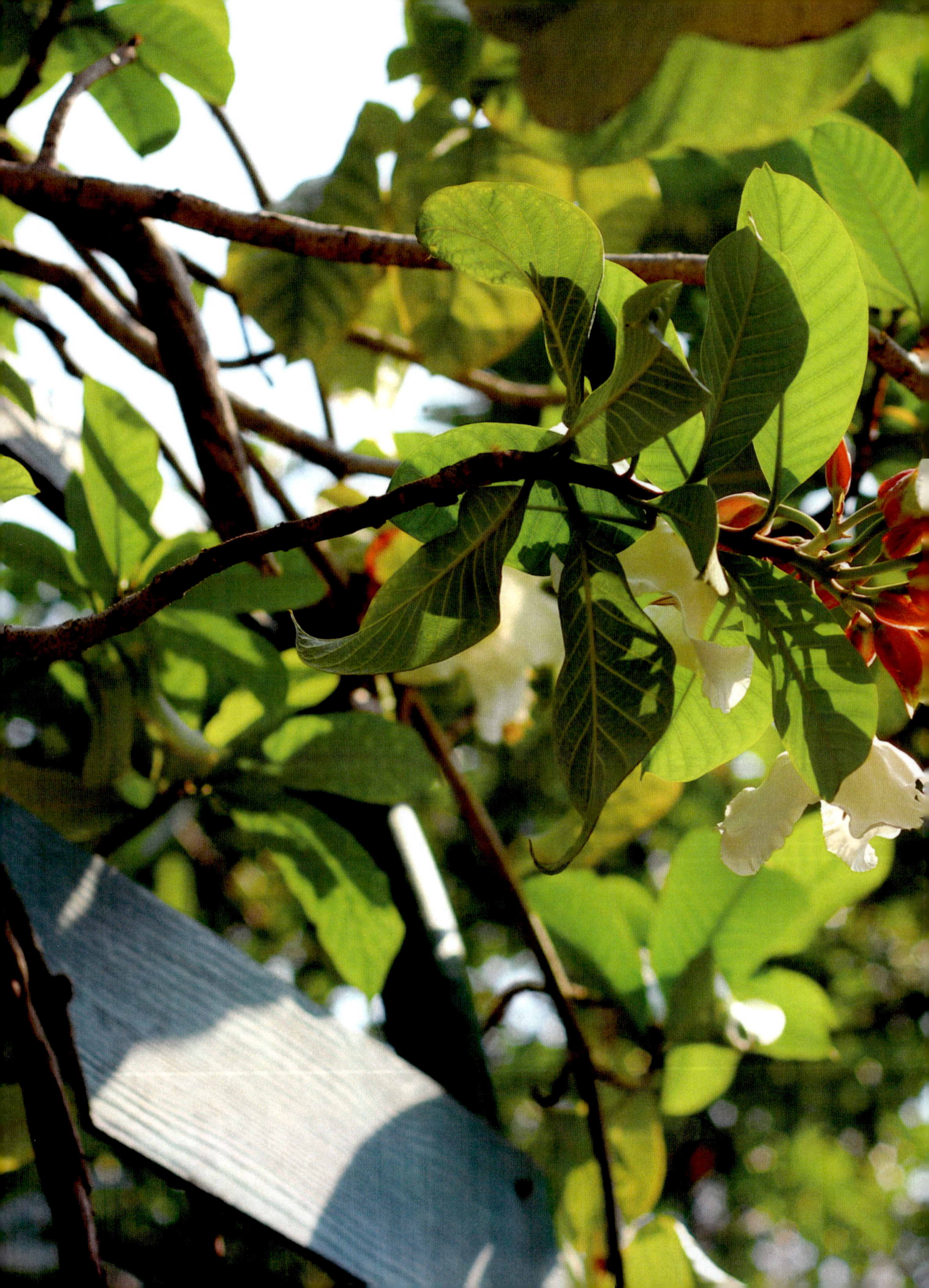

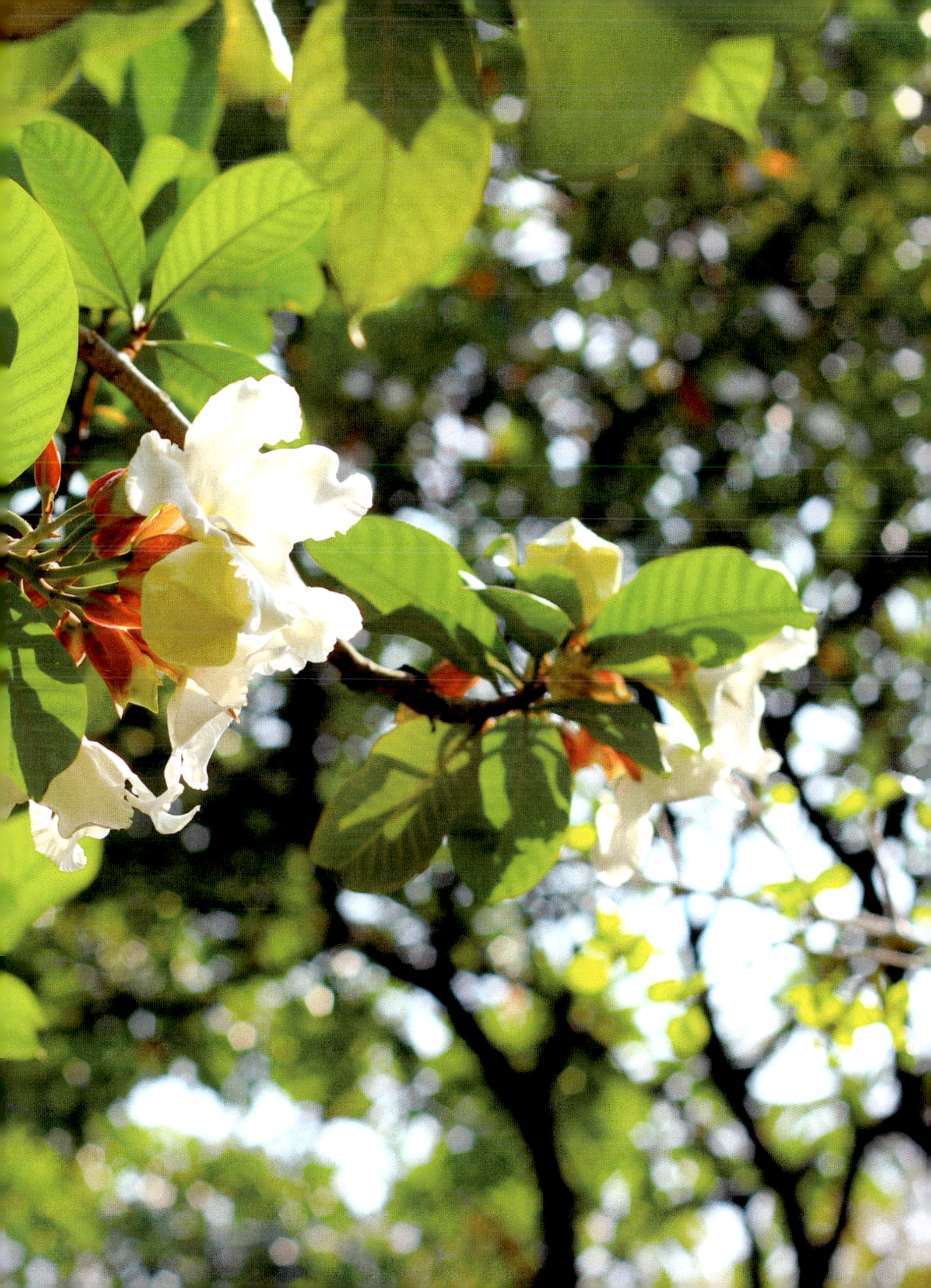

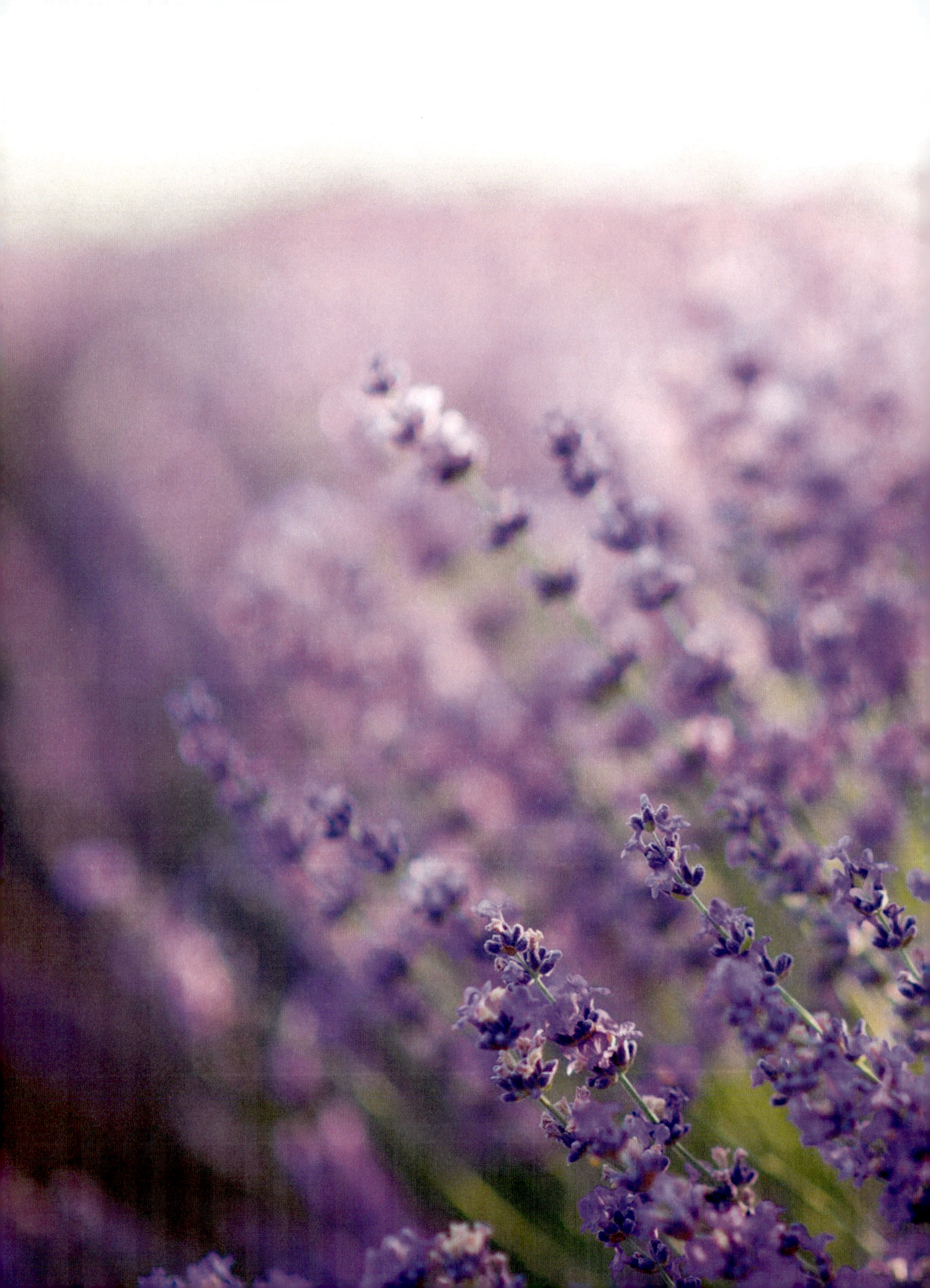

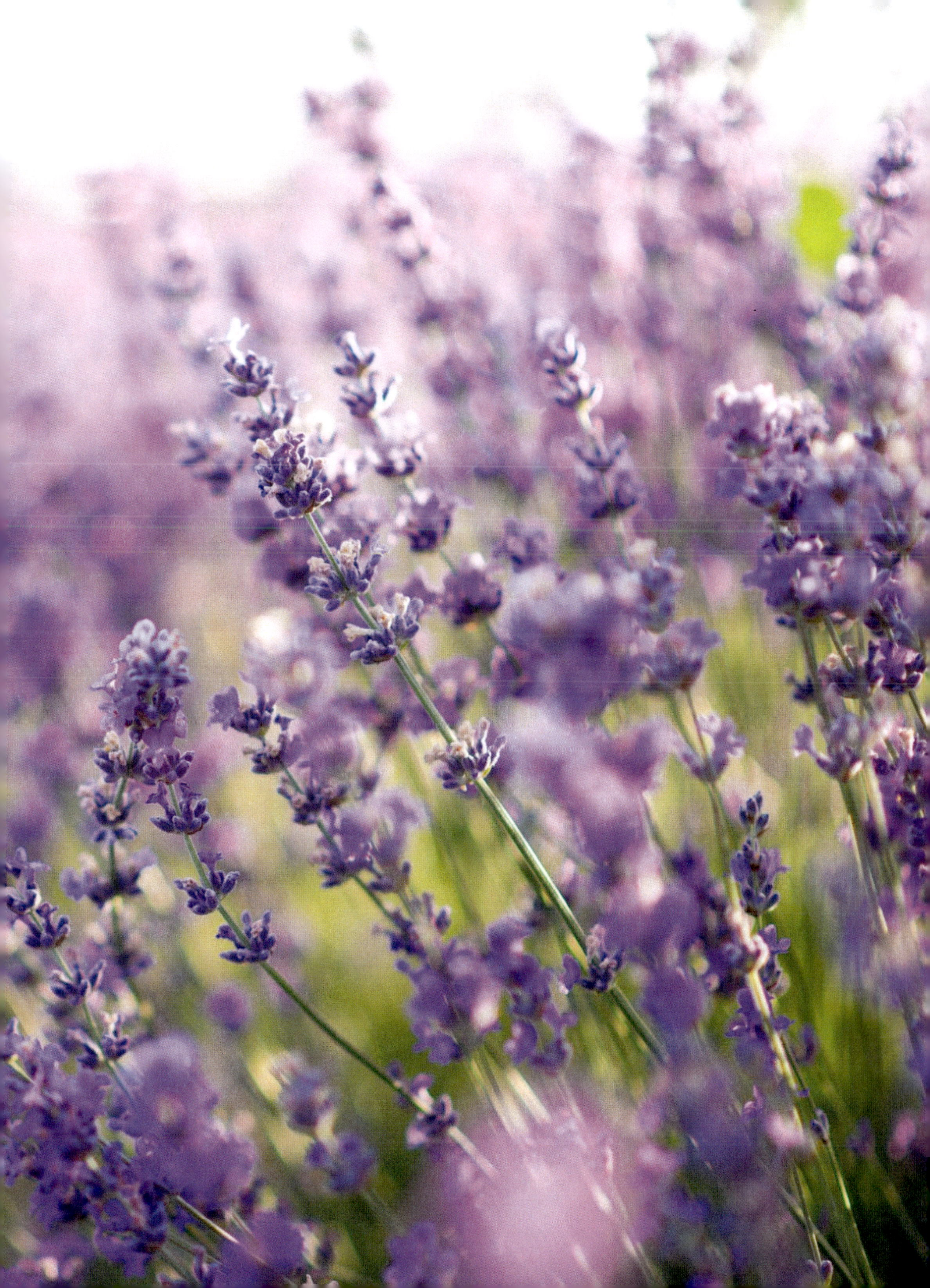

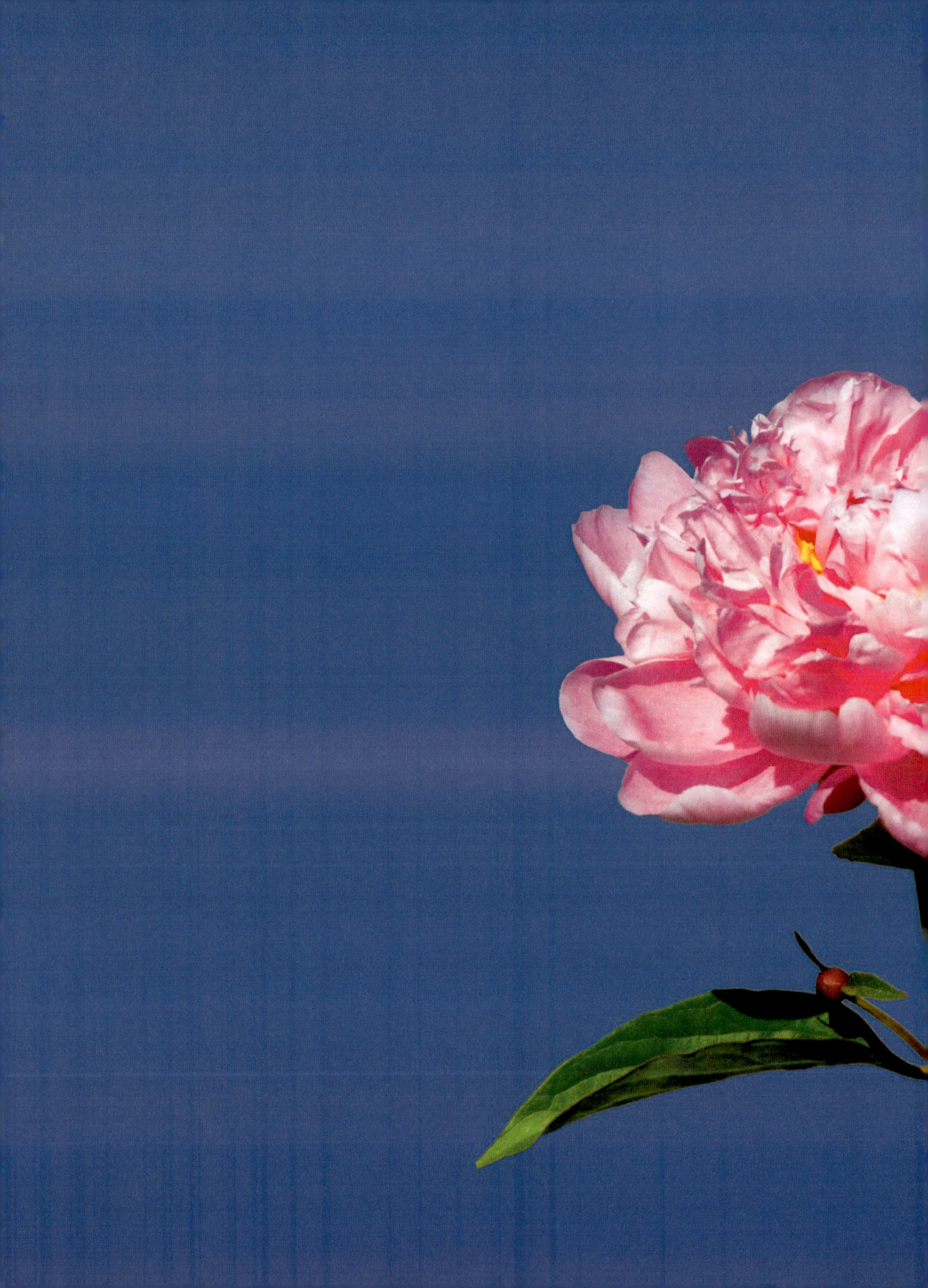

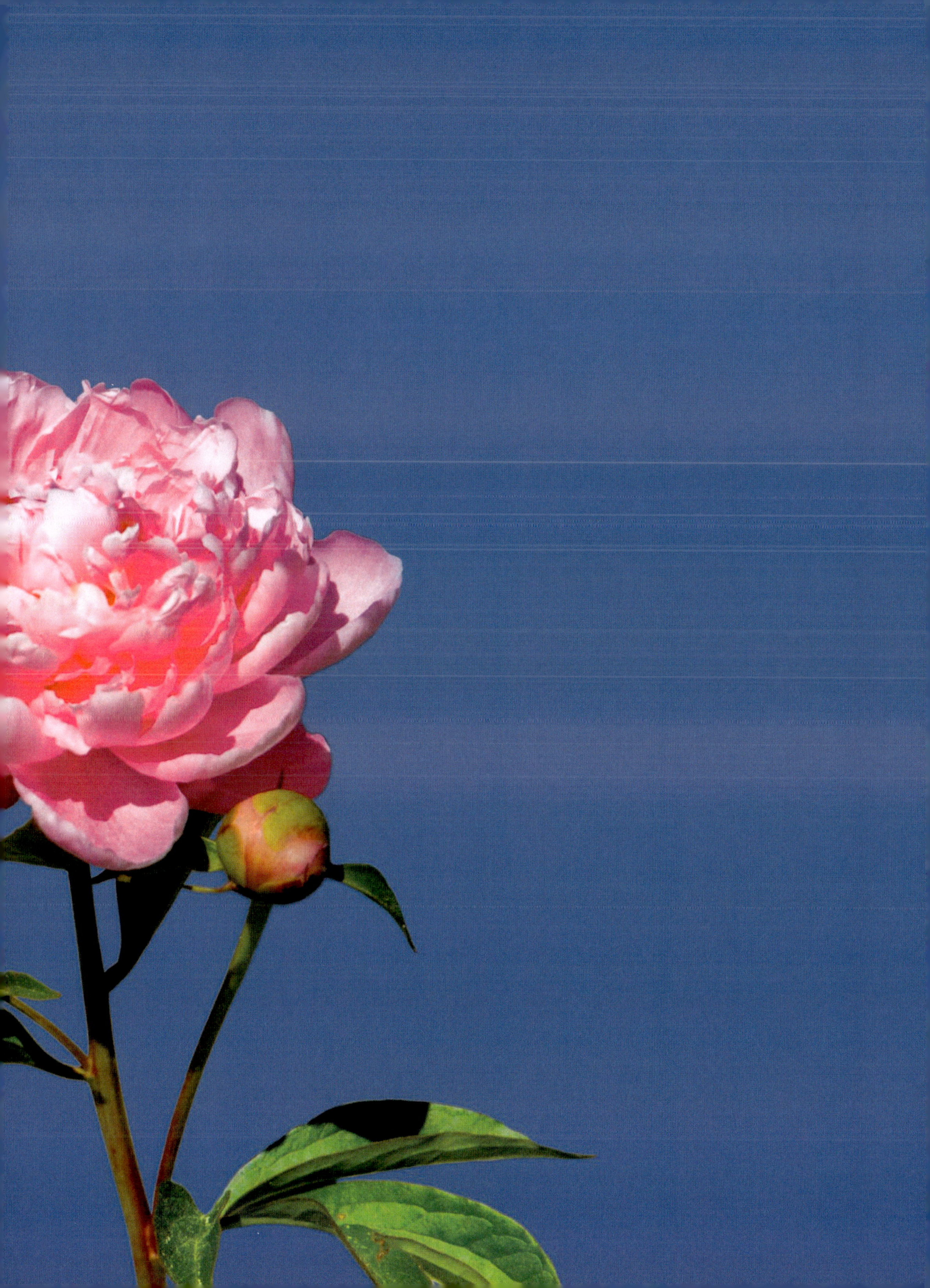

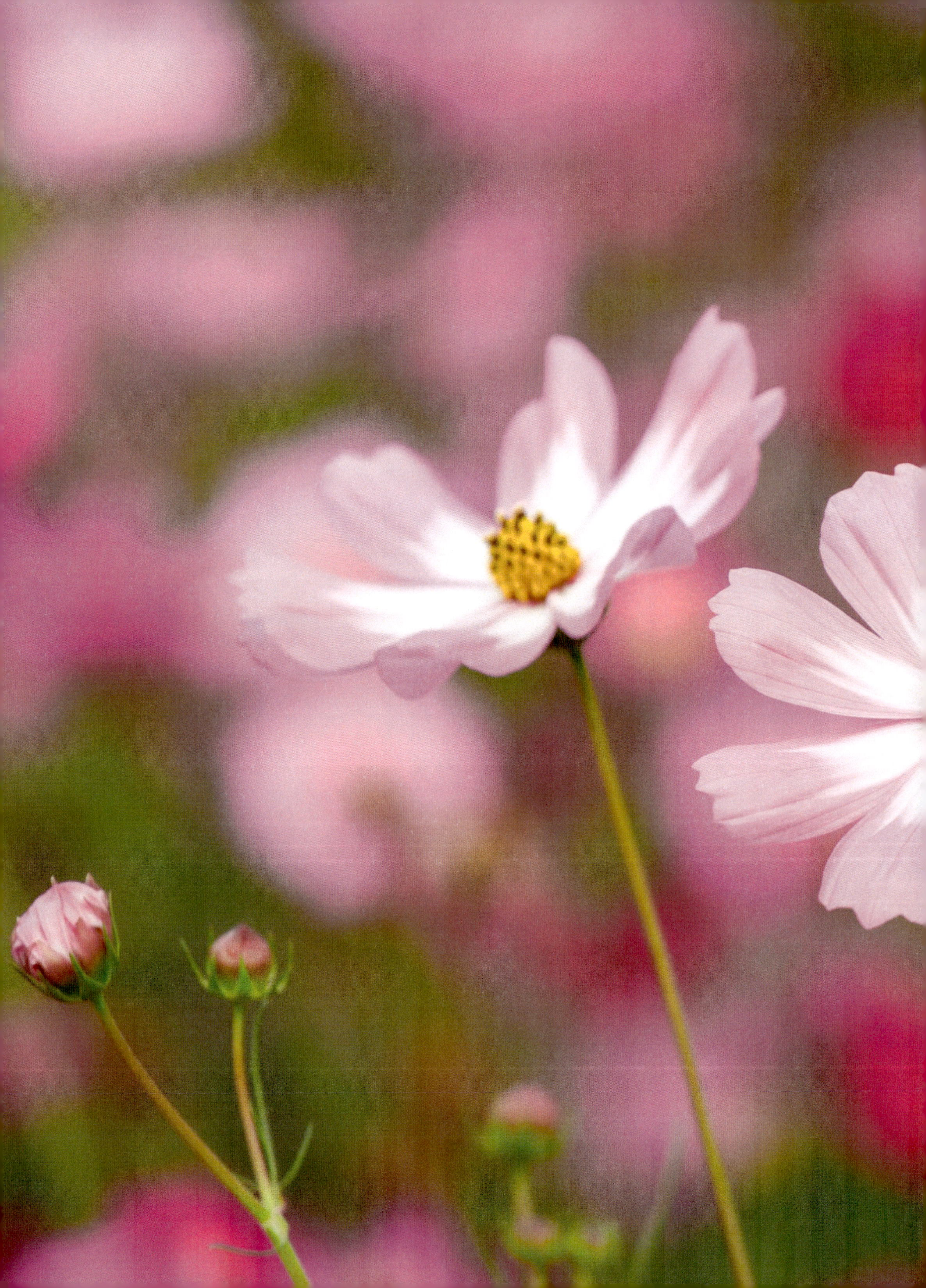

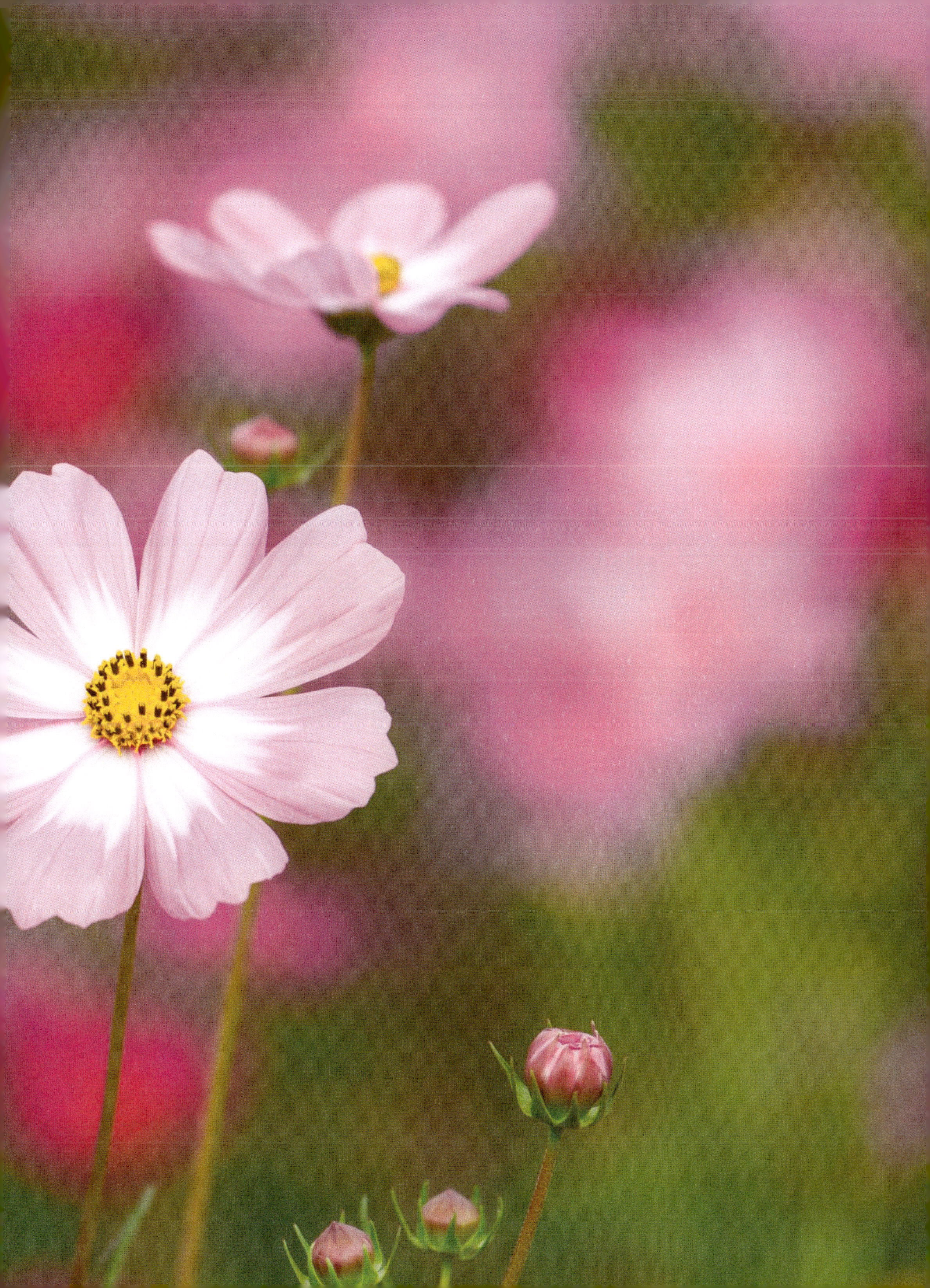

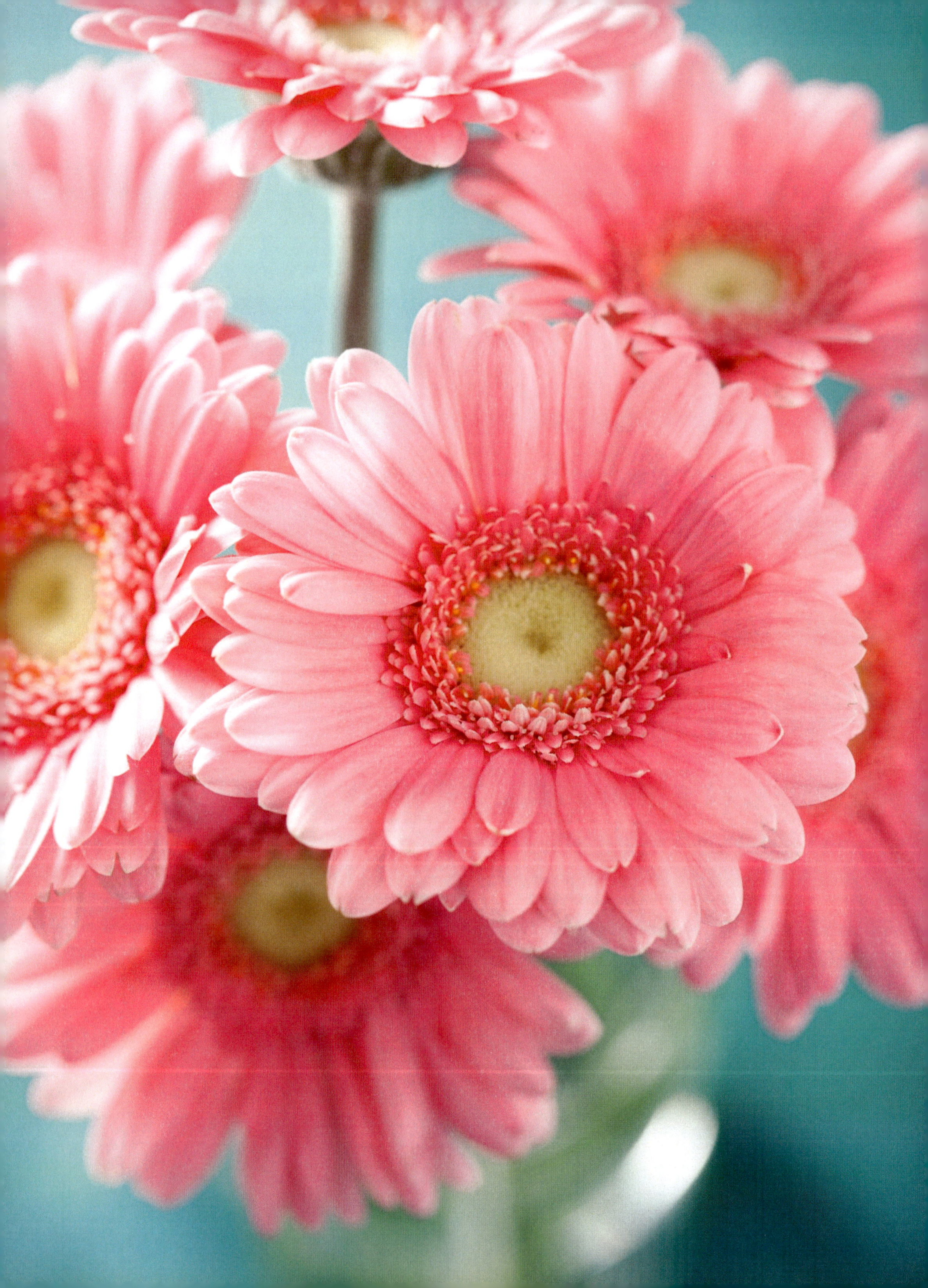

As the days grow longer and the weather warms, most people like to go outside and take the sunlight. This is the season of green places with flowers and gorgeous landscapes. And the season to go for a walk and do some exercise too.

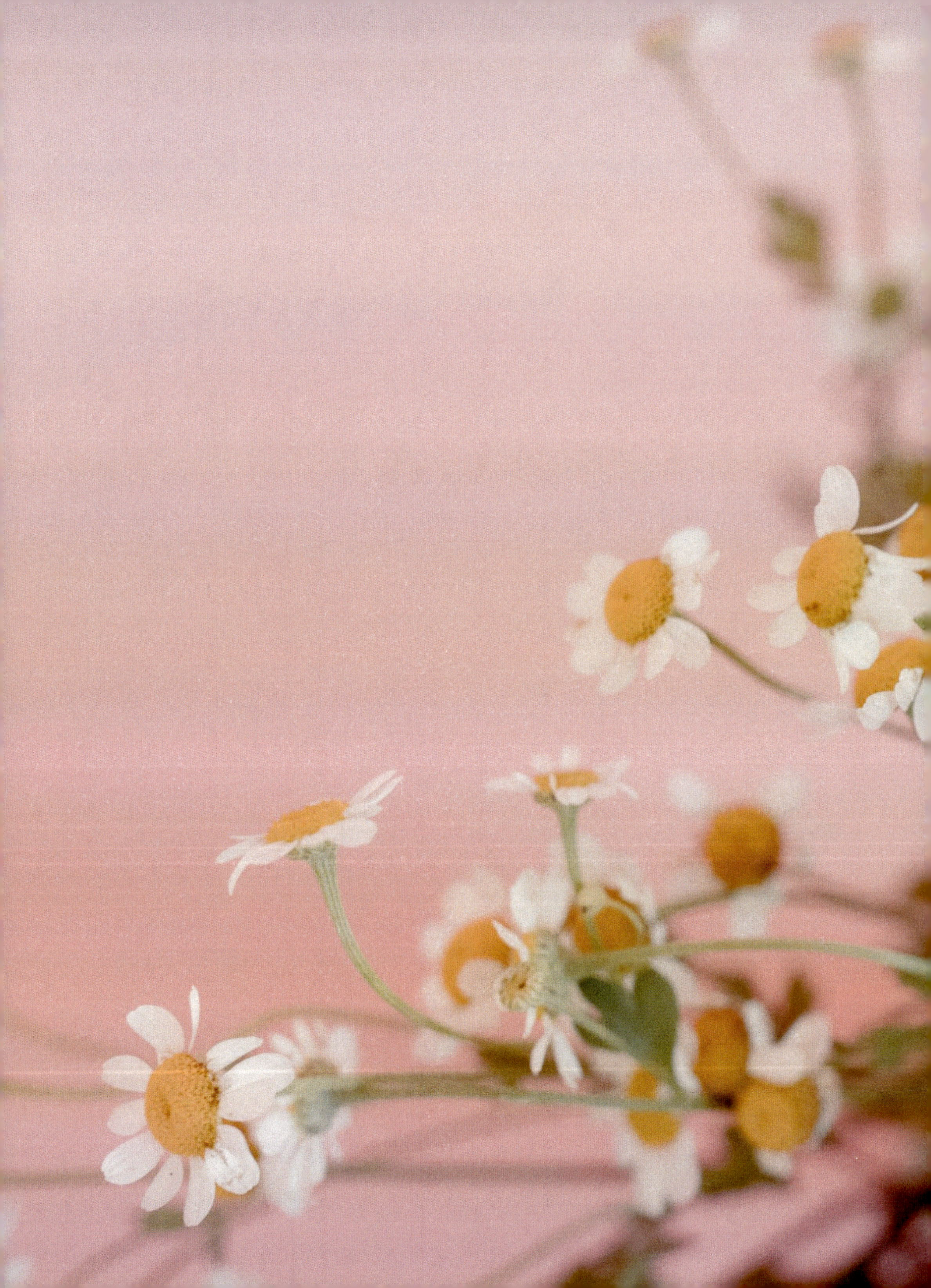

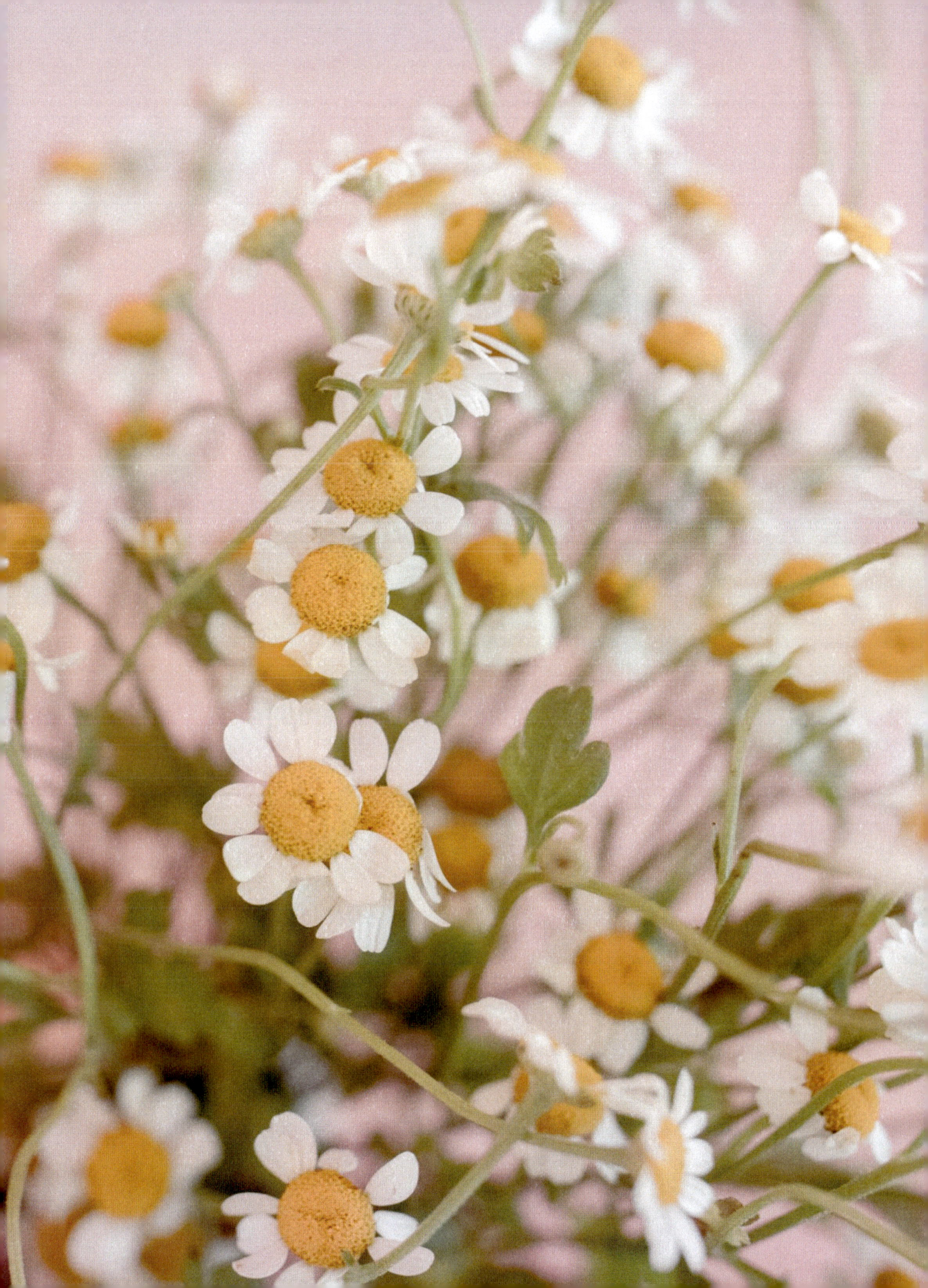

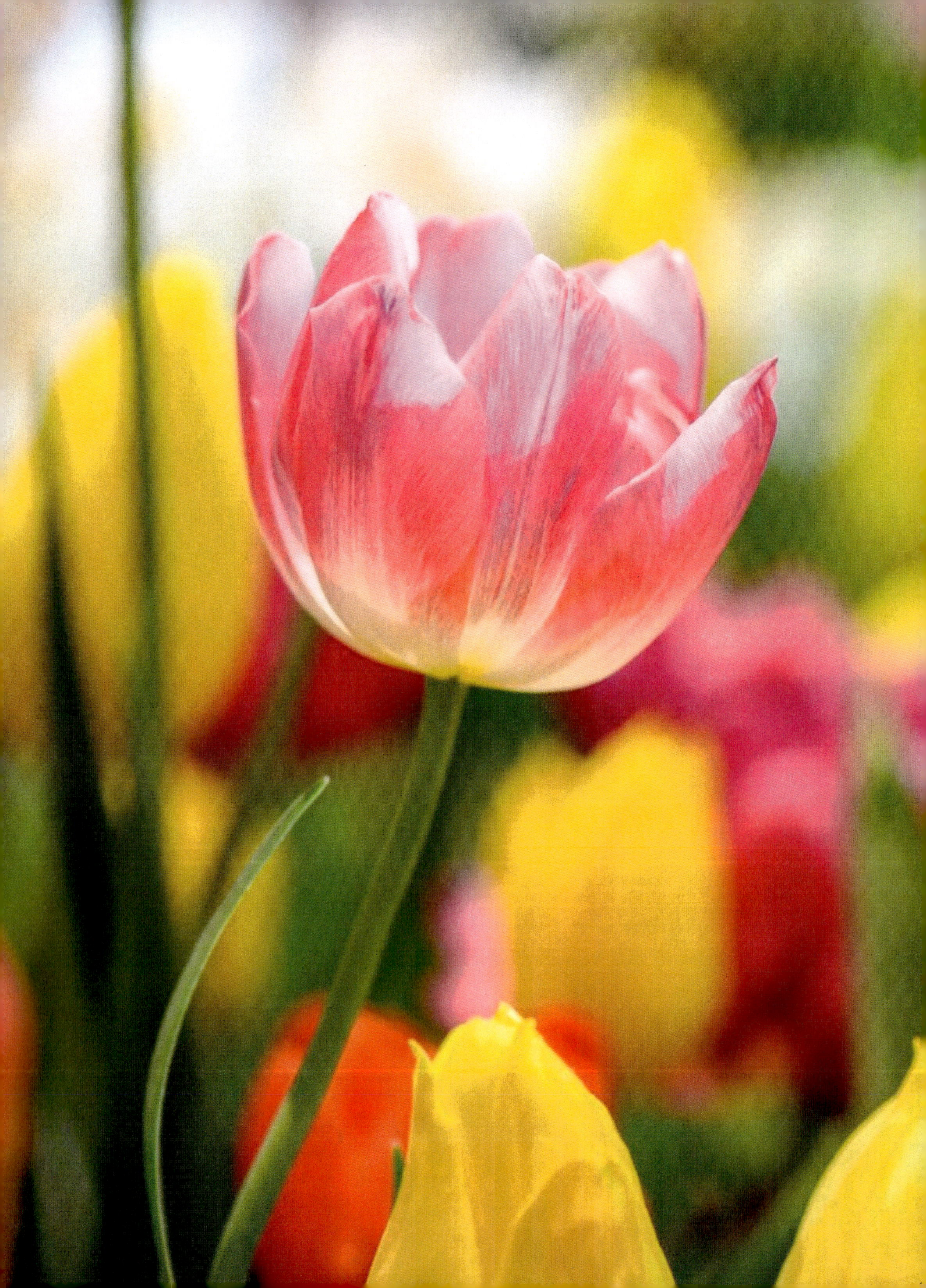

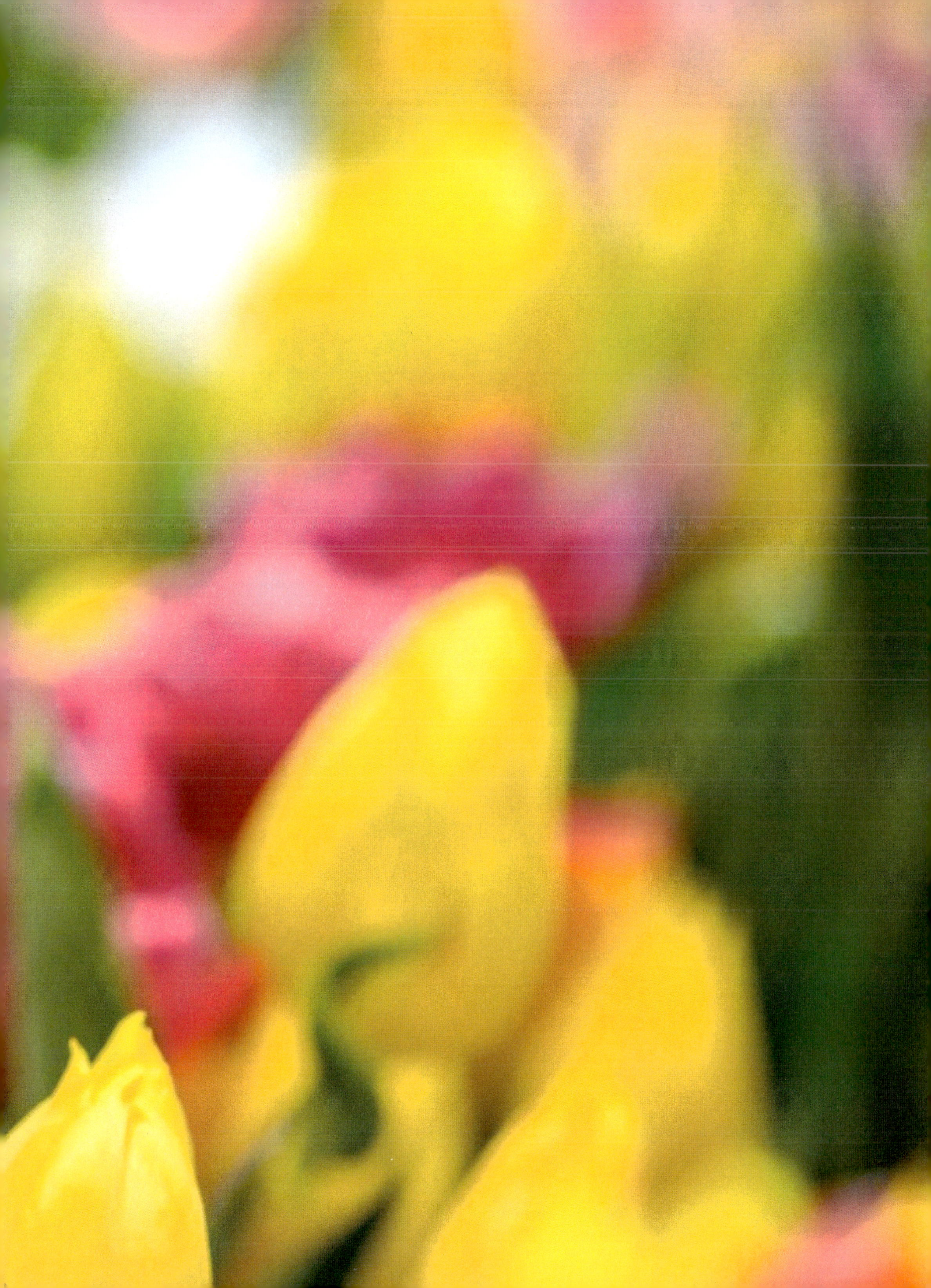

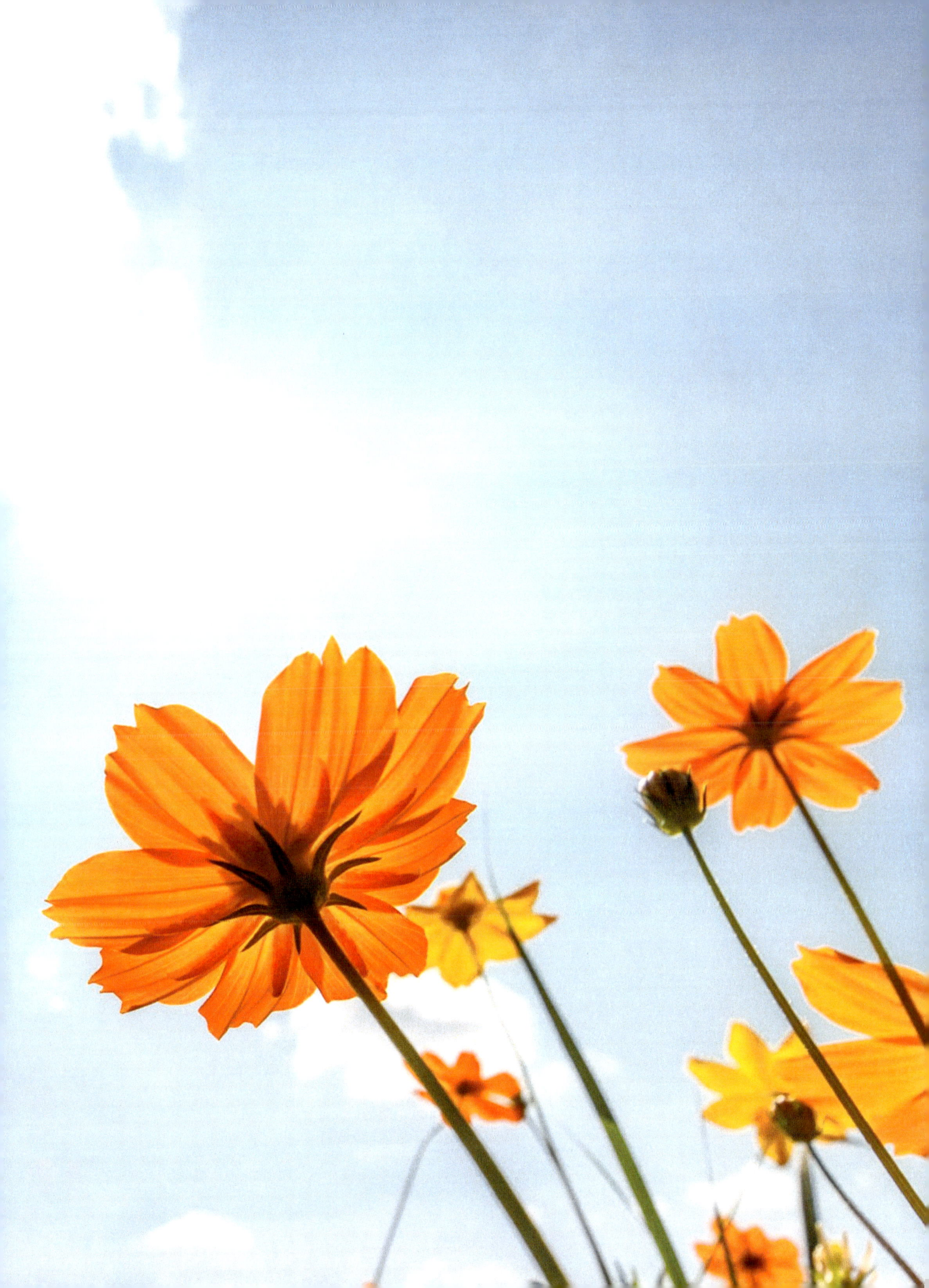

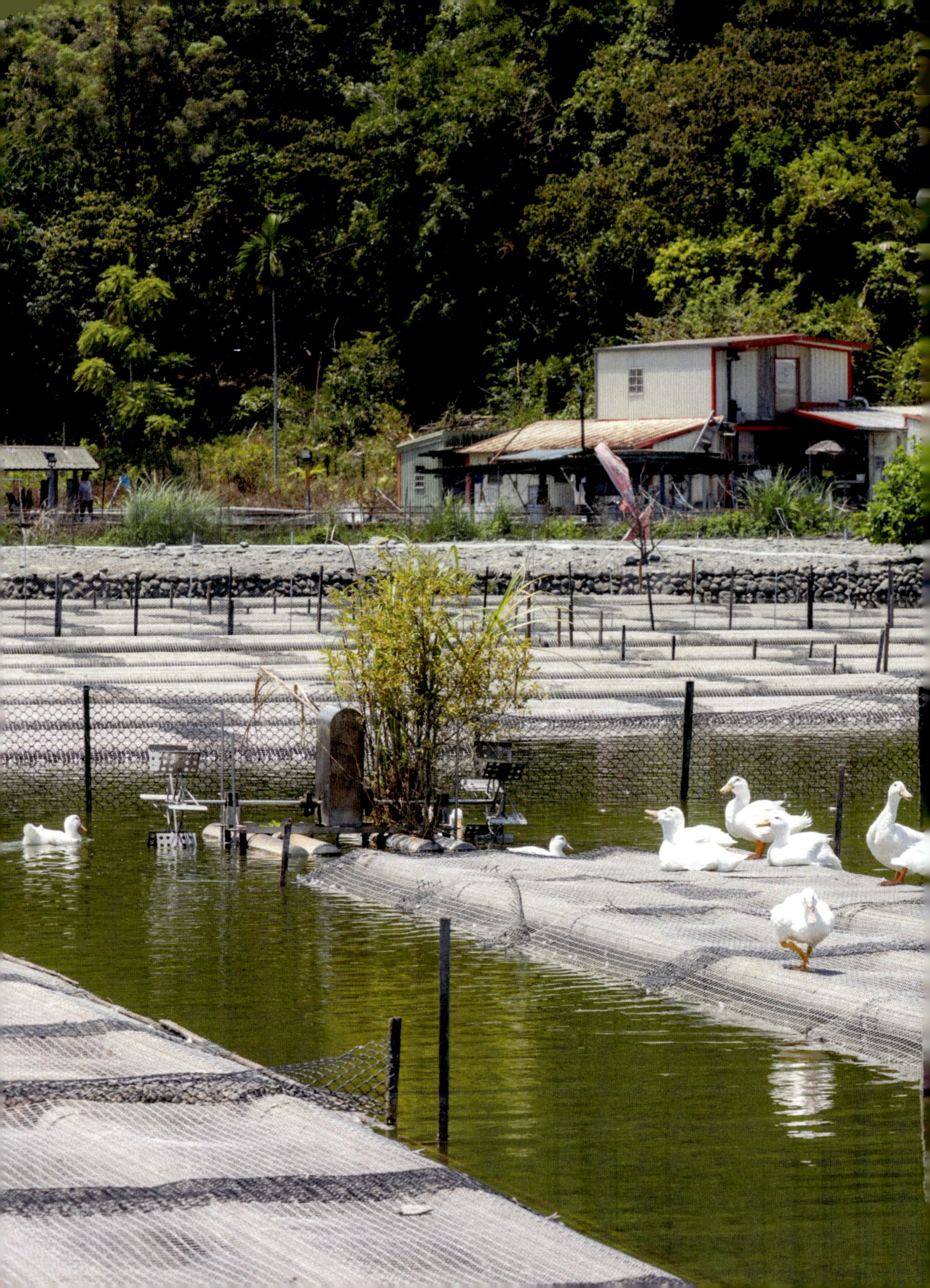

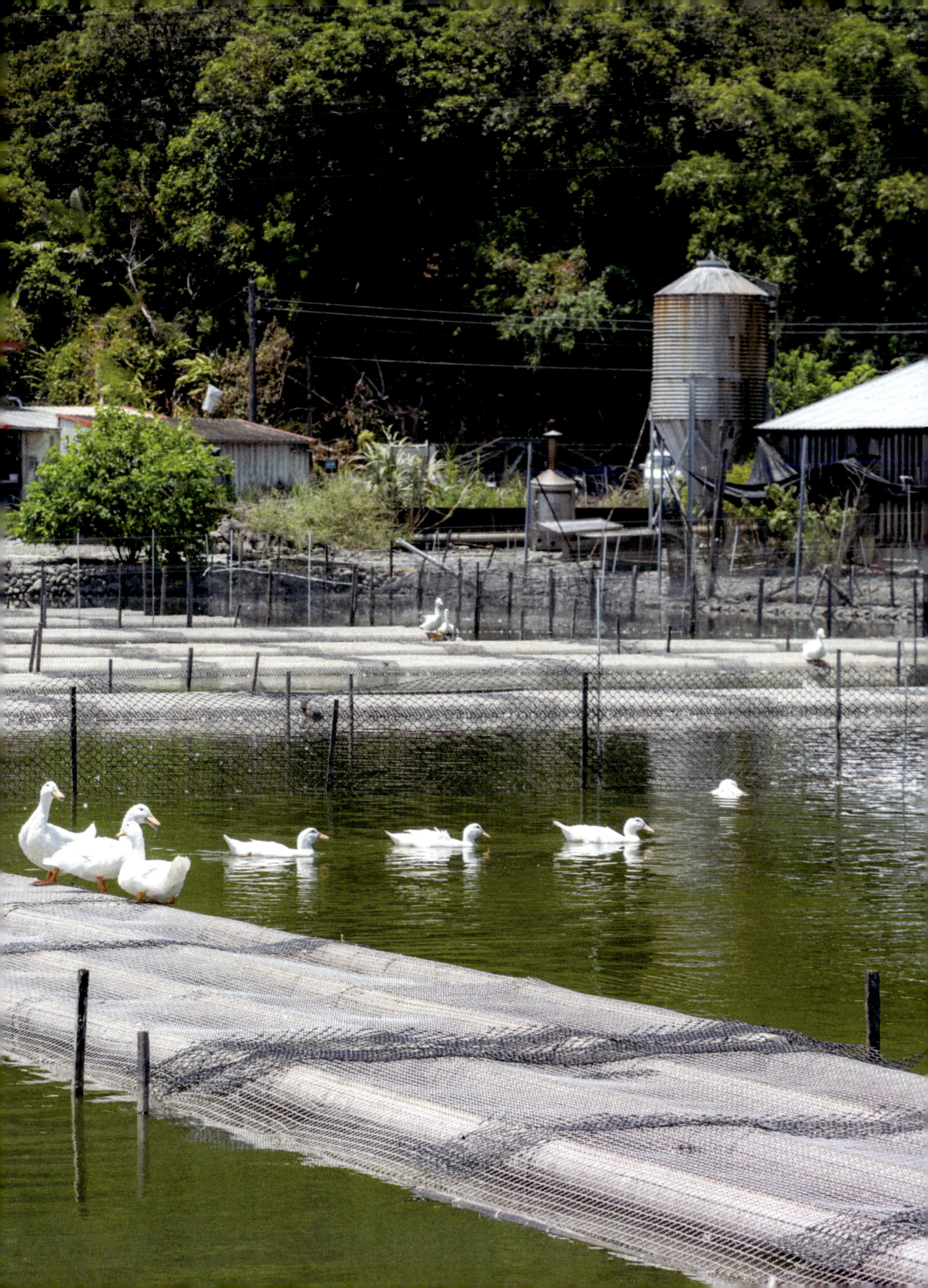

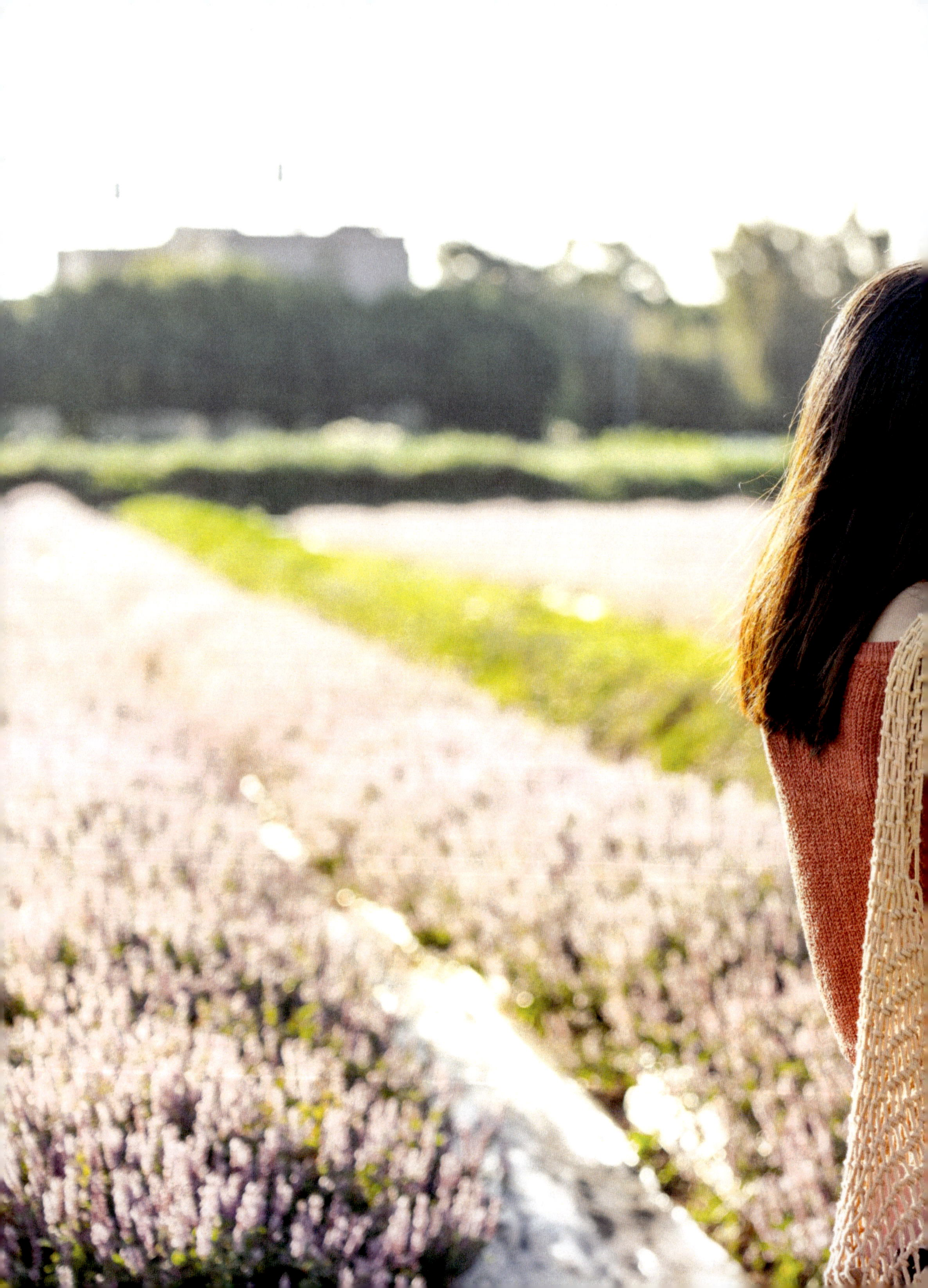

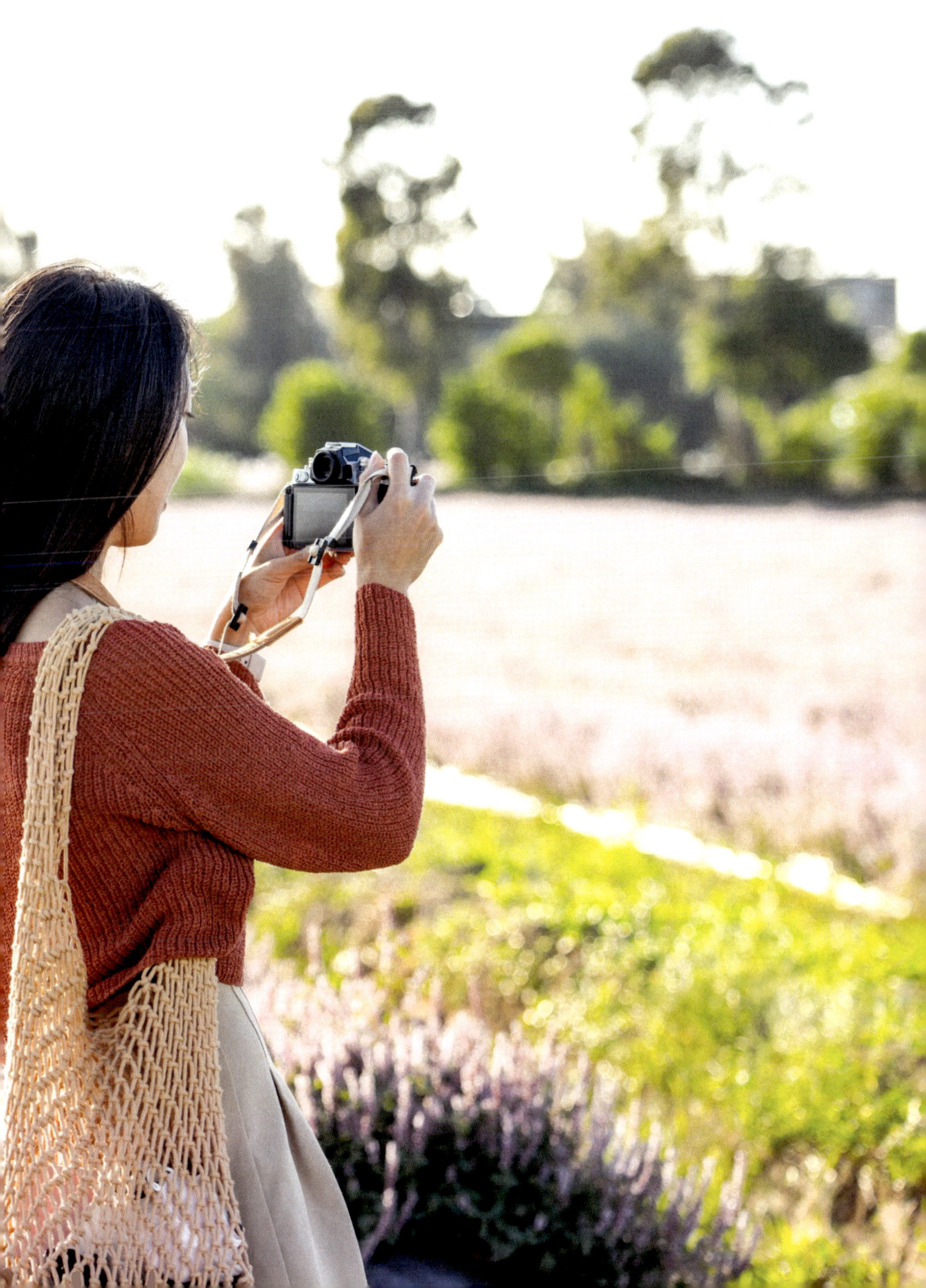

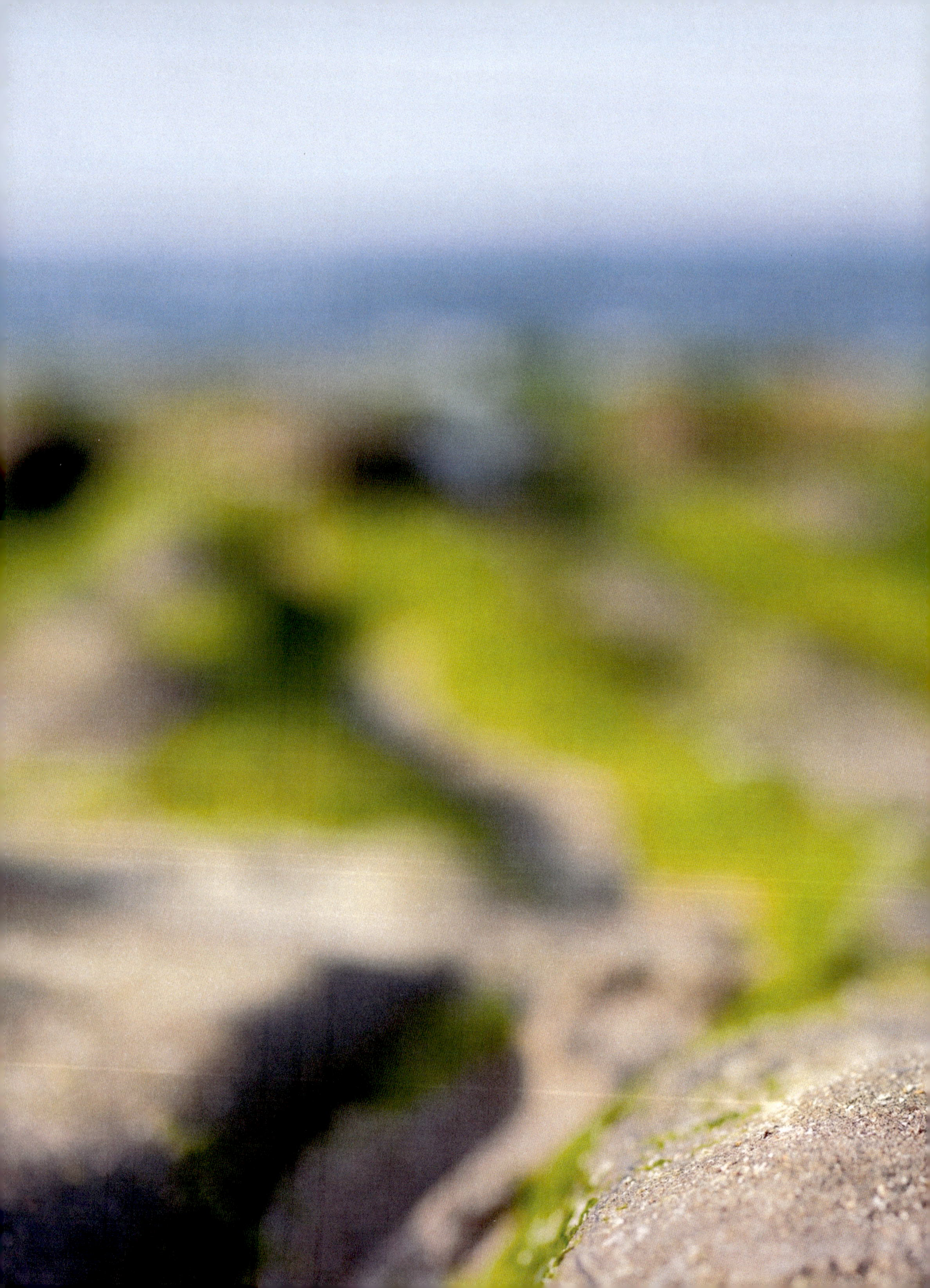

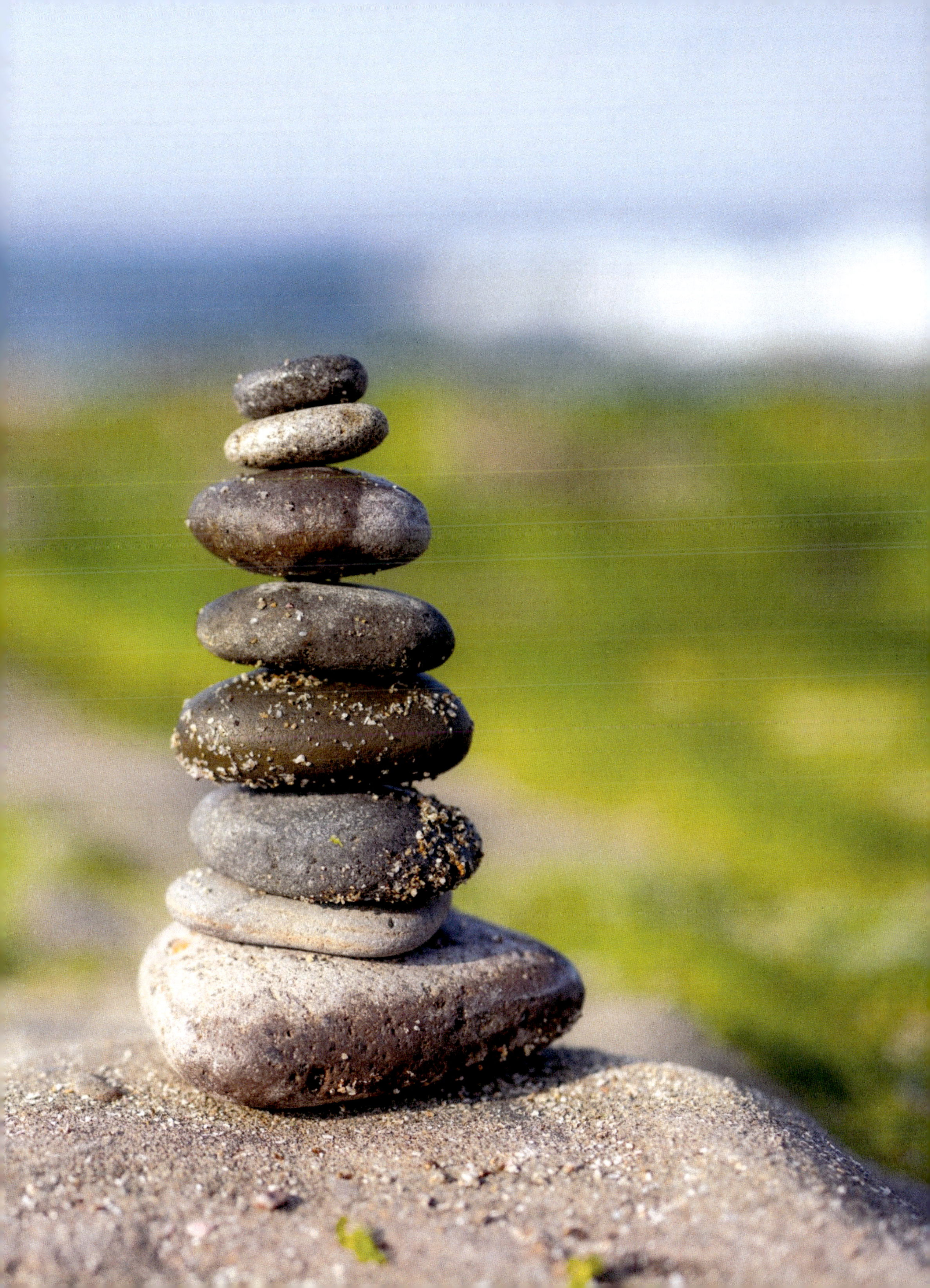

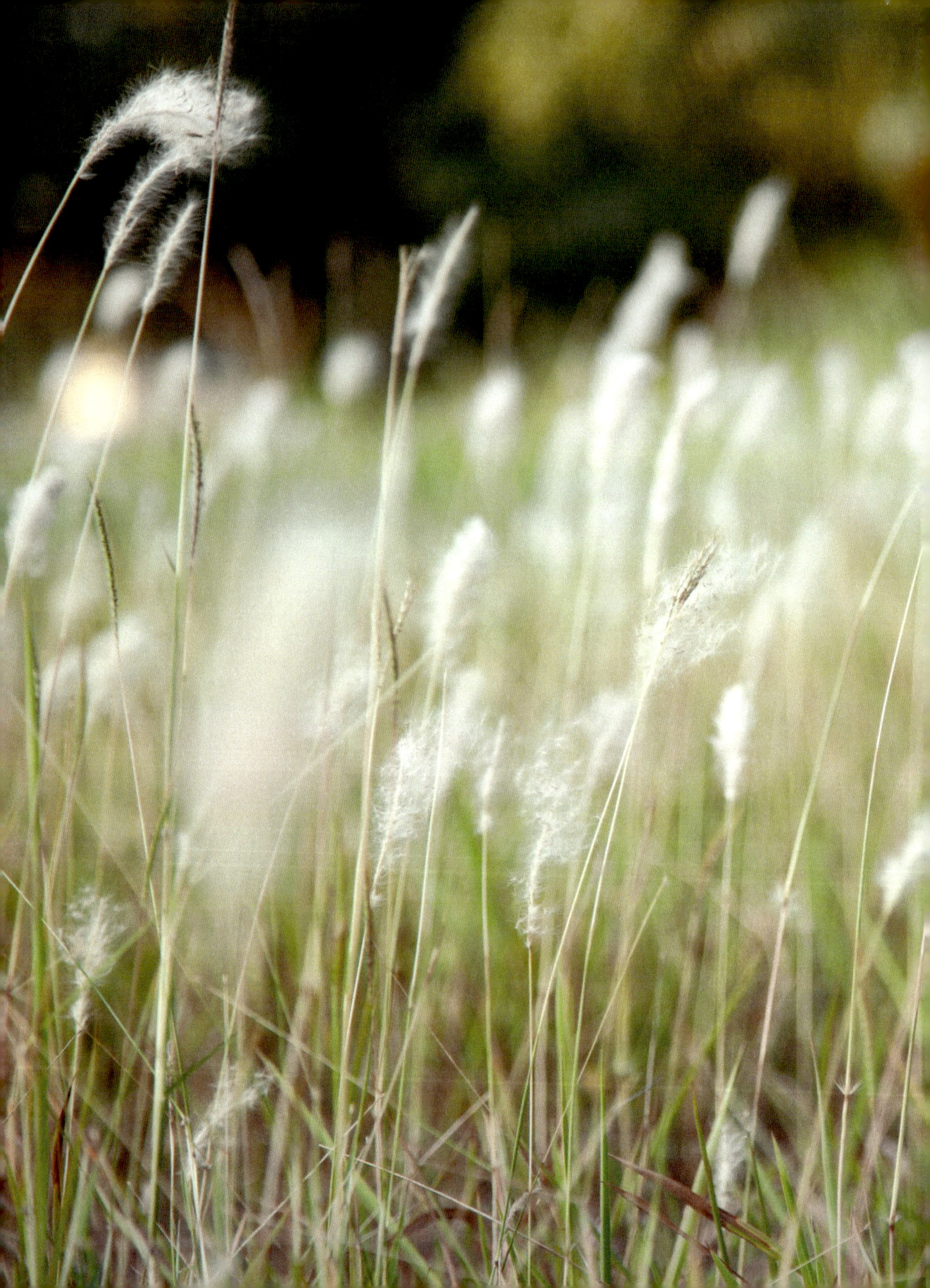

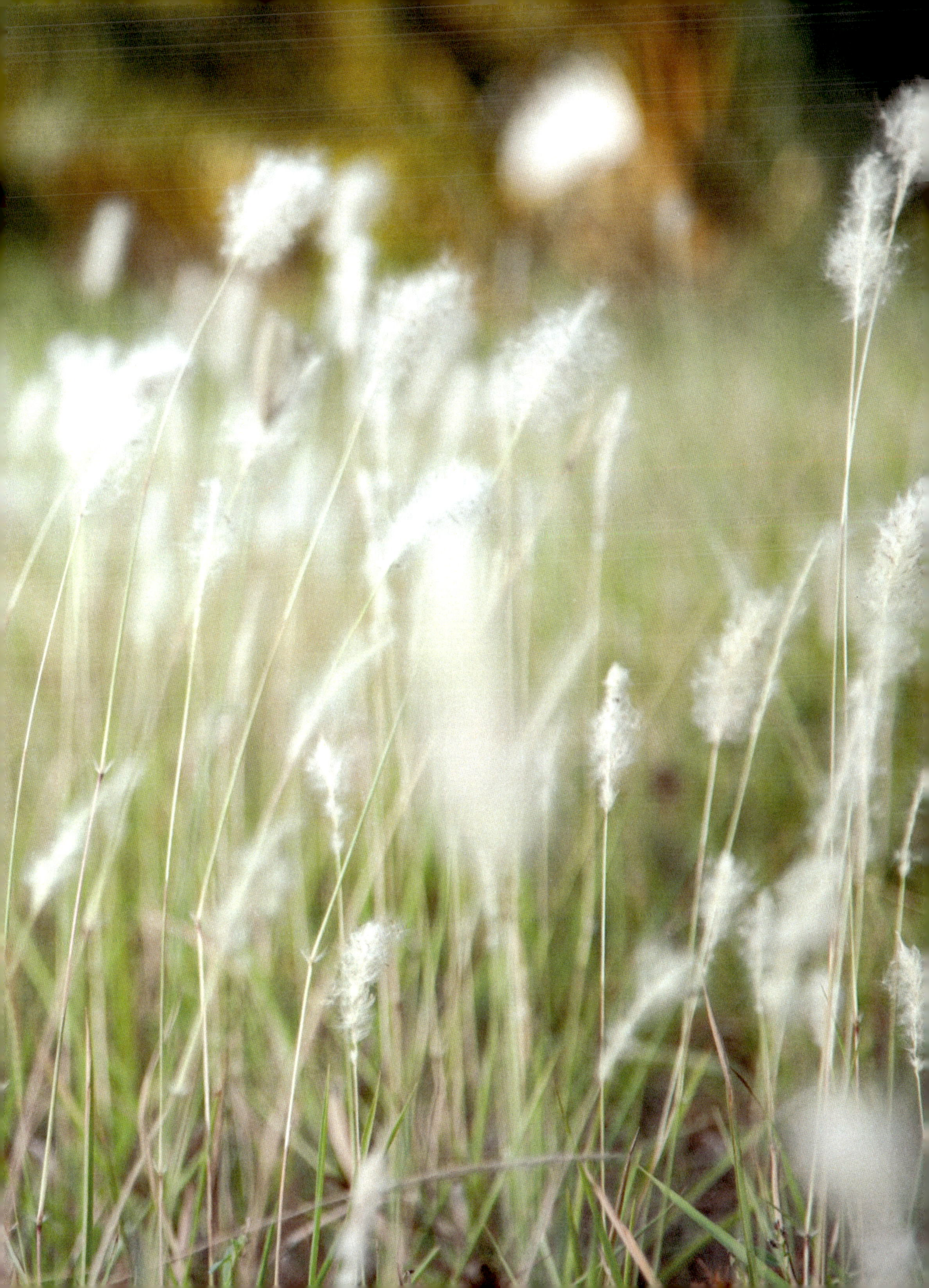

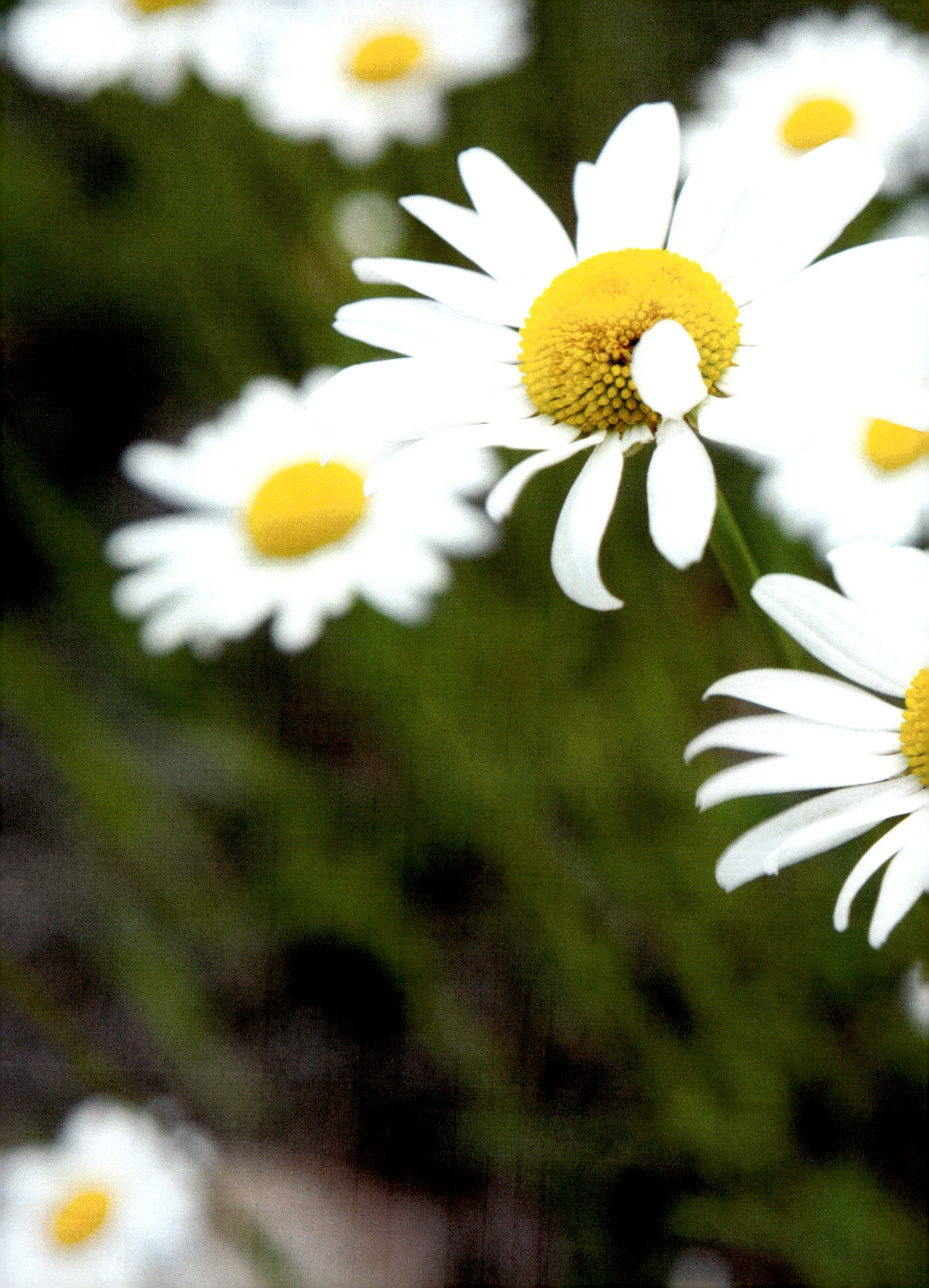

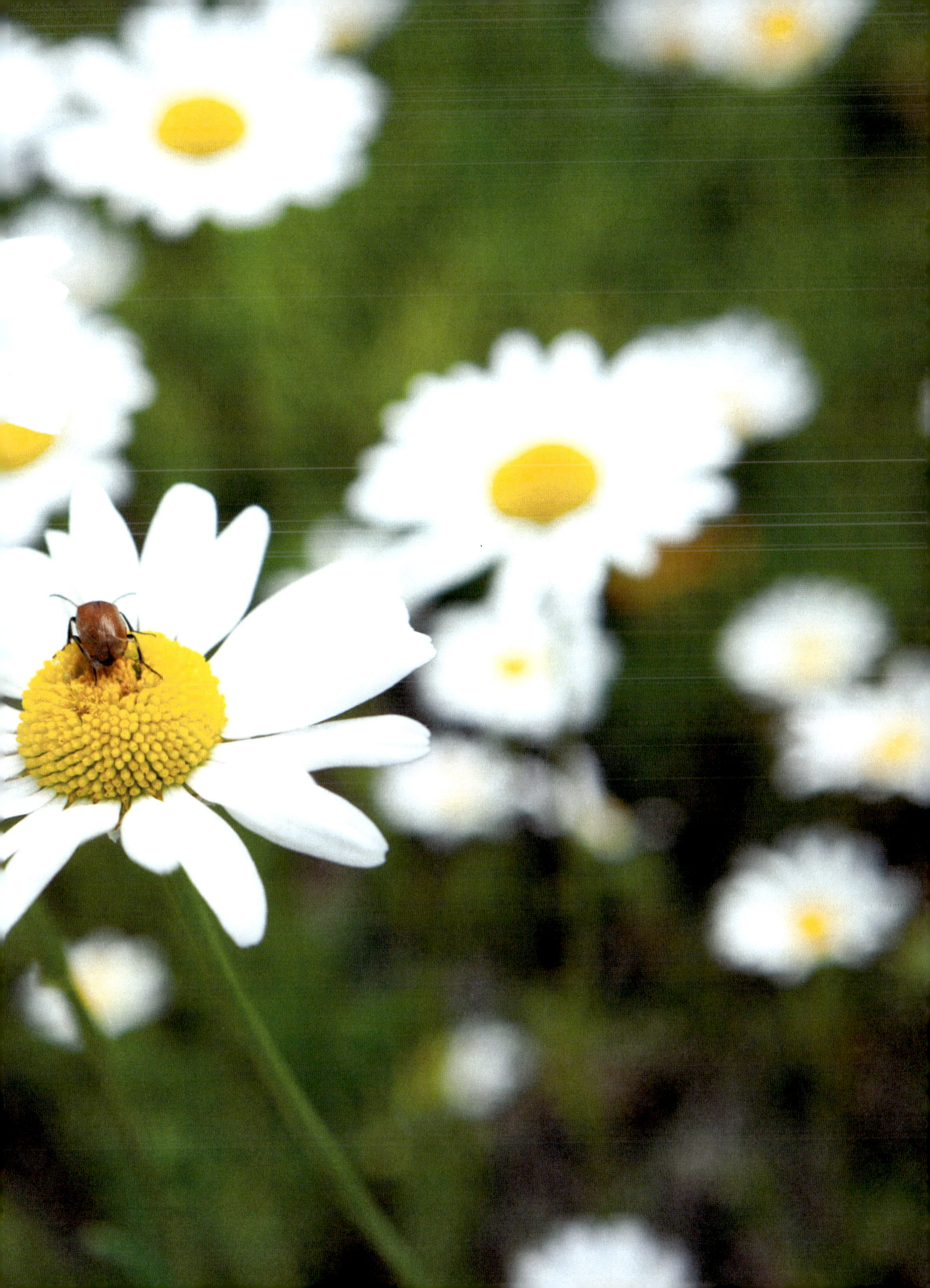

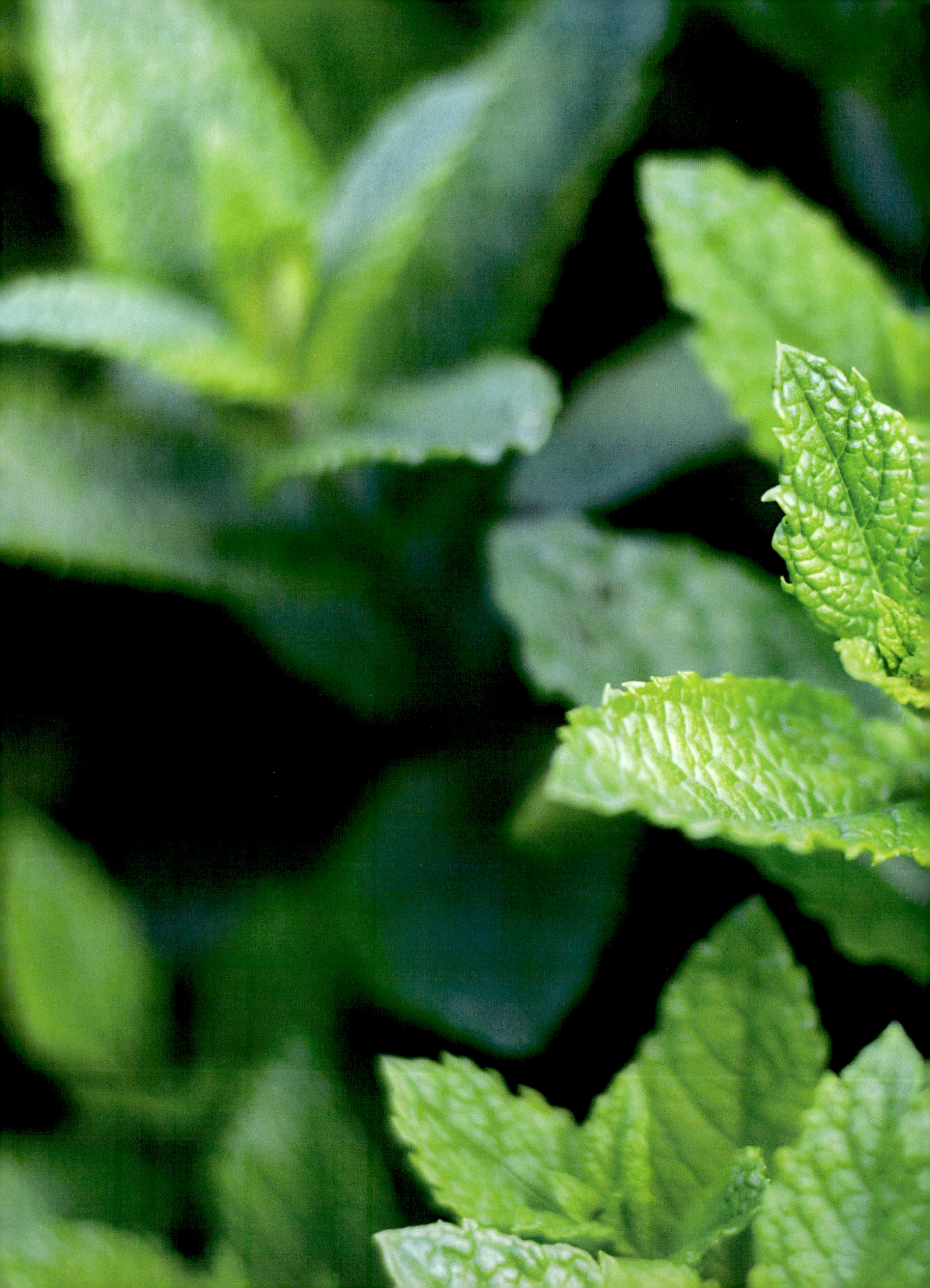

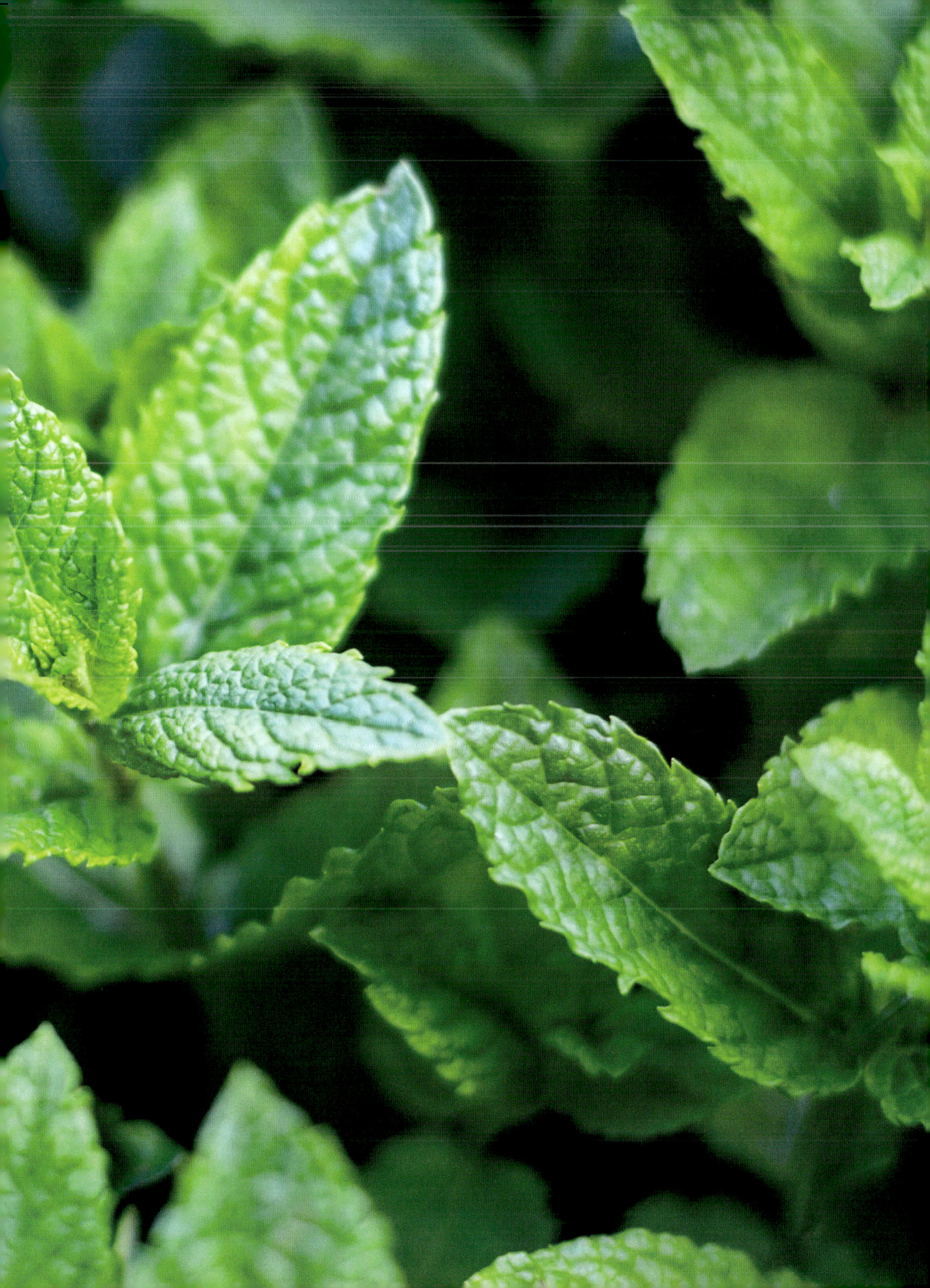

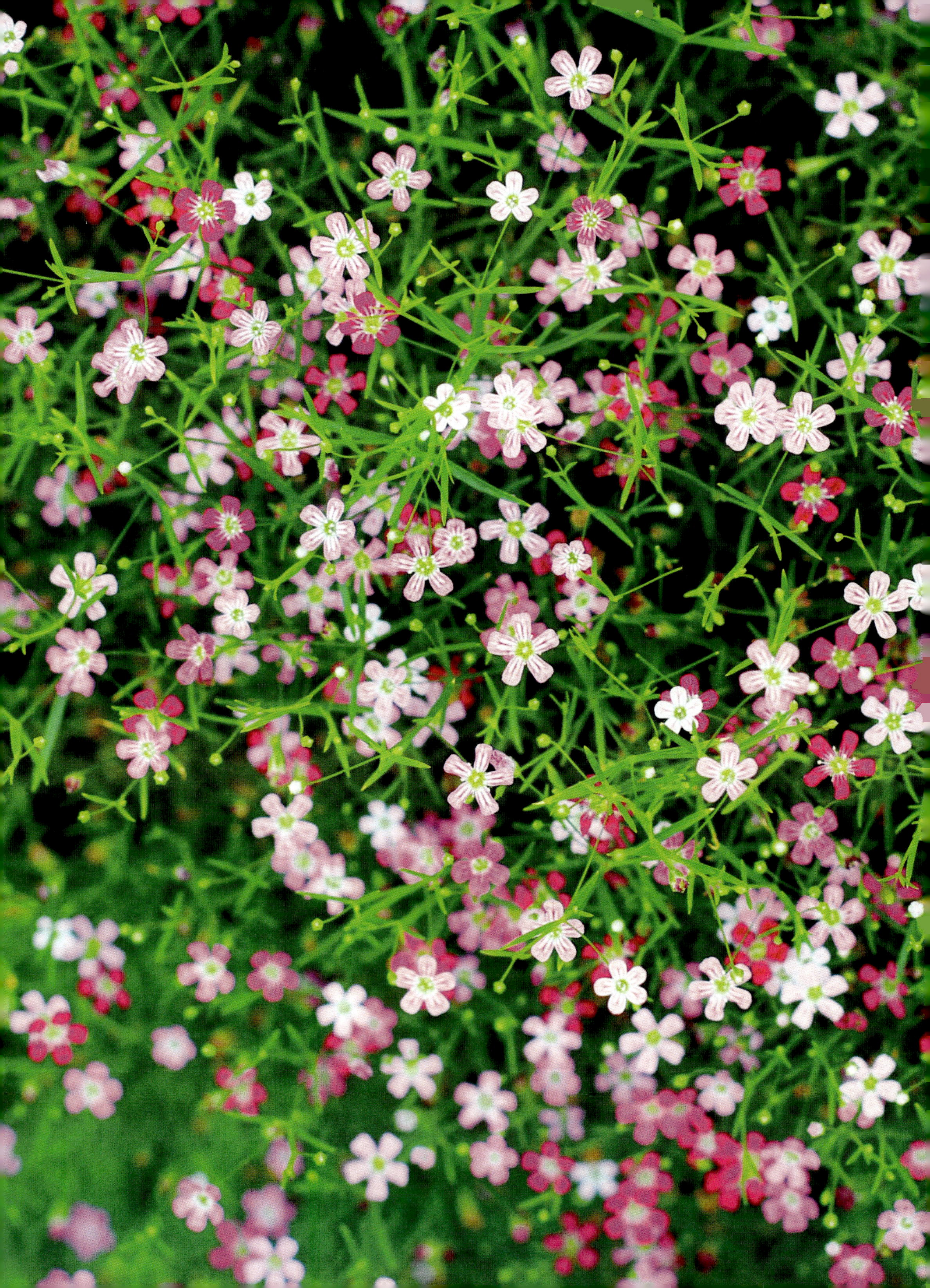

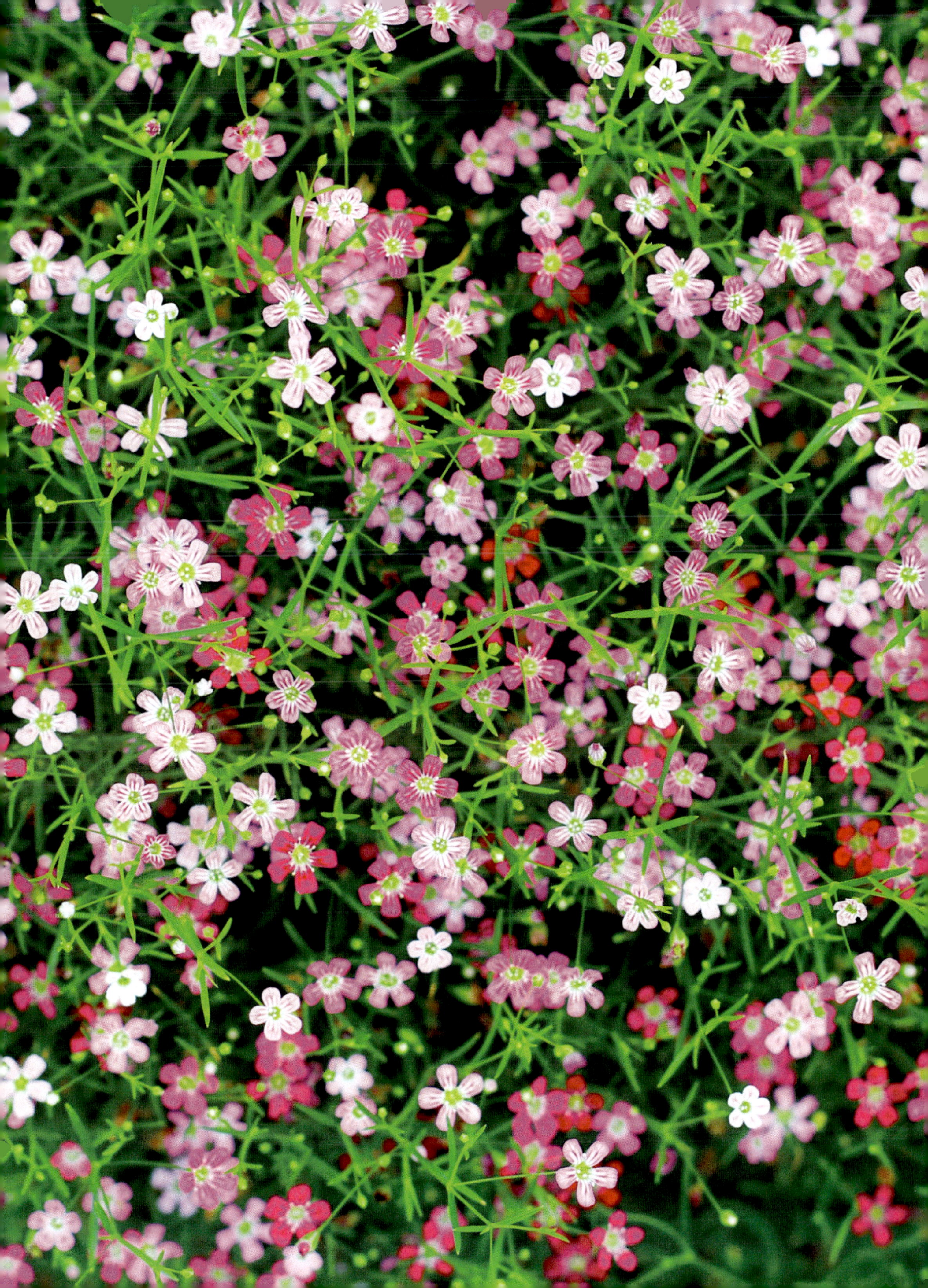

Spring offers the feeling of freshness and lightness after the cold and dark feeling of winter. In spring, we can take away the heavy clothes and be more natural-dressed, with more skin exposed to the sunlight. This season invites us to be outside more often and enjoy the light of the sun.

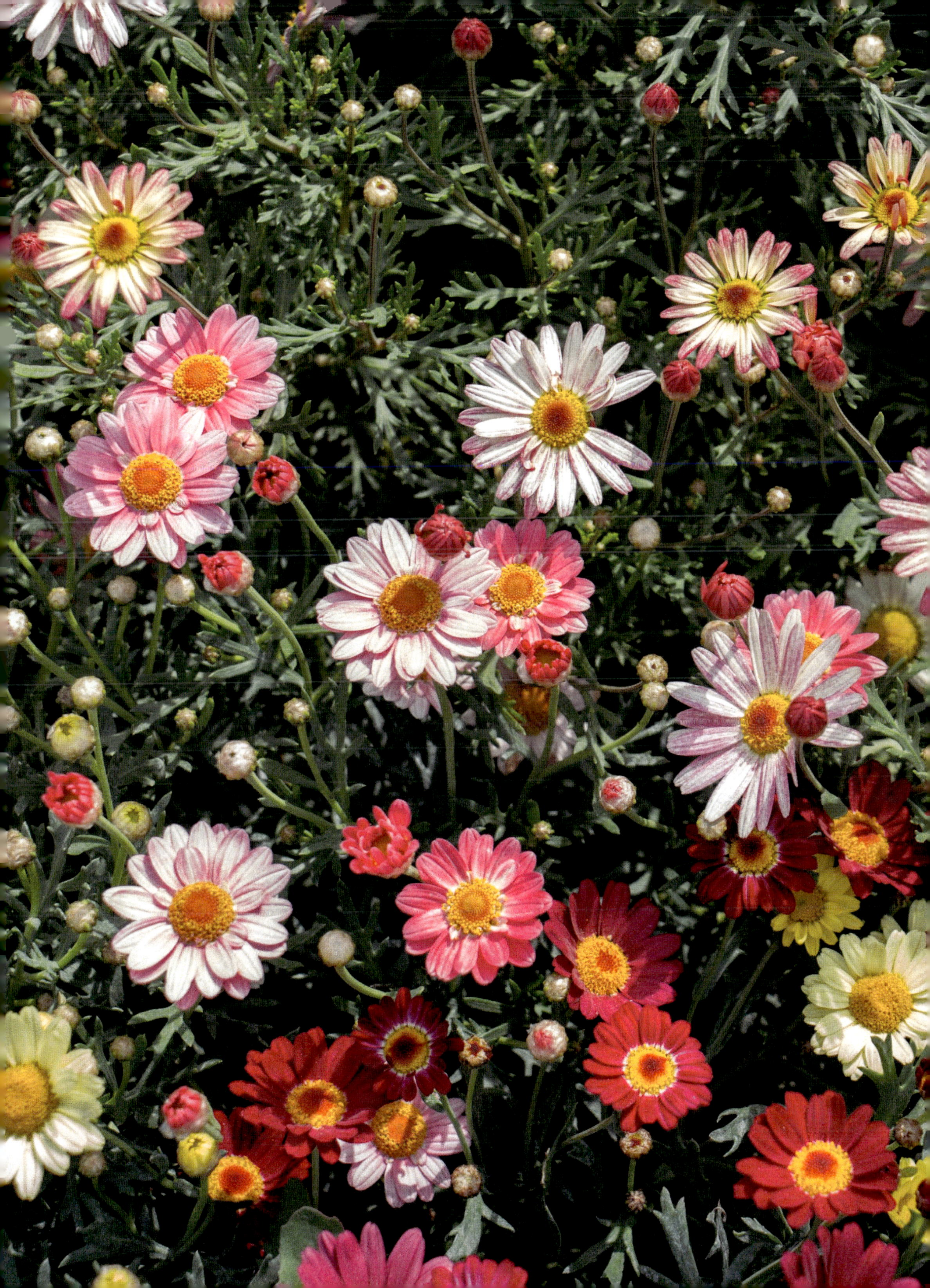

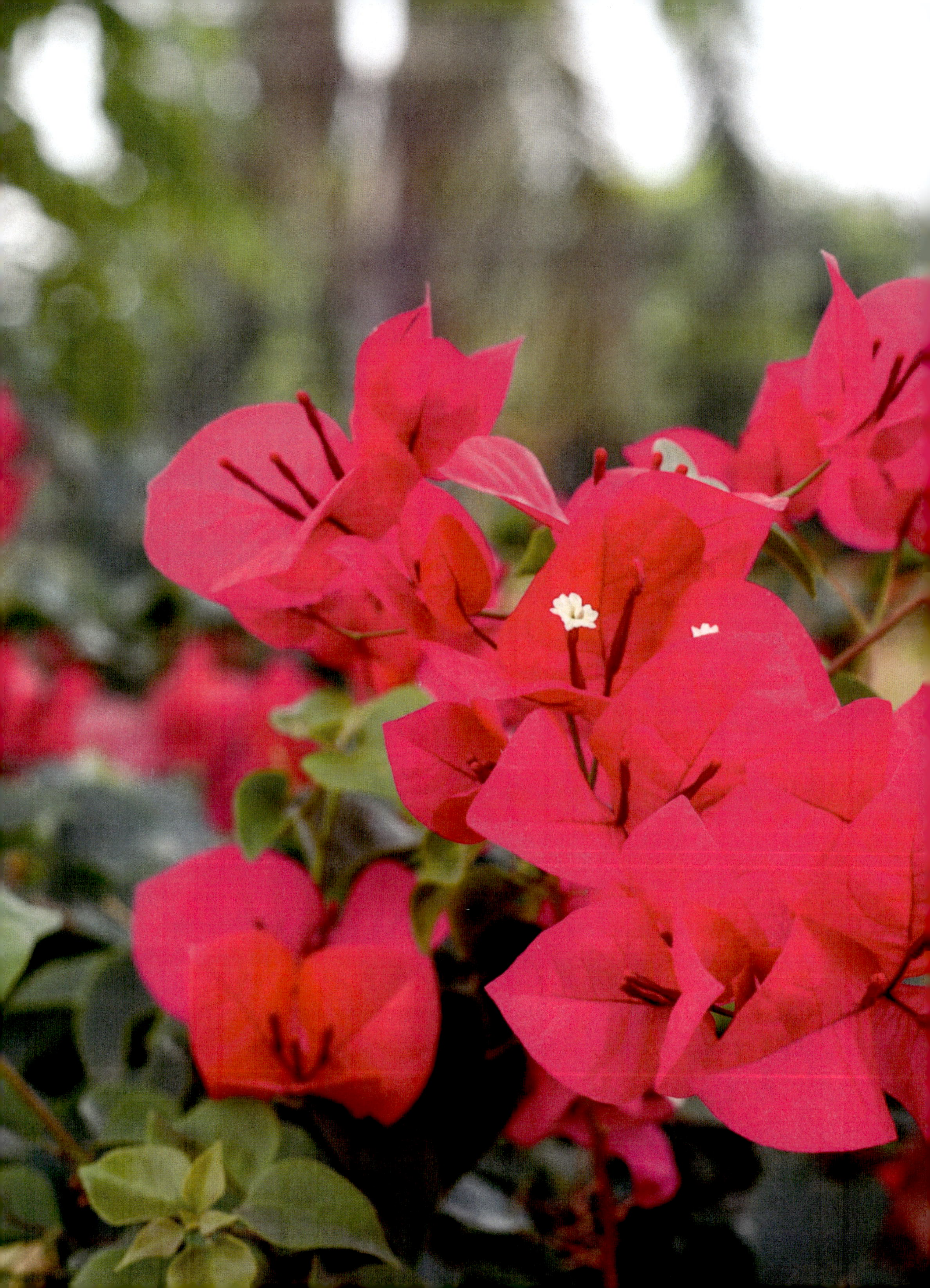

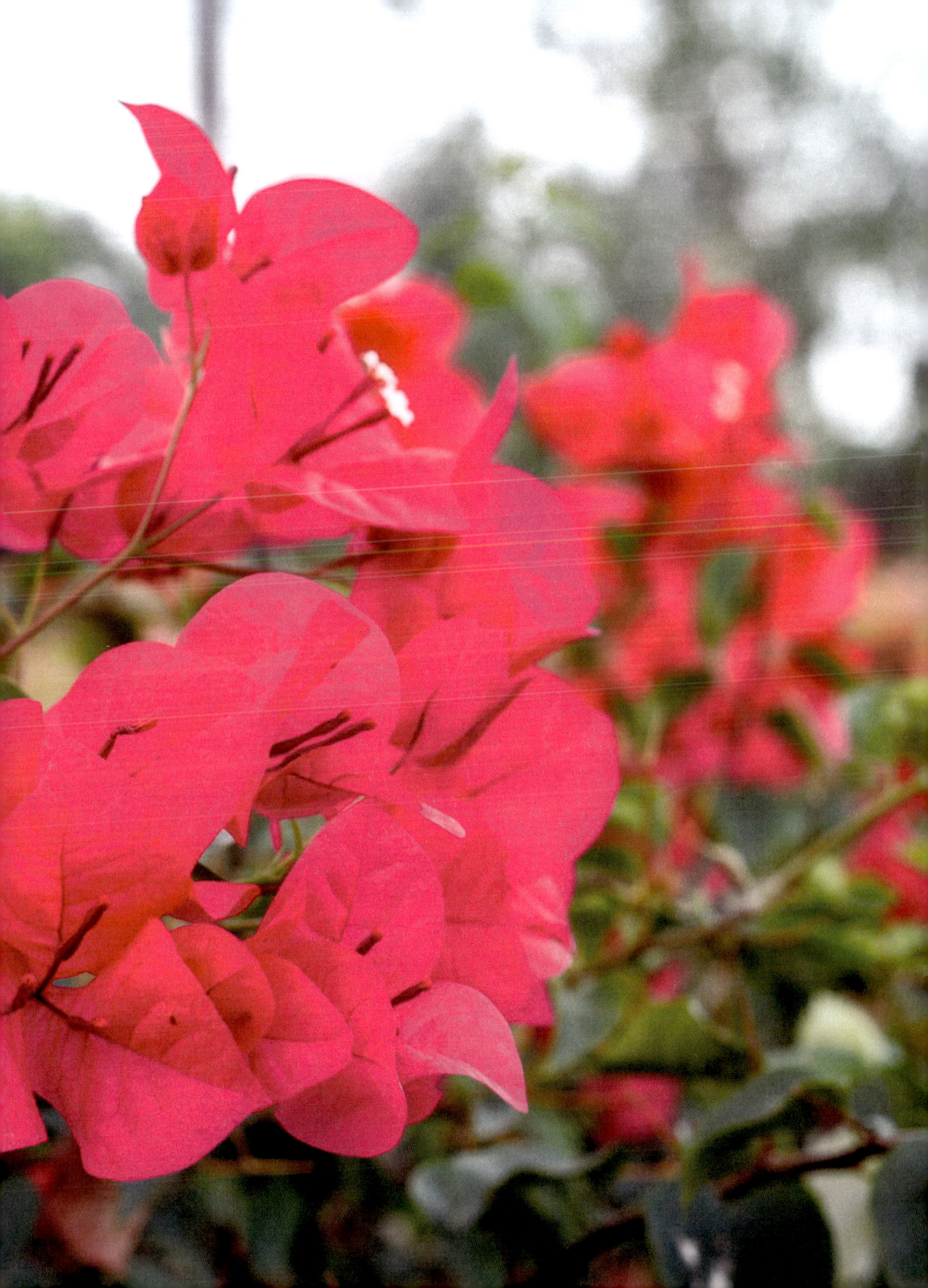

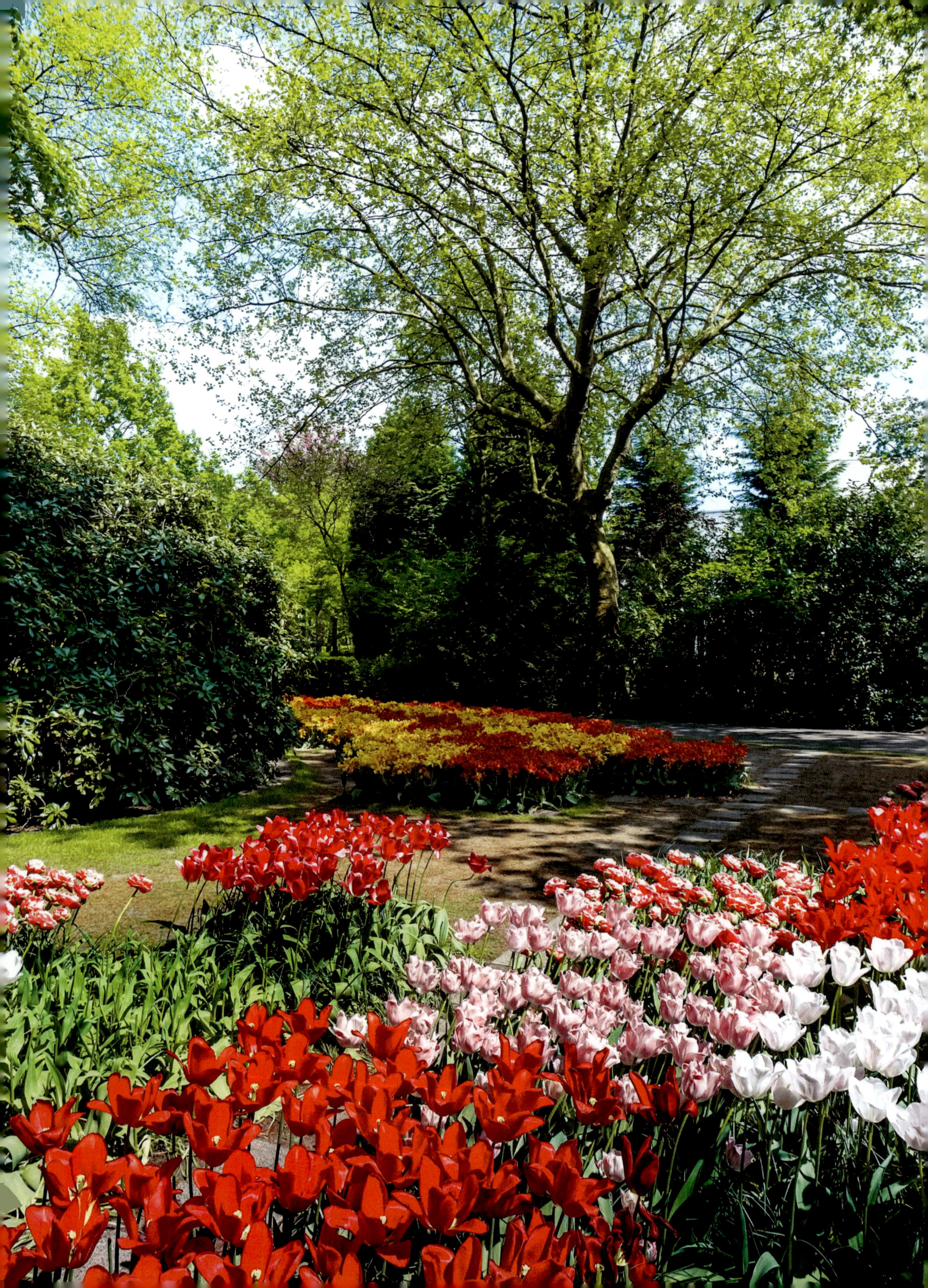

landscape

In spring, the landscape became a masterpiece of nature's artistry with the colorful scenes, the sweet smells and scents of the flowers, and the sound of the birds.

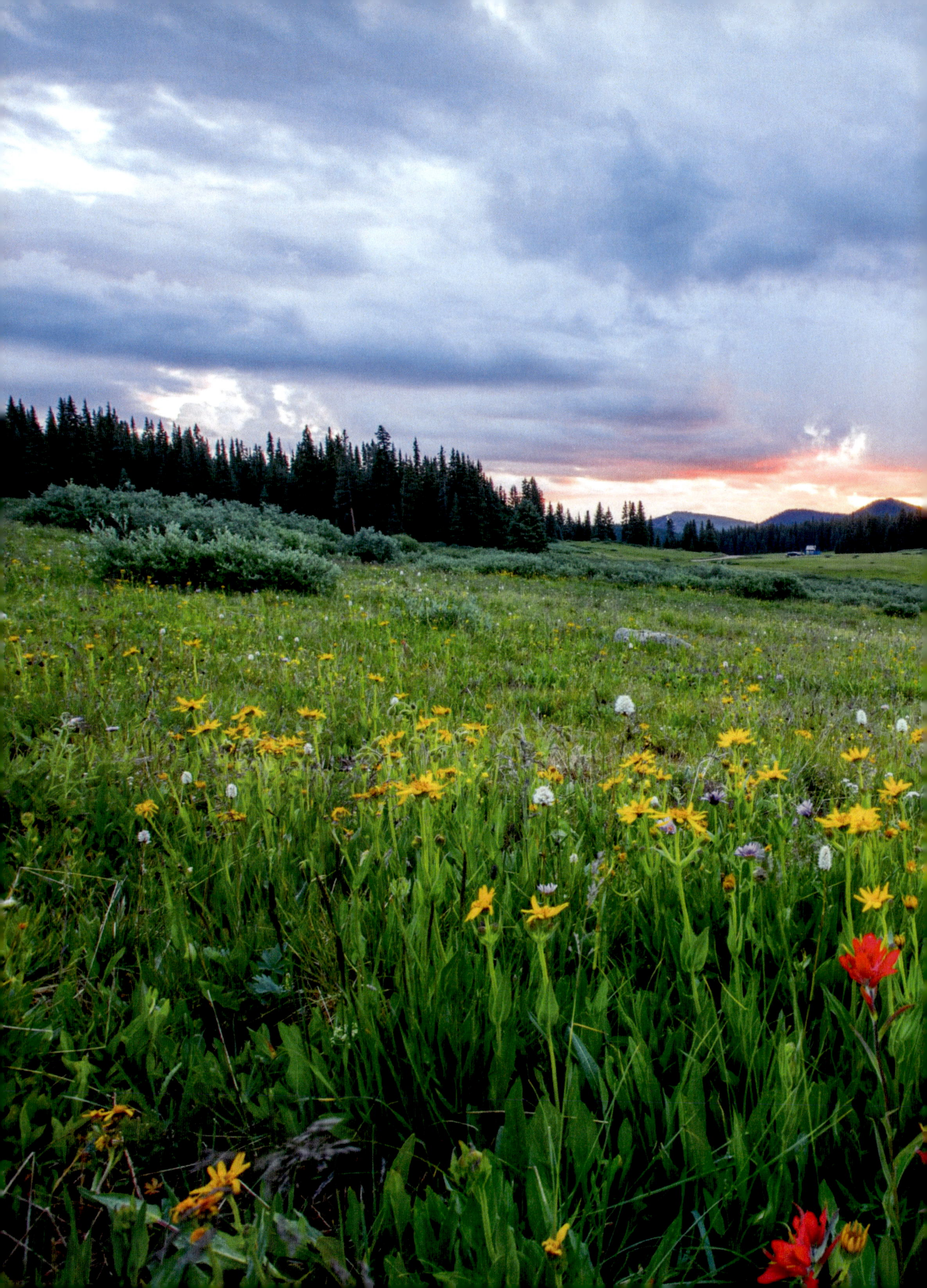

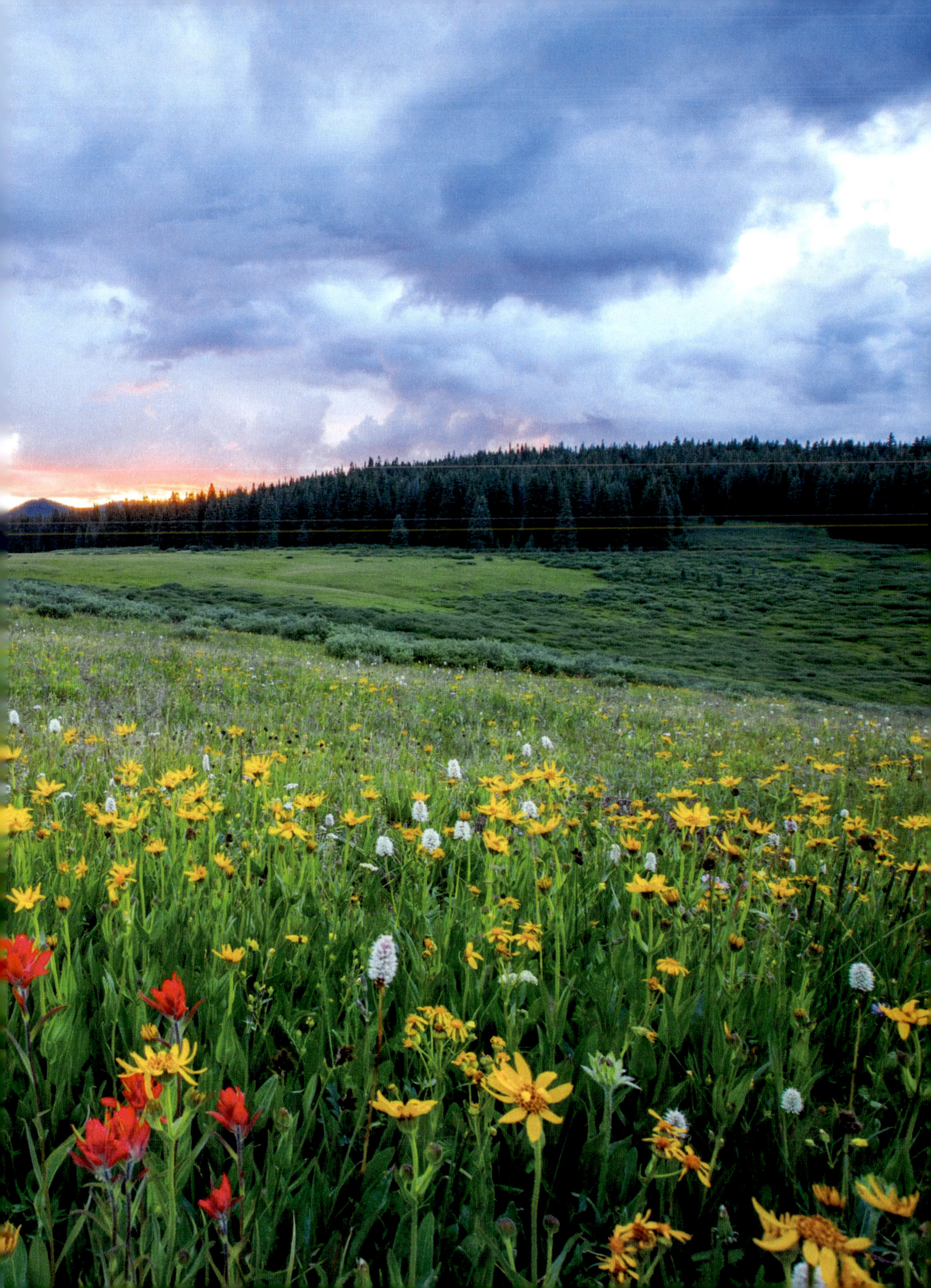

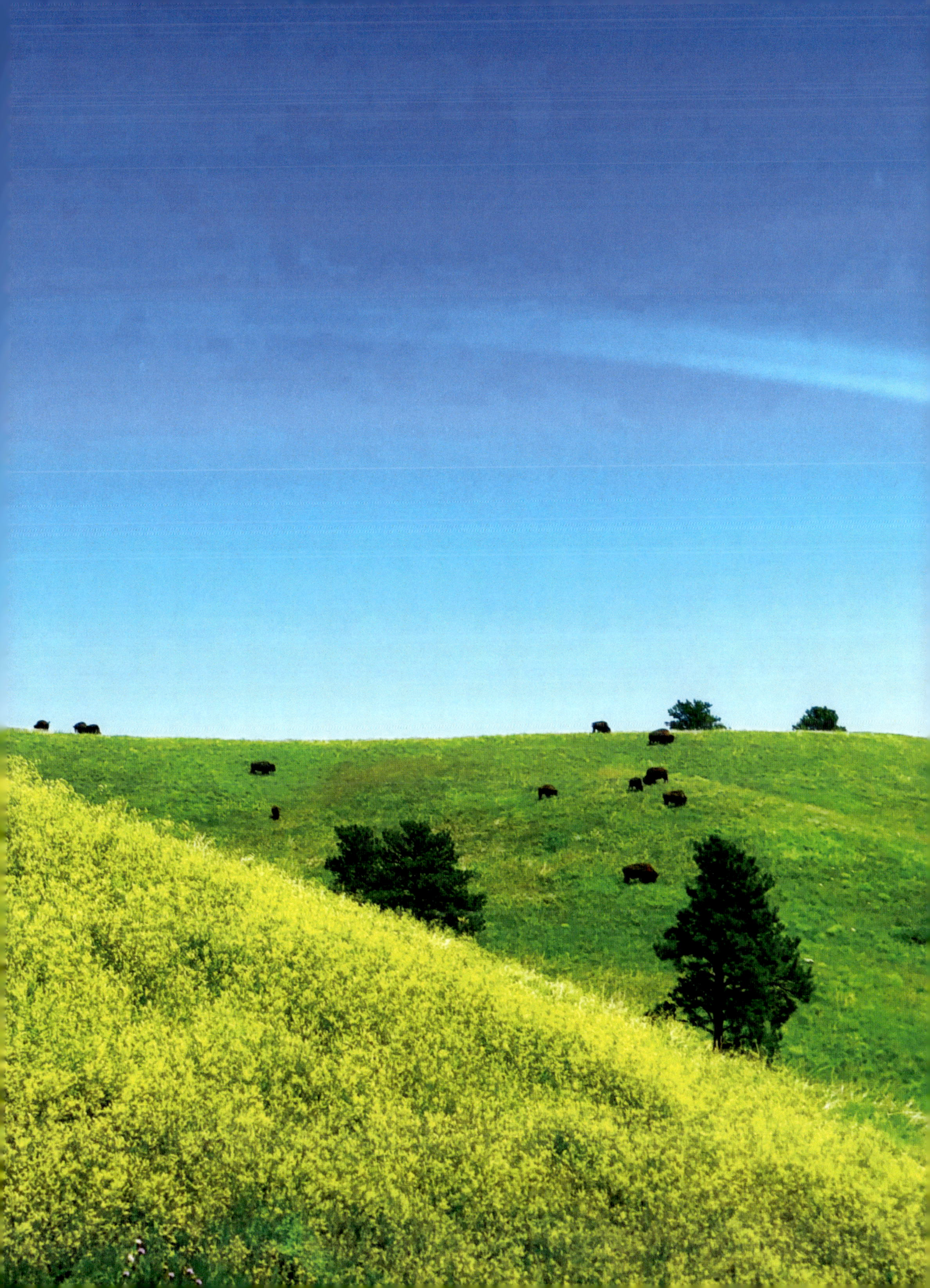

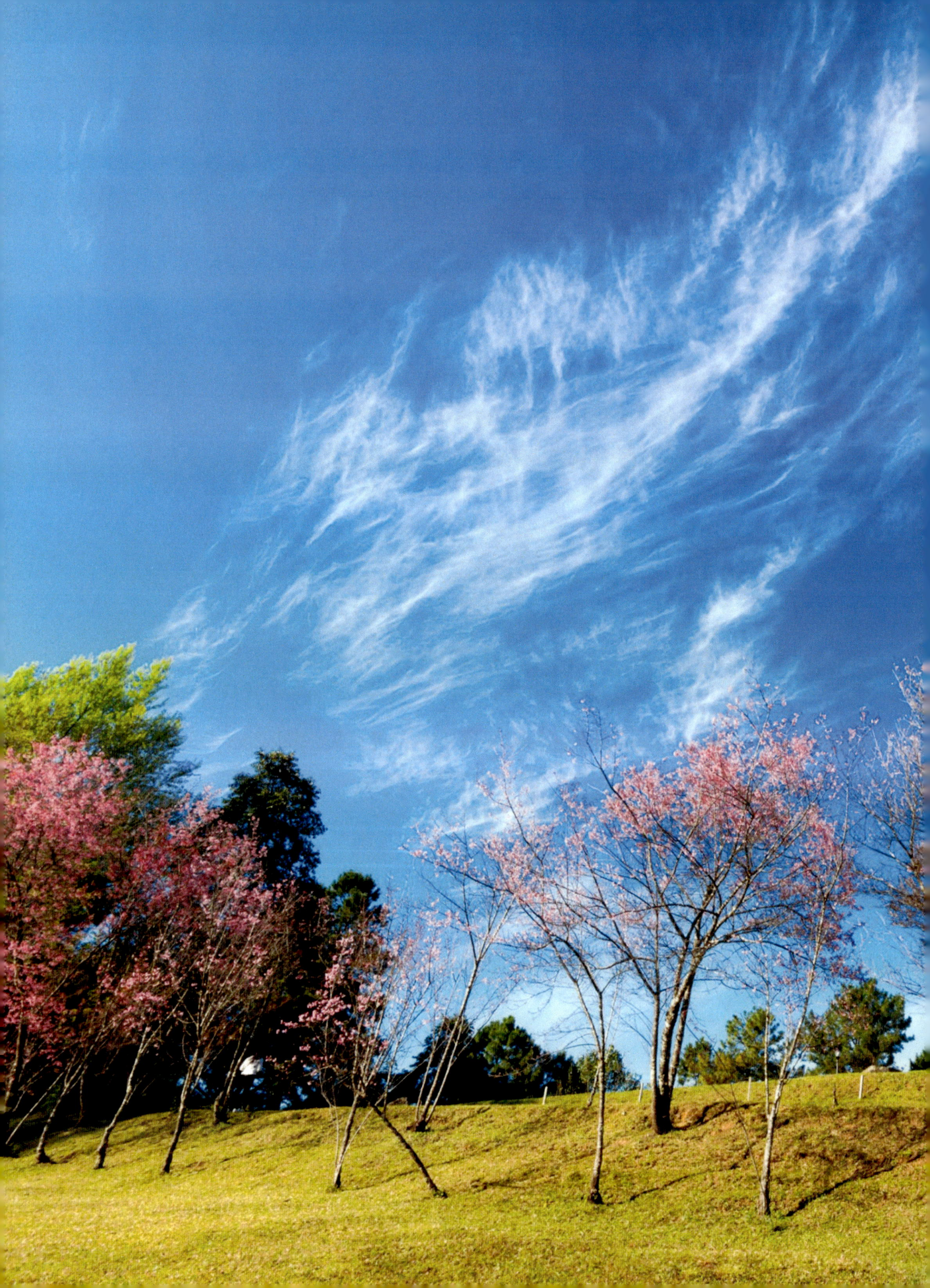

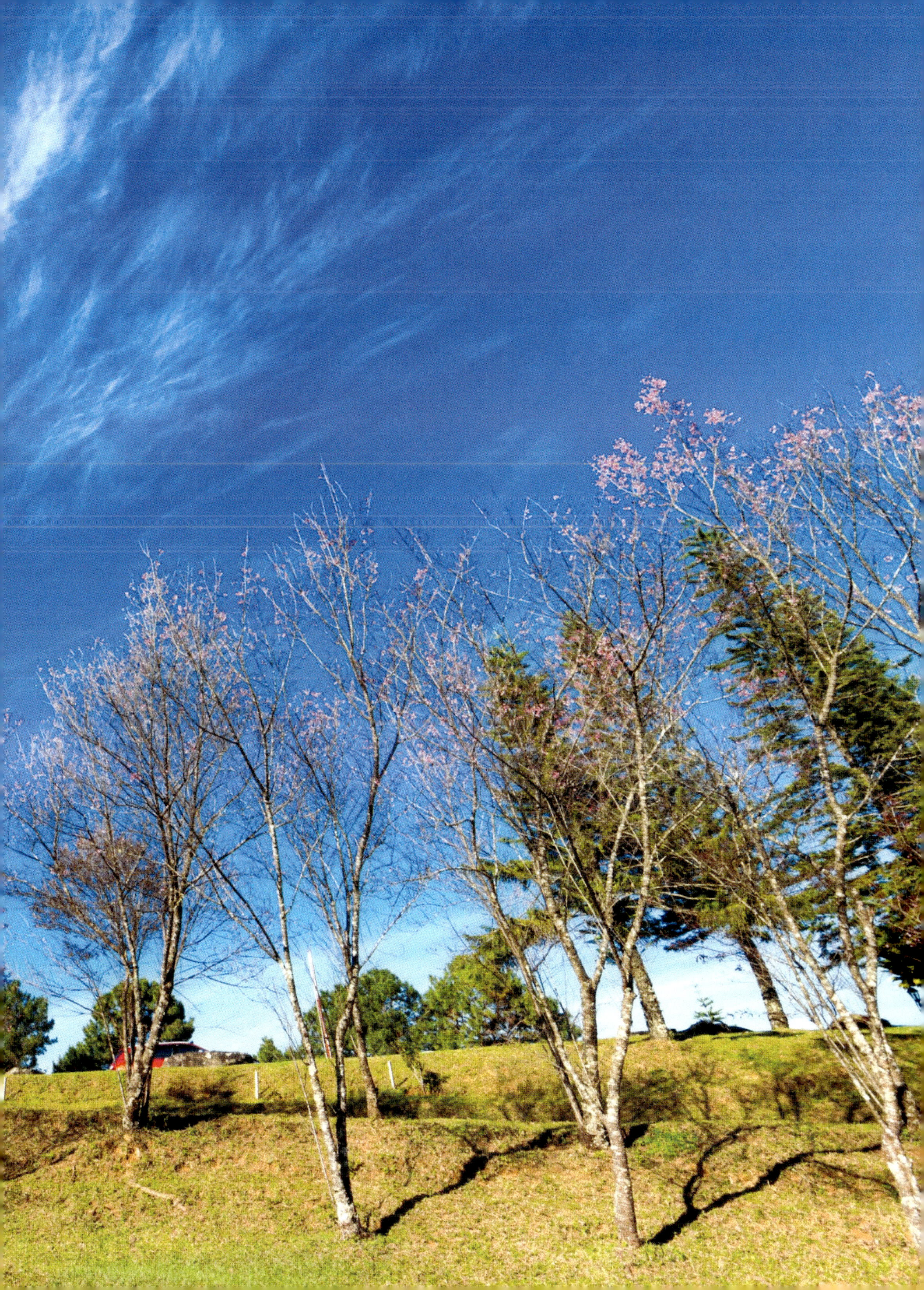

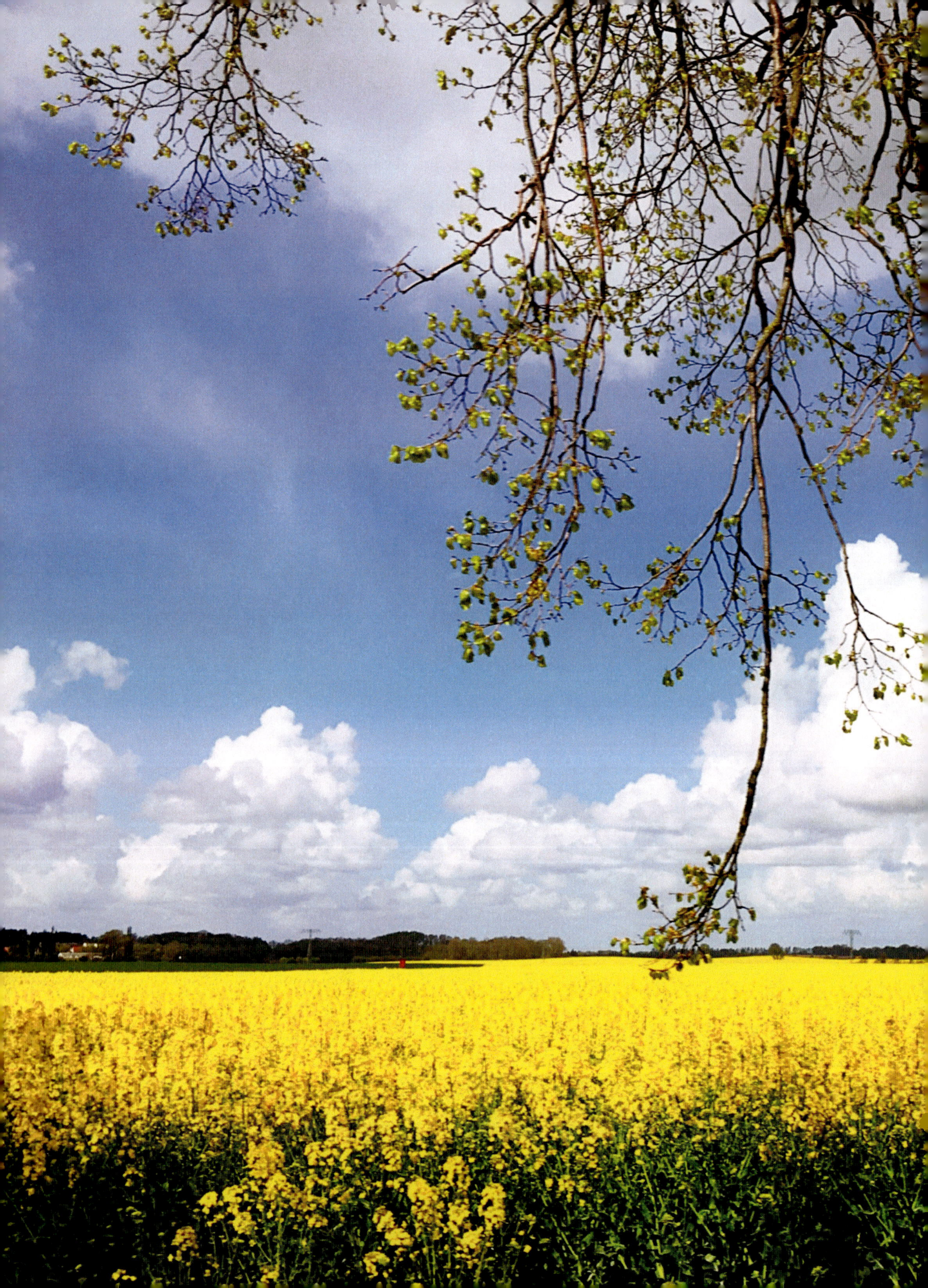

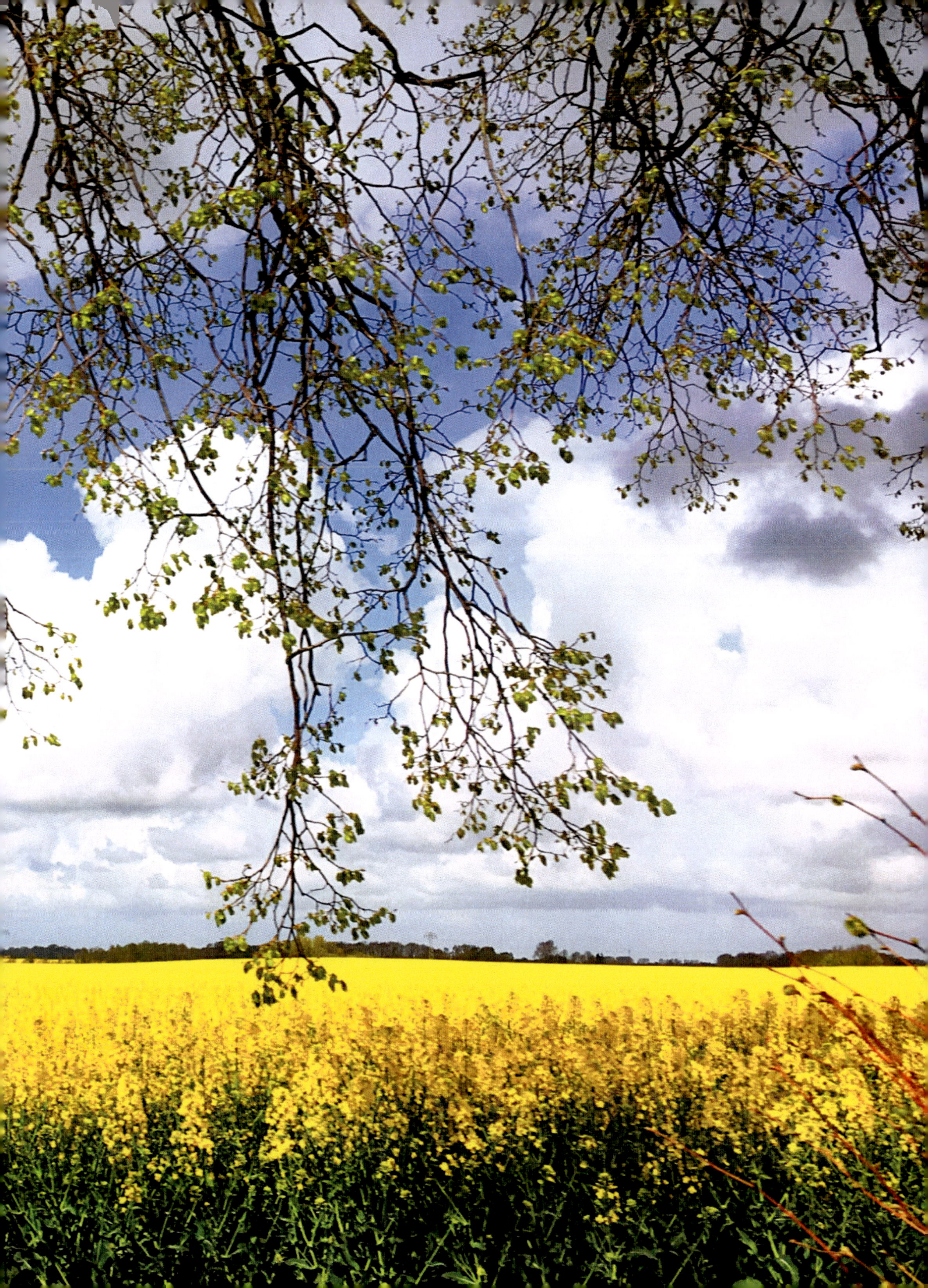

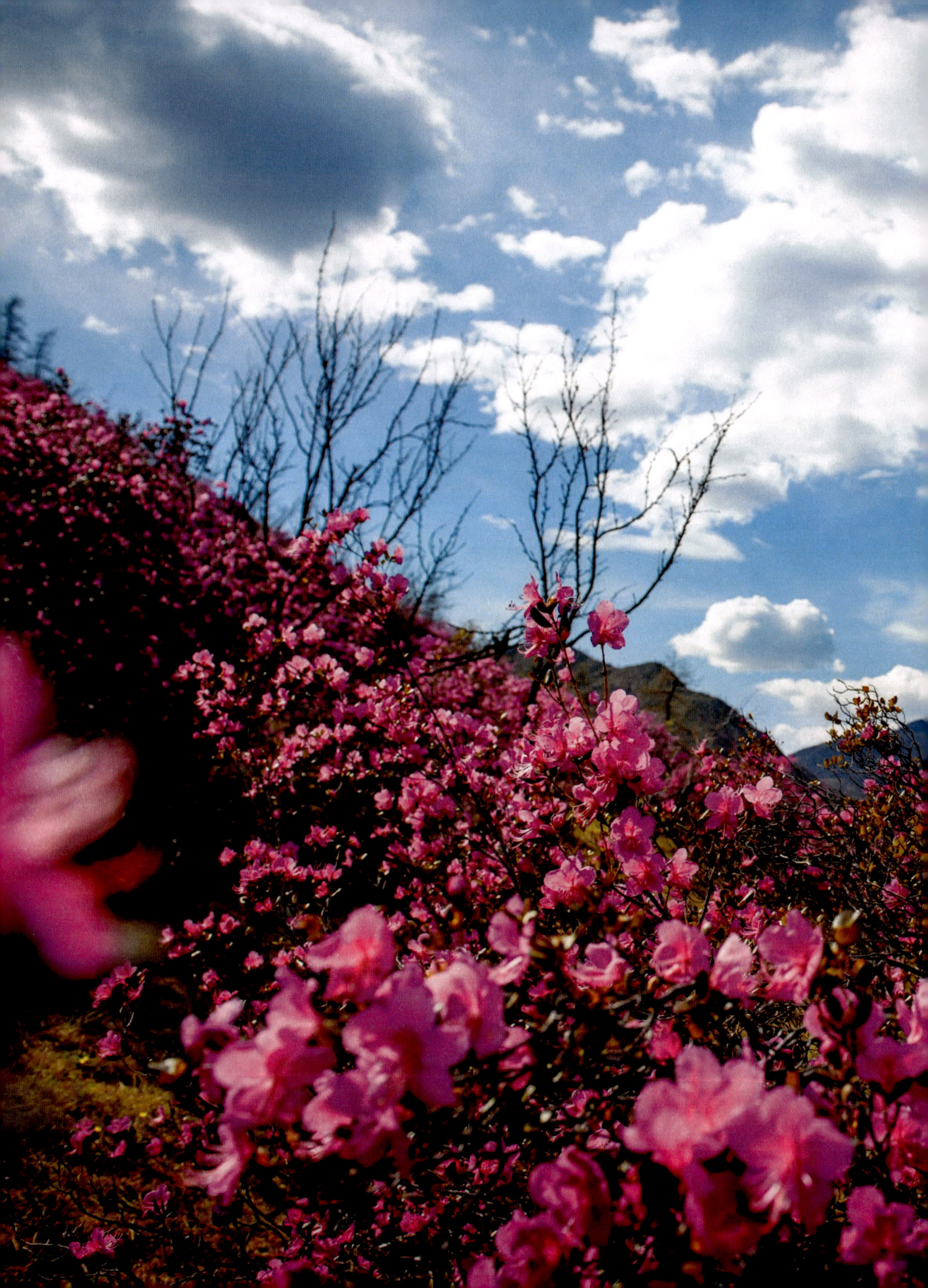

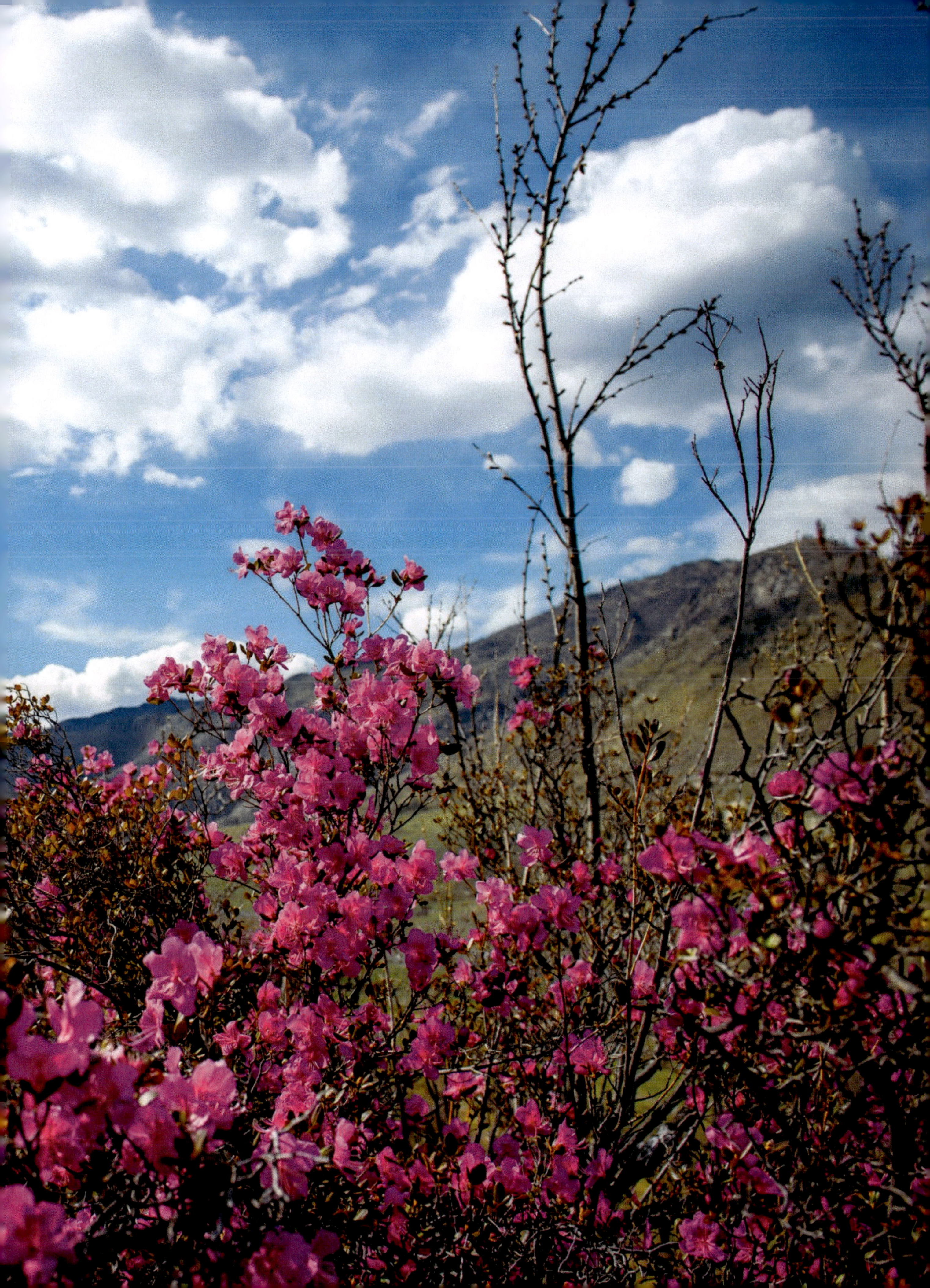

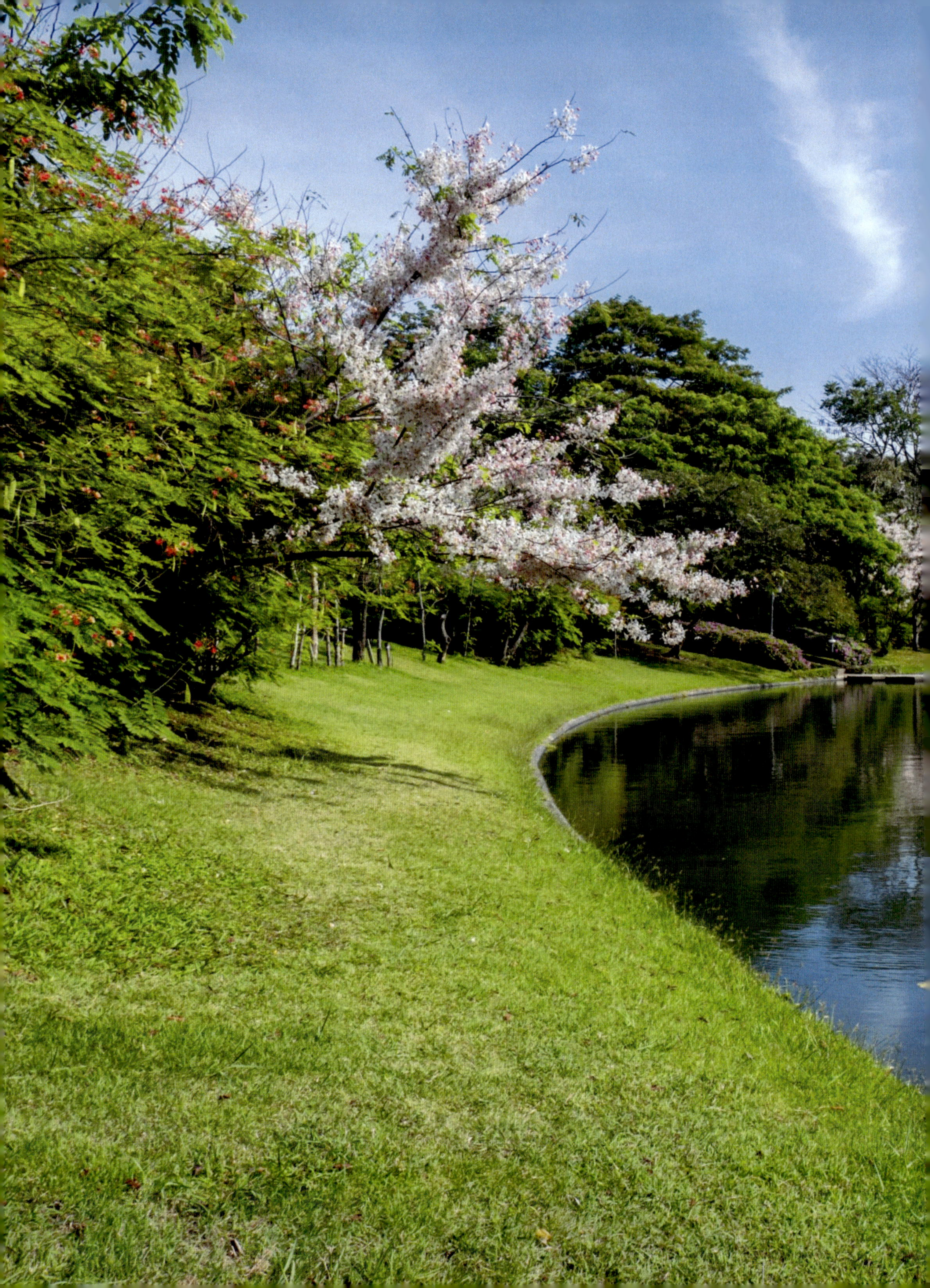

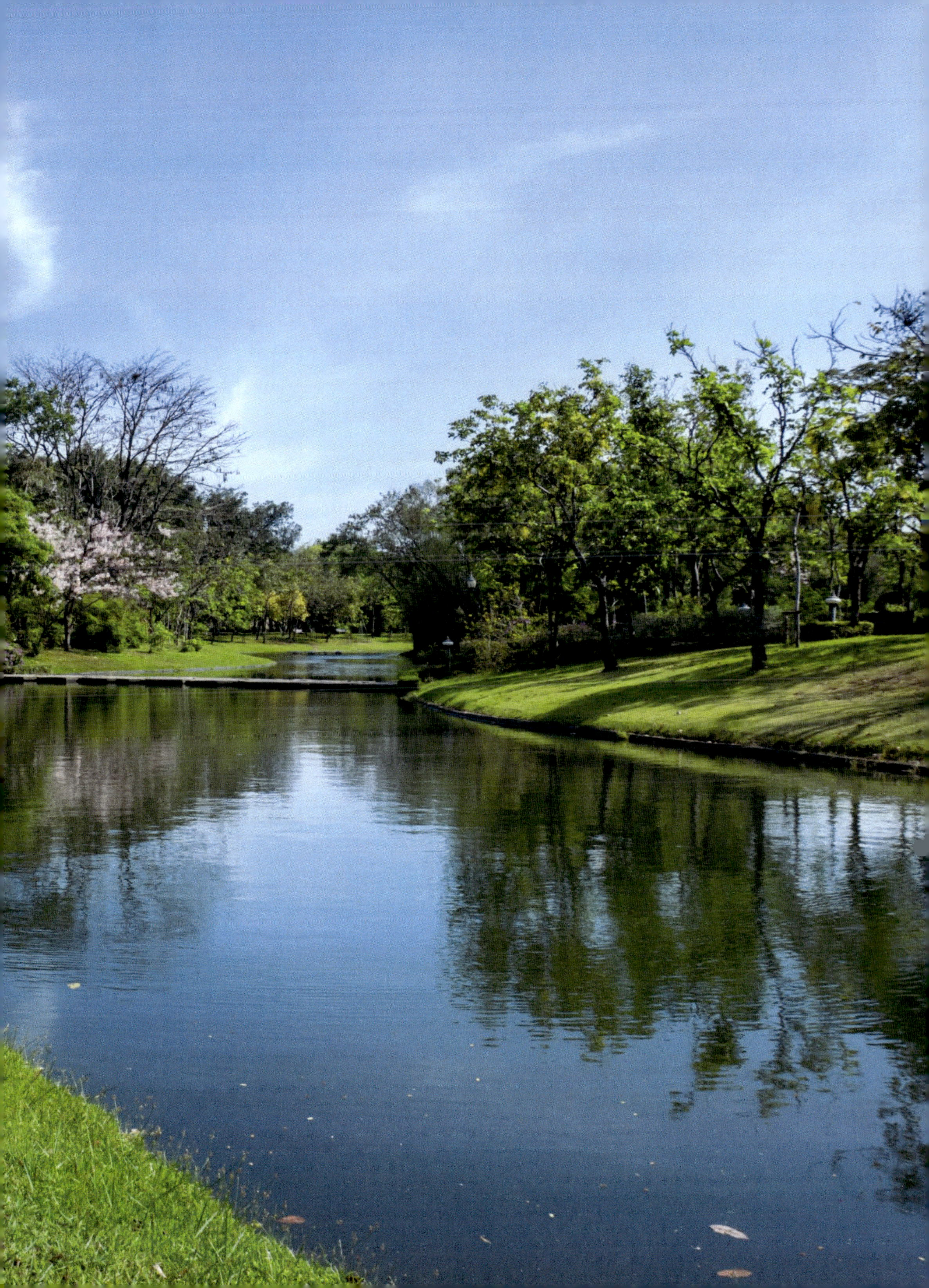

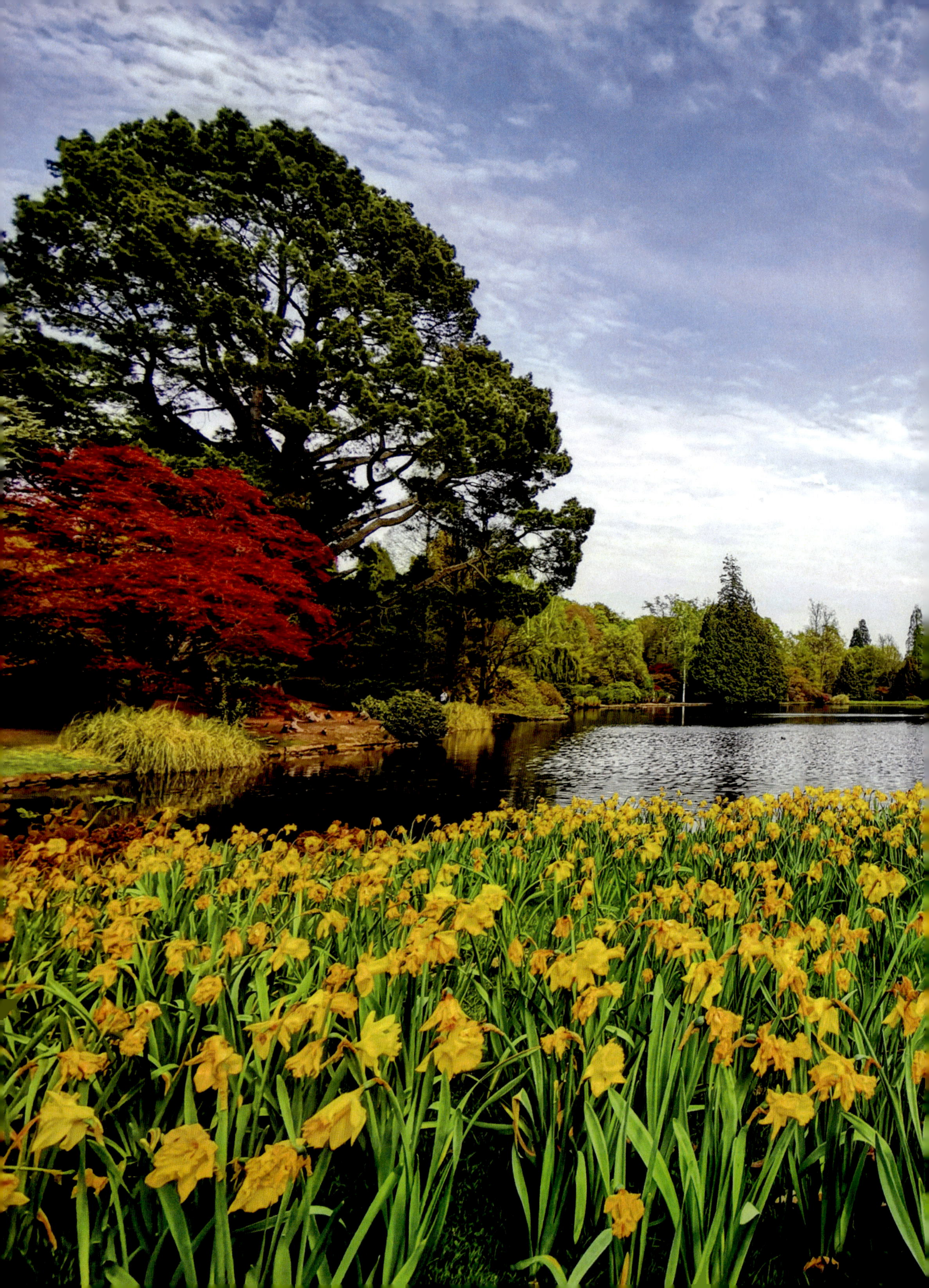

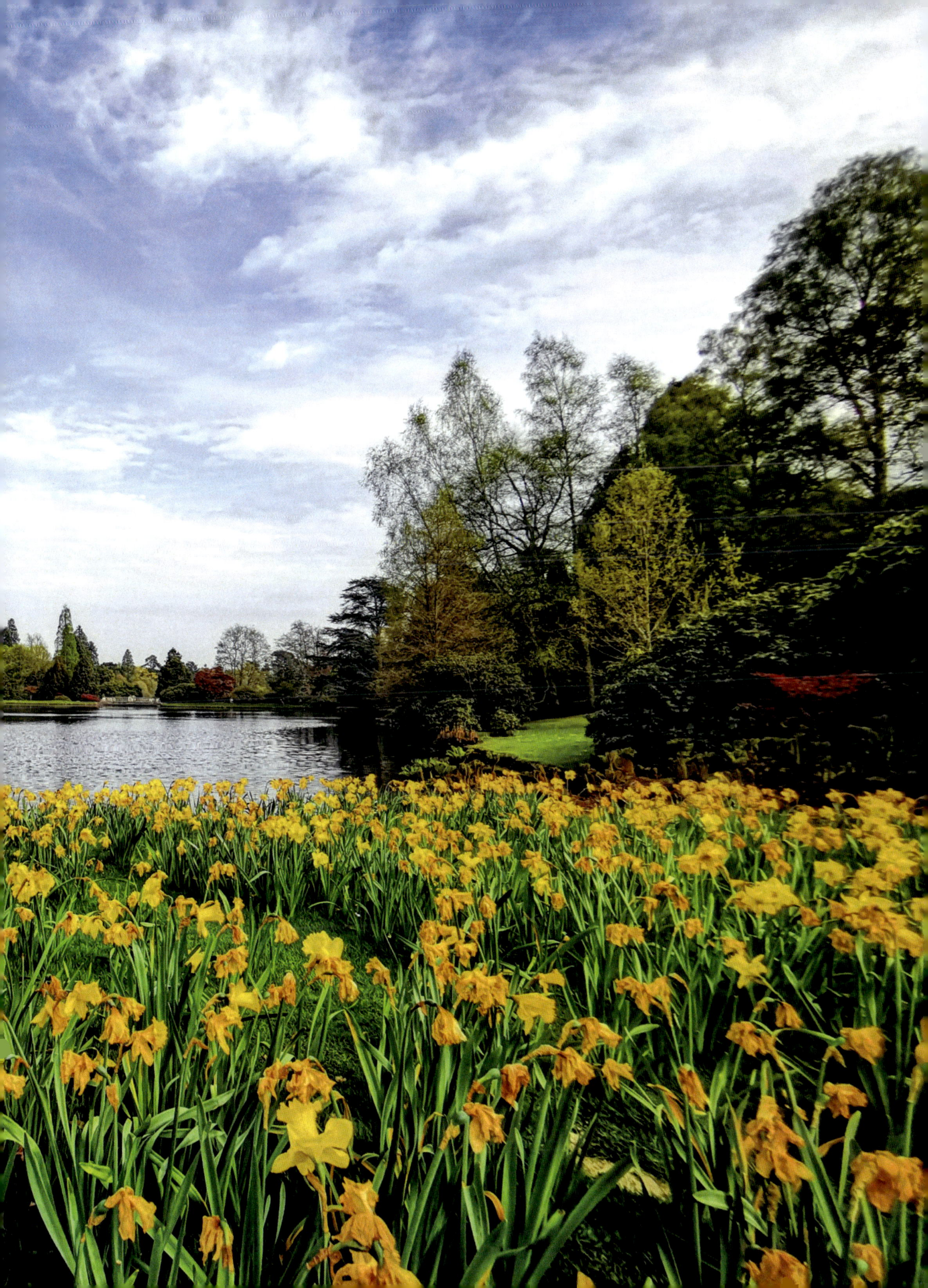

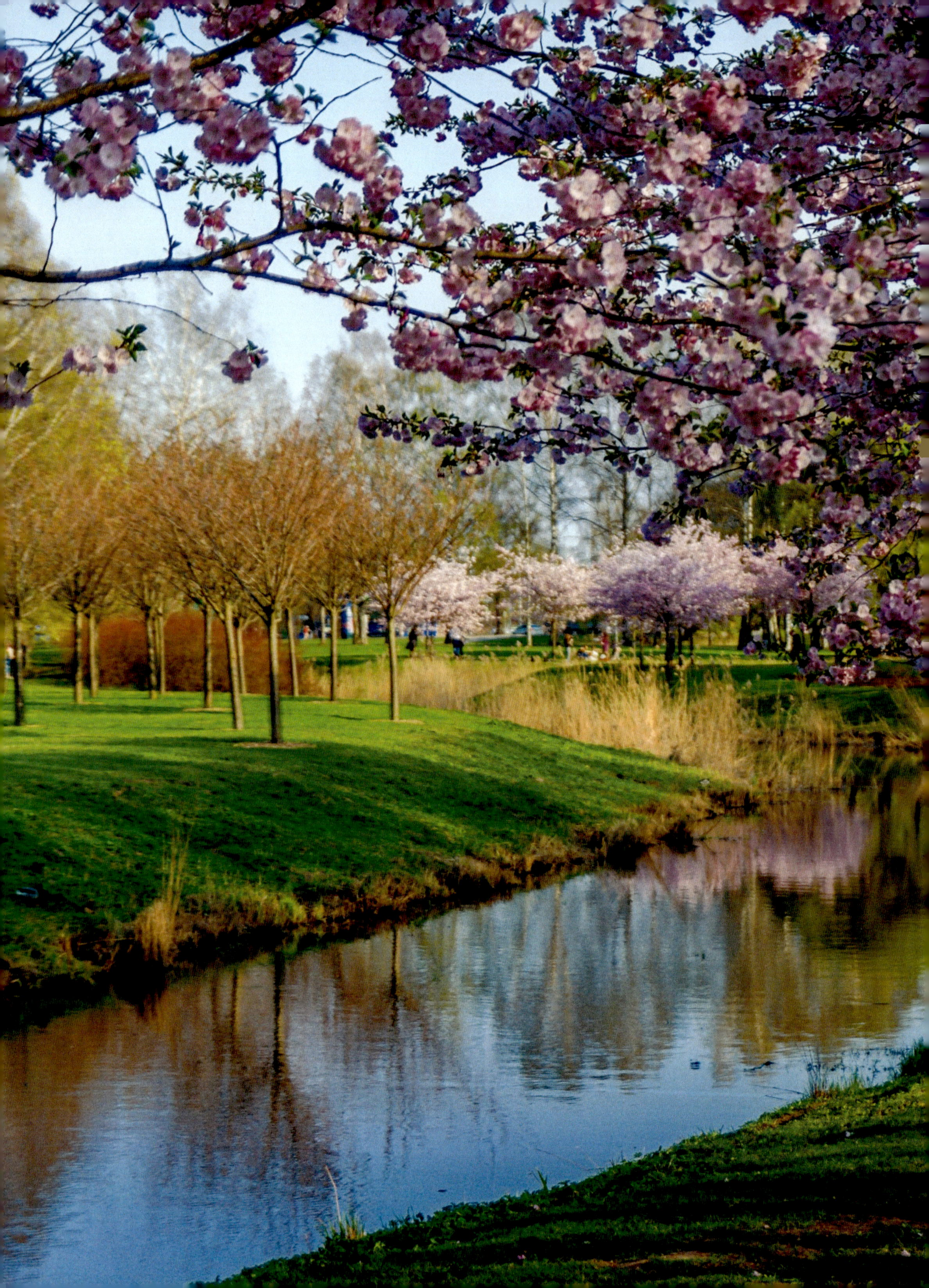

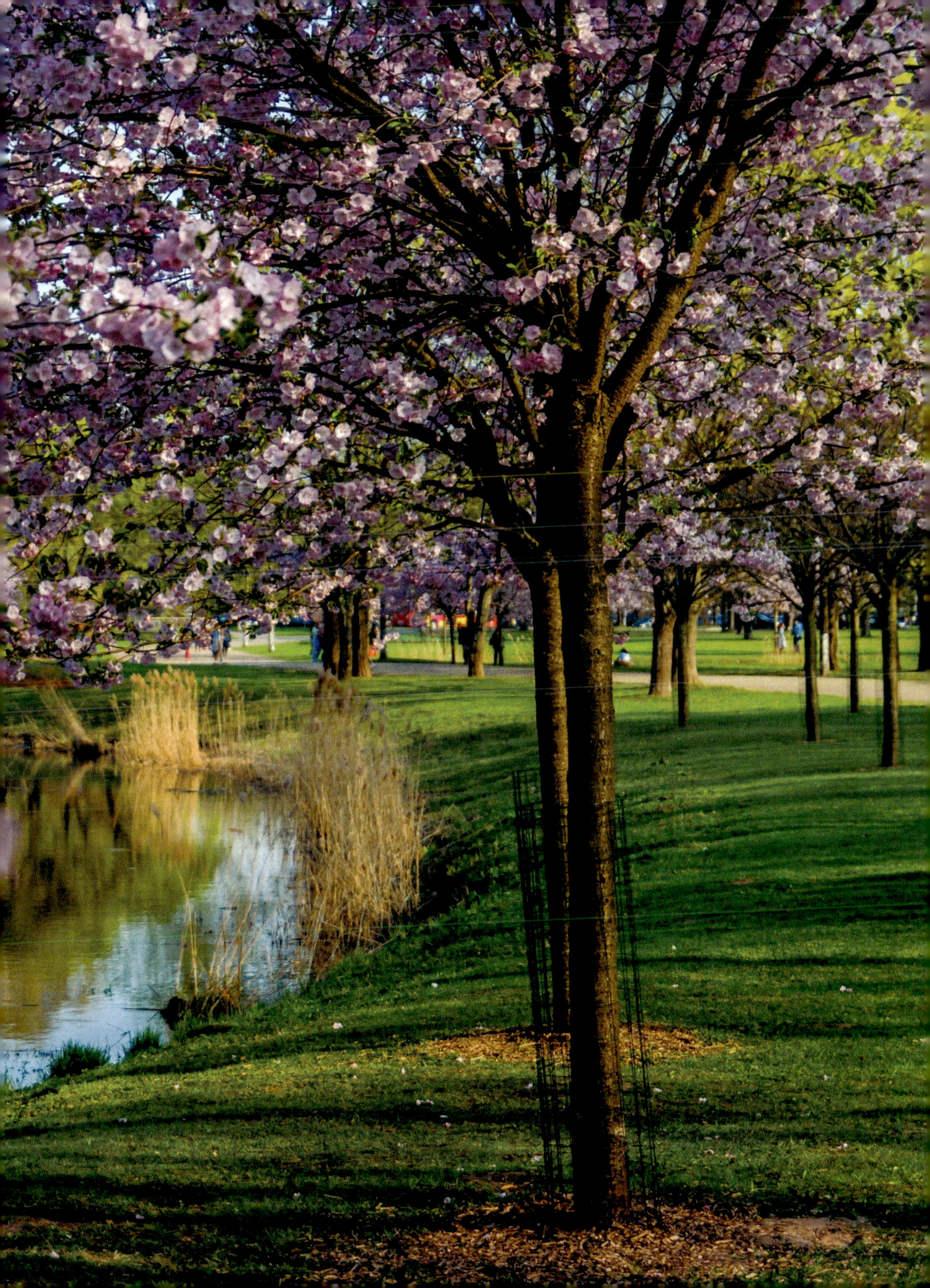

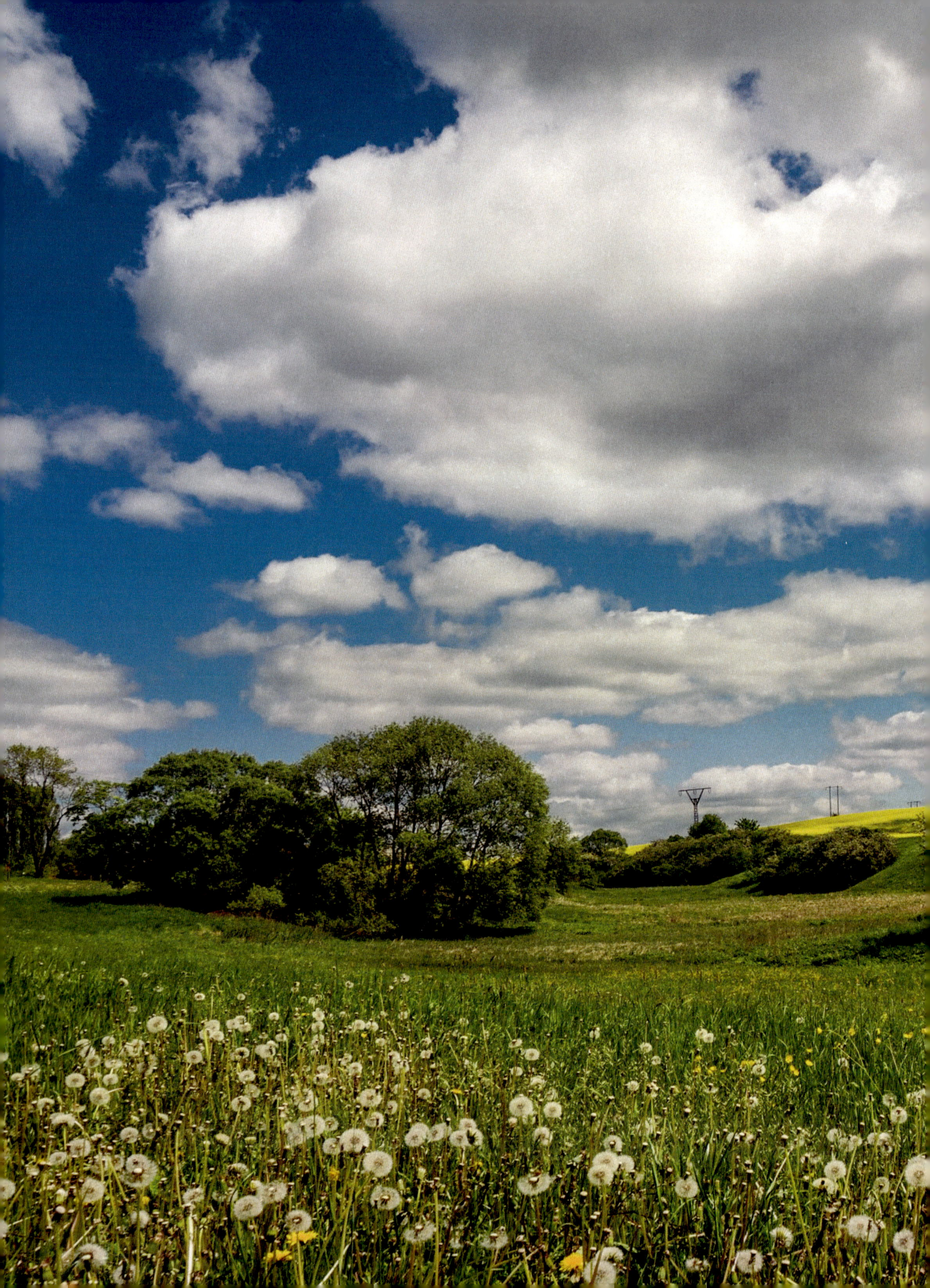

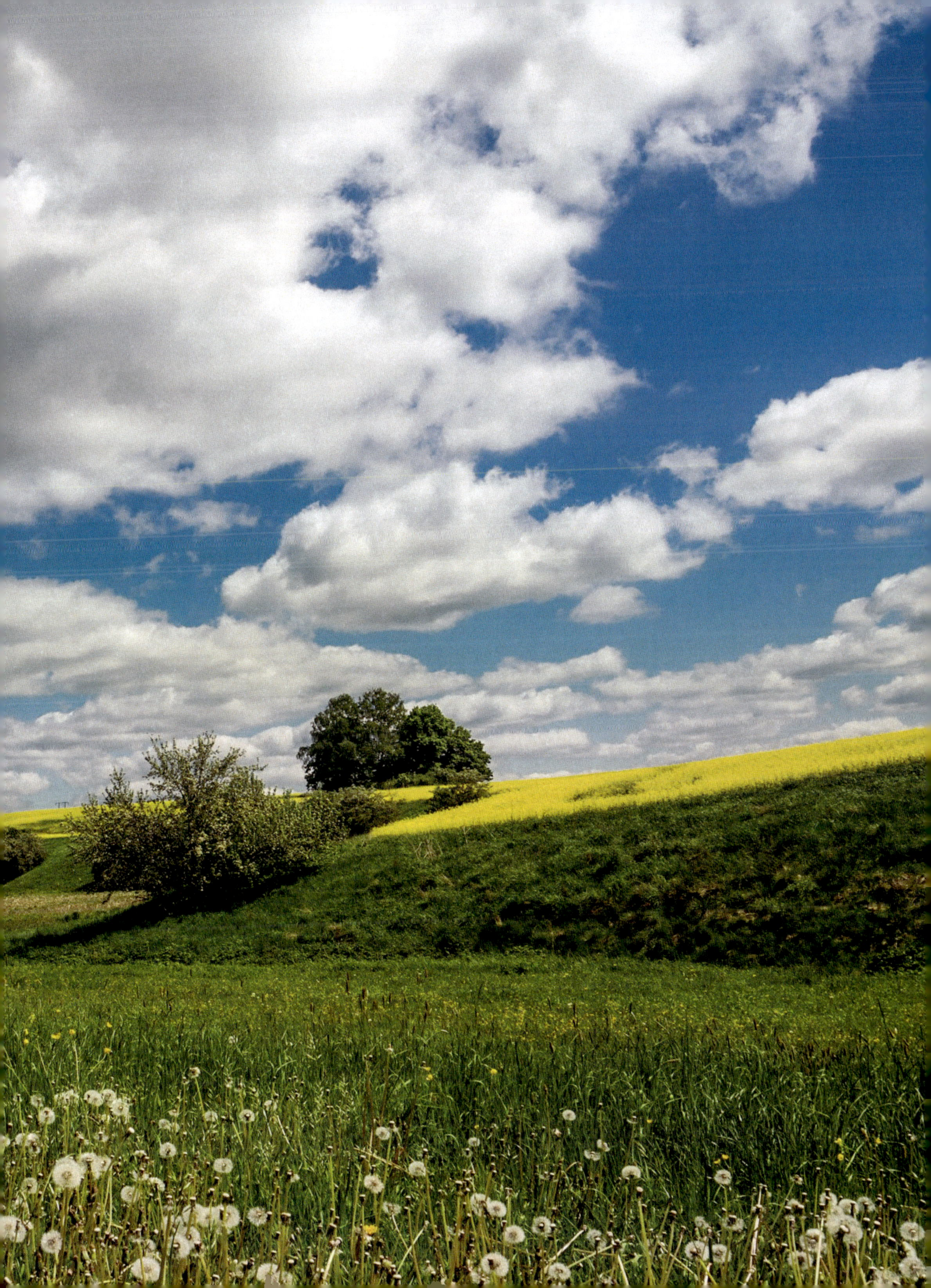

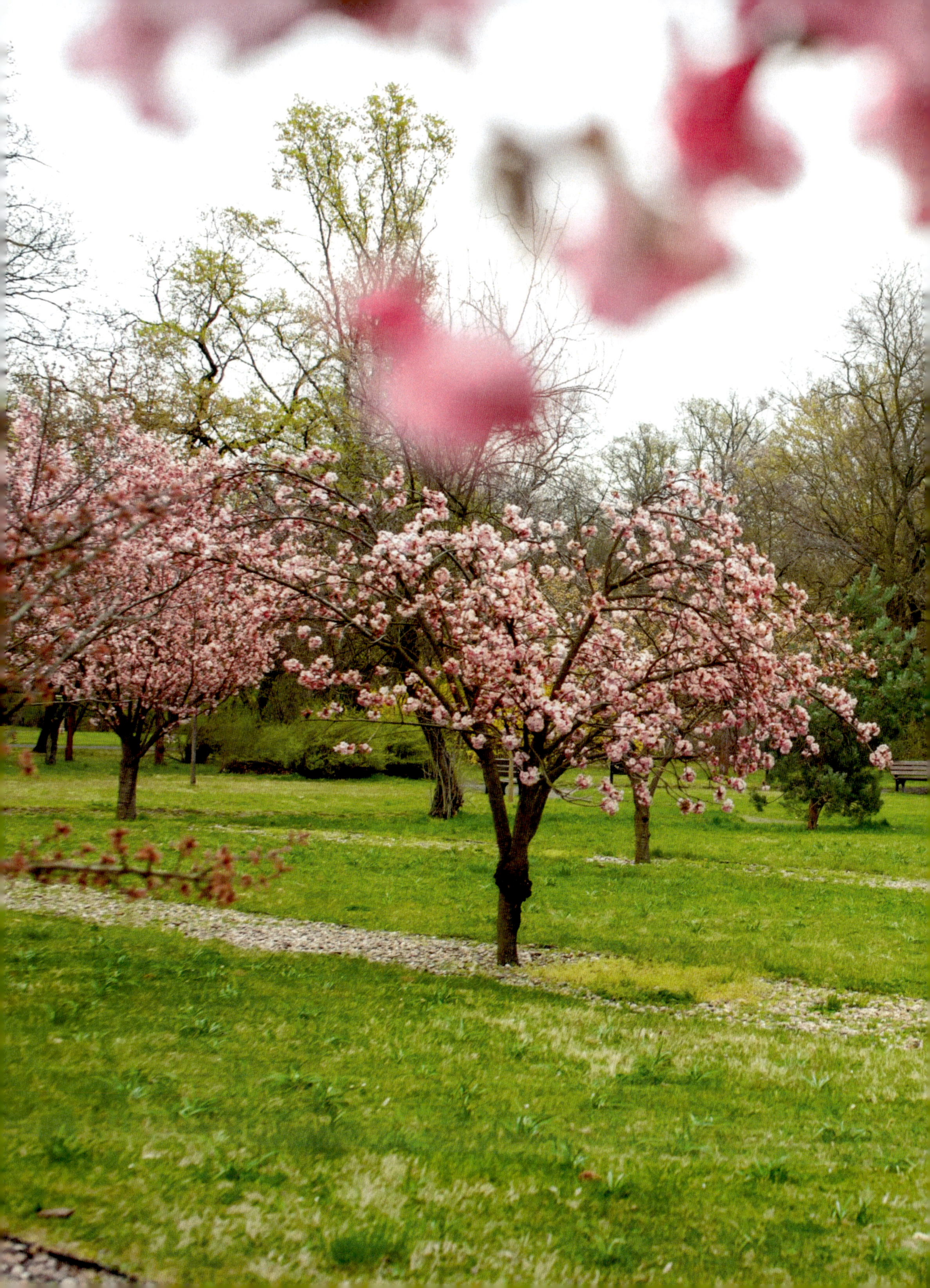

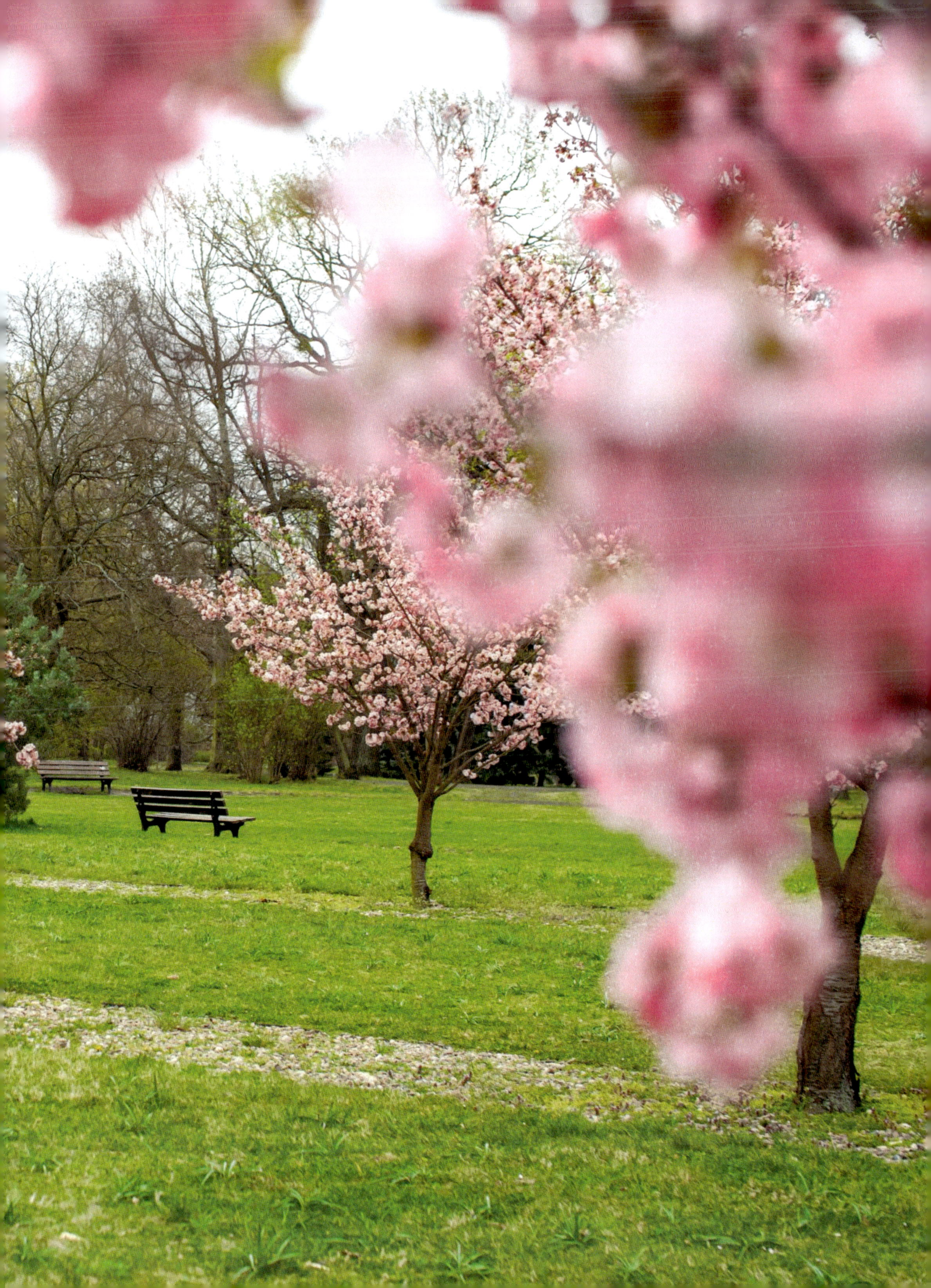

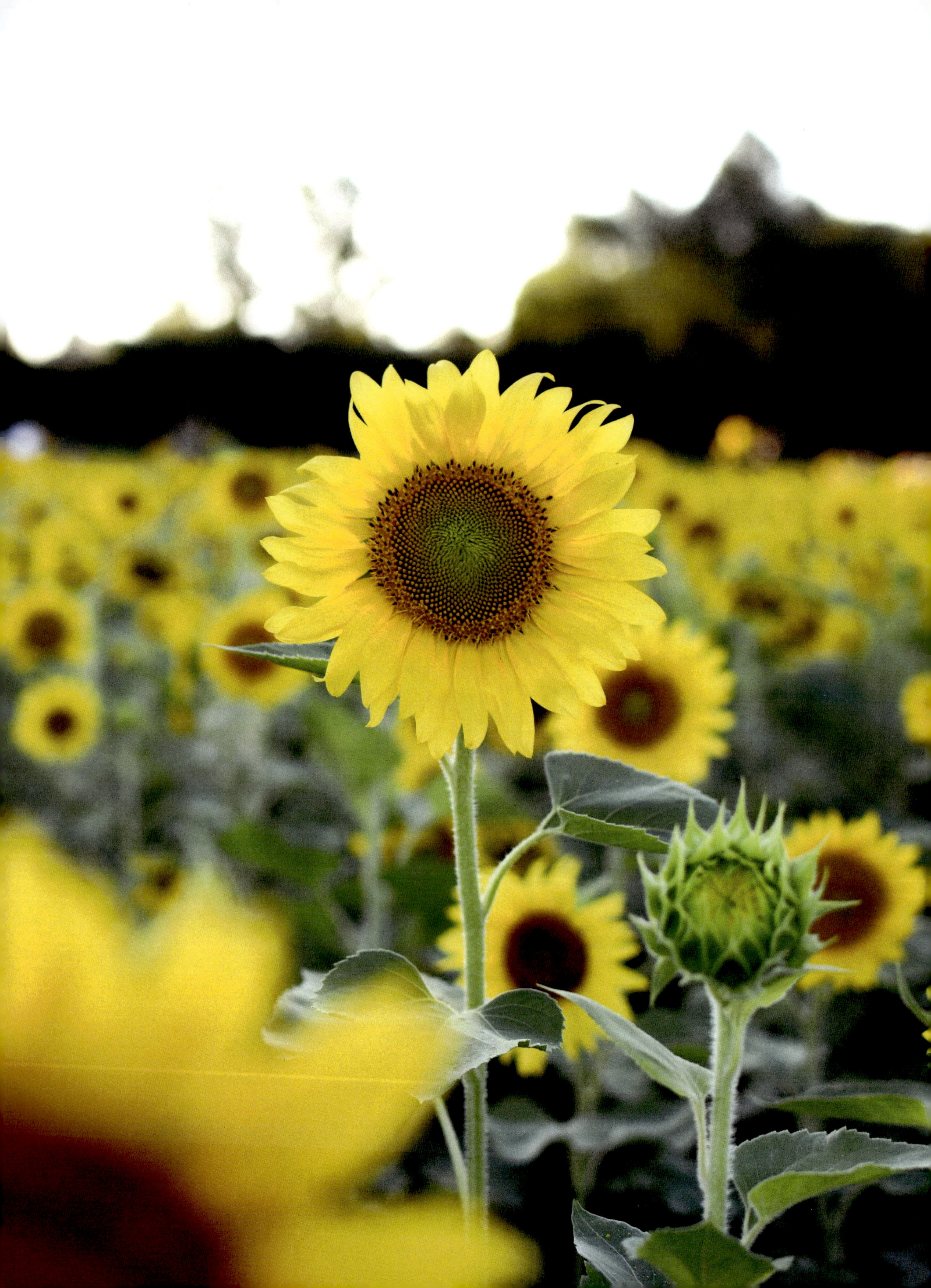

During spring, the landscape is alive and has those gorgeous bursts of magical colors as the flowers bloom and the trees sprout new tiny little leaves in shades of green, pink, purple, and yellow.

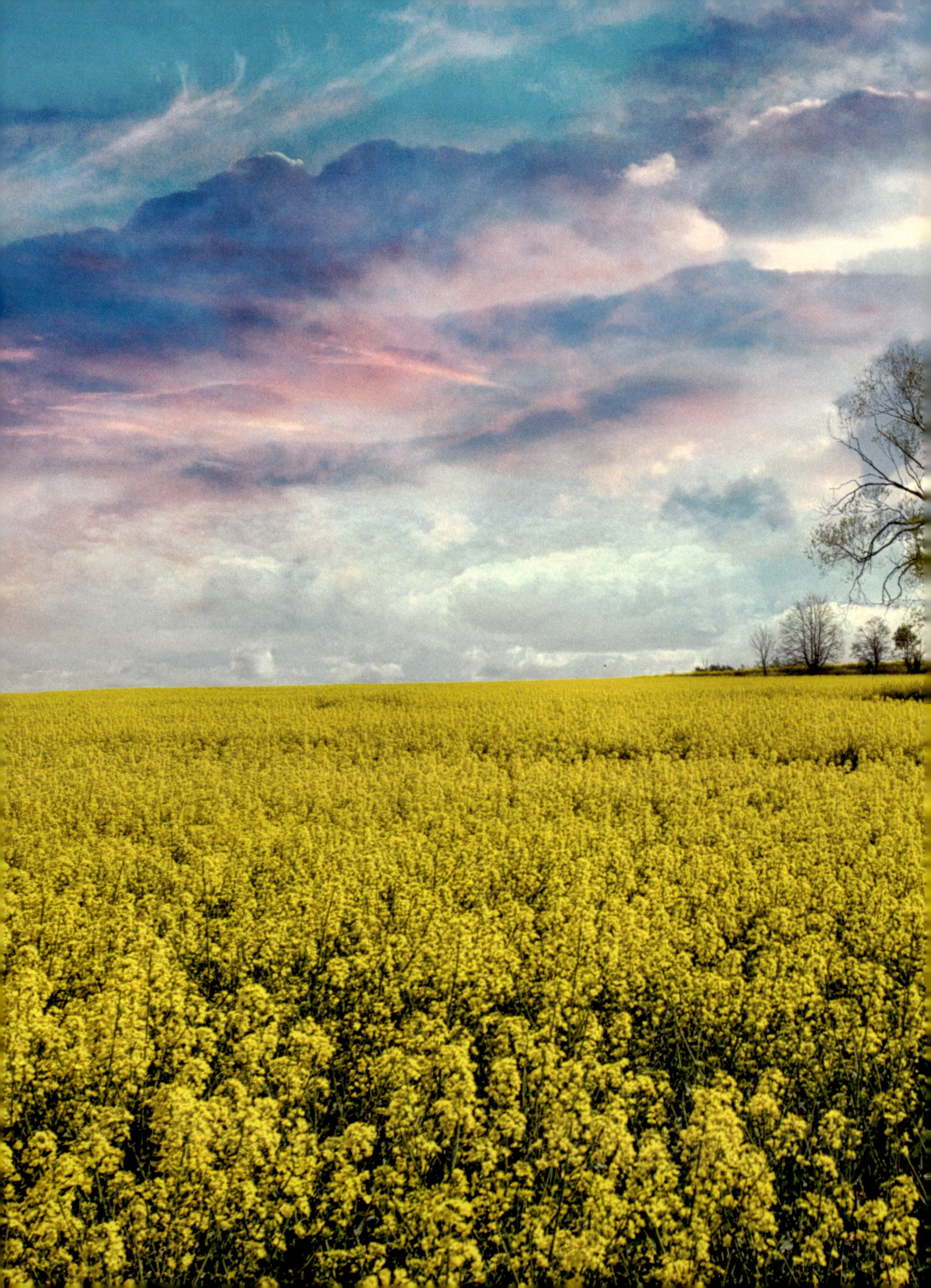

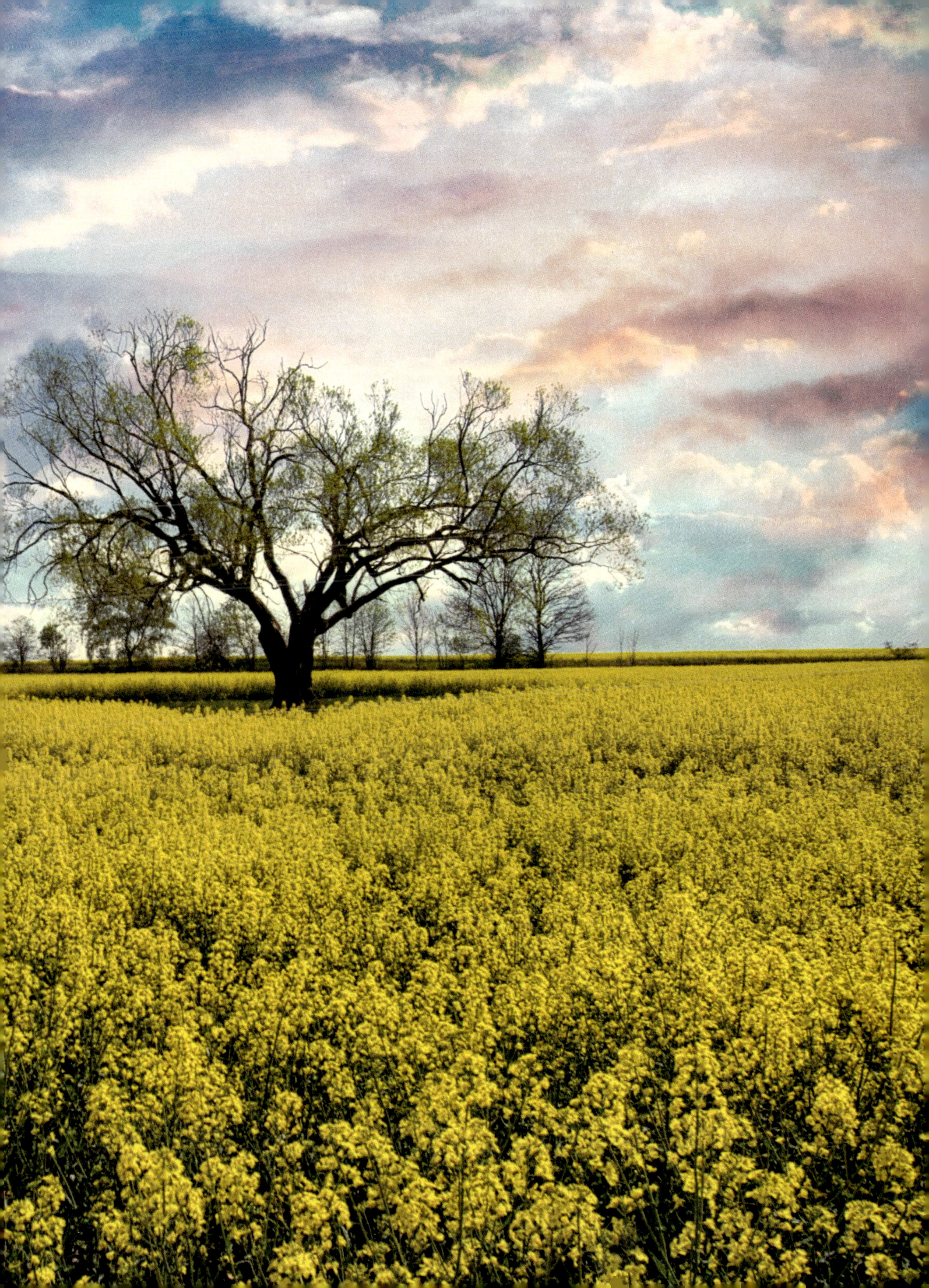

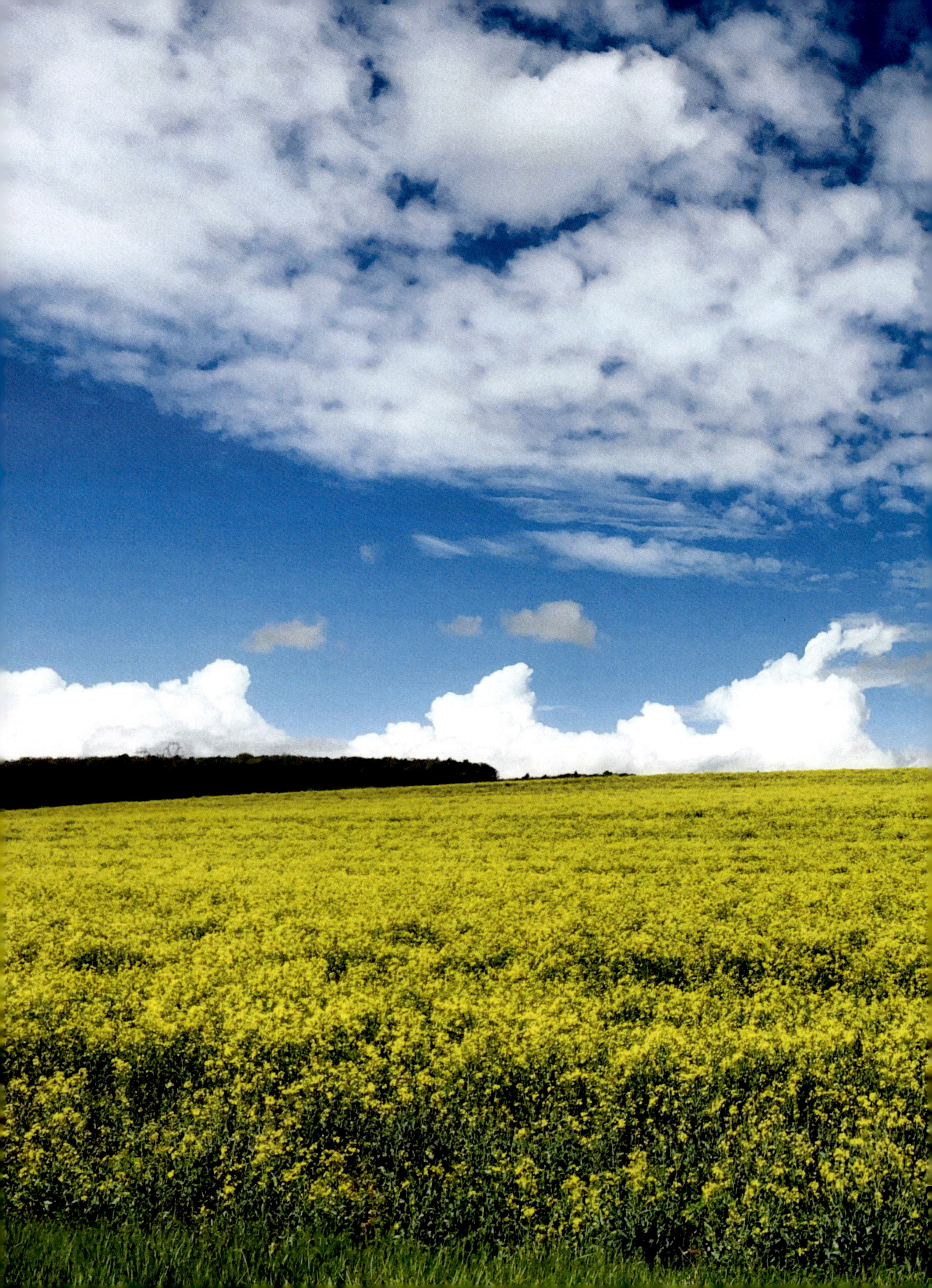

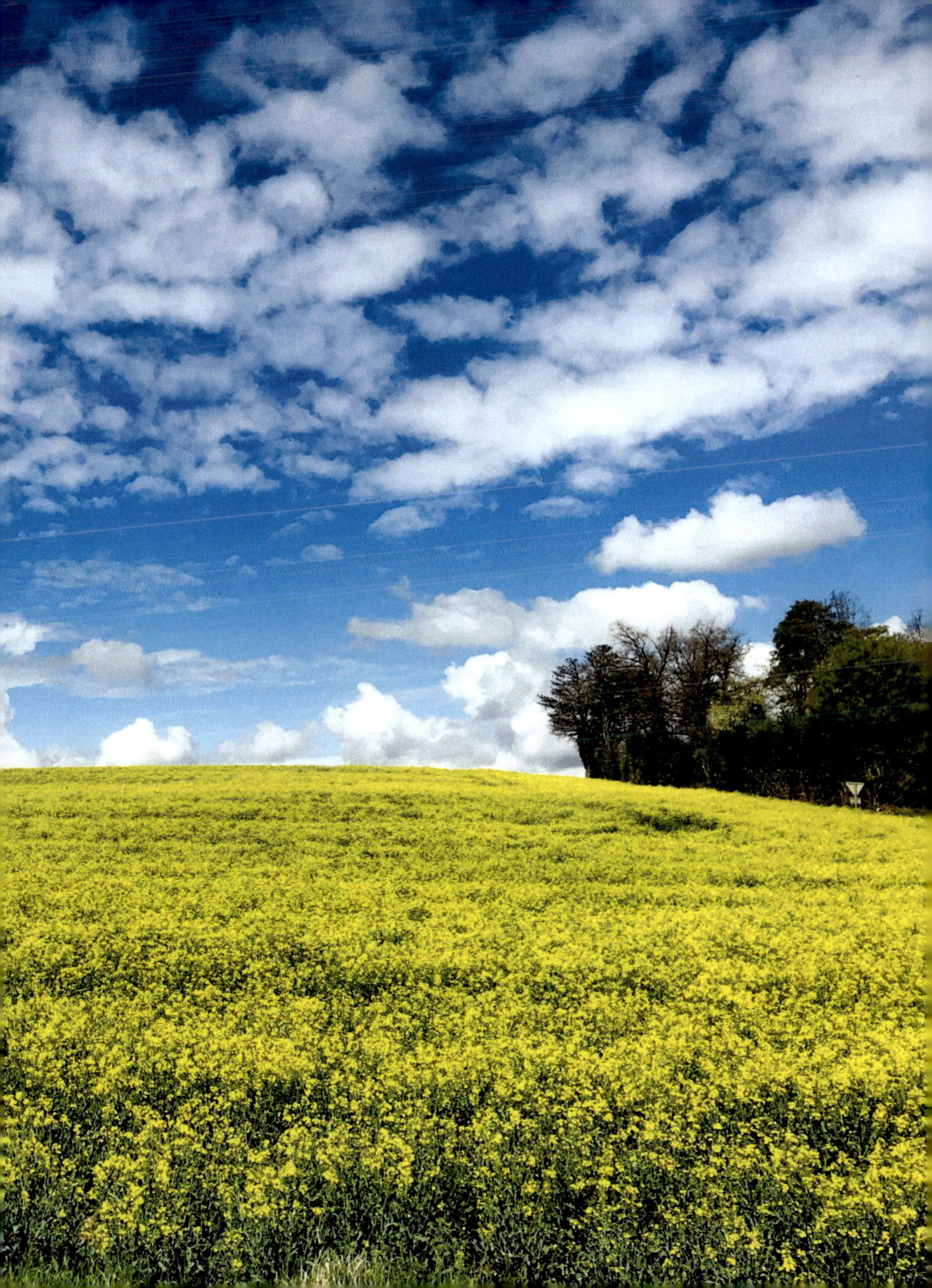

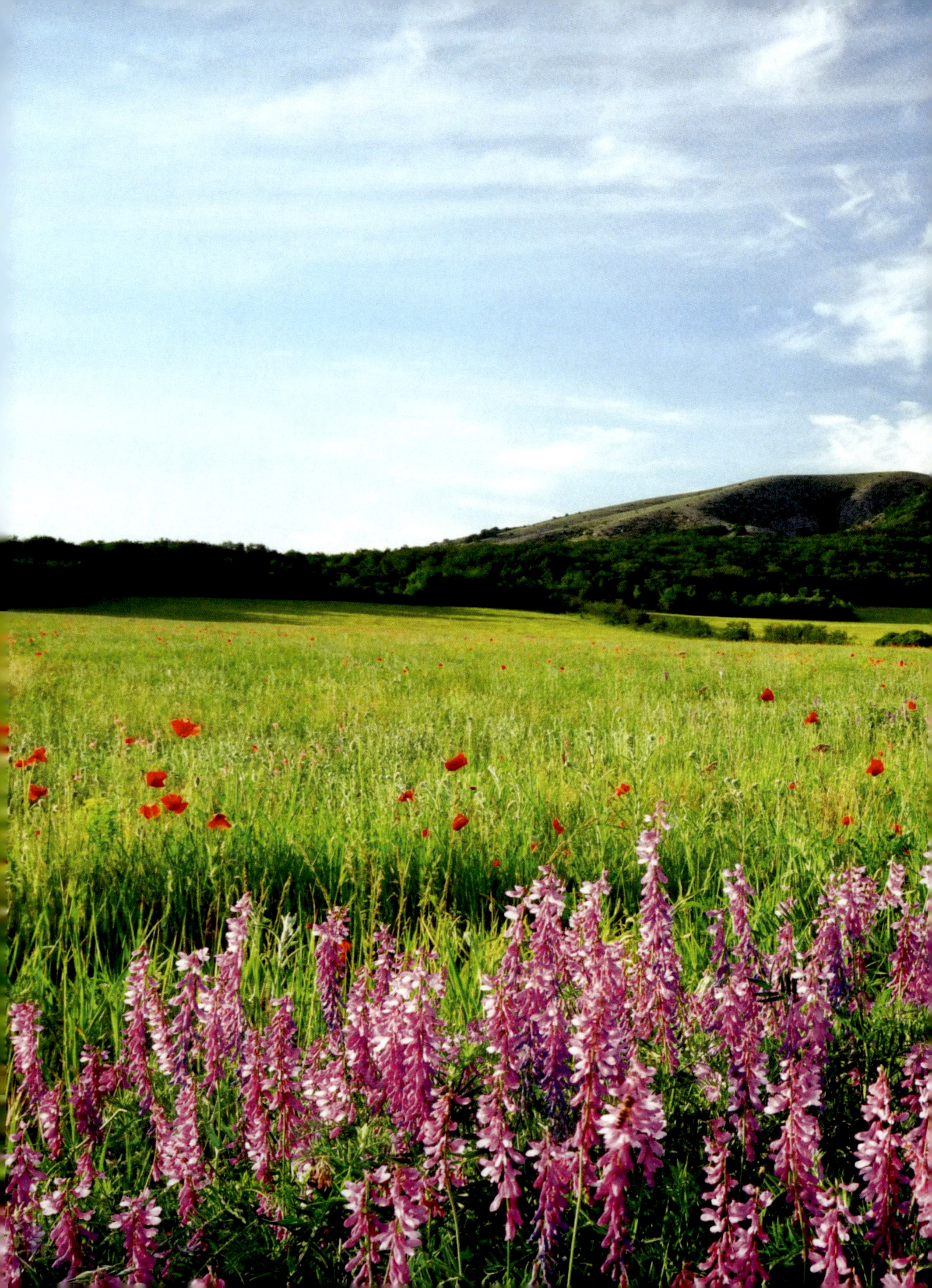

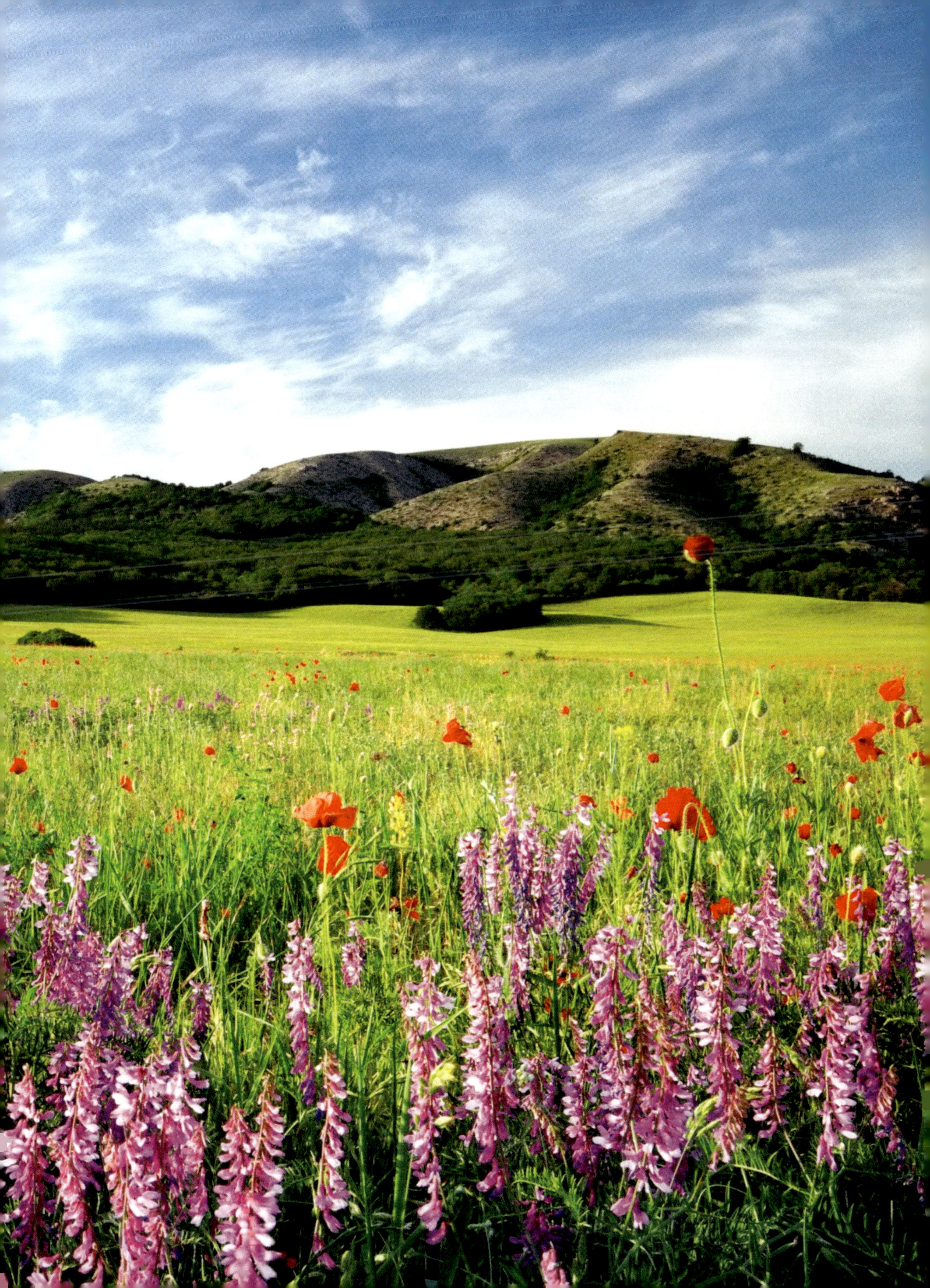

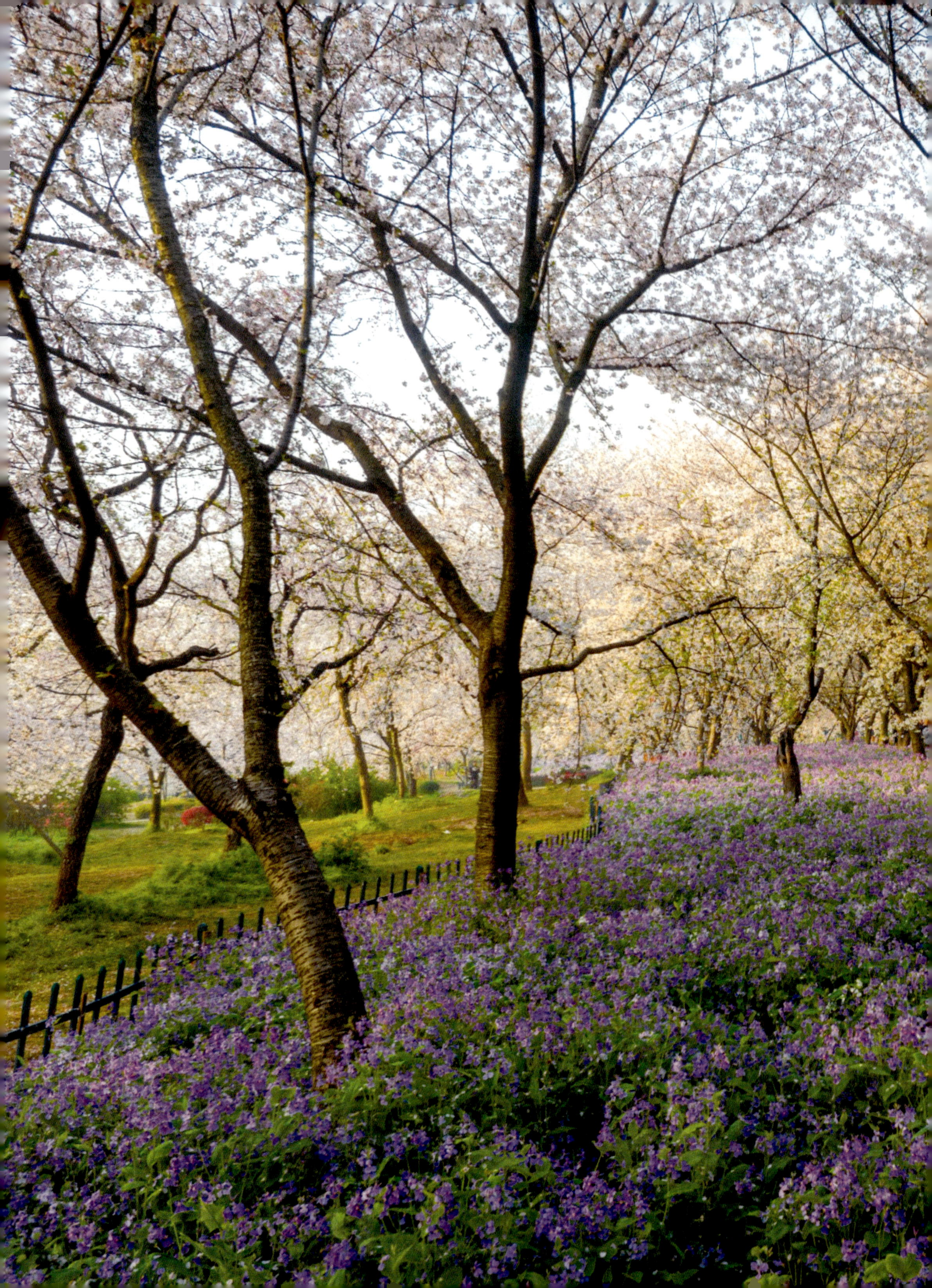

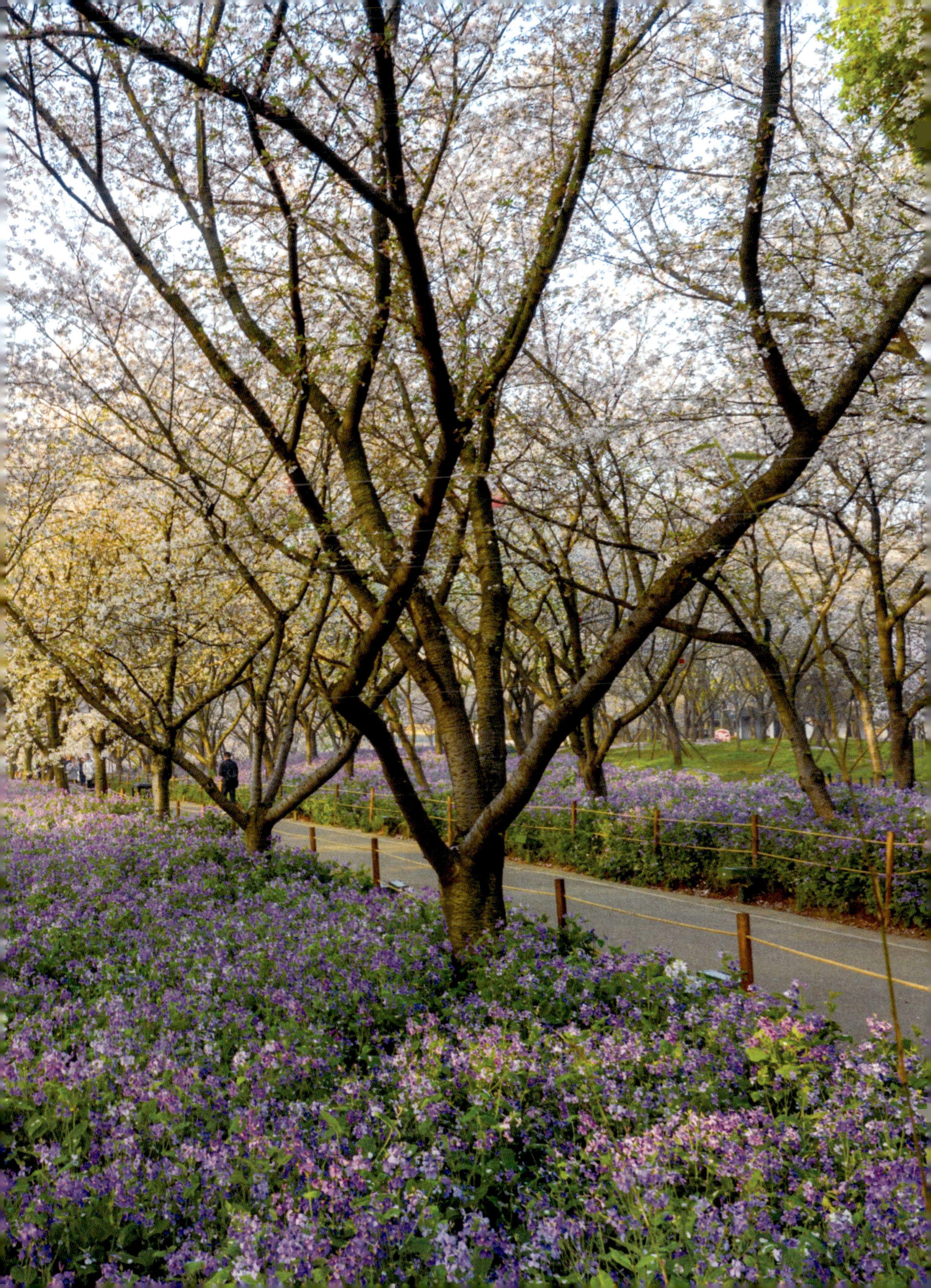

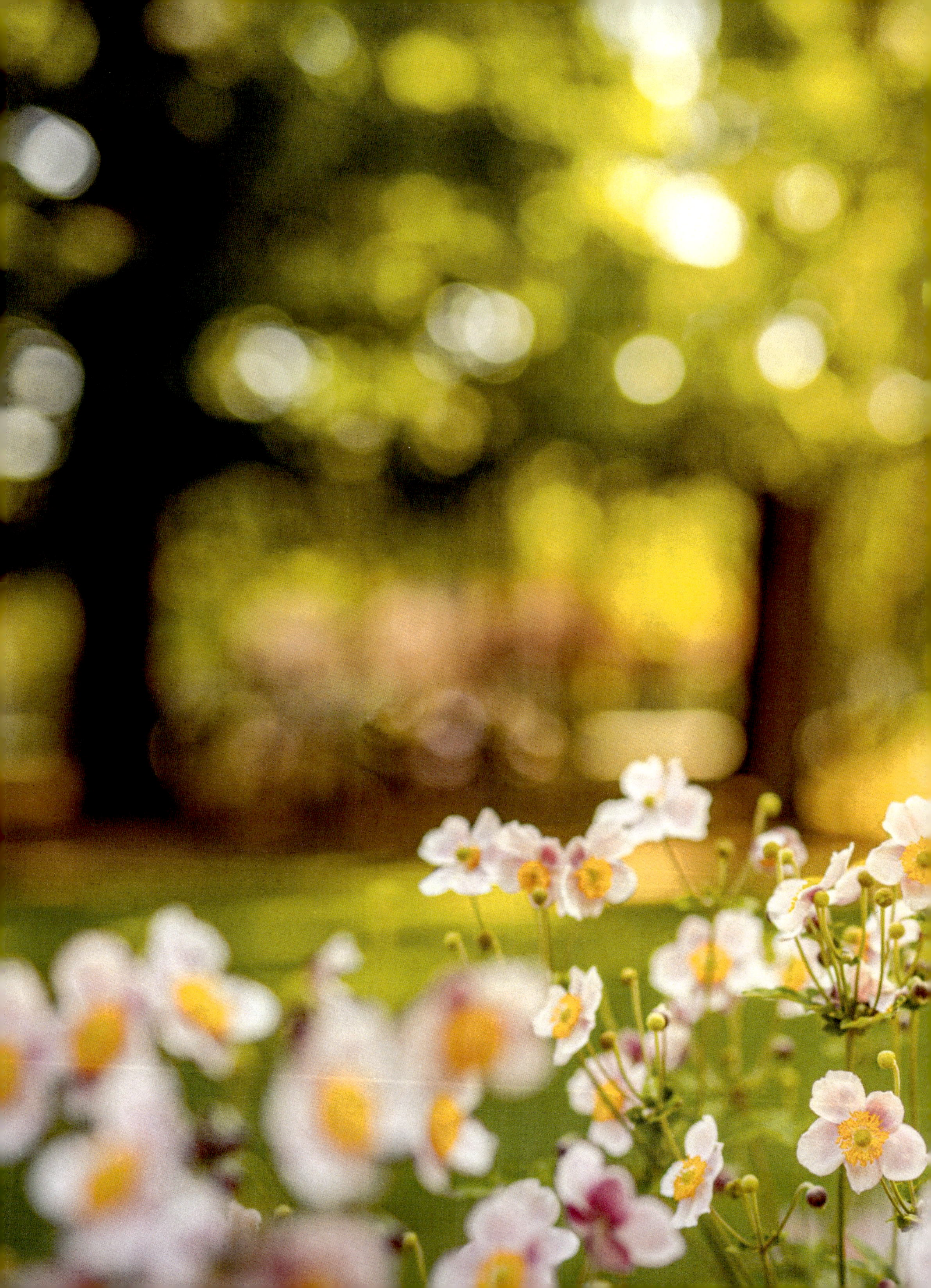

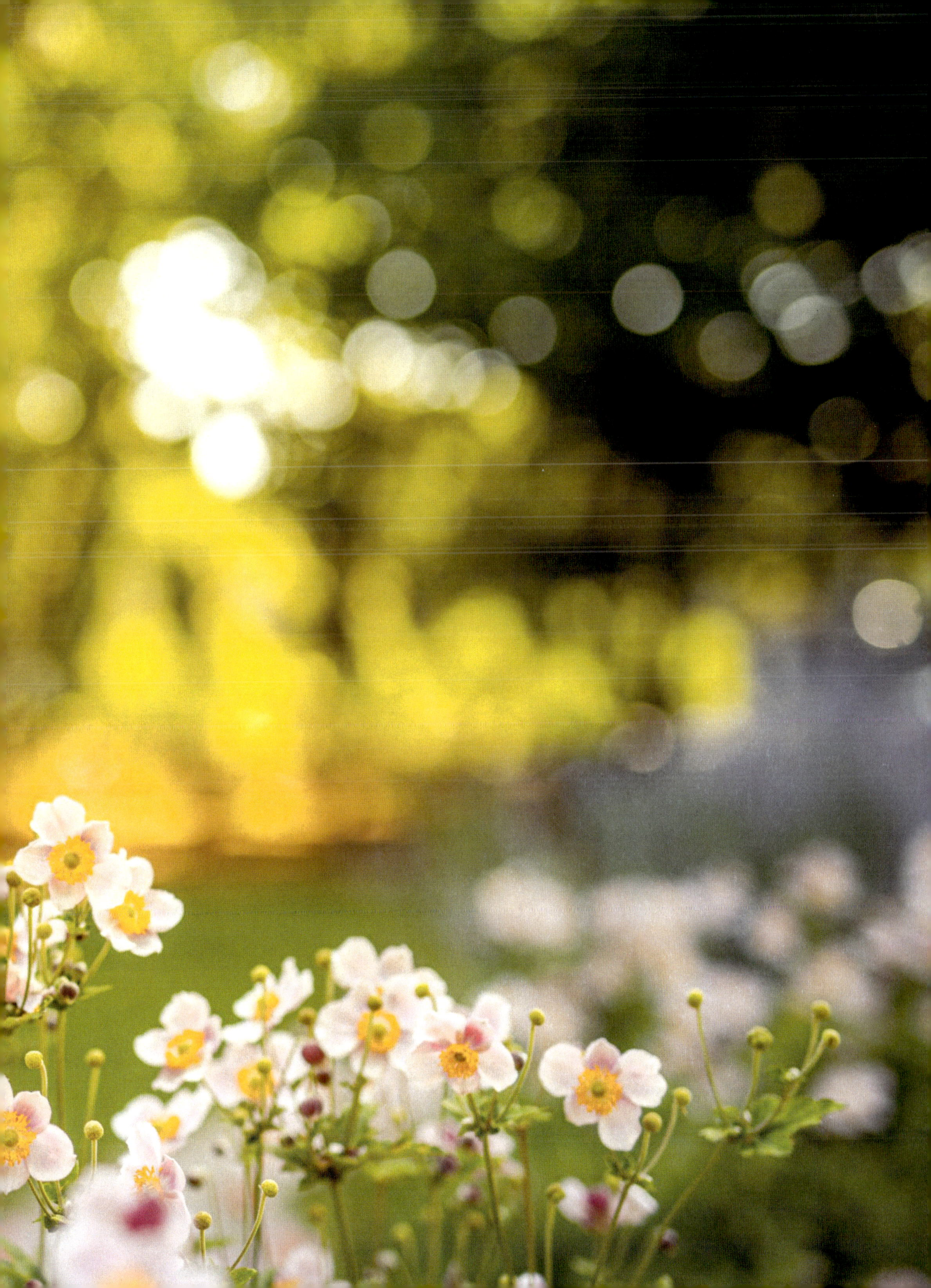

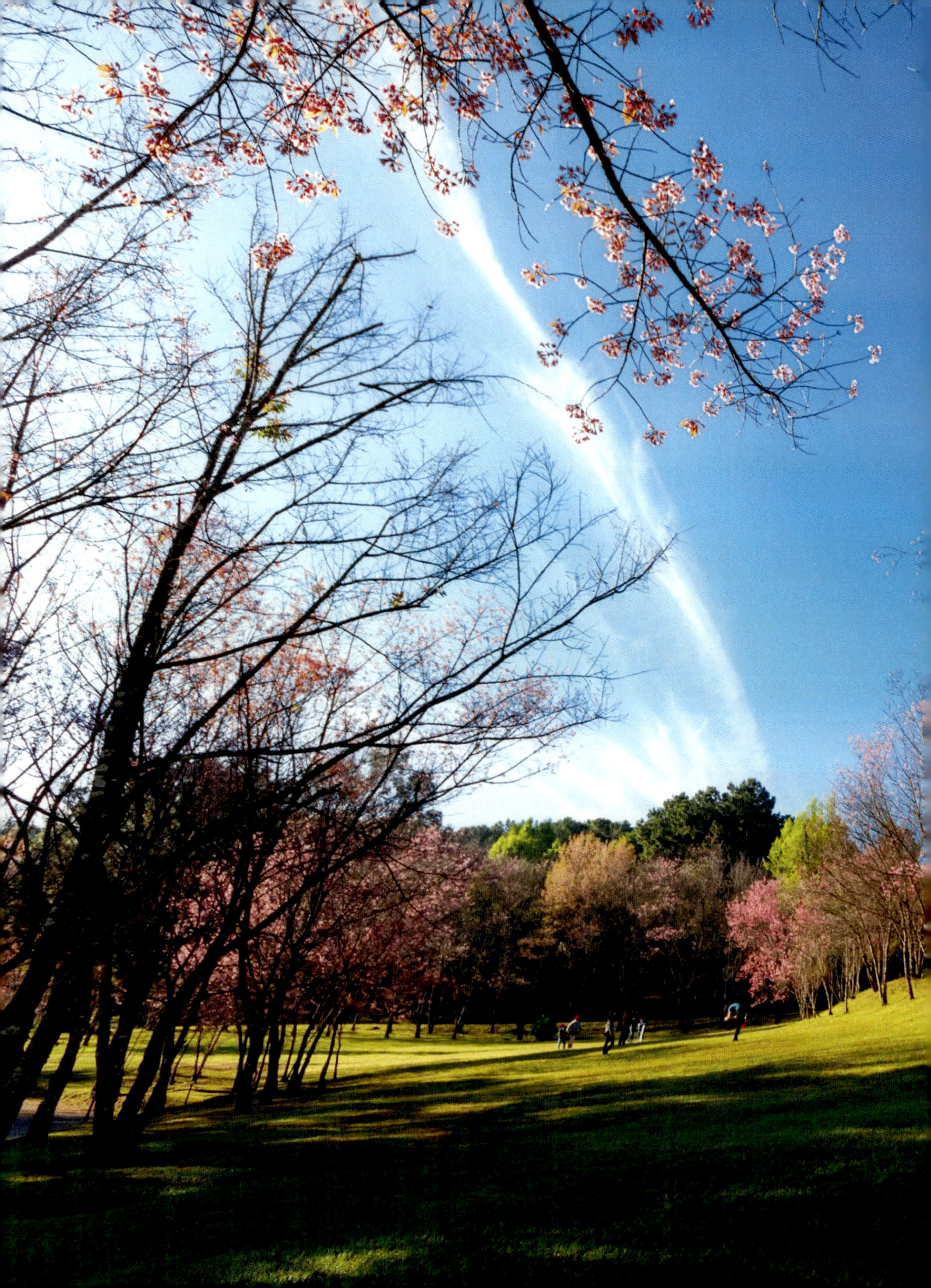

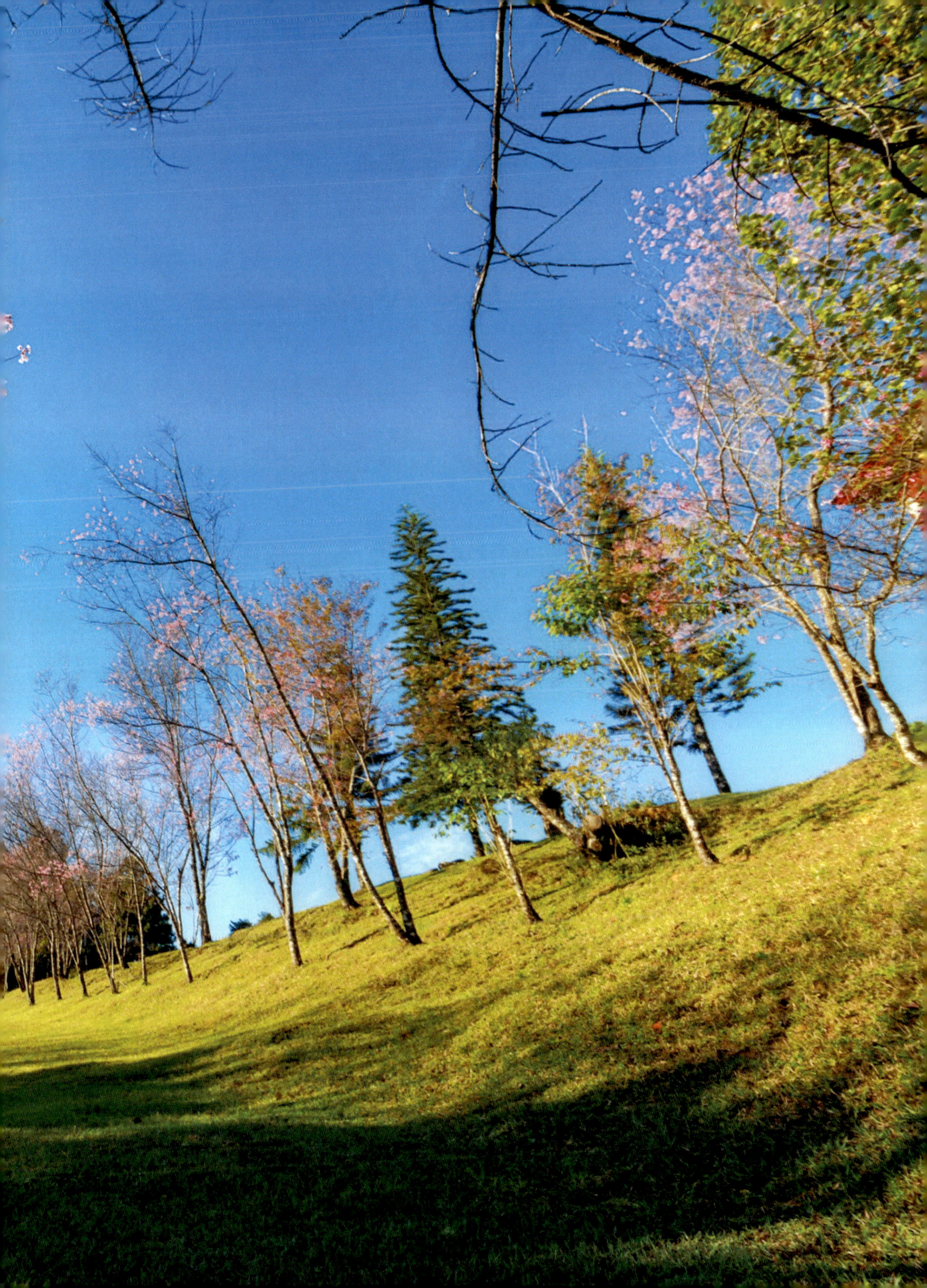

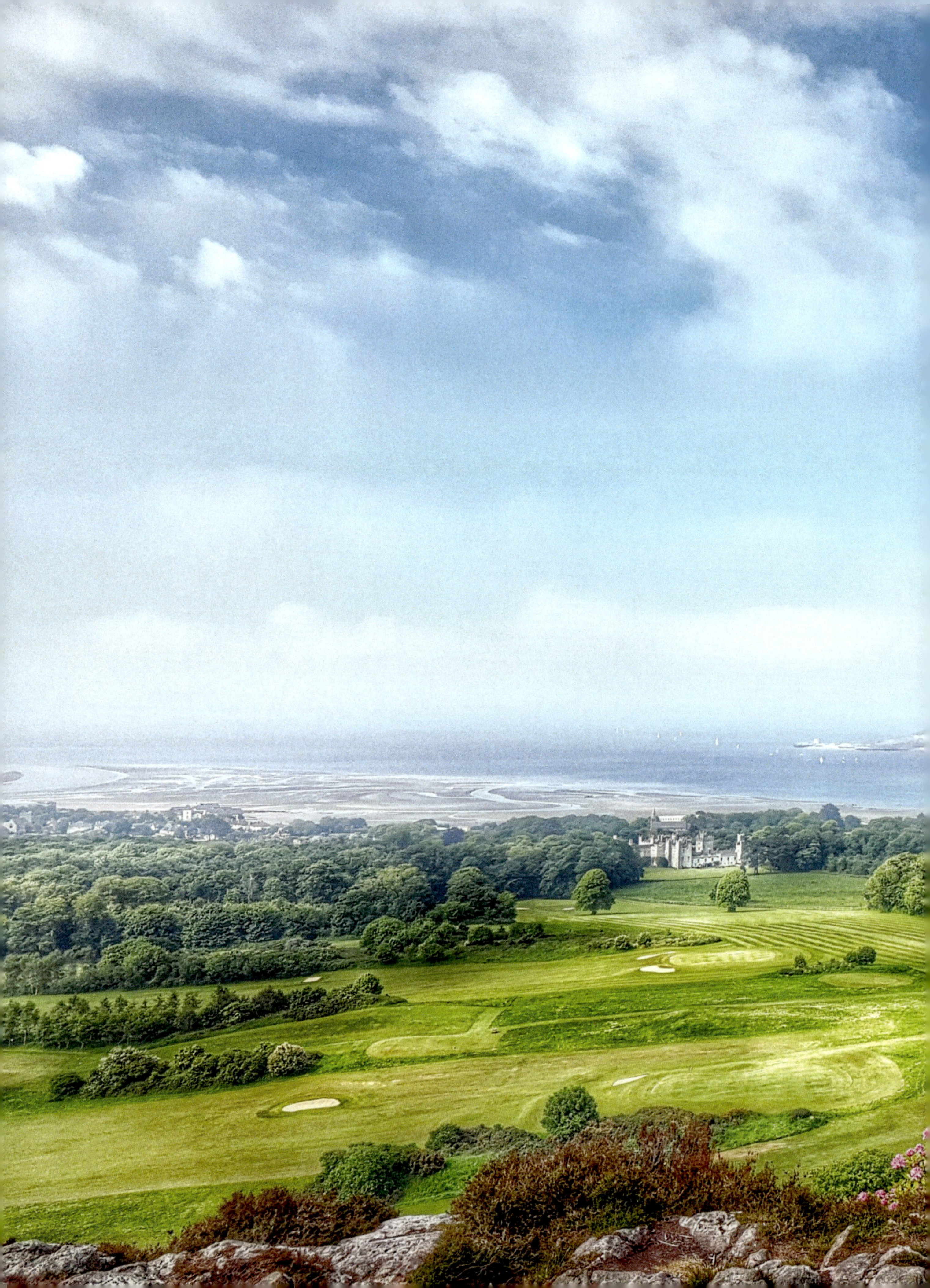

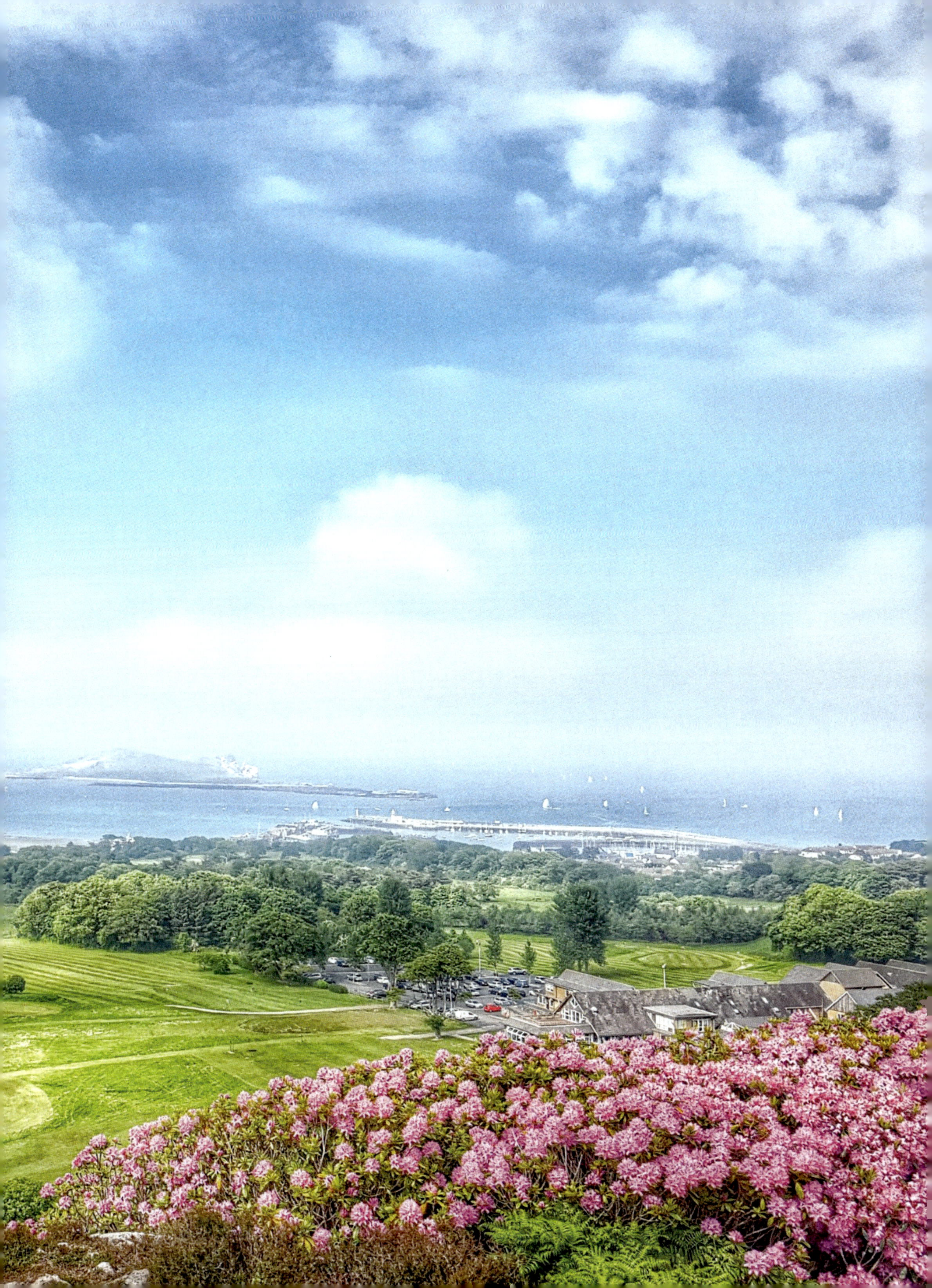

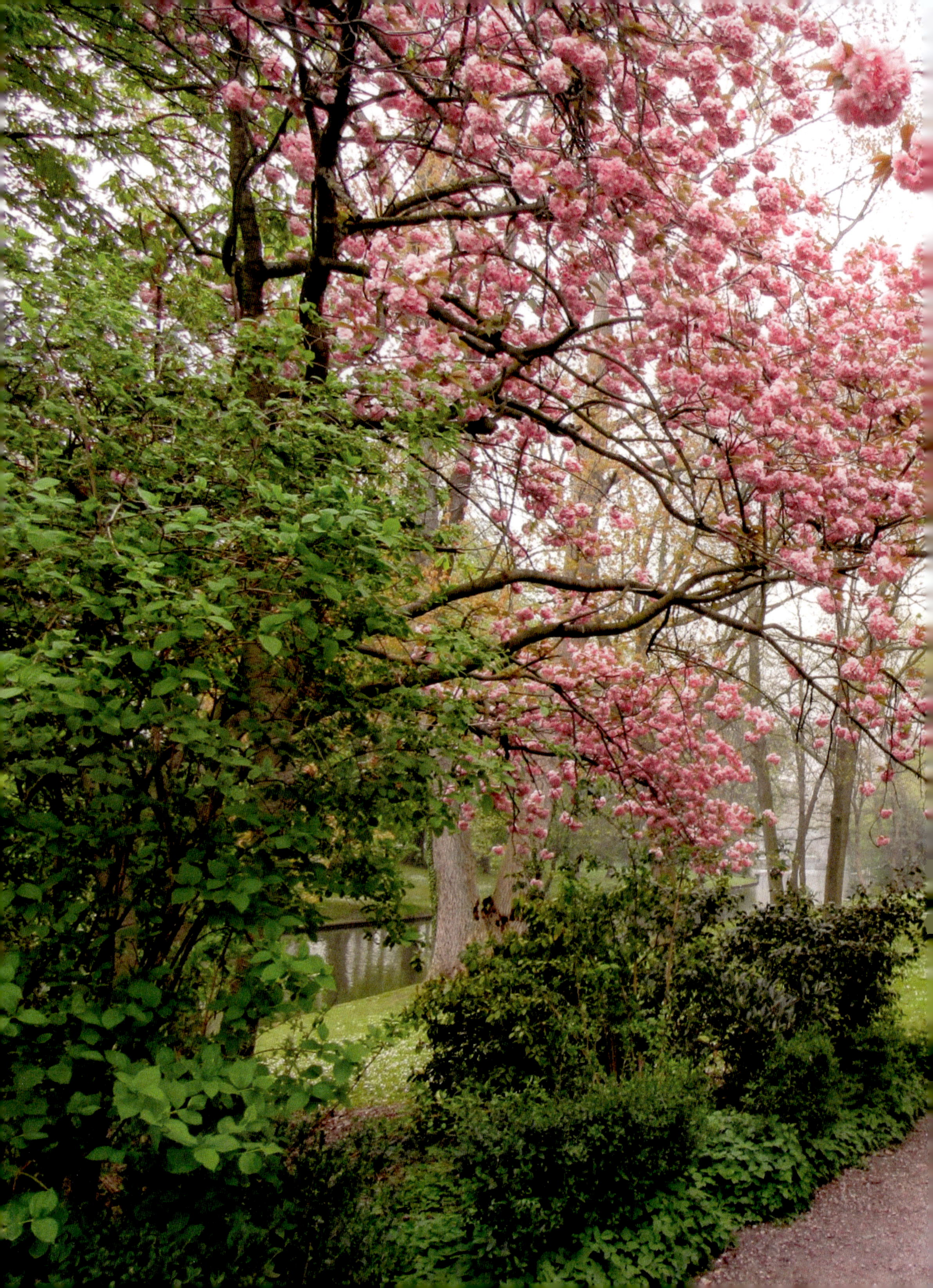

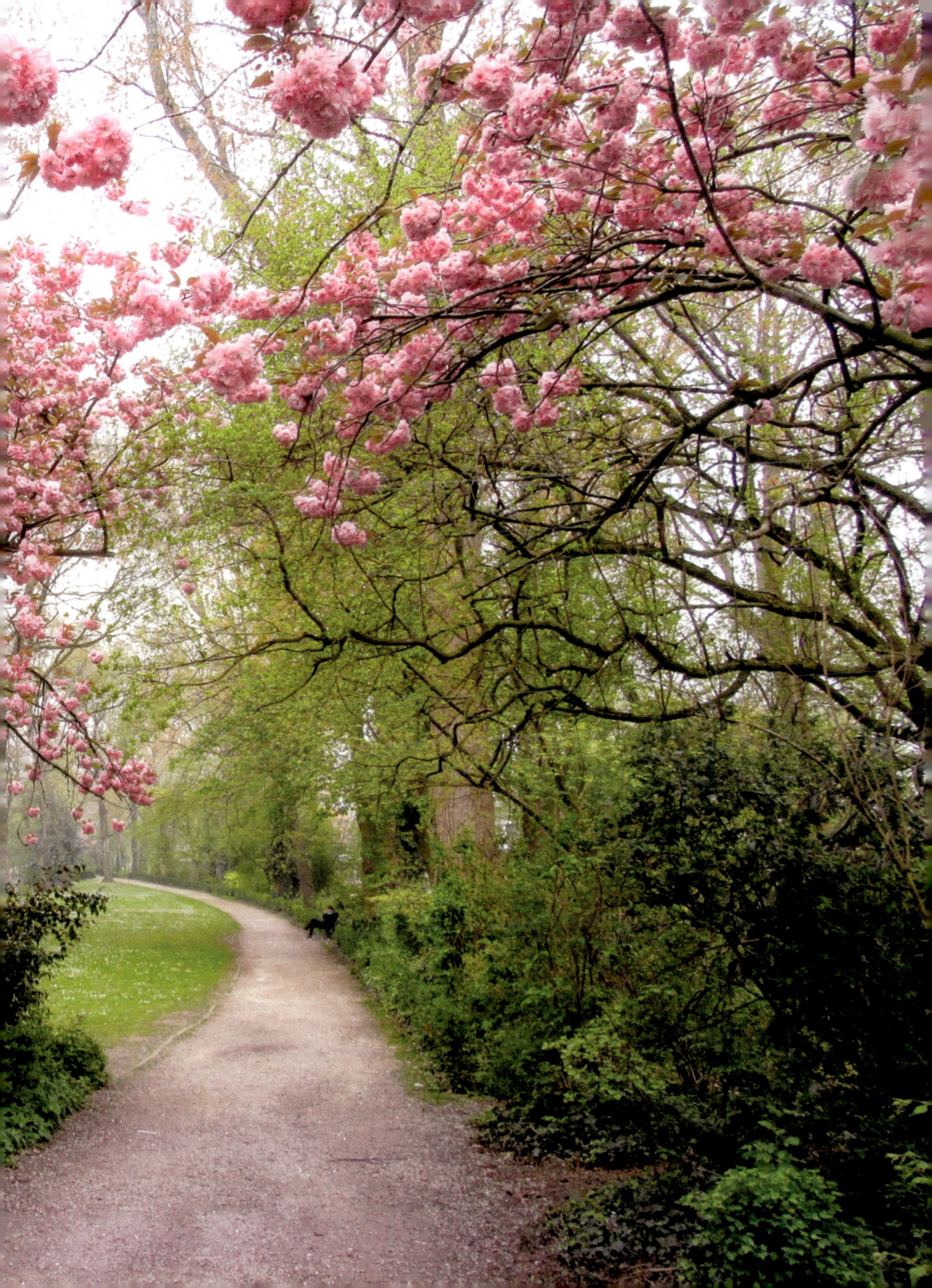

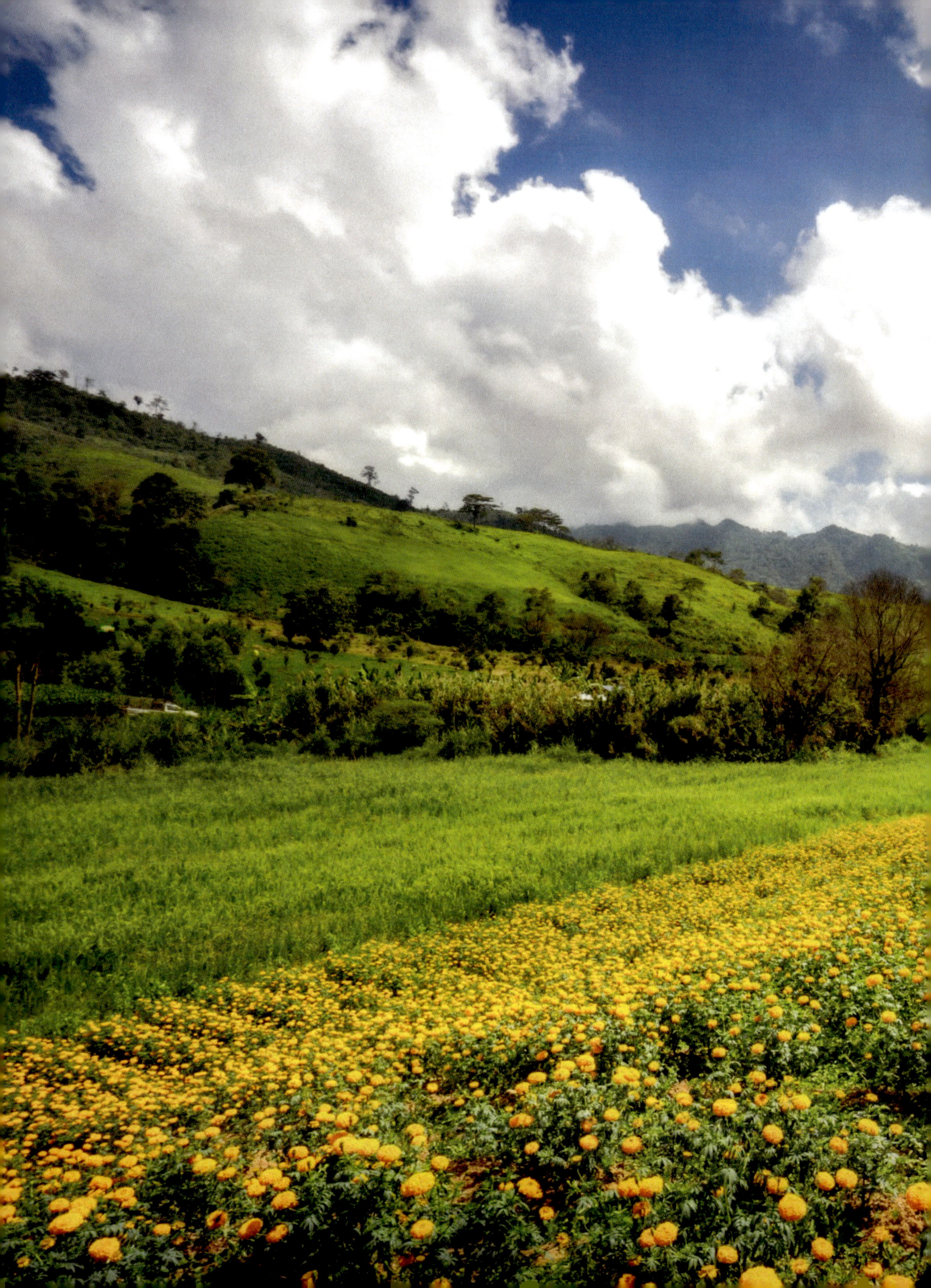

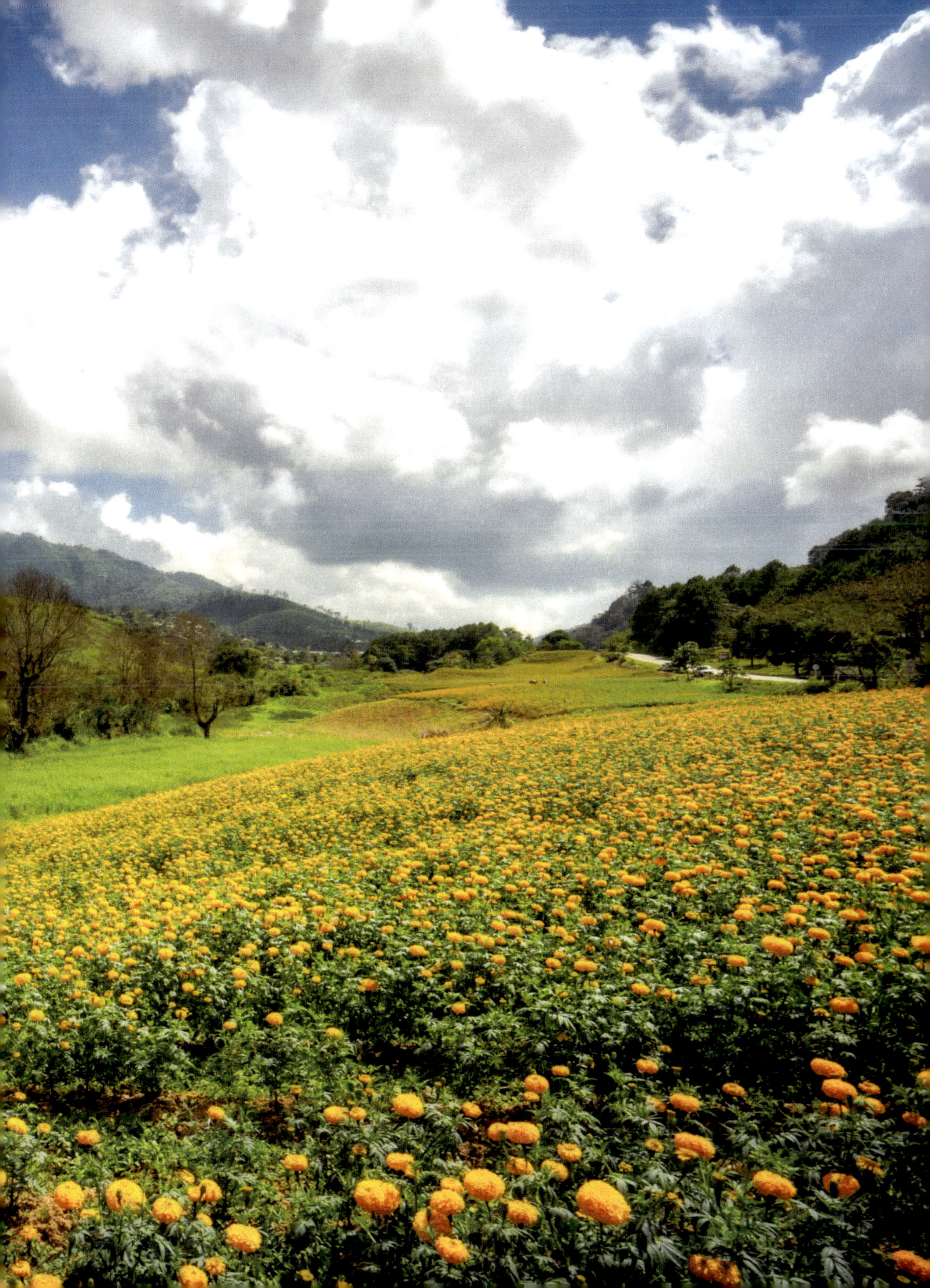

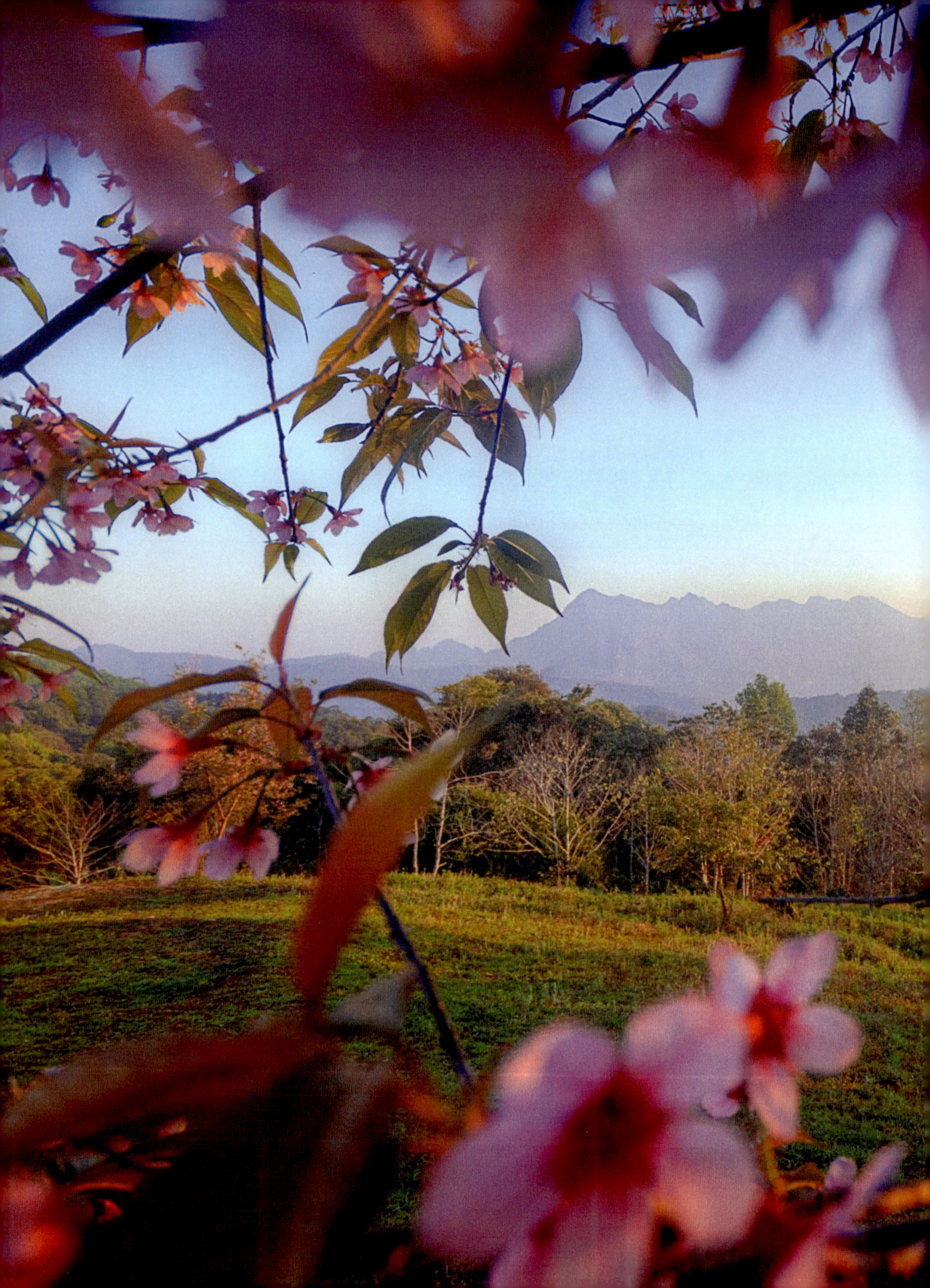

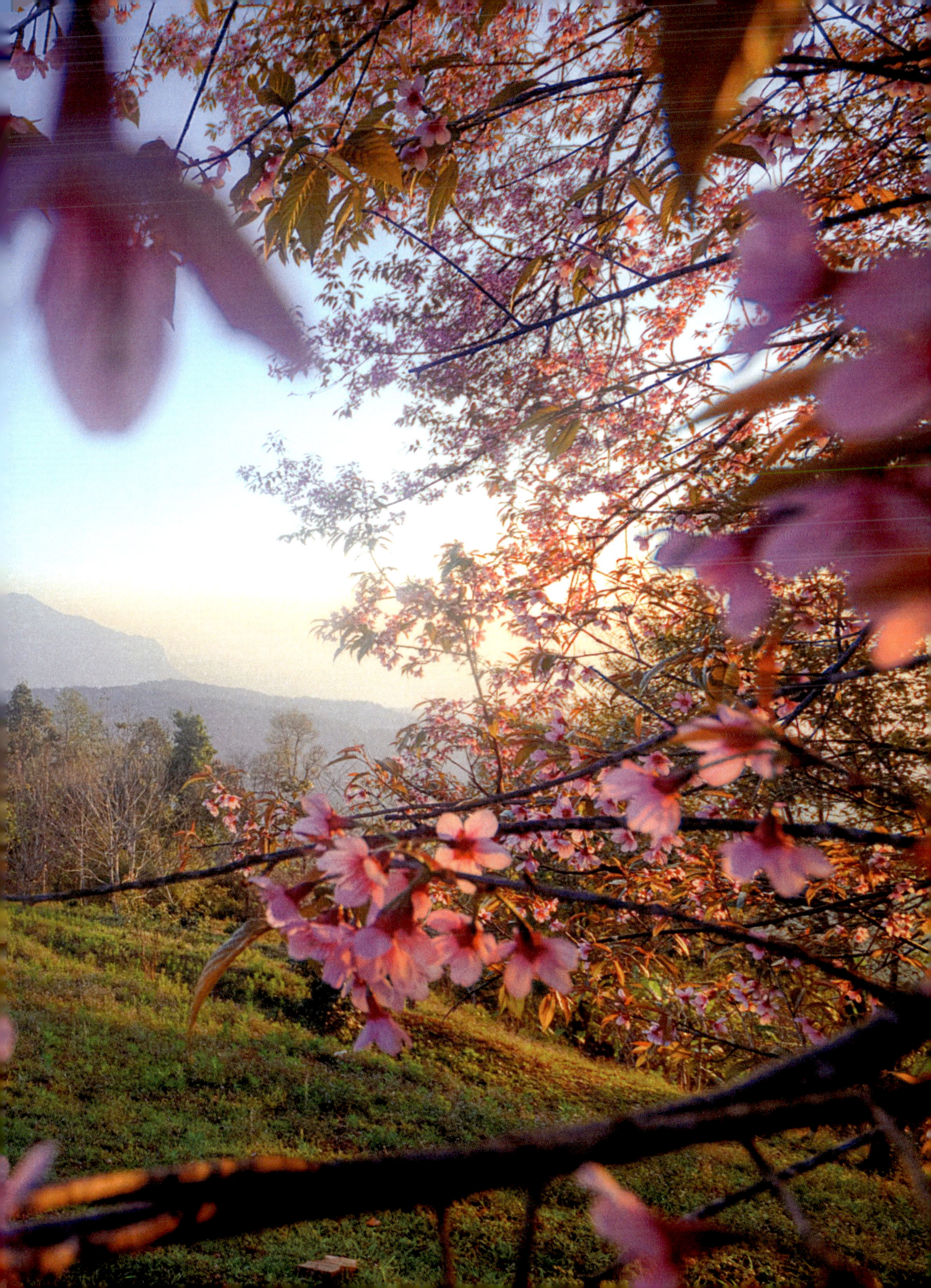

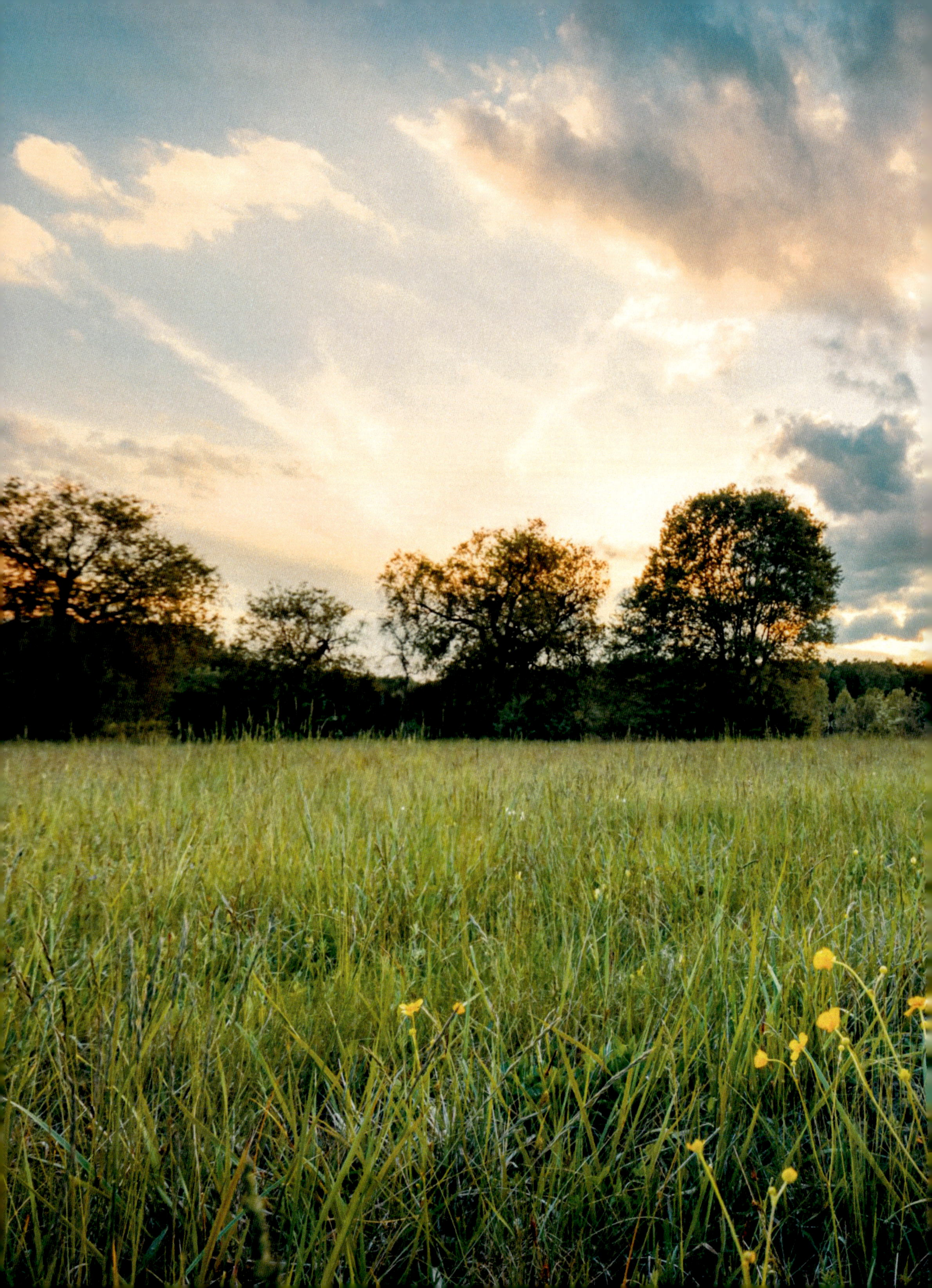

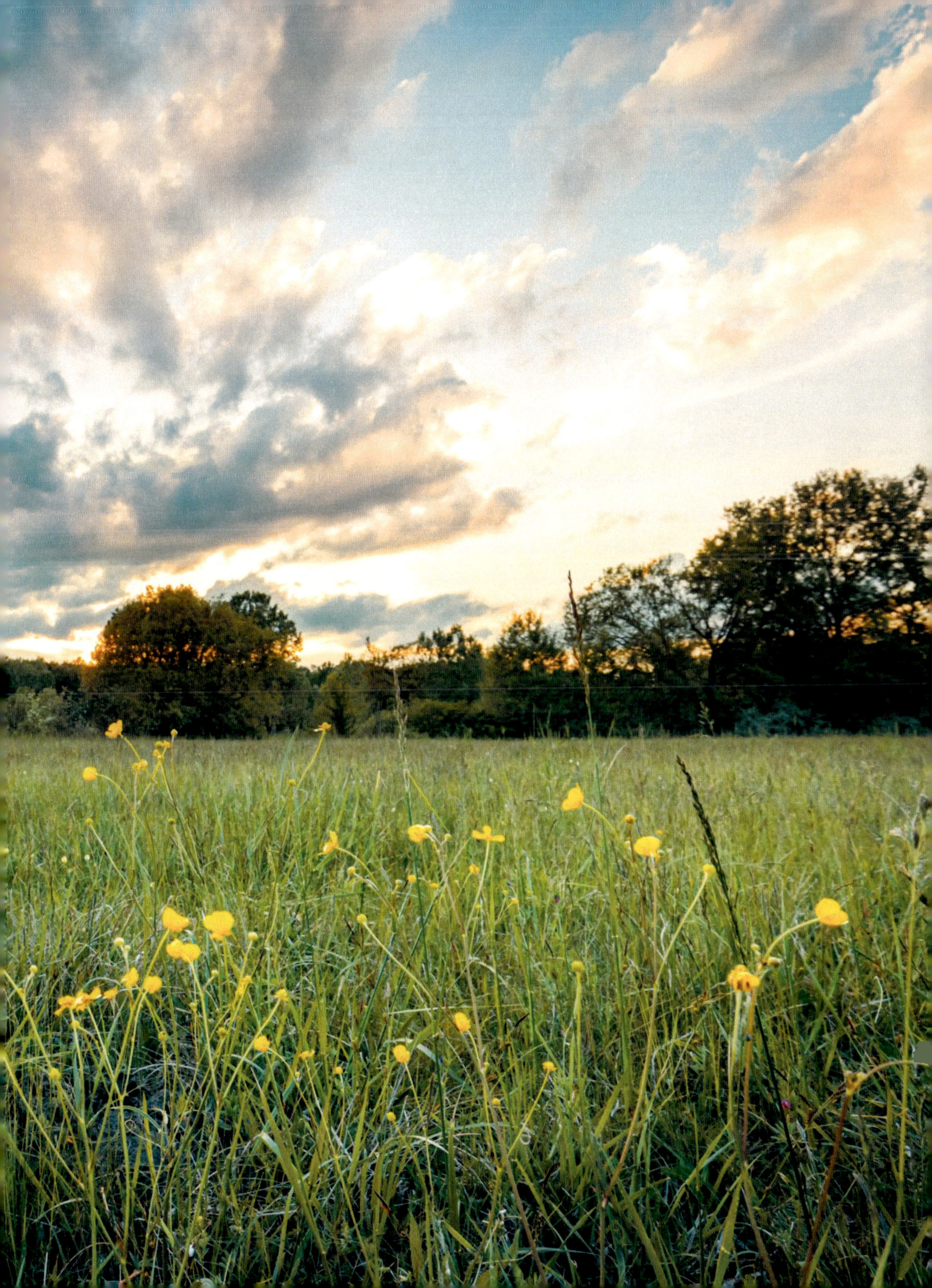

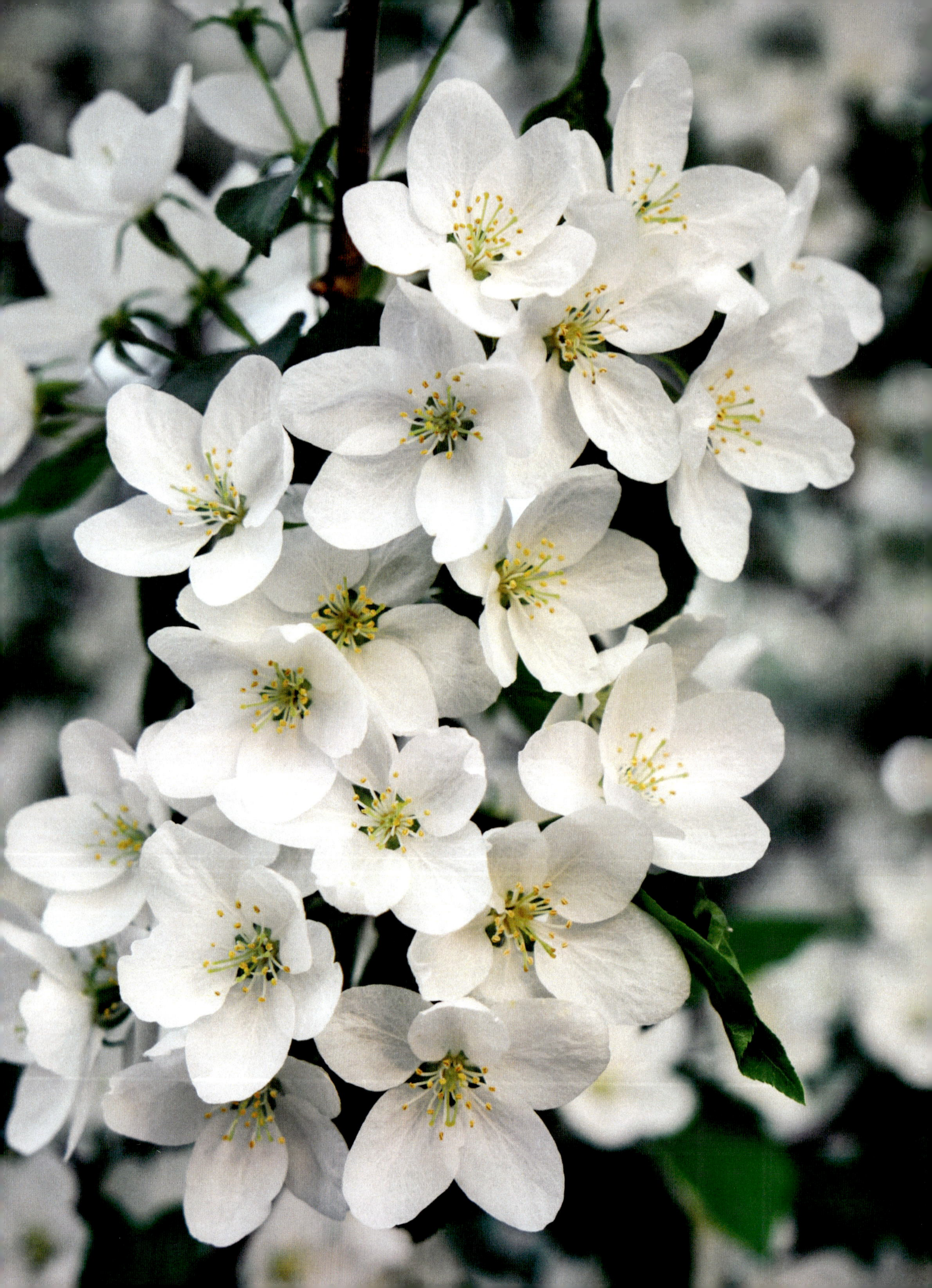

In spring, the blooming flowers, budding trees, and chirping birds come together to create a symphony and a sensory feast that captivates our soul and inspires us to immerse ourselves in the beauty of the season.

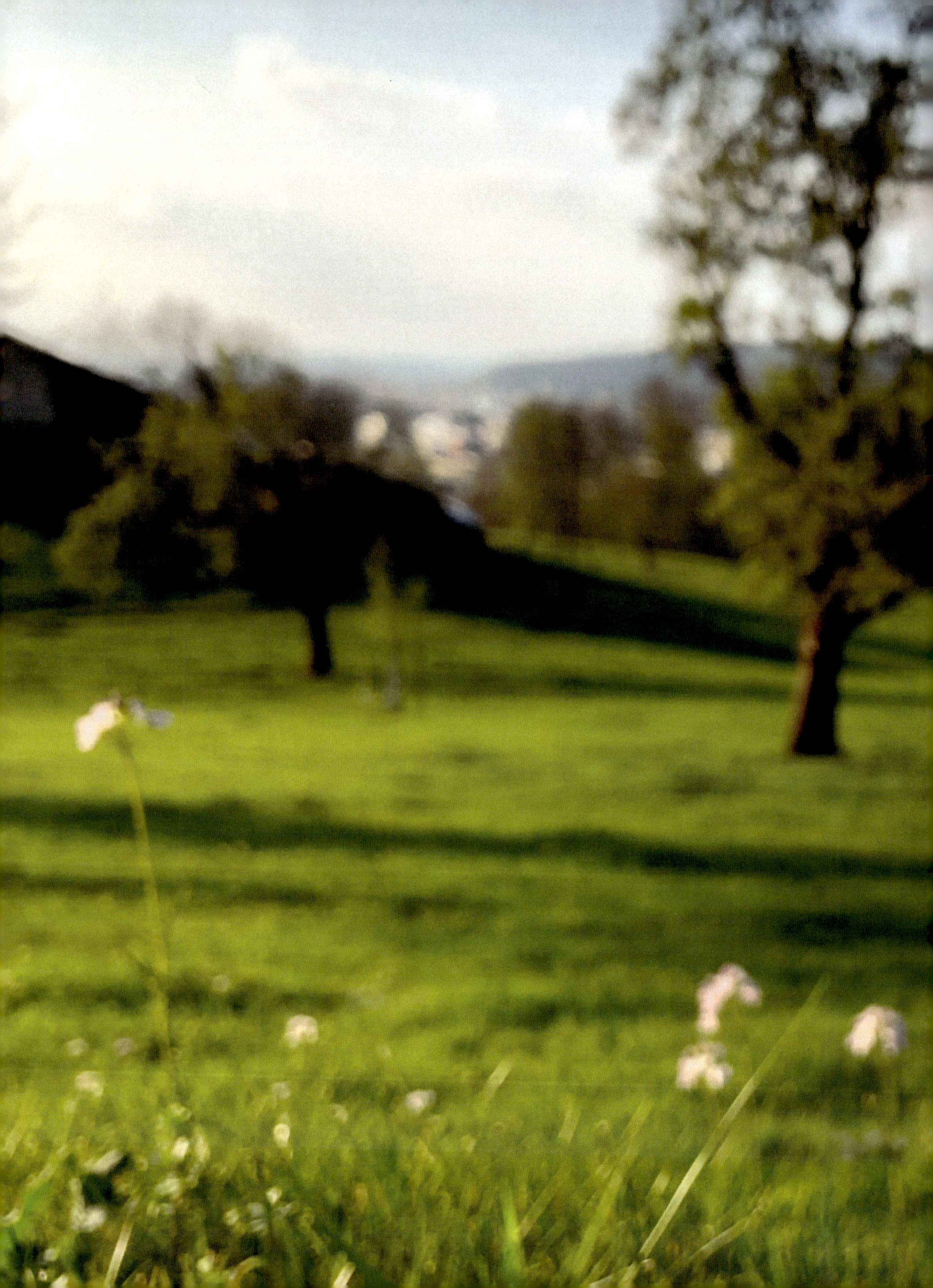

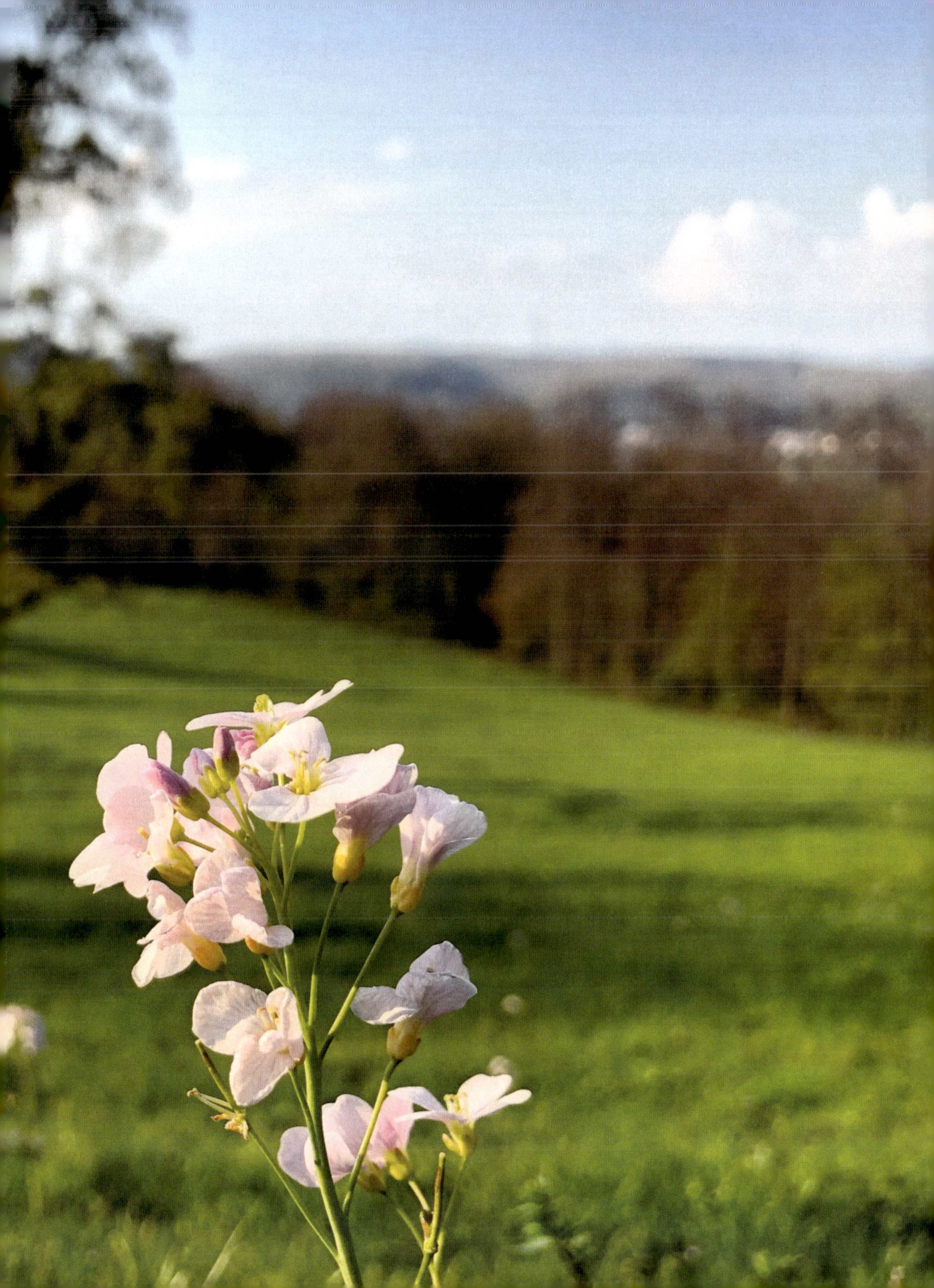

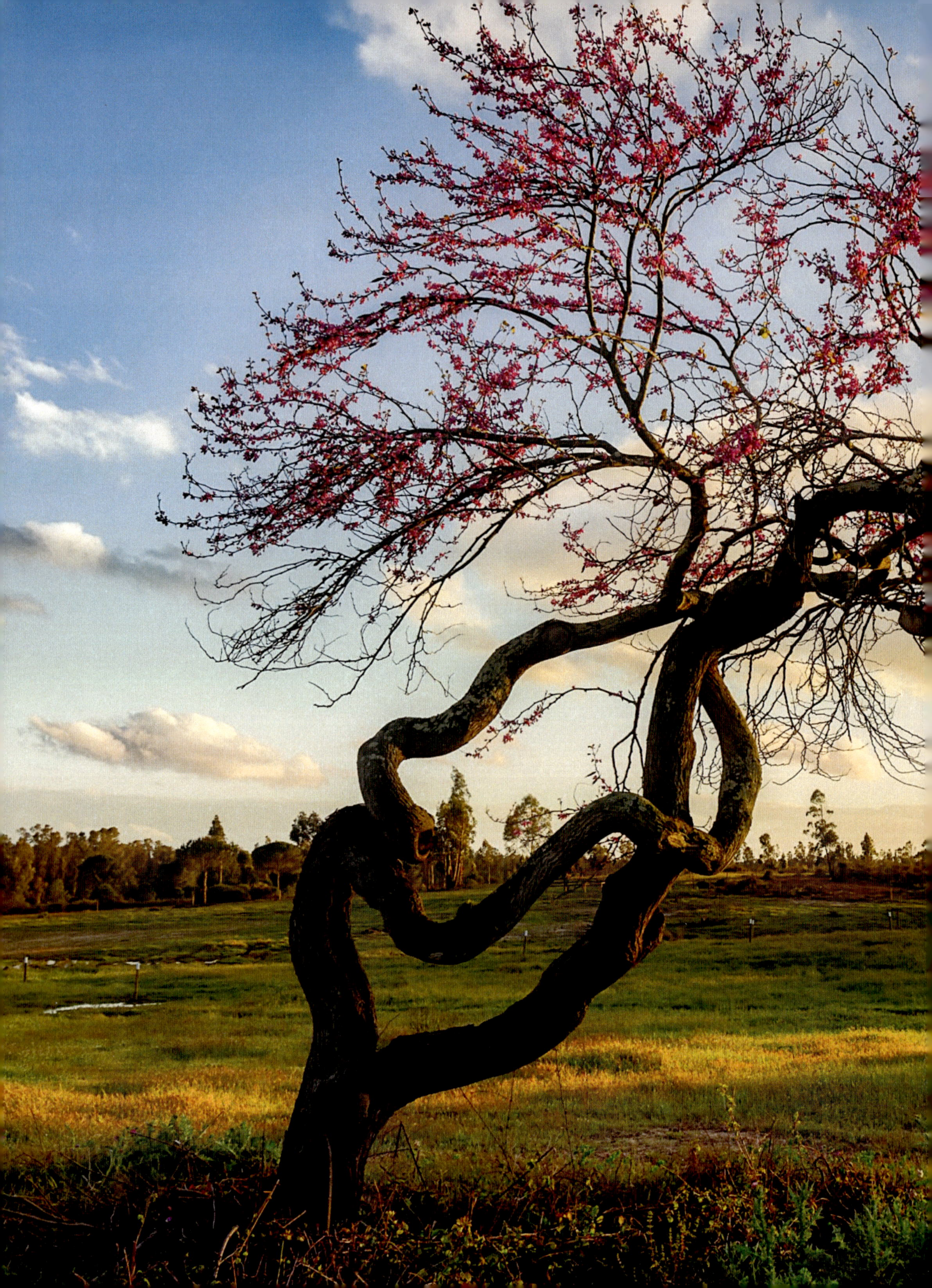

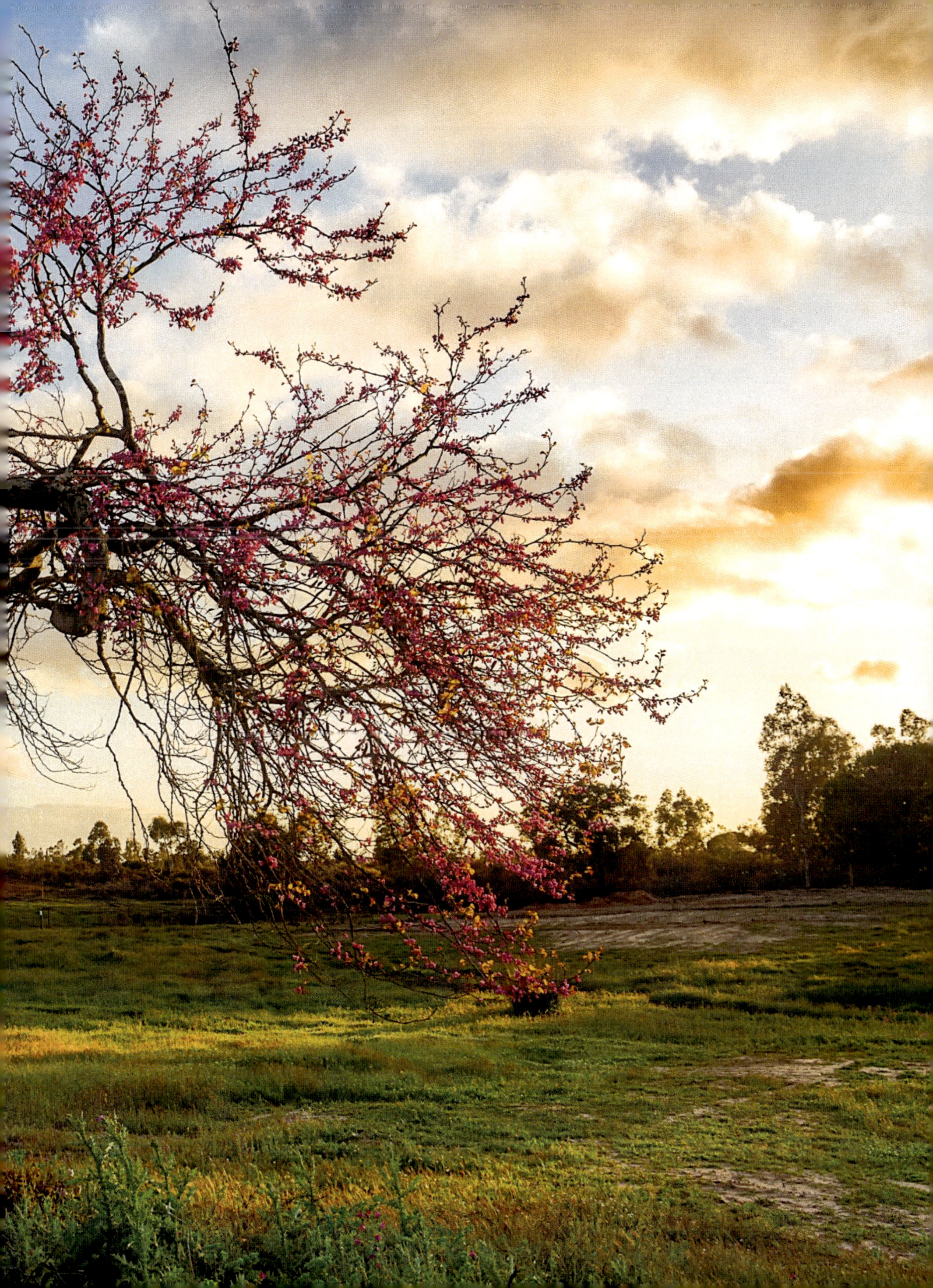

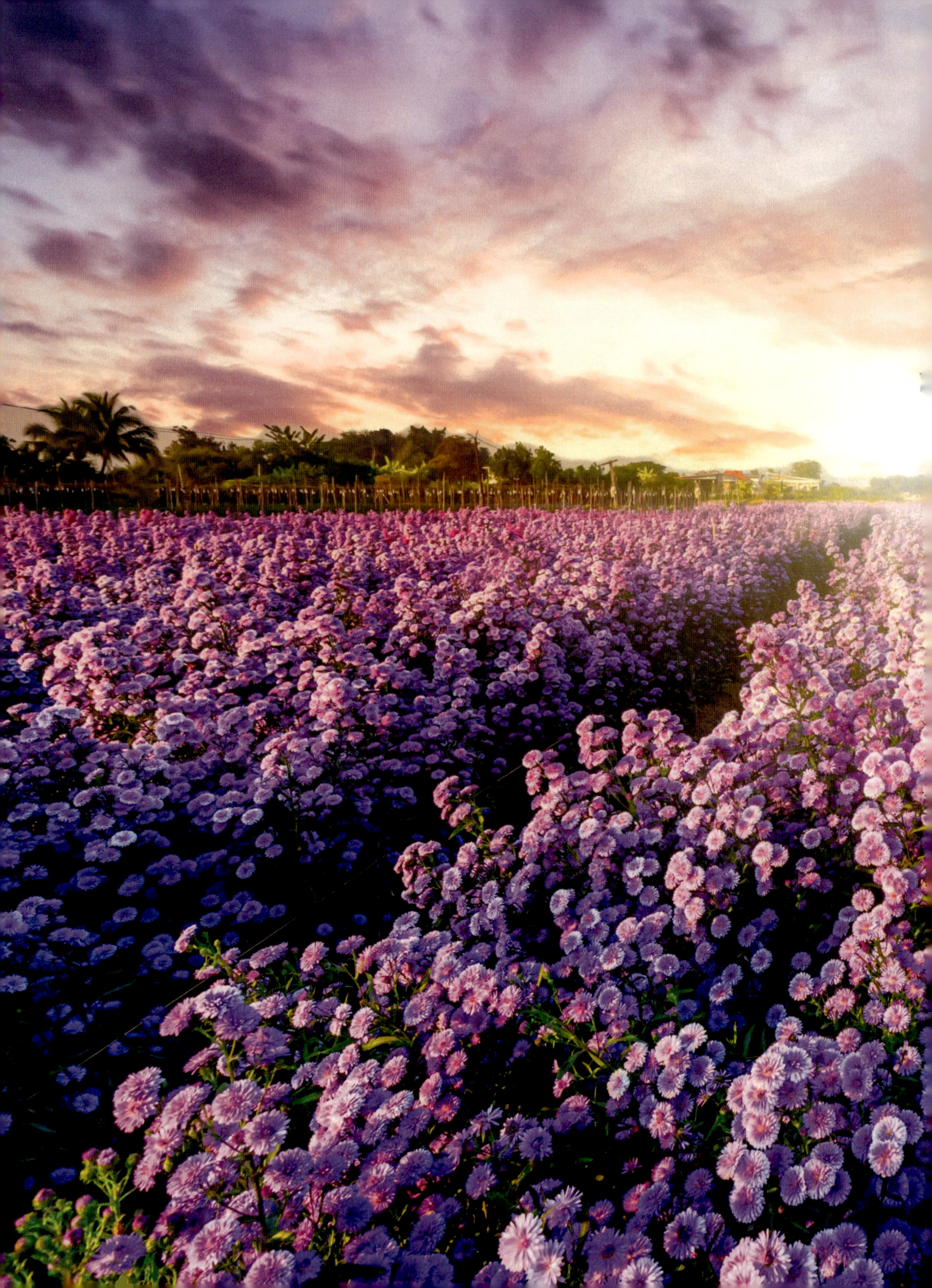

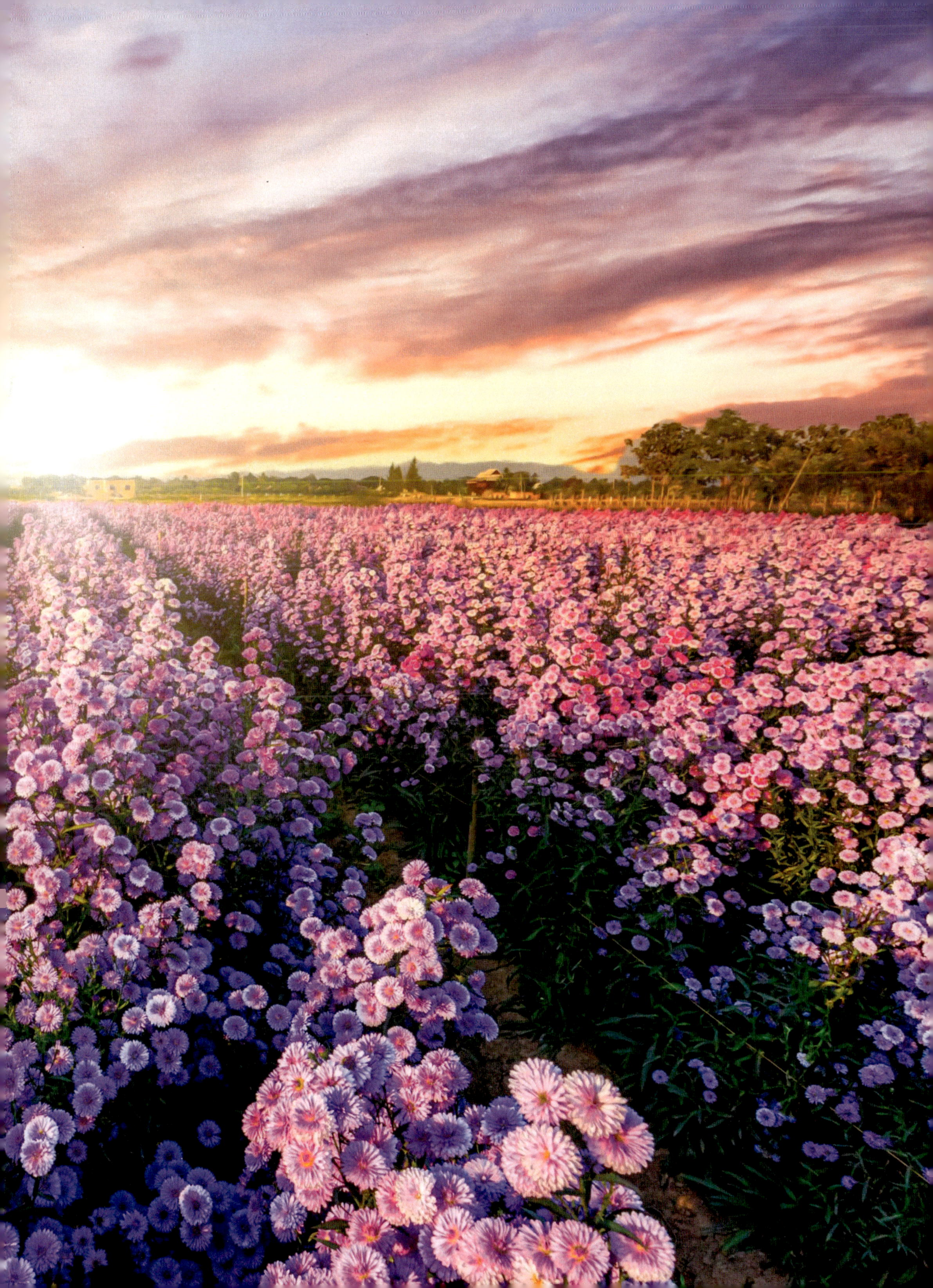

Made in the USA
Las Vegas, NV
21 April 2025

Made in the USA
Las Vegas, NV
21 April 2025

17657117-10d7-458f-a52f-77b06e28abc8R01